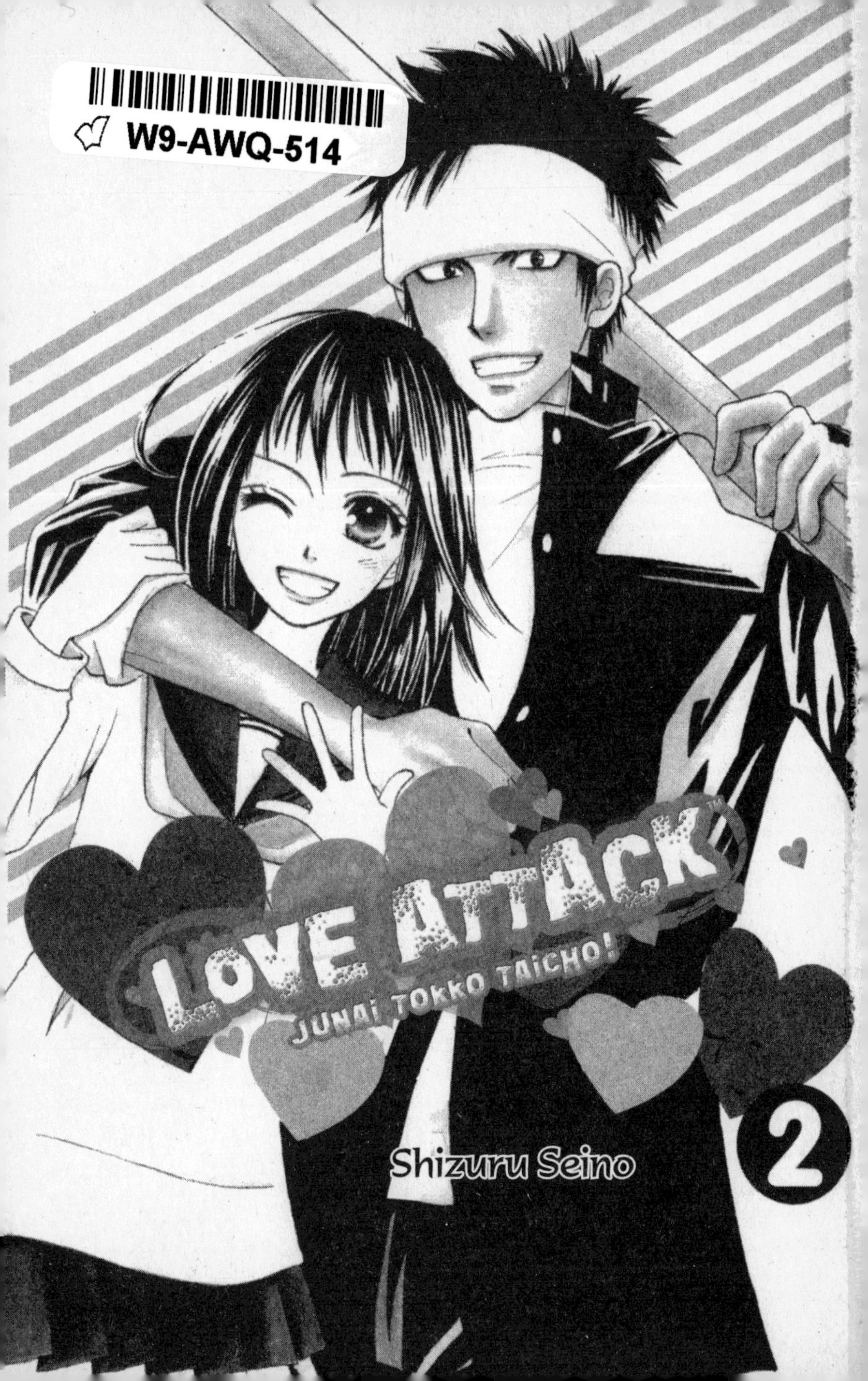
LOVE ATTACK™
JUNAI TOKKO TAICHO!
2
Shizuru Seino

Love Attack Volume 2
Created by Shizuru Seino

Translation - Adrienne Beck
English Adaptation - Magdalena Sniegocki
Retouch and Lettering - Star Print Brokers
Production Artist - Mike Estacio
Graphic Designer - James Lee

Editor - Hyun Joo Kim
Digital Imaging Manager - Chris Buford
Pre-Production Supervisor - Erika Terriquez
Production Manager - Elisabeth Brizzi
Managing Editor - Vy Nguyen
Creative Director - Anne Marie Horne
Editor-in-Chief - Rob Tokar
Publisher - Mike Kiley
President and C.O.O. - John Parker
C.E.O. and Chief Creative Officer - Stu Levy

A ⊚ TOKYOPOP Manga

TOKYOPOP and ⊚ are trademarks or registered trademarks of TOKYOPOP Inc.

TOKYOPOP Inc.
5900 Wilshire Blvd. Suite 2000
Los Angeles, CA 90036

E-mail: info@TOKYOPOP.com
Come visit us online at www.TOKYOPOP.com

ISBN: 978-1-4278-0295-8

First TOKYOPOP printing: April 2008
10 9 8 7 6 5 4 3 2 1
Printed in the USA

LOVE ATTACK™

JUNAI TOKKO TAICHO!

Vol. 2

by

Shizuru Seino

TOKYOPOP®

HAMBURG // LONDON // LOS ANGELES // TOKYO

LOVE ATTACK
JUNAI TOKKO TAICHO!

Ch. 4 Father on Fire Special

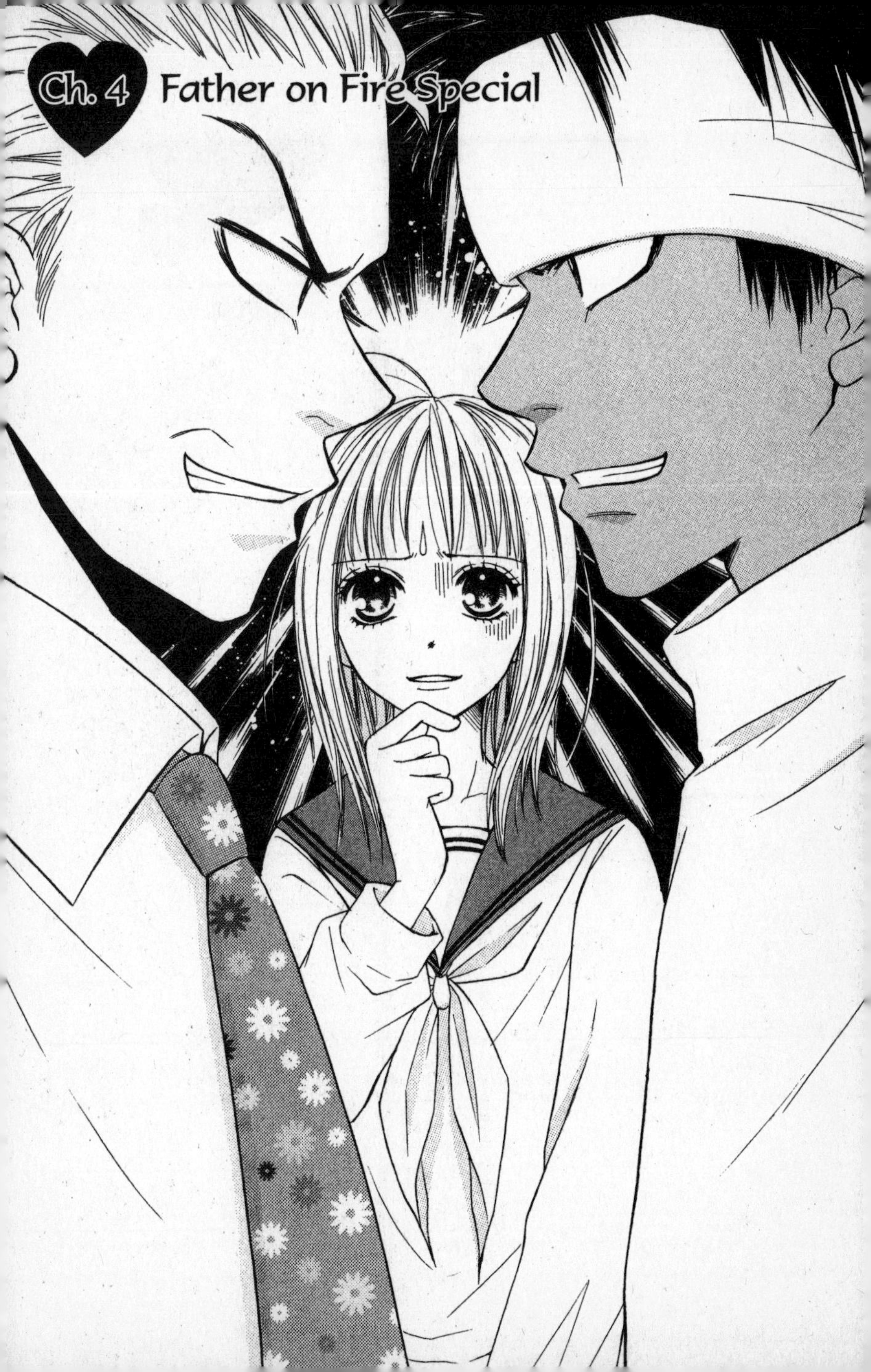

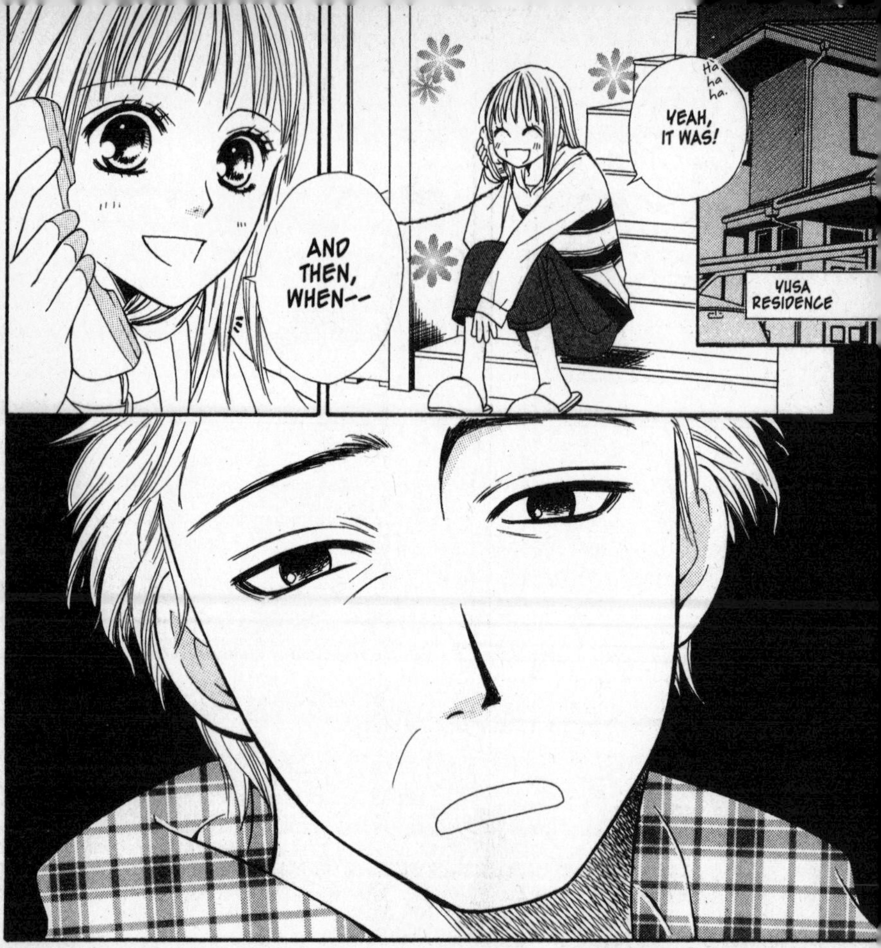
YUSA RESIDENCE
Ha ha ha.
YEAH, IT WAS!
AND THEN, WHEN--

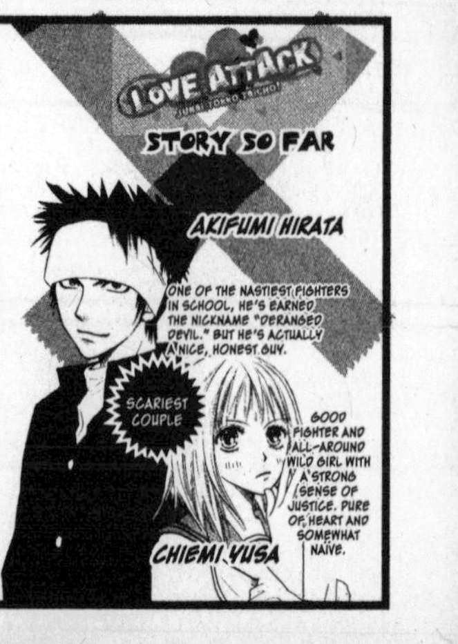
LOVE ATTACK
STORY SO FAR
AKIFUMI HIRATA
ONE OF THE NASTIEST FIGHTERS IN SCHOOL, HE'S EARNED THE NICKNAME "DERANGED DEVIL." BUT HE'S ACTUALLY A NICE, HONEST GUY.
SCARIEST COUPLE
GOOD FIGHTER AND ALL-AROUND WILD GIRL WITH A STRONG SENSE OF JUSTICE. PURE OF HEART AND SOMEWHAT NAÏVE.
CHIEMI YUSA

★WITH HER SCHOOL-RECORD FILE JAM-PACKED WITH WARNINGS FOR FIGHTING, CHIEMI IS GIVEN A CHOICE: REFORM PROBLEM-CHILD HIRATA OR GET EXPELLED! BUT WHEN CHIEMI DISCOVERS THAT HIRATA IS REALLY JUST A NICE GUY STUCK WITH A BAD REP, THE TWO END UP GOING OUT!

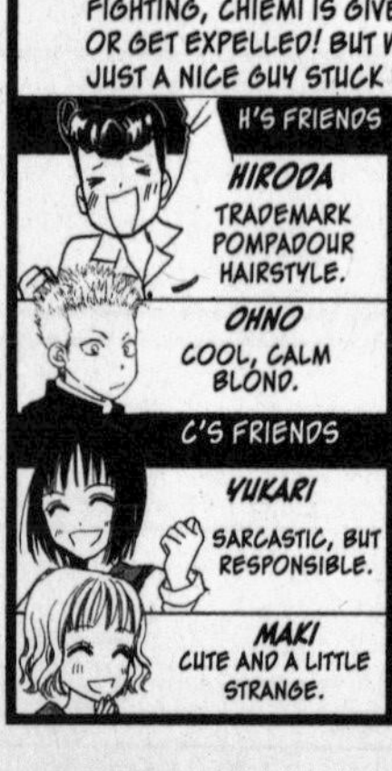
H'S FRIENDS
HIRODA
TRADEMARK POMPADOUR HAIRSTYLE.
OHNO
COOL, CALM BLOND.
C'S FRIENDS
YUKARI
SARCASTIC, BUT RESPONSIBLE.
MAKI
CUTE AND A LITTLE STRANGE.

★ AFTER THREE MONTHS, CHIEMI AND HIRATA FINALLY GOT TO GO ON THEIR FIRST REAL DATE. BUT THANKS TO CHIEMI'S IMAGINATION, THINGS DIDN'T GO AS PLANNED. CHIEMI THEN GOT JUMPED BY A GANG OF UPPERCLASSMEN WITH A GRUDGE AGAINST HIRATA, BUT HIS TIMELY ARRIVAL SENT THEM PACKING!

★ CHIEMI'S COUSIN MIZUKI TRANSFERRED TO THEIR SCHOOL AND THREW A MONKEY WRENCH INTO CHIEMI AND HIRATA'S RELATIONSHIP. ONE EXPLOSIVE ARGUMENT LATER, HIRATA DUMPED CHIEMI! DUE TO CIRCUMSTANCES BEYOND THEIR CONTROL, CHIEMI AND MIZUKI WOUND UP IN BIG TROUBLE, BUT HIRATA ONCE AGAIN CAME TO THE RESCUE. HE AND CHIEMI GOT BACK TOGETHER, AND THINGS RETURNED TO NORMAL, UNTIL...

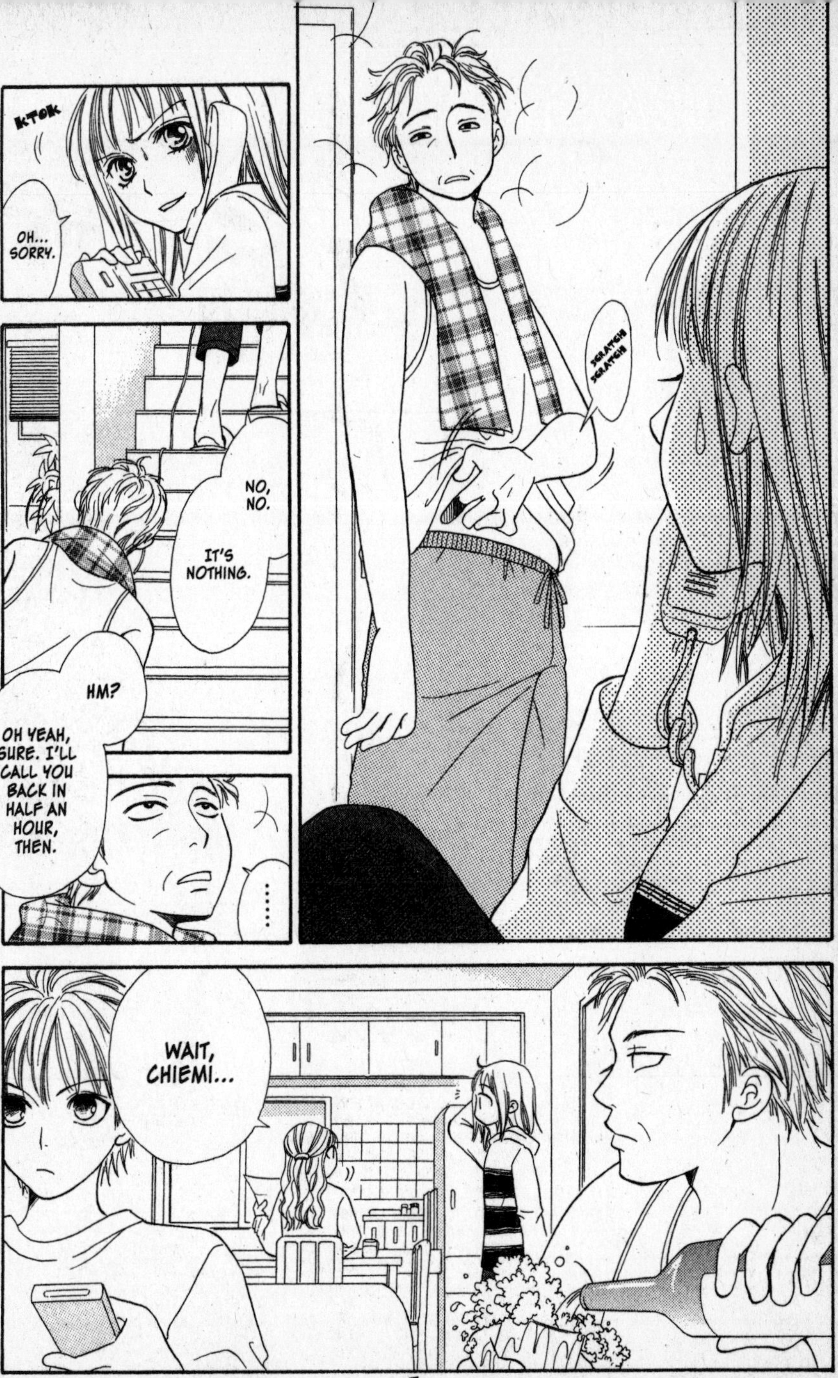
SCRATCH SCRATCH
KTOK
OH... SORRY.
NO, NO.
IT'S NOTHING.
HM?
OH YEAH, SURE. I'LL CALL YOU BACK IN HALF AN HOUR, THEN.
......
WAIT, CHIEMI...

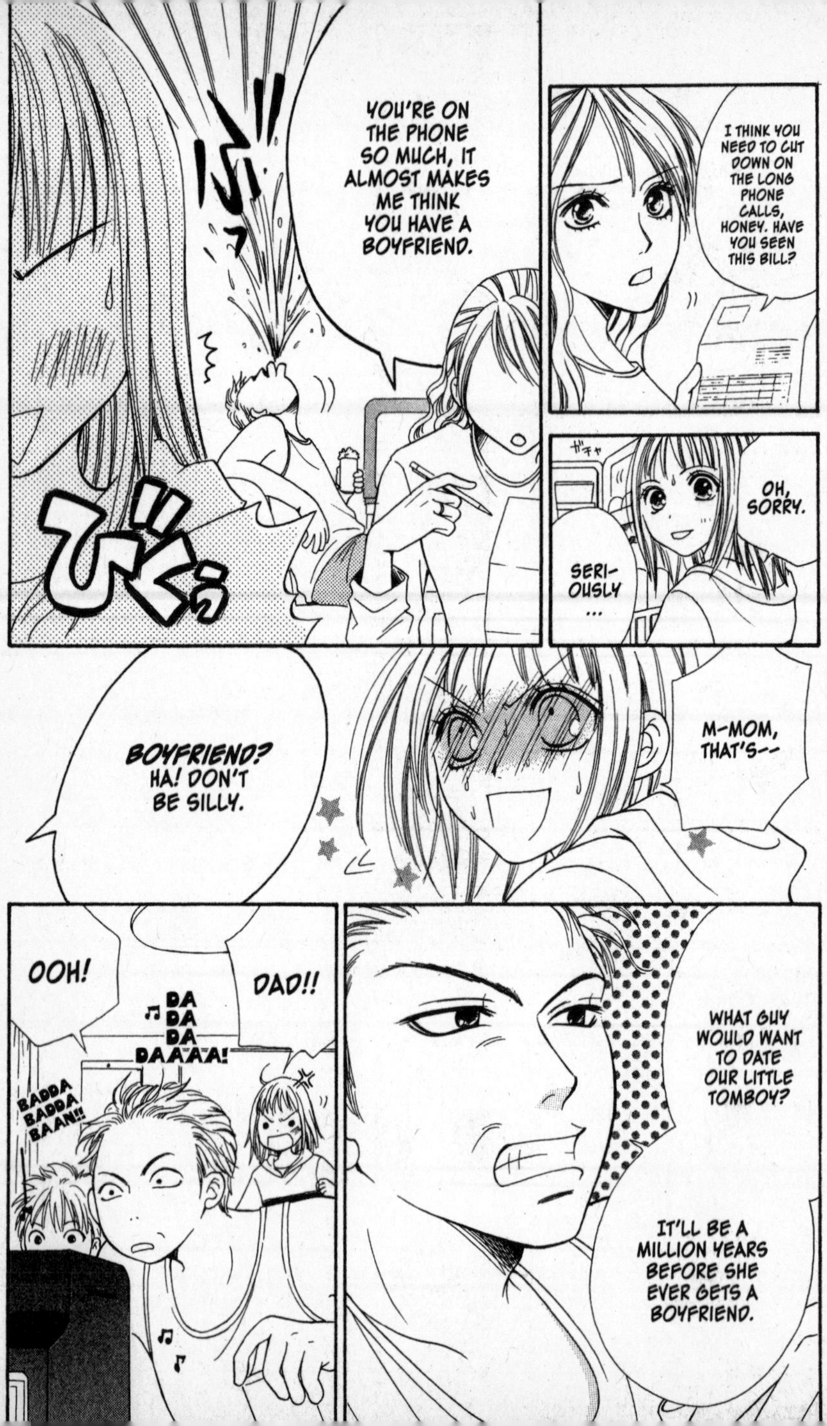
I THINK YOU NEED TO CUT DOWN ON THE LONG PHONE CALLS, HONEY. HAVE YOU SEEN THIS BILL?
ガチャ
OH, SORRY.
SERI-OUSLY...
YOU'RE ON THE PHONE SO MUCH, IT ALMOST MAKES ME THINK YOU HAVE A BOYFRIEND.
M-MOM, THAT'S--
BOYFRIEND? HA! DON'T BE SILLY.
WHAT GUY WOULD WANT TO DATE OUR LITTLE TOMBOY?
IT'LL BE A MILLION YEARS BEFORE SHE EVER GETS A BOYFRIEND.
DAD!!
DA DA DA DAAAA!
OOH!
BADDA BADDA BAAN!!

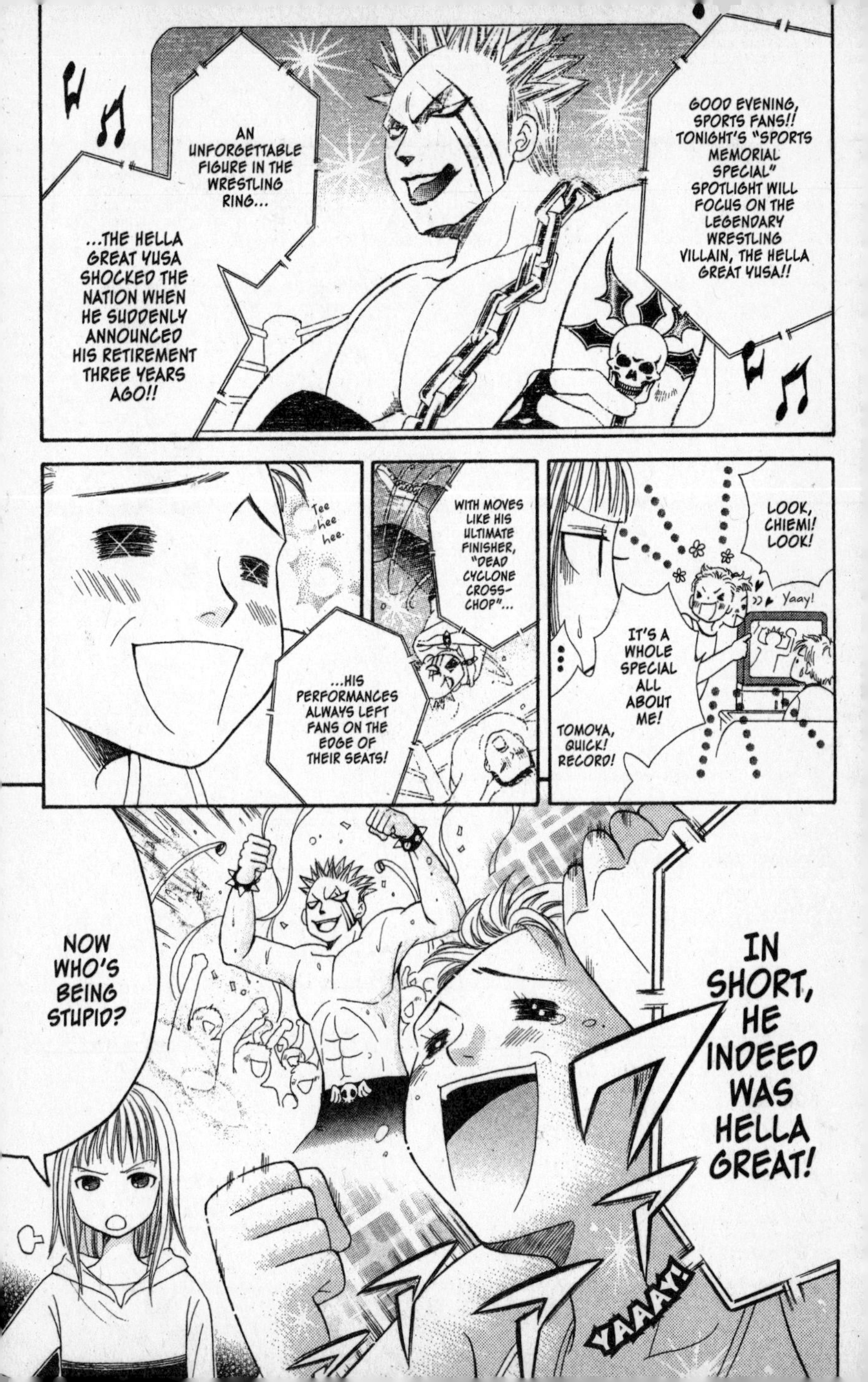
GOOD EVENING, SPORTS FANS!! TONIGHT'S "SPORTS MEMORIAL SPECIAL" SPOTLIGHT WILL FOCUS ON THE LEGENDARY WRESTLING VILLAIN, THE HELLA GREAT YUSA!!
AN UNFORGETTABLE FIGURE IN THE WRESTLING RING...
...THE HELLA GREAT YUSA SHOCKED THE NATION WHEN HE SUDDENLY ANNOUNCED HIS RETIREMENT THREE YEARS AGO!!
LOOK, CHIEMI! LOOK!
Yaay!
IT'S A WHOLE SPECIAL ALL ABOUT ME!
TOMOYA, QUICK! RECORD!
...
WITH MOVES LIKE HIS ULTIMATE FINISHER, "DEAD CYCLONE CROSS-CHOP"...
...HIS PERFORMANCES ALWAYS LEFT FANS ON THE EDGE OF THEIR SEATS!
Tee hee hee.
IN SHORT, HE INDEED WAS HELLA GREAT!
YAAAY!
NOW WHO'S BEING STUPID?

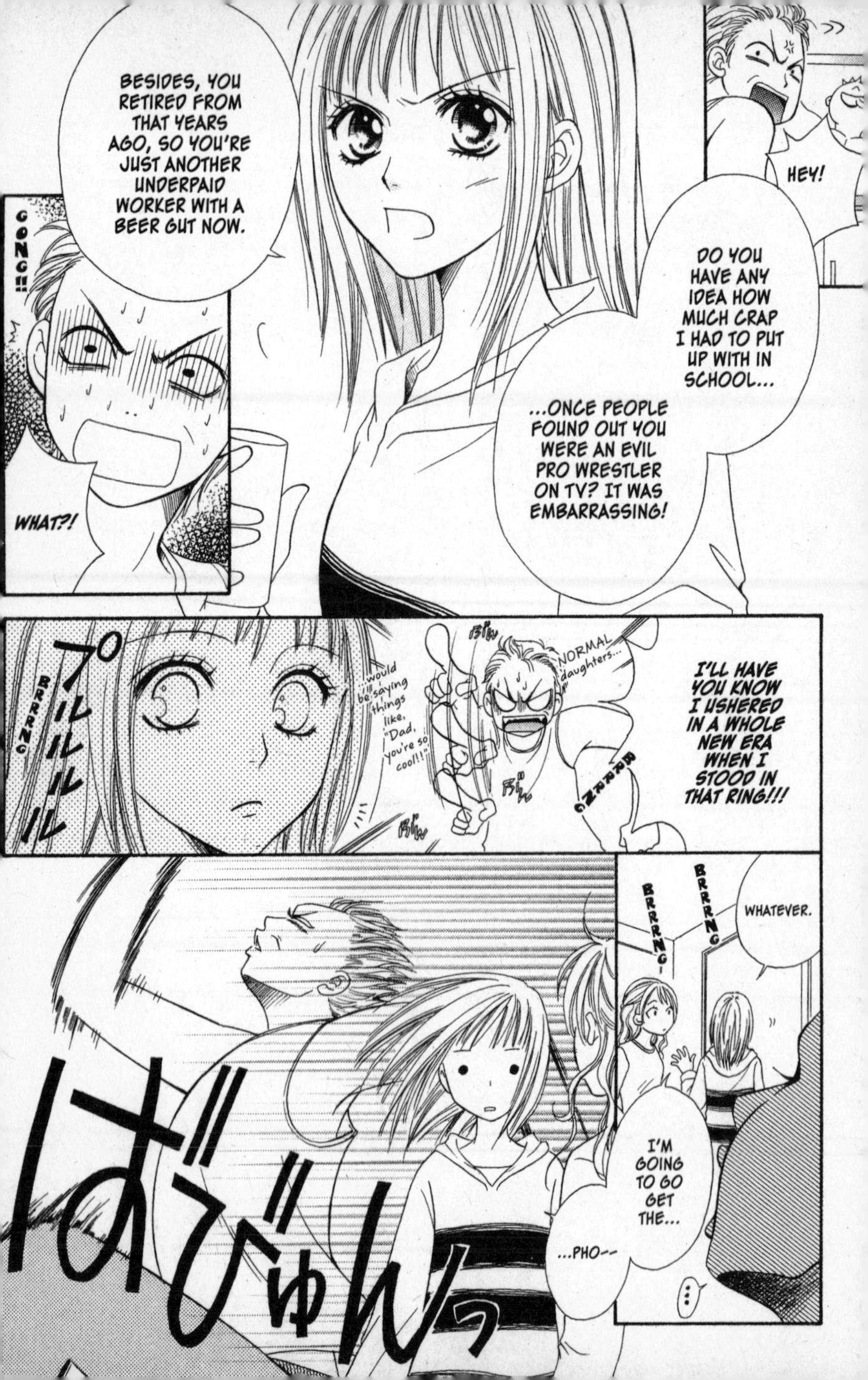
HEY!
DO YOU HAVE ANY IDEA HOW MUCH CRAP I HAD TO PUT UP WITH IN SCHOOL...
...ONCE PEOPLE FOUND OUT YOU WERE AN EVIL PRO WRESTLER ON TV? IT WAS EMBARRASSING!
BESIDES, YOU RETIRED FROM THAT YEARS AGO, SO YOU'RE JUST ANOTHER UNDERPAID WORKER WITH A BEER GUT NOW.
GONG!!
WHAT?!
I'LL HAVE YOU KNOW I USHERED IN A WHOLE NEW ERA WHEN I STOOD IN THAT RING!!!
"NORMAL daughters...
would be saying things like, "Dad, you're so cool!!""
プルルル
BRRRNG
WHATEVER.
BRRRNG
BRRRNG!
I'M GOING TO GO GET THE...
...PHO--
...
ばびゅんっ

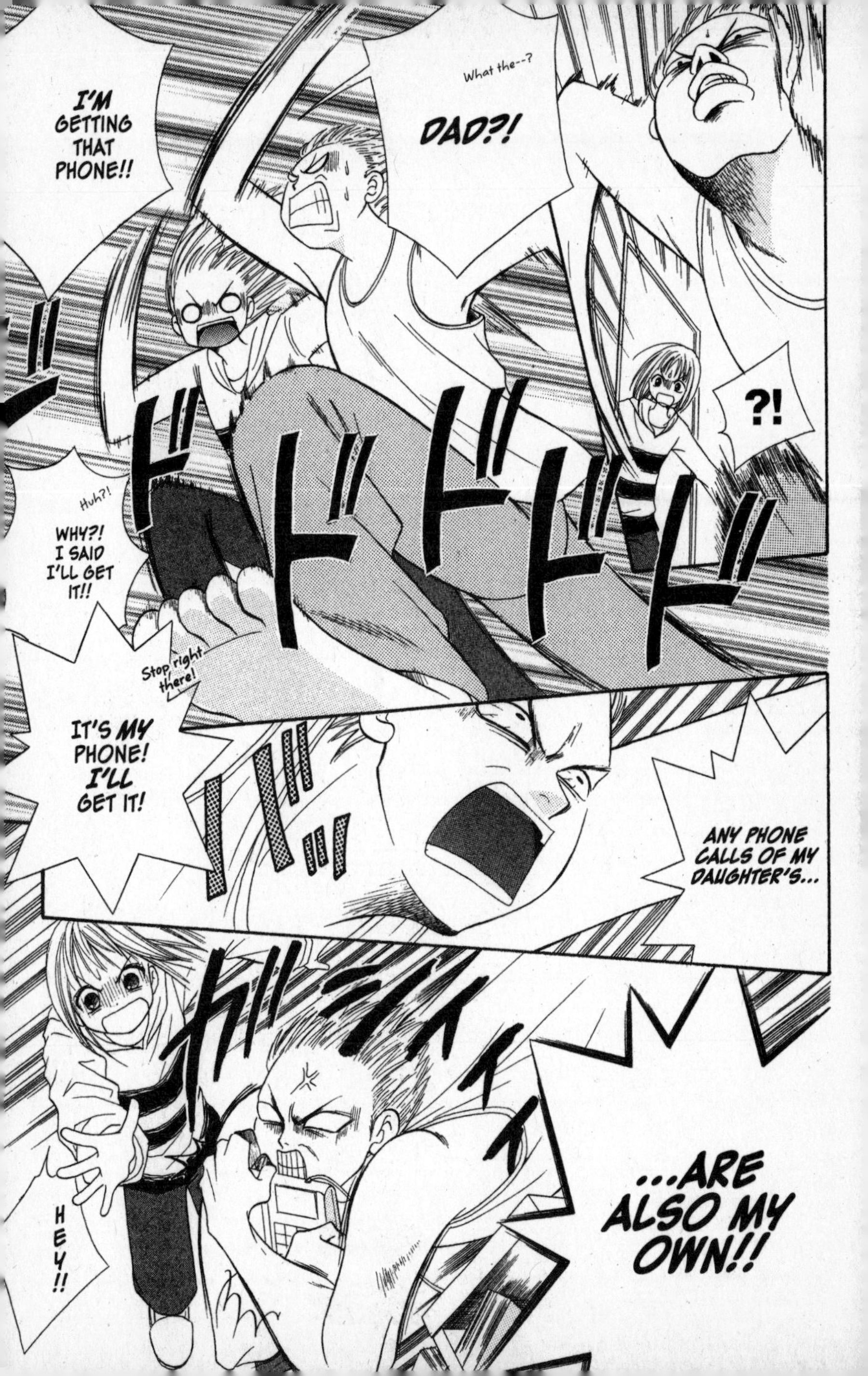
What the--?
DAD?!
I'M GETTING THAT PHONE!!
?!
Huh?!
WHY?! I SAID I'LL GET IT!!
Stop right there!
IT'S MY PHONE! I'LL GET IT!
ANY PHONE CALLS OF MY DAUGHTER'S...
...ARE ALSO MY OWN!!
HEY!!

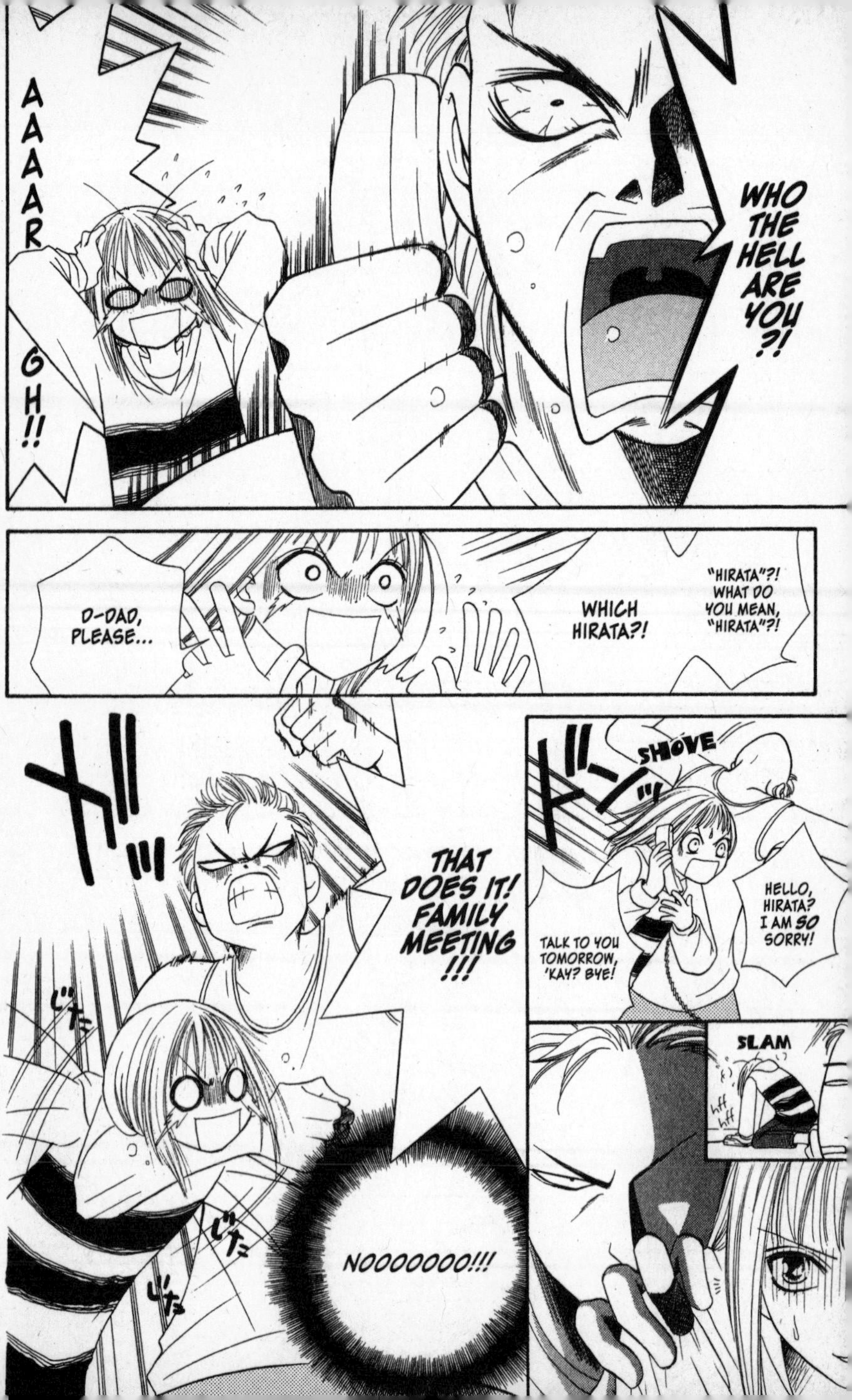
WHO THE HELL ARE YOU?!
AAAARGH!!
"HIRATA"?! WHAT DO YOU MEAN, "HIRATA"?!
WHICH HIRATA?!
D-DAD, PLEASE...
SHOVE
HELLO, HIRATA? I AM SO SORRY!
TALK TO YOU TOMORROW, 'KAY? BYE!
SLAM
THAT DOES IT! FAMILY MEETING!!!
NOOOOOOO!!!

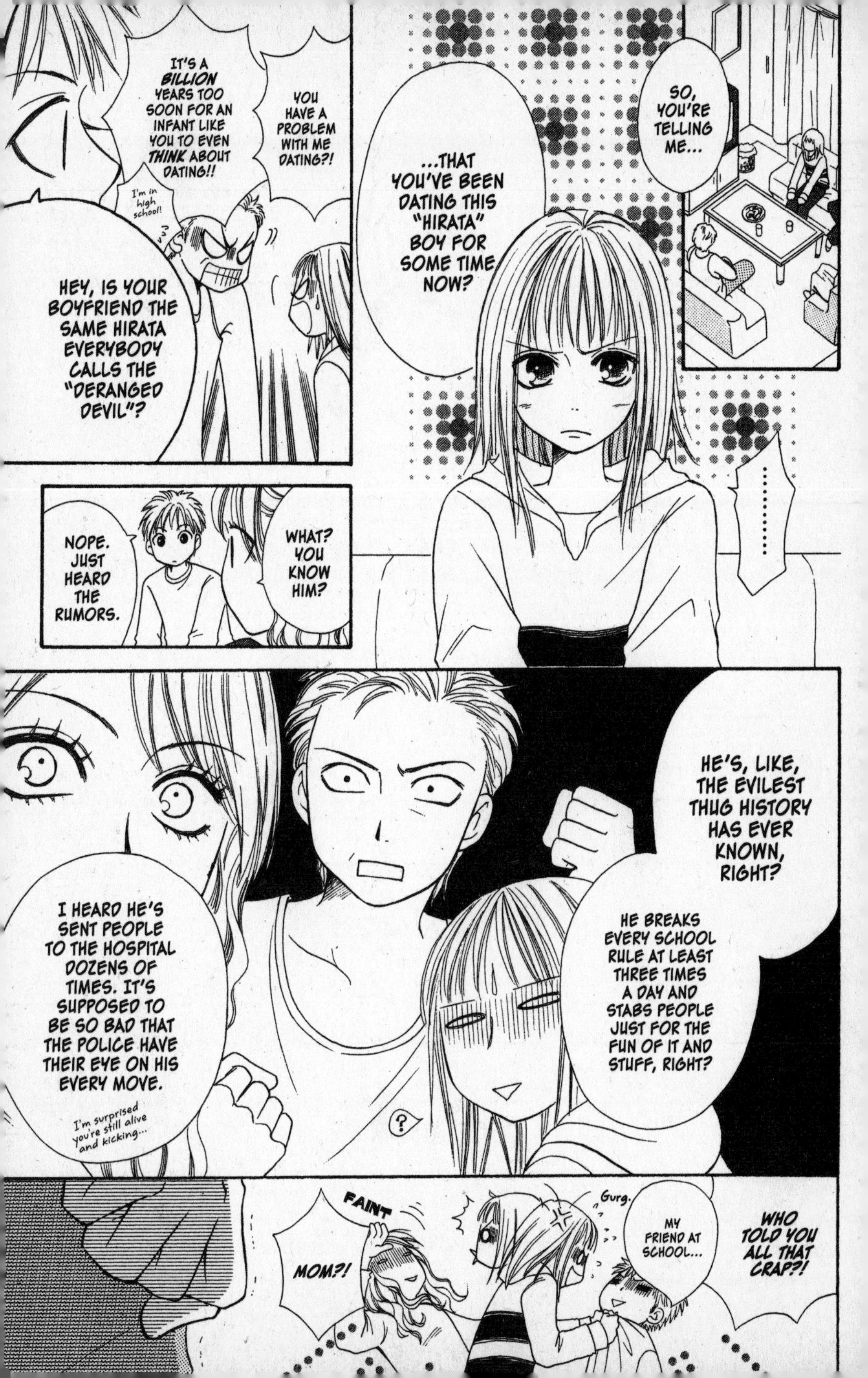
SO, YOU'RE TELLING ME...
...THAT YOU'VE BEEN DATING THIS "HIRATA" BOY FOR SOME TIME NOW?
......
YOU HAVE A PROBLEM WITH ME DATING?!
IT'S A BILLION YEARS TOO SOON FOR AN INFANT LIKE YOU TO EVEN THINK ABOUT DATING!!
I'm in high school!
HEY, IS YOUR BOYFRIEND THE SAME HIRATA EVERYBODY CALLS THE "DERANGED DEVIL"?
WHAT? YOU KNOW HIM?
NOPE. JUST HEARD THE RUMORS.
HE'S, LIKE, THE EVILEST THUG HISTORY HAS EVER KNOWN, RIGHT?
HE BREAKS EVERY SCHOOL RULE AT LEAST THREE TIMES A DAY AND STABS PEOPLE JUST FOR THE FUN OF IT AND STUFF, RIGHT?
I HEARD HE'S SENT PEOPLE TO THE HOSPITAL DOZENS OF TIMES. IT'S SUPPOSED TO BE SO BAD THAT THE POLICE HAVE THEIR EYE ON HIS EVERY MOVE.
I'm surprised you're still alive and kicking...
?
WHO TOLD YOU ALL THAT CRAP?!
Gurg.
MY FRIEND AT SCHOOL...
MOM?!
FAINT

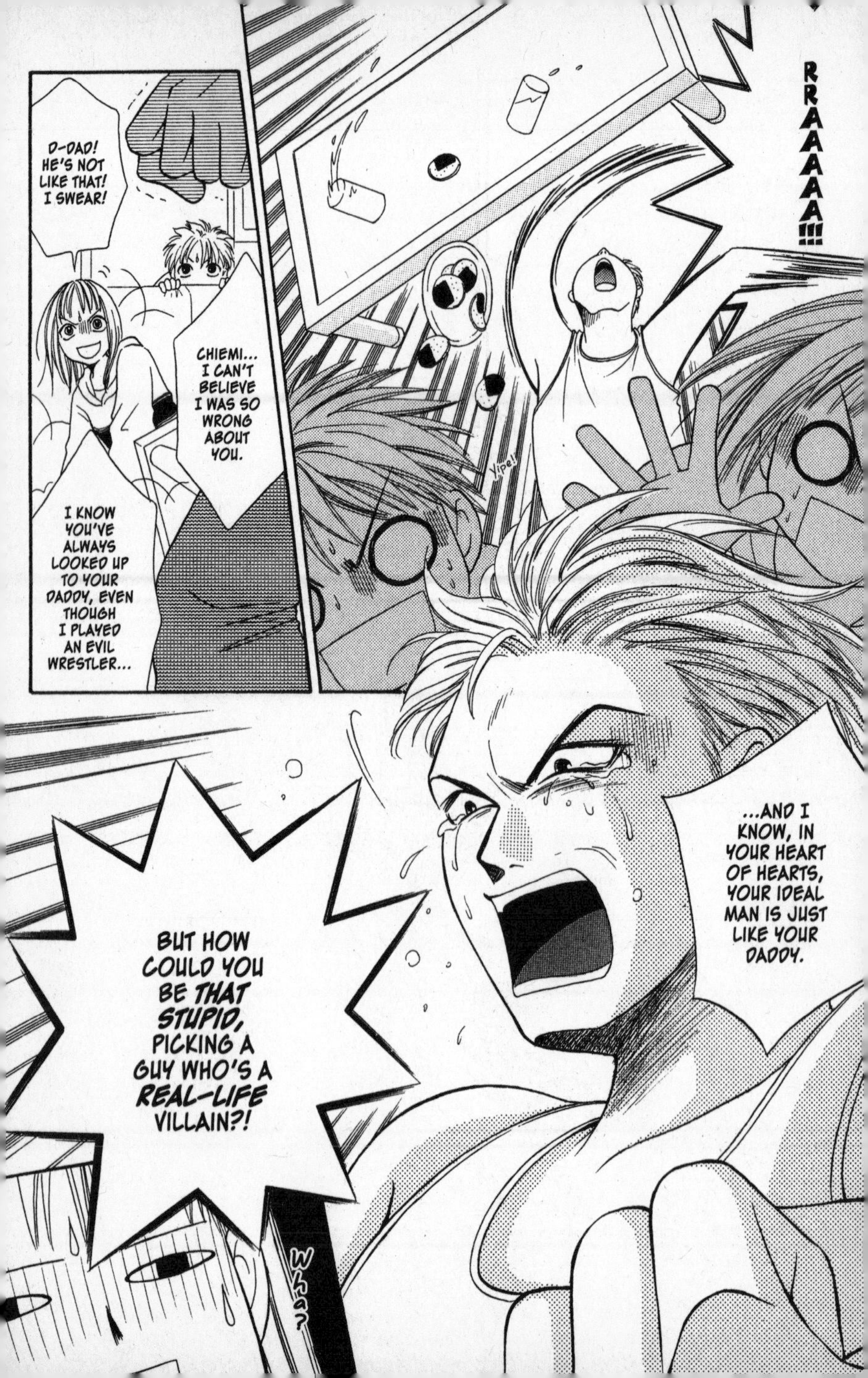
RRAAAAA!!!
Yipe!
D-DAD! HE'S NOT LIKE THAT! I SWEAR!
CHIEMI... I CAN'T BELIEVE I WAS SO WRONG ABOUT YOU.
I KNOW YOU'VE ALWAYS LOOKED UP TO YOUR DADDY, EVEN THOUGH I PLAYED AN EVIL WRESTLER...
...AND I KNOW, IN YOUR HEART OF HEARTS, YOUR IDEAL MAN IS JUST LIKE YOUR DADDY.
BUT HOW COULD YOU BE *THAT STUPID*, PICKING A GUY WHO'S A *REAL-LIFE* VILLAIN?!
Wha?

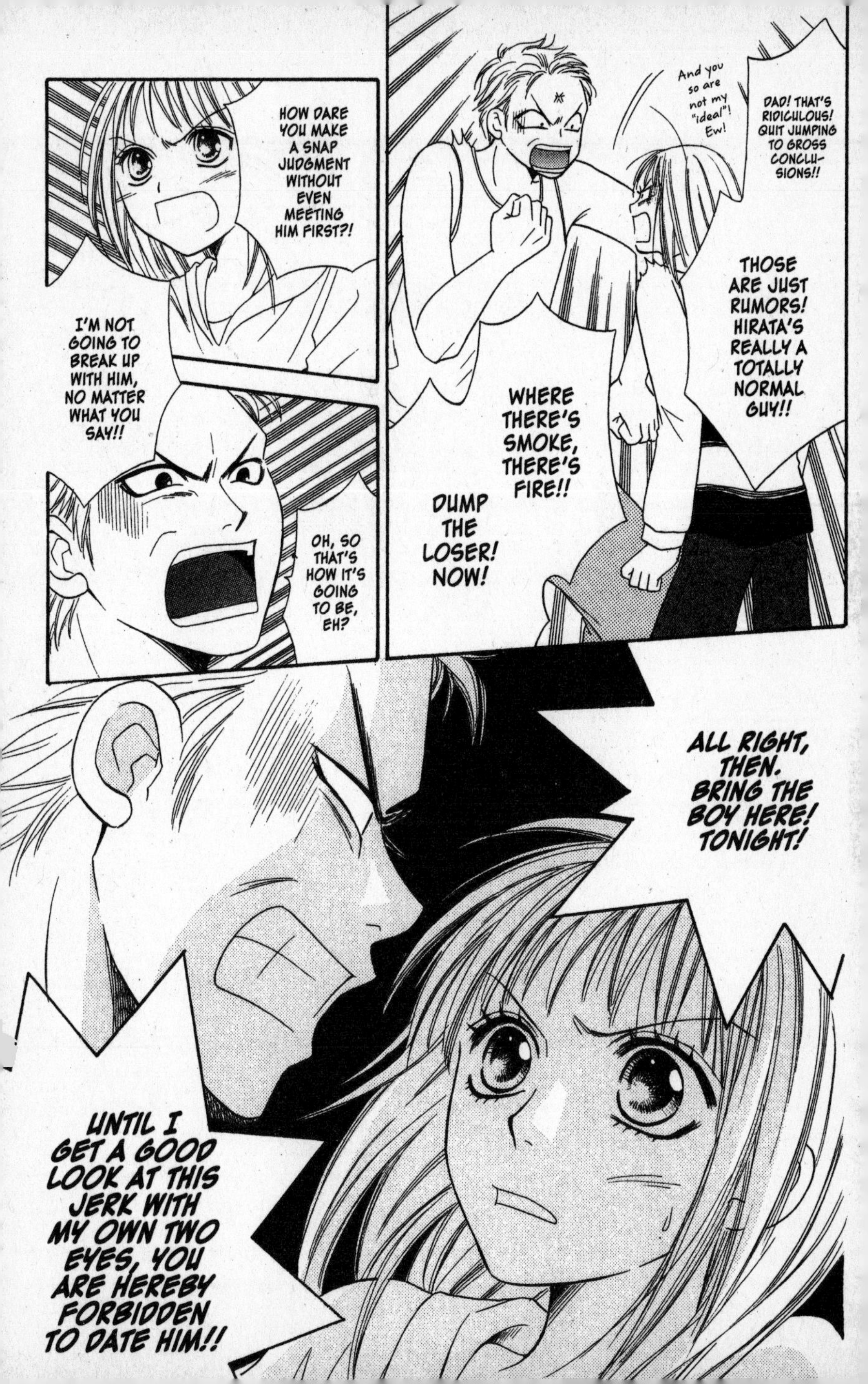
DAD! THAT'S RIDICULOUS! QUIT JUMPING TO GROSS CONCLU-SIONS!!
And you so are not my "ideal"! Ew!
THOSE ARE JUST RUMORS! HIRATA'S REALLY A TOTALLY NORMAL GUY!!
WHERE THERE'S SMOKE, THERE'S FIRE!!
DUMP THE LOSER! NOW!
HOW DARE YOU MAKE A SNAP JUDGMENT WITHOUT EVEN MEETING HIM FIRST?!
I'M NOT GOING TO BREAK UP WITH HIM, NO MATTER WHAT YOU SAY!!
OH, SO THAT'S HOW IT'S GOING TO BE, EH?
ALL RIGHT, THEN. BRING THE BOY HERE! TONIGHT!
UNTIL I GET A GOOD LOOK AT THIS JERK WITH MY OWN TWO EYES, YOU ARE HEREBY FORBIDDEN TO DATE HIM!!

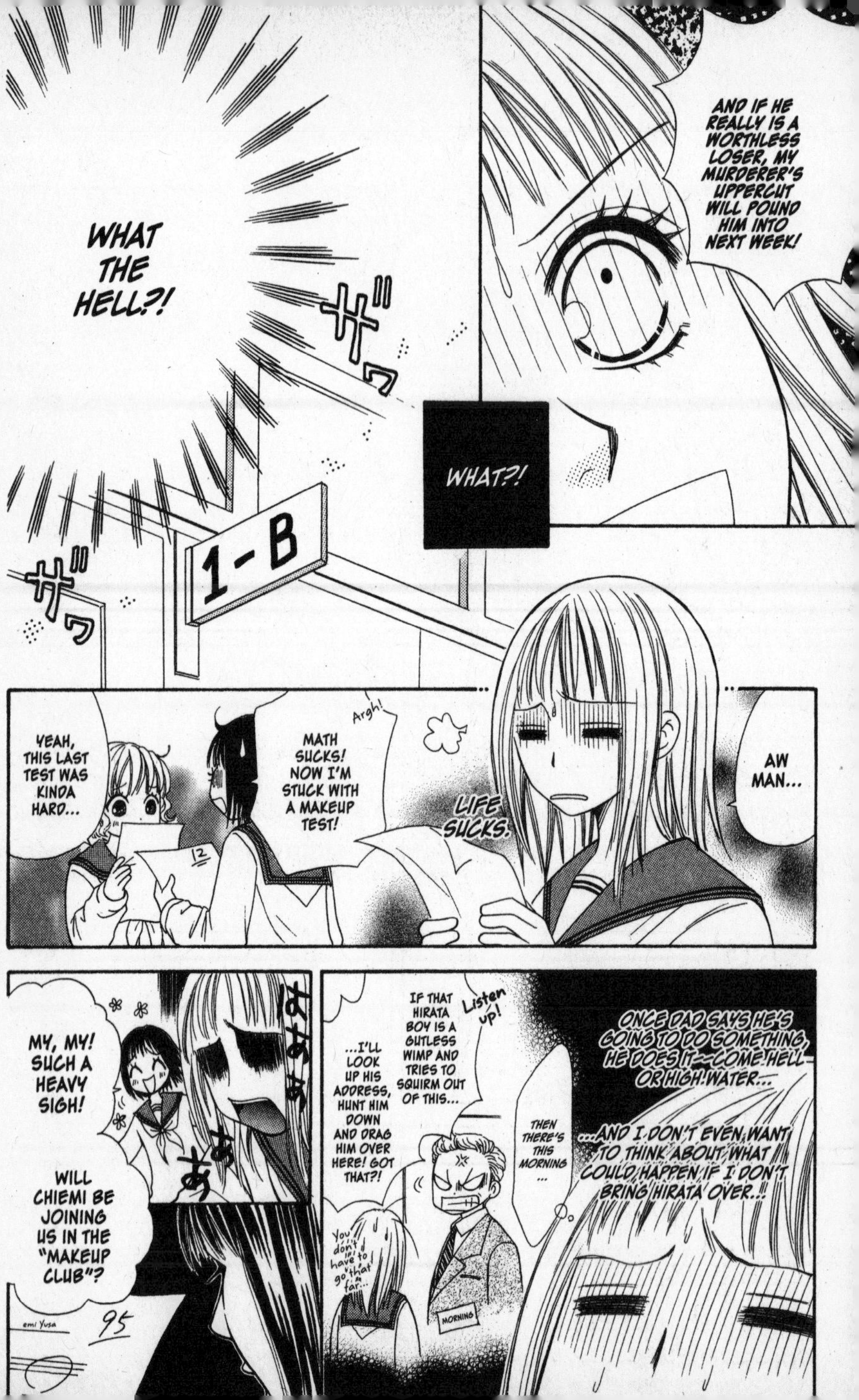
AND IF HE REALLY IS A WORTHLESS LOSER, MY MURDERER'S UPPERCUT WILL POUND HIM INTO NEXT WEEK!
WHAT?!
ザワ
WHAT THE HELL?!
ザワ
AW MAN...
LIFE SUCKS.
Argh!
MATH SUCKS! NOW I'M STUCK WITH A MAKEUP TEST!
12
YEAH, THIS LAST TEST WAS KINDA HARD...
ONCE DAD SAYS HE'S GOING TO DO SOMETHING, HE DOES IT—COME HELL OR HIGH WATER...
...AND I DON'T EVEN WANT TO THINK ABOUT WHAT COULD HAPPEN IF I DON'T BRING HIRATA OVER...!
THEN THERE'S THIS MORNING...
Listen up!
IF THAT HIRATA BOY IS A GUTLESS WIMP AND TRIES TO SQUIRM OUT OF THIS...
...I'LL LOOK UP HIS ADDRESS, HUNT HIM DOWN AND DRAG HIM OVER HERE! GOT THAT?!
You don't have to go that far...
MORNING
はあああ
MY, MY! SUCH A HEAVY SIGH!
WILL CHIEMI BE JOINING US IN THE "MAKEUP CLUB"?
emi Yusa

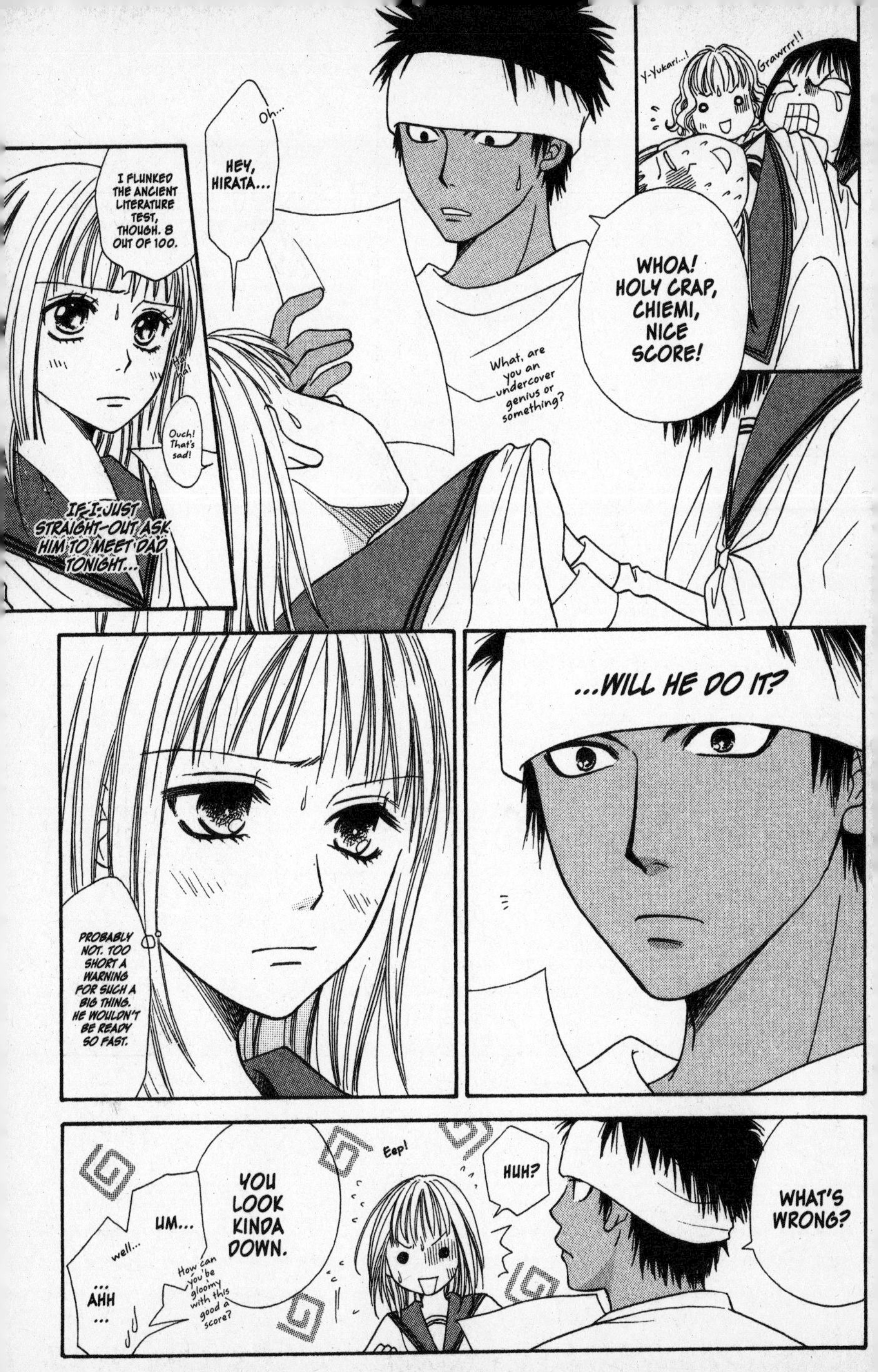
Y-Yukari...!
Grawrrr!!
WHOA! HOLY CRAP, CHIEMI, NICE SCORE!
What, are you an undercover genius or something?
Oh...
HEY, HIRATA...
I FLUNKED THE ANCIENT LITERATURE TEST, THOUGH. 8 OUT OF 100.
Ha ha!
Ouch! That's sad!
IF I JUST STRAIGHT-OUT ASK HIM TO MEET DAD TONIGHT...
...WILL HE DO IT?
PROBABLY NOT. TOO SHORT A WARNING FOR SUCH A BIG THING. HE WOULDN'T BE READY SO FAST.
WHAT'S WRONG?
HUH?
Eep!
YOU LOOK KINDA DOWN.
How can you be gloomy with this good a score?
UM...
well...
...AHH...

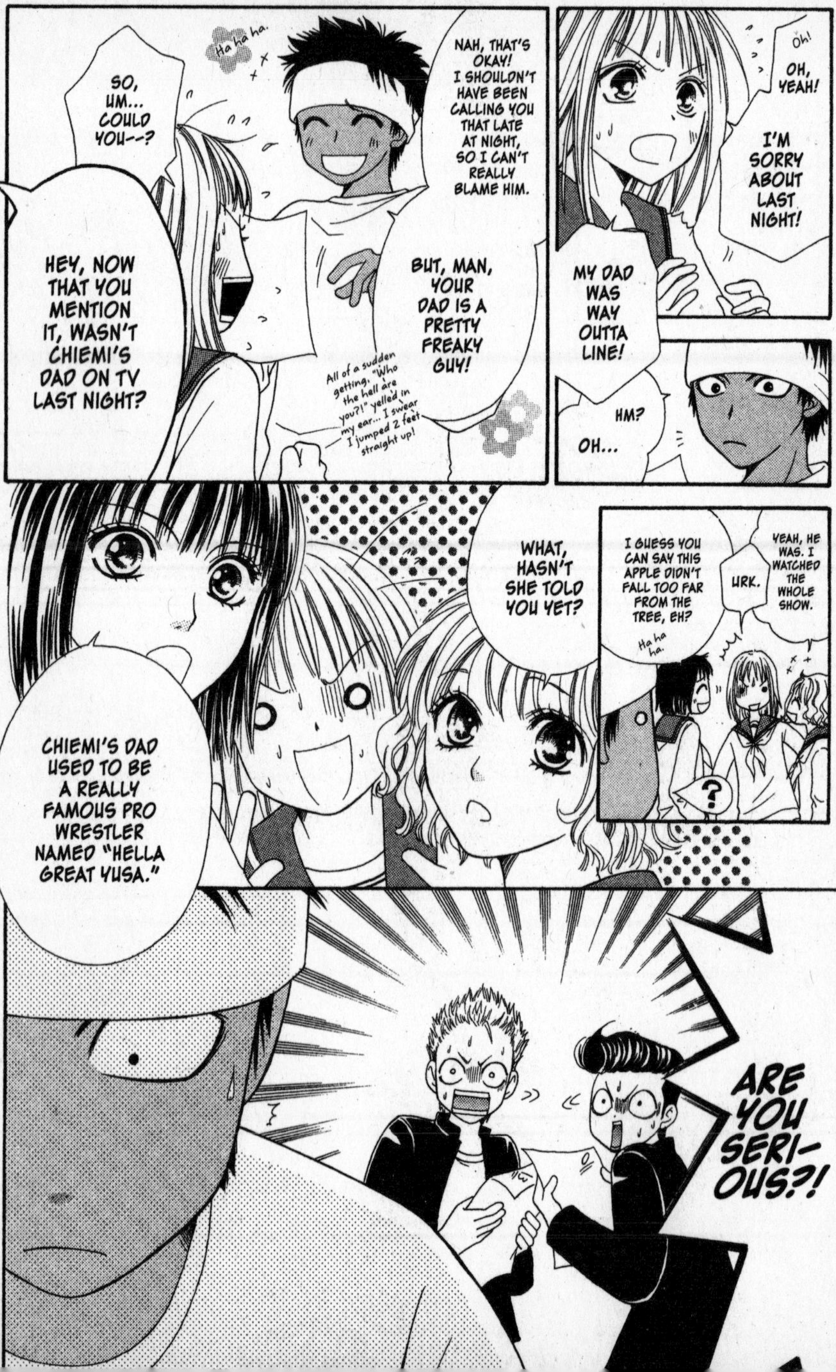
Oh!
OH, YEAH!
I'M SORRY ABOUT LAST NIGHT!
MY DAD WAS WAY OUTTA LINE!
HM?
OH...
NAH, THAT'S OKAY! I SHOULDN'T HAVE BEEN CALLING YOU THAT LATE AT NIGHT, SO I CAN'T REALLY BLAME HIM.
Ha ha ha.
SO, UM... COULD YOU--?
BUT, MAN, YOUR DAD IS A PRETTY FREAKY GUY!
All of a sudden getting, "Who the hell are you?!" yelled in my ear... I swear I jumped 2 feet straight up!
HEY, NOW THAT YOU MENTION IT, WASN'T CHIEMI'S DAD ON TV LAST NIGHT?
YEAH, HE WAS. I WATCHED THE WHOLE SHOW.
URK.
I GUESS YOU CAN SAY THIS APPLE DIDN'T FALL TOO FAR FROM THE TREE, EH?
Ha ha ha.
?
WHAT, HASN'T SHE TOLD YOU YET?
CHIEMI'S DAD USED TO BE A REALLY FAMOUS PRO WRESTLER NAMED "HELLA GREAT YUSA."
ARE YOU SERI-OUS?!

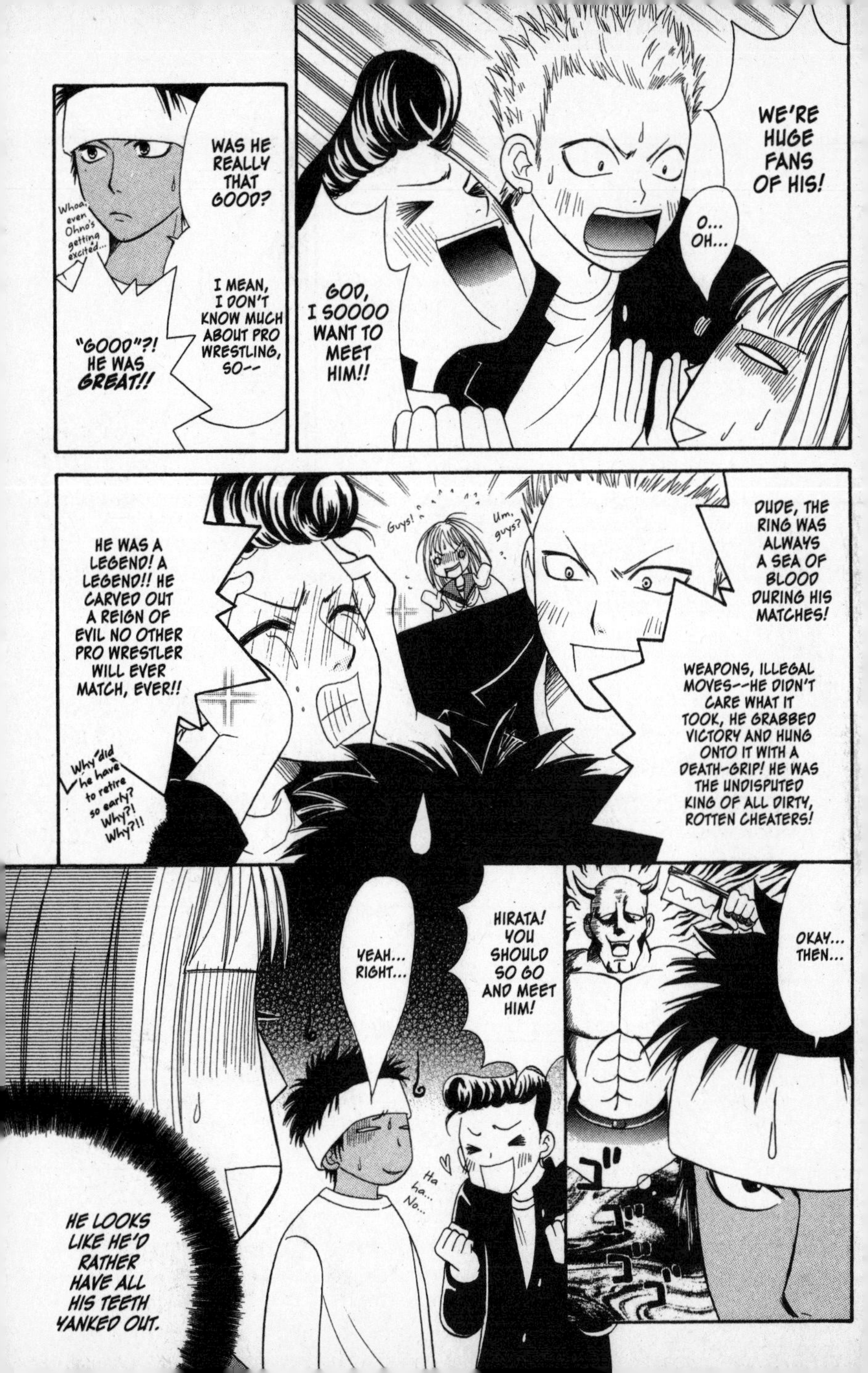

WE'RE HUGE FANS OF HIS!
O... OH...
GOD, I SOOOO WANT TO MEET HIM!!
WAS HE REALLY THAT GOOD?
I MEAN, I DON'T KNOW MUCH ABOUT PRO WRESTLING, SO--
Whoa, even Ohno's getting excited...
"GOOD"?! HE WAS GREAT!!
DUDE, THE RING WAS ALWAYS A SEA OF BLOOD DURING HIS MATCHES!
WEAPONS, ILLEGAL MOVES--HE DIDN'T CARE WHAT IT TOOK, HE GRABBED VICTORY AND HUNG ONTO IT WITH A DEATH-GRIP! HE WAS THE UNDISPUTED KING OF ALL DIRTY, ROTTEN CHEATERS!
Um, guys?
Guys!
HE WAS A LEGEND! A LEGEND!! HE CARVED OUT A REIGN OF EVIL NO OTHER PRO WRESTLER WILL EVER MATCH, EVER!!
Why did he have to retire so early? Why?! Why?!!
OKAY... THEN...
HIRATA! YOU SHOULD SO GO AND MEET HIM!
YEAH... RIGHT...
Ha ha... No...
HE LOOKS LIKE HE'D RATHER HAVE ALL HIS TEETH YANKED OUT.

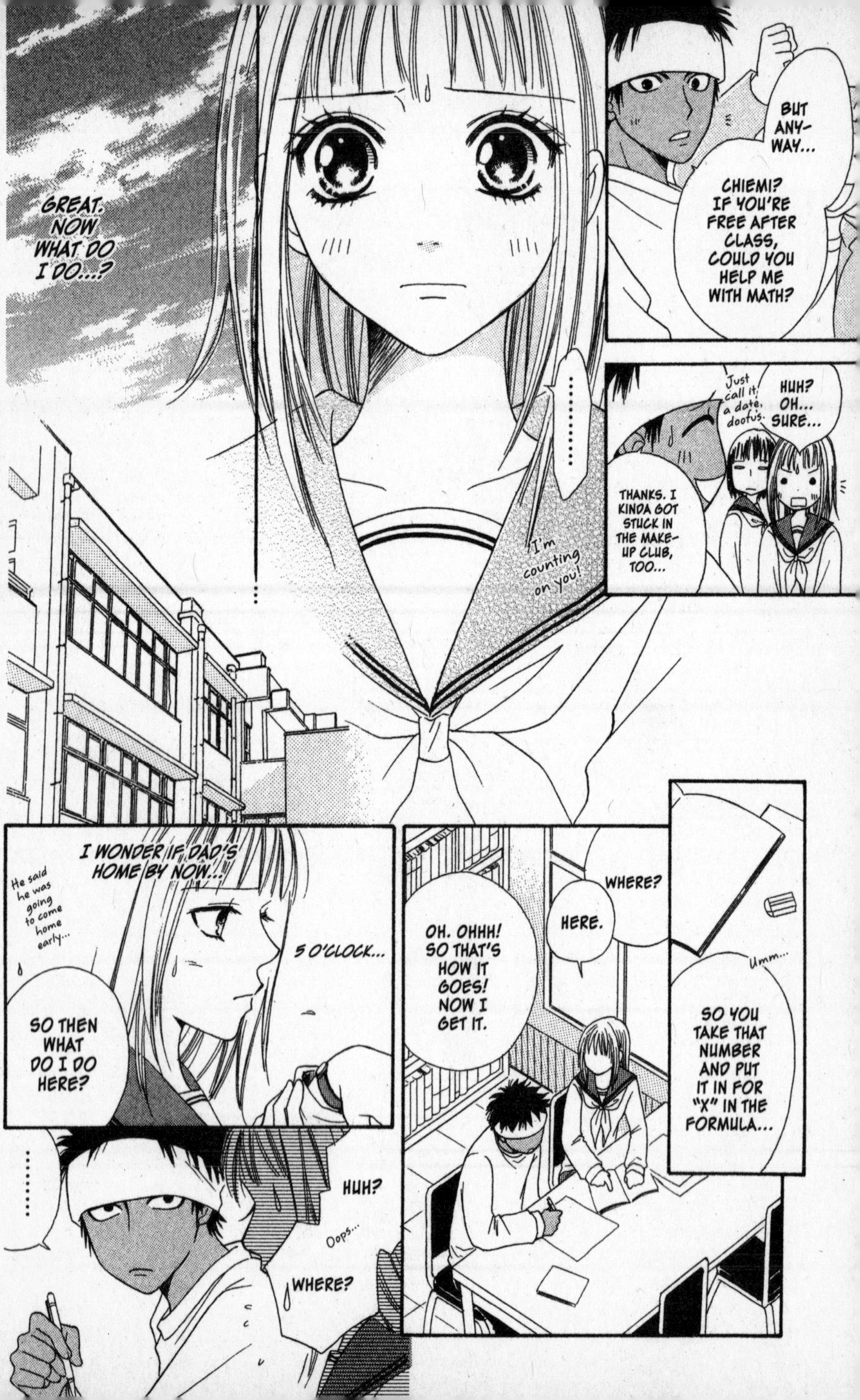

BUT ANY-WAY...
CHIEMI? IF YOU'RE FREE AFTER CLASS, COULD YOU HELP ME WITH MATH?
HUH? OH... SURE...
Just call it a date, doofus.
THANKS. I KINDA GOT STUCK IN THE MAKE-UP CLUB, TOO...
......
I'm counting on you!
GREAT. NOW WHAT DO I DO...?
......
Umm...
SO YOU TAKE THAT NUMBER AND PUT IT IN FOR "X" IN THE FORMULA...
WHERE?
HERE.
OH. OHHH! SO THAT'S HOW IT GOES! NOW I GET IT.
I WONDER IF DAD'S HOME BY NOW...
He said he was going to come home early...
5 O'CLOCK...
SO THEN WHAT DO I DO HERE?
HUH?
Oops...
WHERE?
......

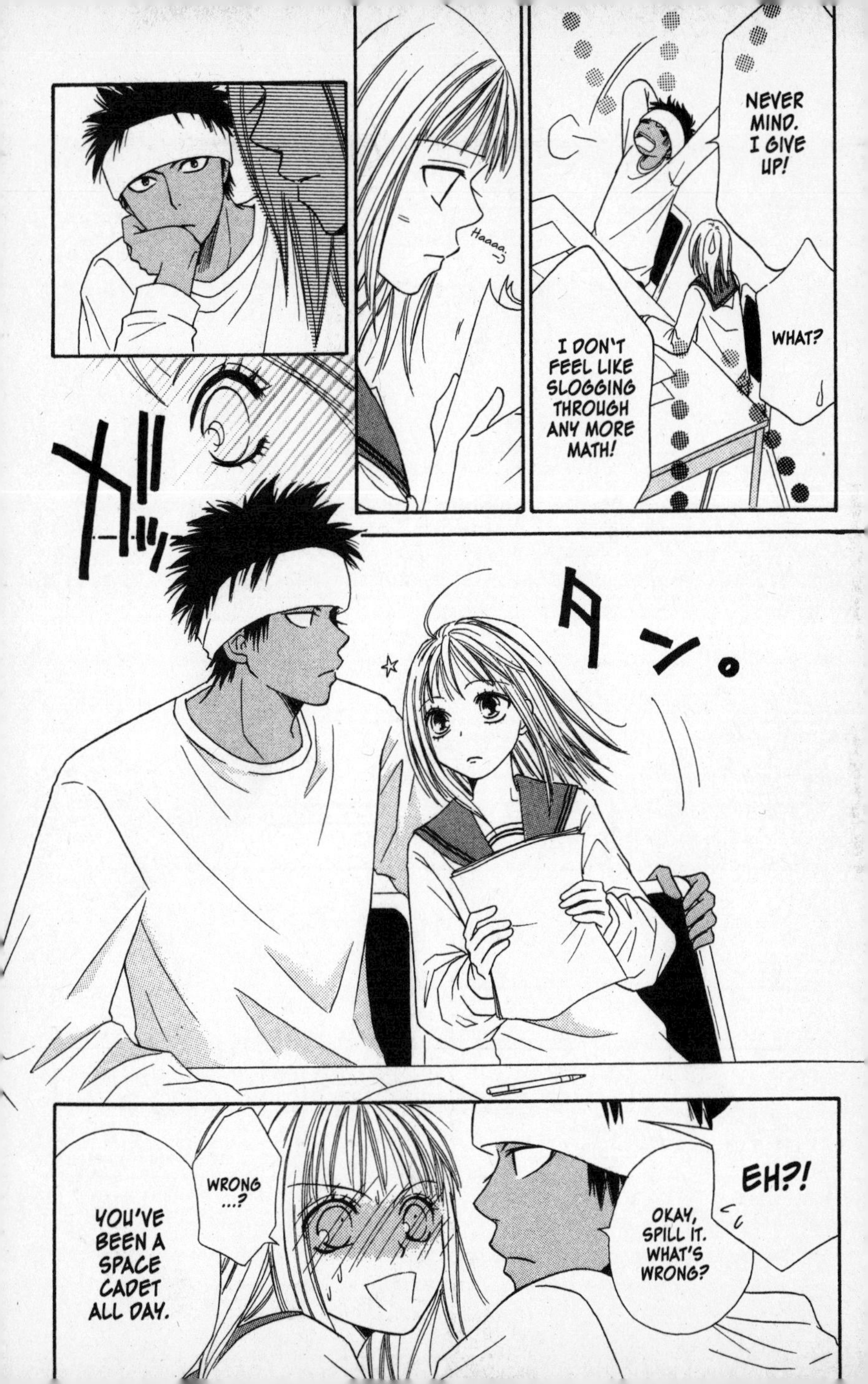
NEVER MIND. I GIVE UP!
WHAT?
I DON'T FEEL LIKE SLOGGING THROUGH ANY MORE MATH!
Haaaa.
ガッ
タン。
EH?!
OKAY, SPILL IT. WHAT'S WRONG?
WRONG ...?
YOU'VE BEEN A SPACE CADET ALL DAY.

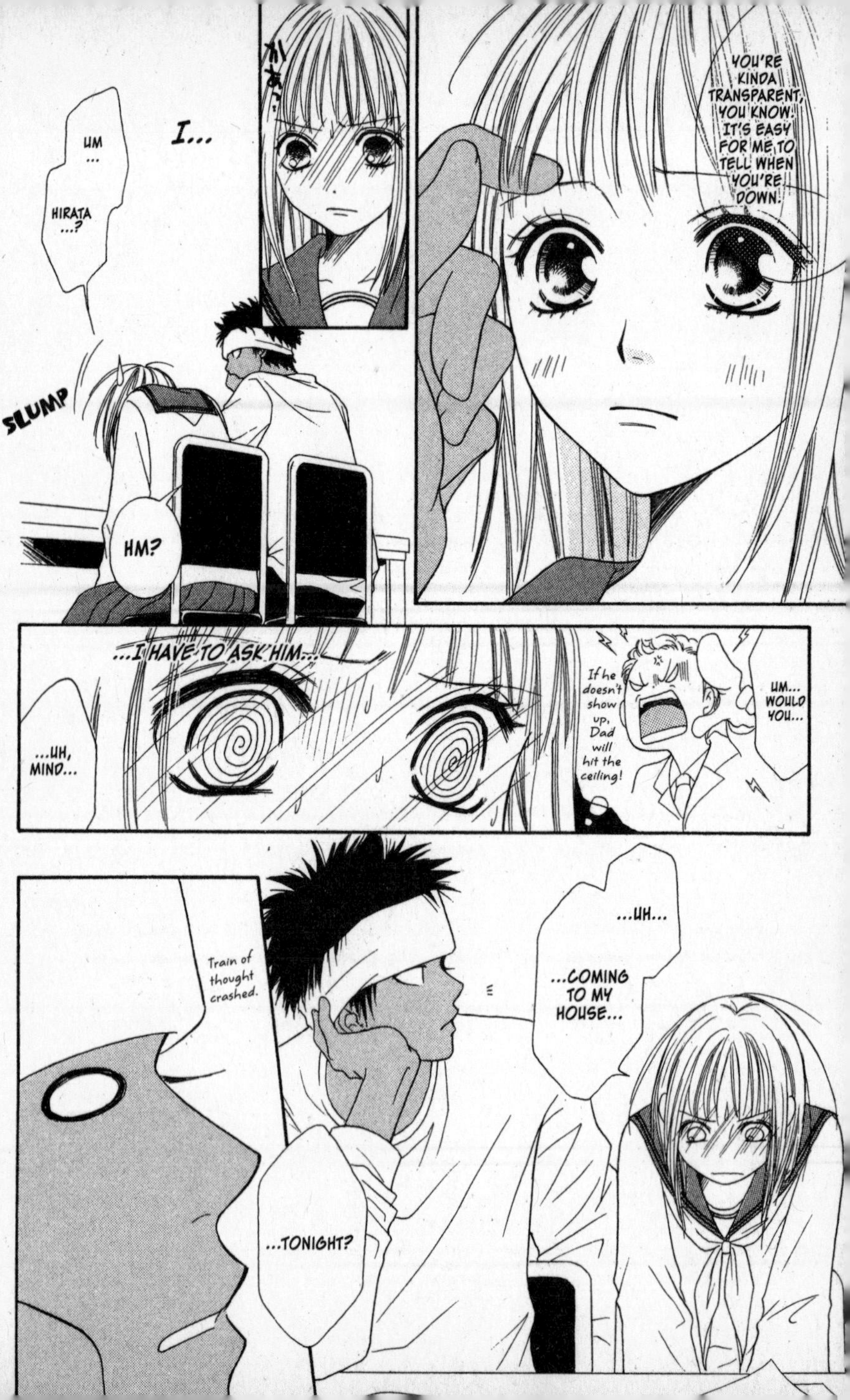
YOU'RE KINDA TRANSPARENT, YOU KNOW. IT'S EASY FOR ME TO TELL WHEN YOU'RE DOWN.
I...
UM ... HIRATA ...?
SLUMP
HM?
UM... WOULD YOU...
If he doesn't show up, Dad will hit the ceiling!
...I HAVE TO ASK HIM...
...UH, MIND...
...UH...
...COMING TO MY HOUSE...
Train of thought crashed.
...TONIGHT?

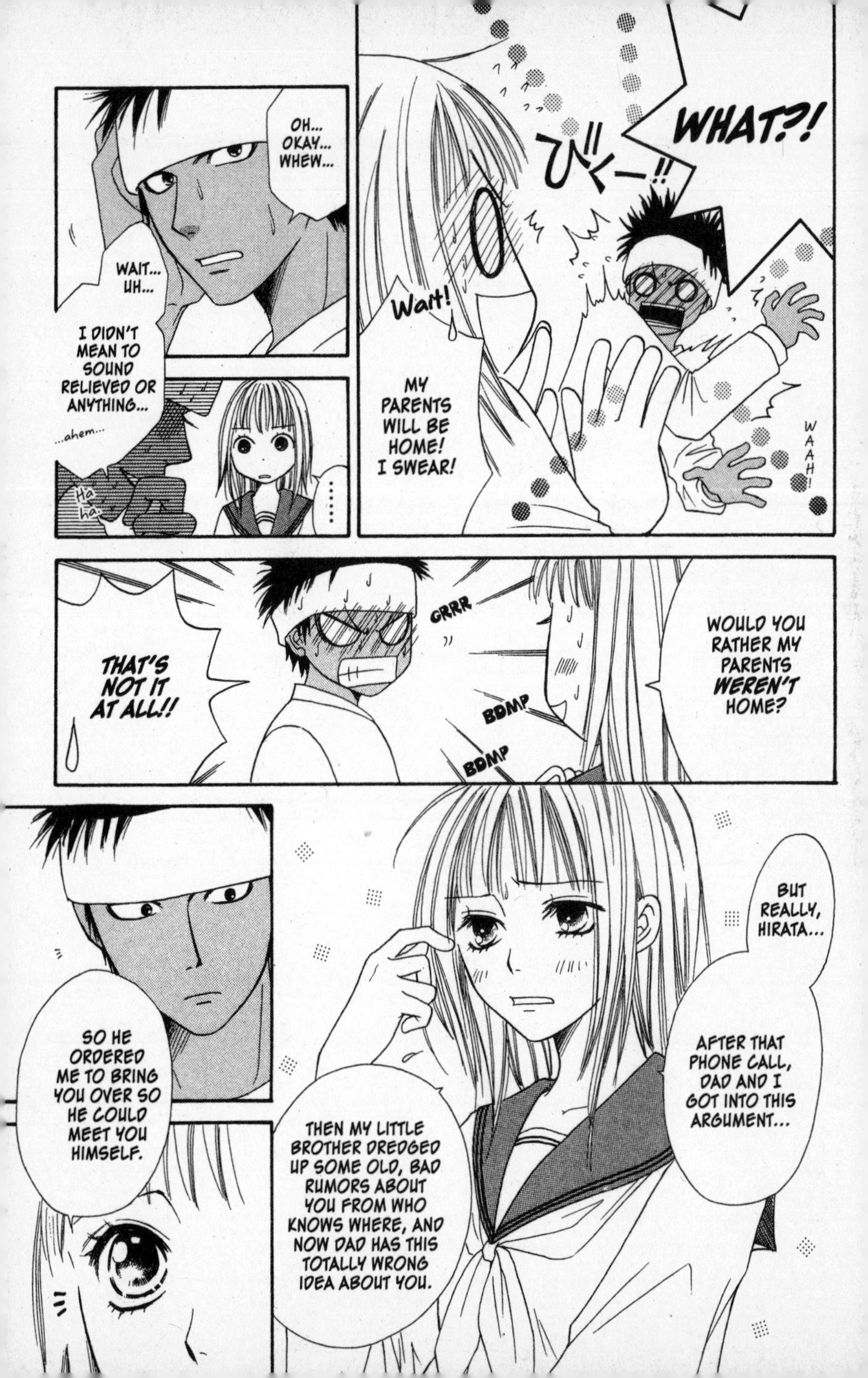
WHAT?!
びくー!!
WAAH!
Wait!
MY PARENTS WILL BE HOME! I SWEAR!
OH... OKAY... WHEW...
WAIT... UH...
I DIDN'T MEAN TO SOUND RELIEVED OR ANYTHING...
...ahem...
Ha ha.
......
WOULD YOU RATHER MY PARENTS WEREN'T HOME?
GRRR
BDMP
BDMP
THAT'S NOT IT AT ALL!!
BUT REALLY, HIRATA...
AFTER THAT PHONE CALL, DAD AND I GOT INTO THIS ARGUMENT...
THEN MY LITTLE BROTHER DREDGED UP SOME OLD, BAD RUMORS ABOUT YOU FROM WHO KNOWS WHERE, AND NOW DAD HAS THIS TOTALLY WRONG IDEA ABOUT YOU.
SO HE ORDERED ME TO BRING YOU OVER SO HE COULD MEET YOU HIMSELF.

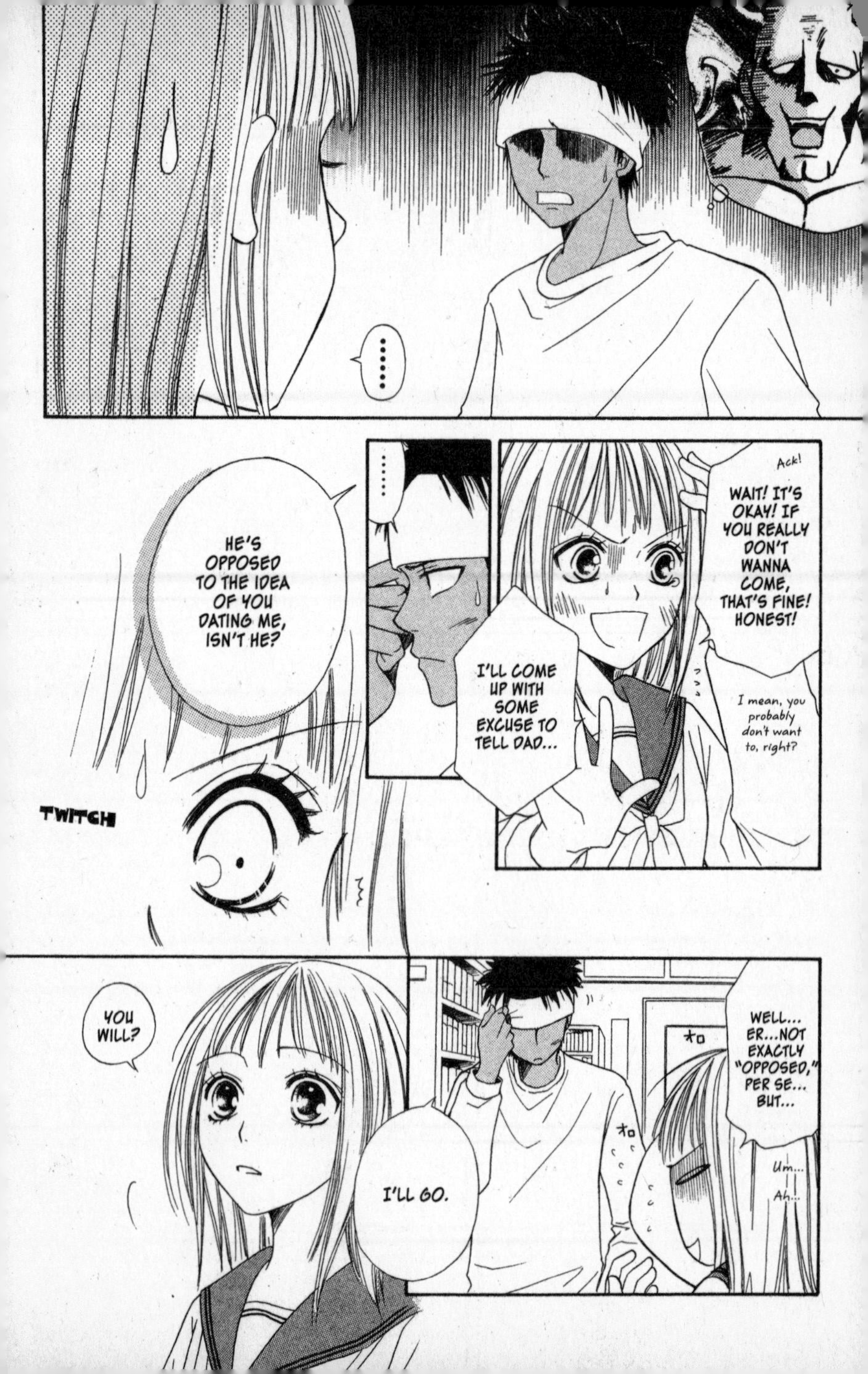
......
Ack!
WAIT! IT'S OKAY! IF YOU REALLY DON'T WANNA COME, THAT'S FINE! HONEST!
I mean, you probably don't want to, right?
I'LL COME UP WITH SOME EXCUSE TO TELL DAD...
......
HE'S OPPOSED TO THE IDEA OF YOU DATING ME, ISN'T HE?
TWITCH
WELL... ER...NOT EXACTLY "OPPOSED," PER SE... BUT...
Um...
Ah...
I'LL GO.
YOU WILL?

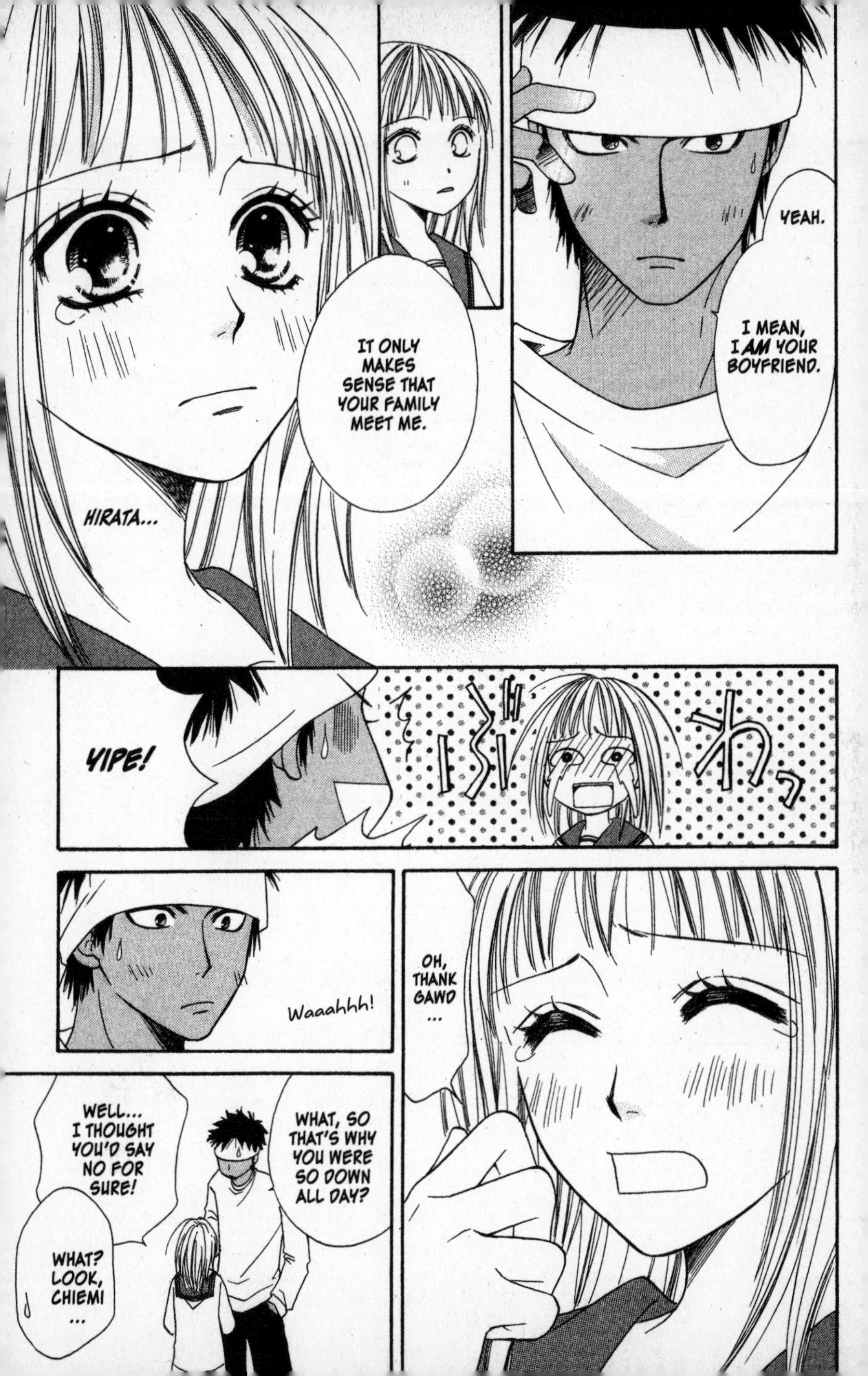
YEAH.
I MEAN, I AM YOUR BOYFRIEND.
IT ONLY MAKES SENSE THAT YOUR FAMILY MEET ME.
HIRATA...
YIPE!
OH, THANK GAWD ...
Waaahhh!
WHAT, SO THAT'S WHY YOU WERE SO DOWN ALL DAY?
WELL... I THOUGHT YOU'D SAY NO FOR SURE!
WHAT? LOOK, CHIEMI ...

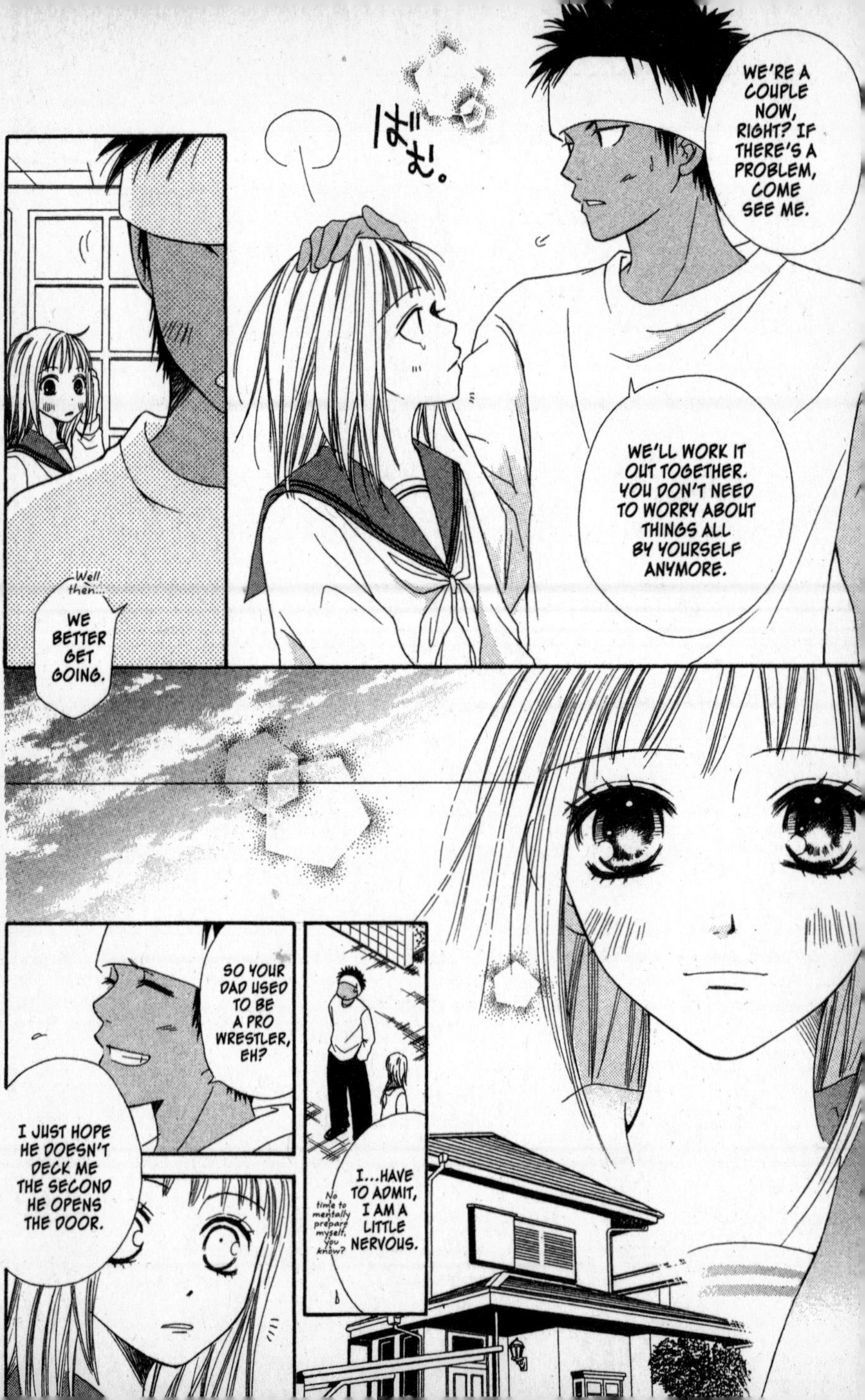

ばむ。
WE'RE A COUPLE NOW, RIGHT? IF THERE'S A PROBLEM, COME SEE ME.
WE'LL WORK IT OUT TOGETHER. YOU DON'T NEED TO WORRY ABOUT THINGS ALL BY YOURSELF ANYMORE.
Well then...
WE BETTER GET GOING.
I...HAVE TO ADMIT, I AM A LITTLE NERVOUS.
No time to mentally prepare myself, you know?
SO YOUR DAD USED TO BE A PRO WRESTLER, EH?
I JUST HOPE HE DOESN'T DECK ME THE SECOND HE OPENS THE DOOR.

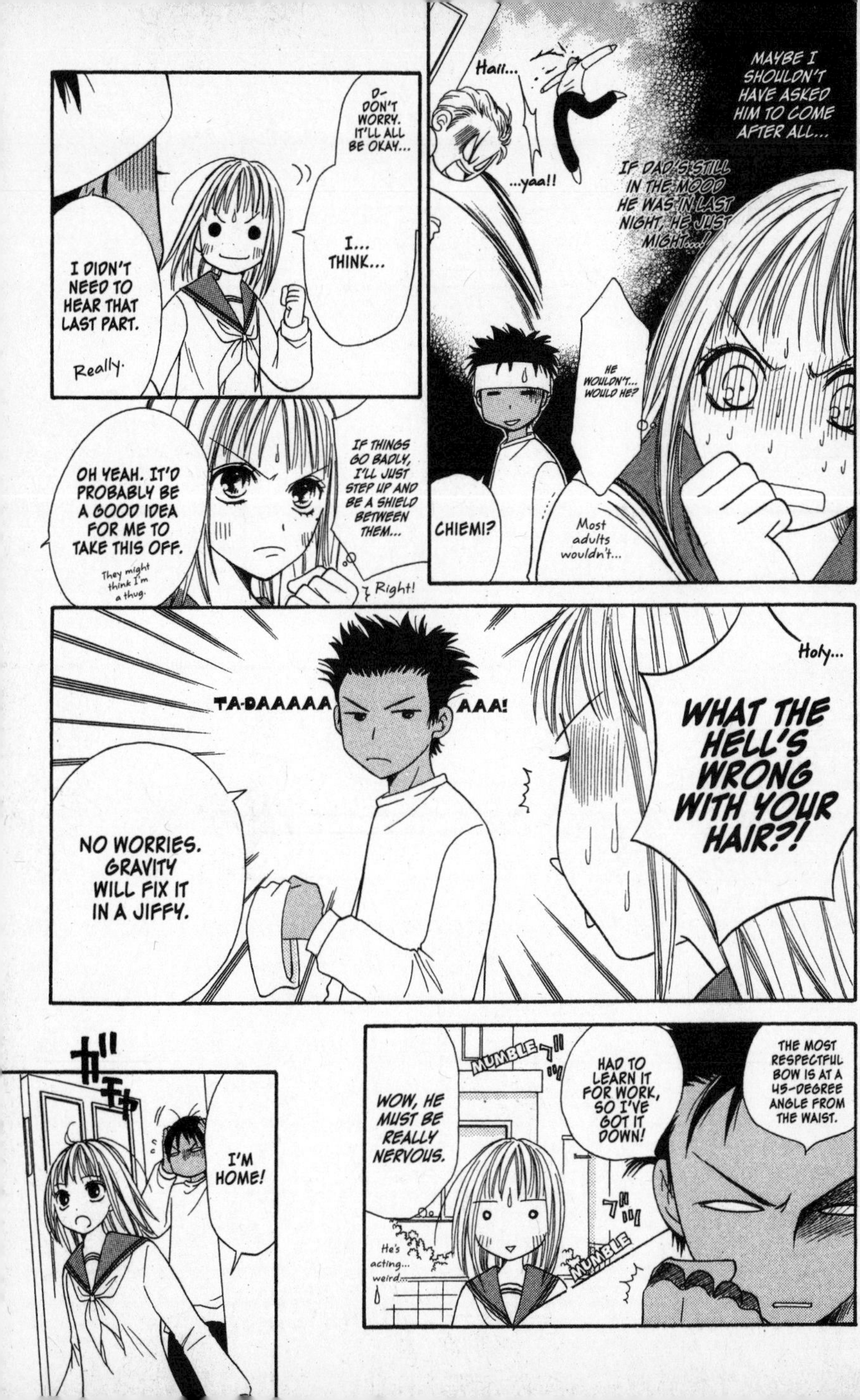
MAYBE I SHOULDN'T HAVE ASKED HIM TO COME AFTER ALL...
Haii...
...yaa!!
IF DAD'S STILL IN THE MOOD HE WAS IN LAST NIGHT, HE JUST MIGHT...!
HE WOULDN'T... WOULD HE?
Most adults wouldn't...
CHIEMI?
D-DON'T WORRY. IT'LL ALL BE OKAY...
I... THINK...
I DIDN'T NEED TO HEAR THAT LAST PART.
Really.
IF THINGS GO BADLY, I'LL JUST STEP UP AND BE A SHIELD BETWEEN THEM...
Right!
OH YEAH. IT'D PROBABLY BE A GOOD IDEA FOR ME TO TAKE THIS OFF.
They might think I'm a thug.
Holy...
WHAT THE HELL'S WRONG WITH YOUR HAIR?!
TA-DAAAAAAAAA!
NO WORRIES. GRAVITY WILL FIX IT IN A JIFFY.
THE MOST RESPECTFUL BOW IS AT A 45-DEGREE ANGLE FROM THE WAIST.
HAD TO LEARN IT FOR WORK, SO I'VE GOT IT DOWN!
MUMBLE
WOW, HE MUST BE REALLY NERVOUS.
He's acting... weird...
MUMBLE
I'M HOME!
ガチャ

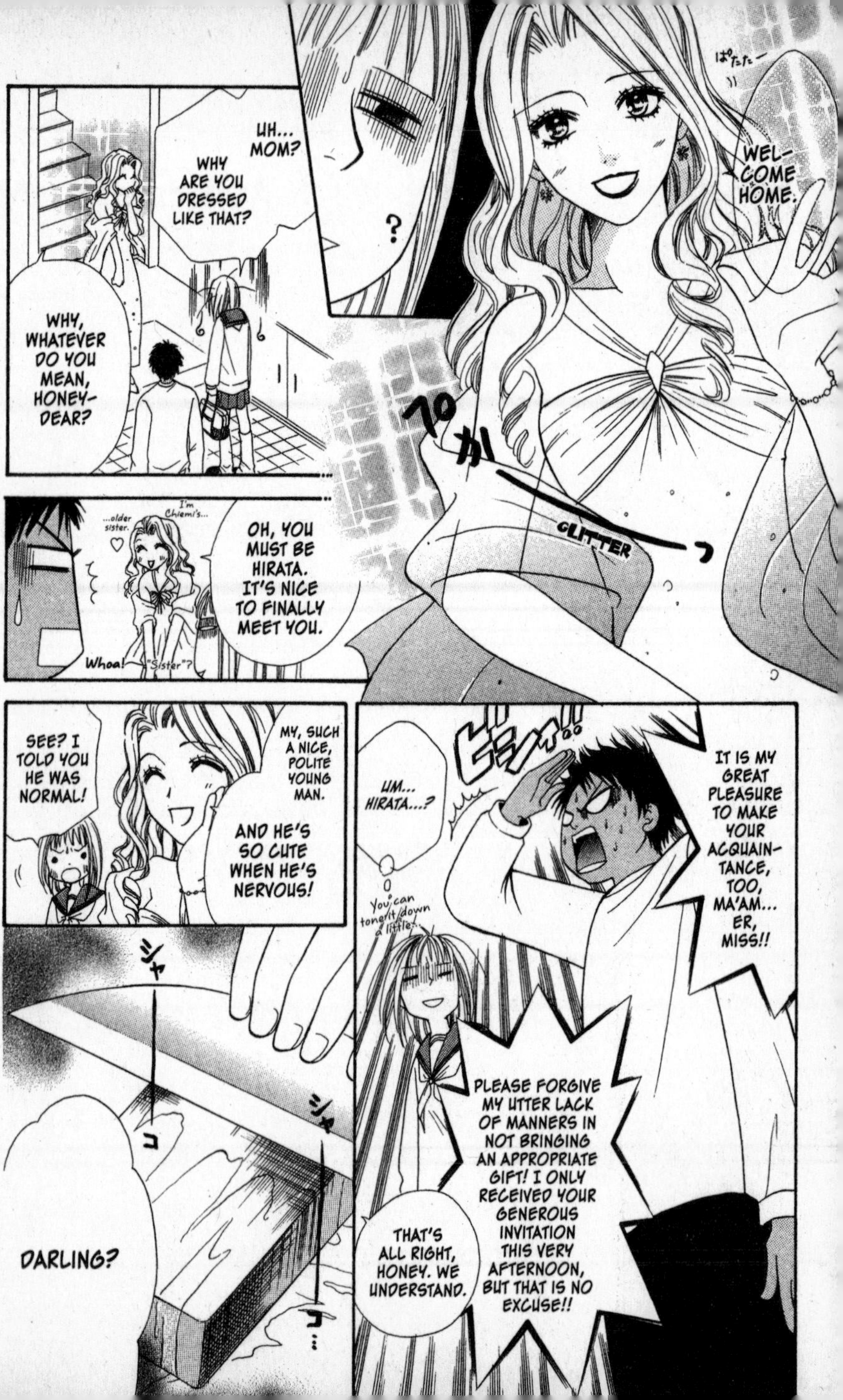
?
ぱたたー
WEL-COME HOME.
GLITTER
UH... MOM?
WHY ARE YOU DRESSED LIKE THAT?
WHY, WHATEVER DO YOU MEAN, HONEY-DEAR?
OH, YOU MUST BE HIRATA. IT'S NICE TO FINALLY MEET YOU.
I'm Chiemi's...
...older sister.
Whoa! "Sister"?
IT IS MY GREAT PLEASURE TO MAKE YOUR ACQUAINTANCE, TOO, MA'AM... ER, MISS!!
UM... HIRATA...?
You can tone it down a little...
PLEASE FORGIVE MY UTTER LACK OF MANNERS IN NOT BRINGING AN APPROPRIATE GIFT! I ONLY RECEIVED YOUR GENEROUS INVITATION THIS VERY AFTERNOON, BUT THAT IS NO EXCUSE!!
THAT'S ALL RIGHT, HONEY. WE UNDERSTAND.
MY, SUCH A NICE, POLITE YOUNG MAN.
AND HE'S SO CUTE WHEN HE'S NERVOUS!
SEE? I TOLD YOU HE WAS NORMAL!
シャ
コ
シャ
コ...
DARLING?

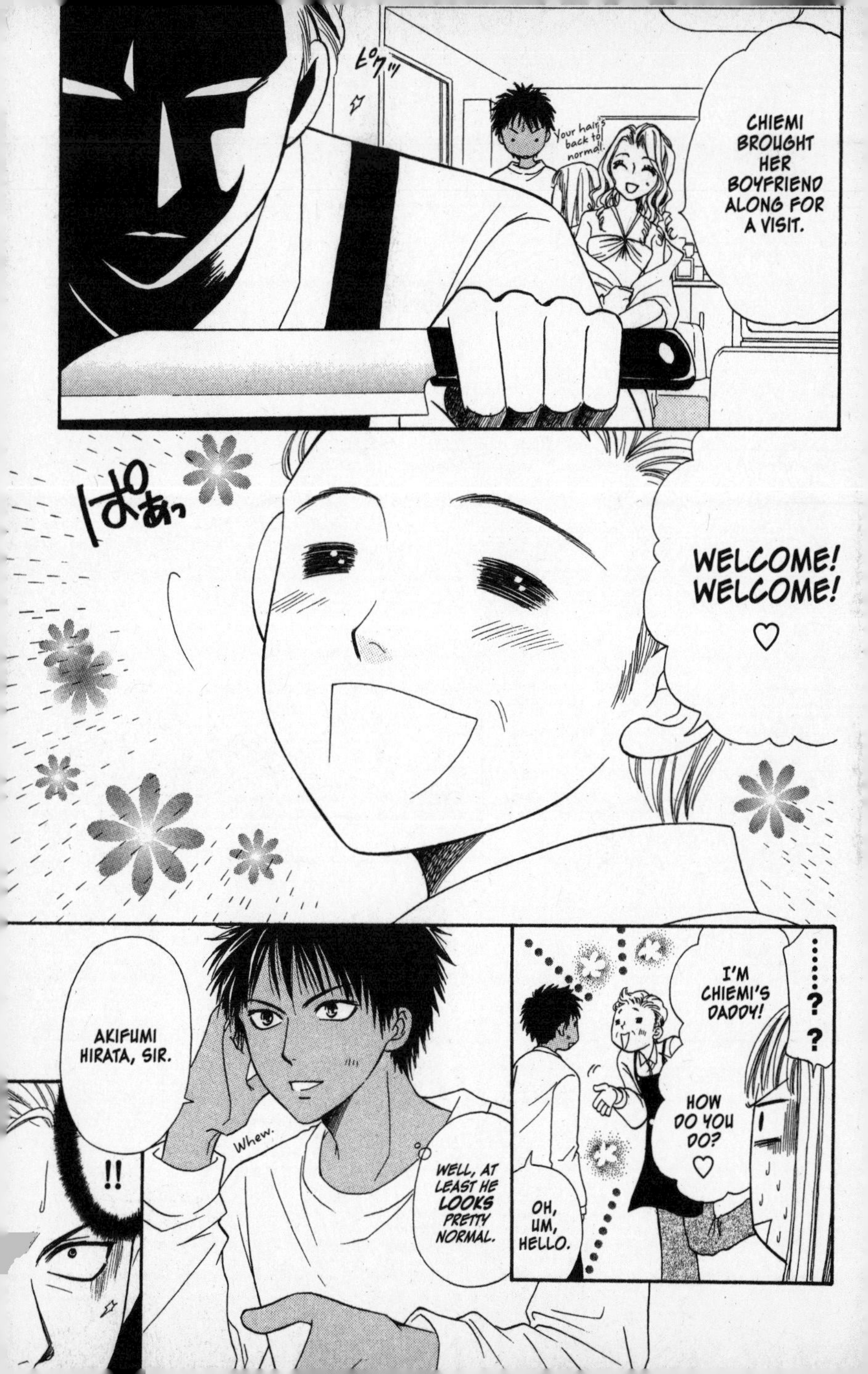
CHIEMI BROUGHT HER BOYFRIEND ALONG FOR A VISIT.
Your hair's back to normal.
ピクッ
WELCOME! WELCOME! ♡
ぱあっ
......??
I'M CHIEMI'S DADDY!
HOW DO YOU DO? ♡
OH, UM, HELLO.
AKIFUMI HIRATA, SIR.
Whew.
WELL, AT LEAST HE LOOKS PRETTY NORMAL.
!!

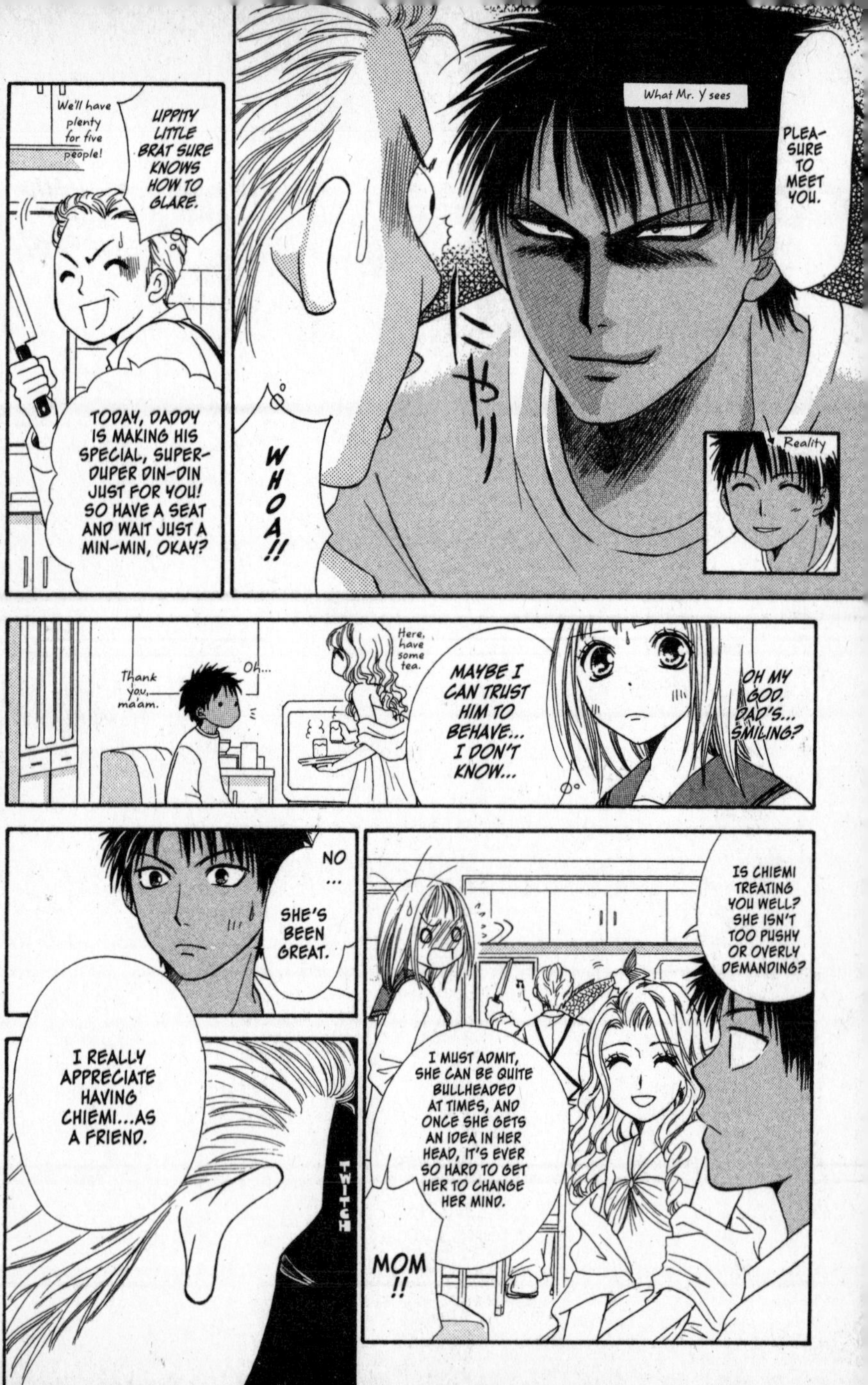
What Mr. Y sees
PLEASURE TO MEET YOU.
Reality
ニヤリ
WHOA!!
UPPITY LITTLE BRAT SURE KNOWS HOW TO GLARE.
We'll have plenty for five people!
TODAY, DADDY IS MAKING HIS SPECIAL, SUPER-DUPER DIN-DIN JUST FOR YOU! SO HAVE A SEAT AND WAIT JUST A MIN-MIN, OKAY?
OH MY GOD. DAD'S... SMILING?
MAYBE I CAN TRUST HIM TO BEHAVE... I DON'T KNOW...
Here, have some tea.
Oh...
Thank you, ma'am.
IS CHIEMI TREATING YOU WELL? SHE ISN'T TOO PUSHY OR OVERLY DEMANDING?
I MUST ADMIT, SHE CAN BE QUITE BULLHEADED AT TIMES, AND ONCE SHE GETS AN IDEA IN HER HEAD, IT'S EVER SO HARD TO GET HER TO CHANGE HER MIND.
MOM!!
NO ...
SHE'S BEEN GREAT.
I REALLY APPRECIATE HAVING CHIEMI...AS A FRIEND.
TWITCH

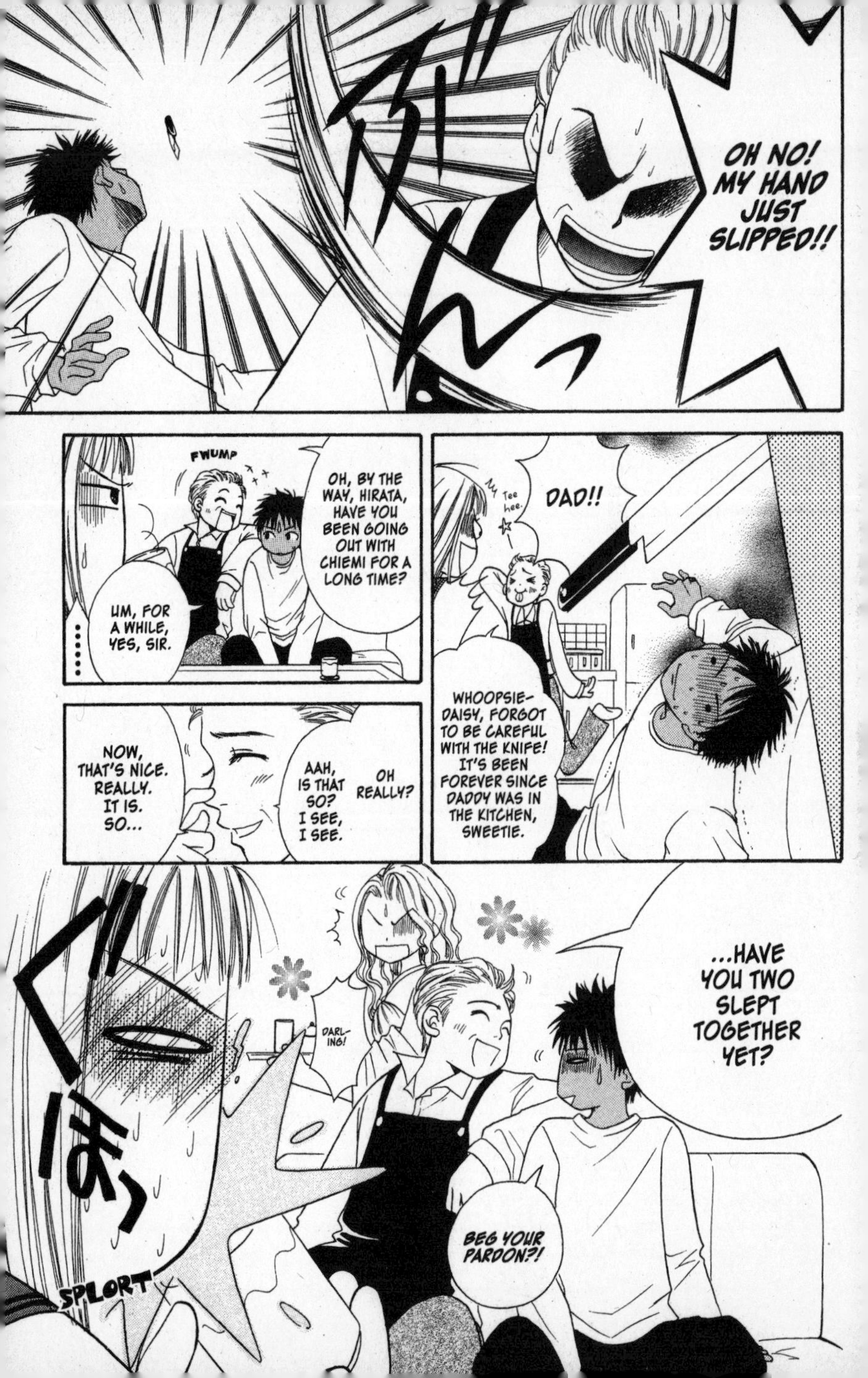
OH NO! MY HAND JUST SLIPPED!!
DAD!!
Tee hee.
WHOOPSIE-DAISY, FORGOT TO BE CAREFUL WITH THE KNIFE! IT'S BEEN FOREVER SINCE DADDY WAS IN THE KITCHEN, SWEETIE.
FWUMP
OH, BY THE WAY, HIRATA, HAVE YOU BEEN GOING OUT WITH CHIEMI FOR A LONG TIME?
UM, FOR A WHILE, YES, SIR.
......
OH REALLY?
AAH, IS THAT SO? I SEE, I SEE.
NOW, THAT'S NICE. REALLY. IT IS. SO...
...HAVE YOU TWO SLEPT TOGETHER YET?
BEG YOUR PARDON?!
DARL-ING!
SPLORT

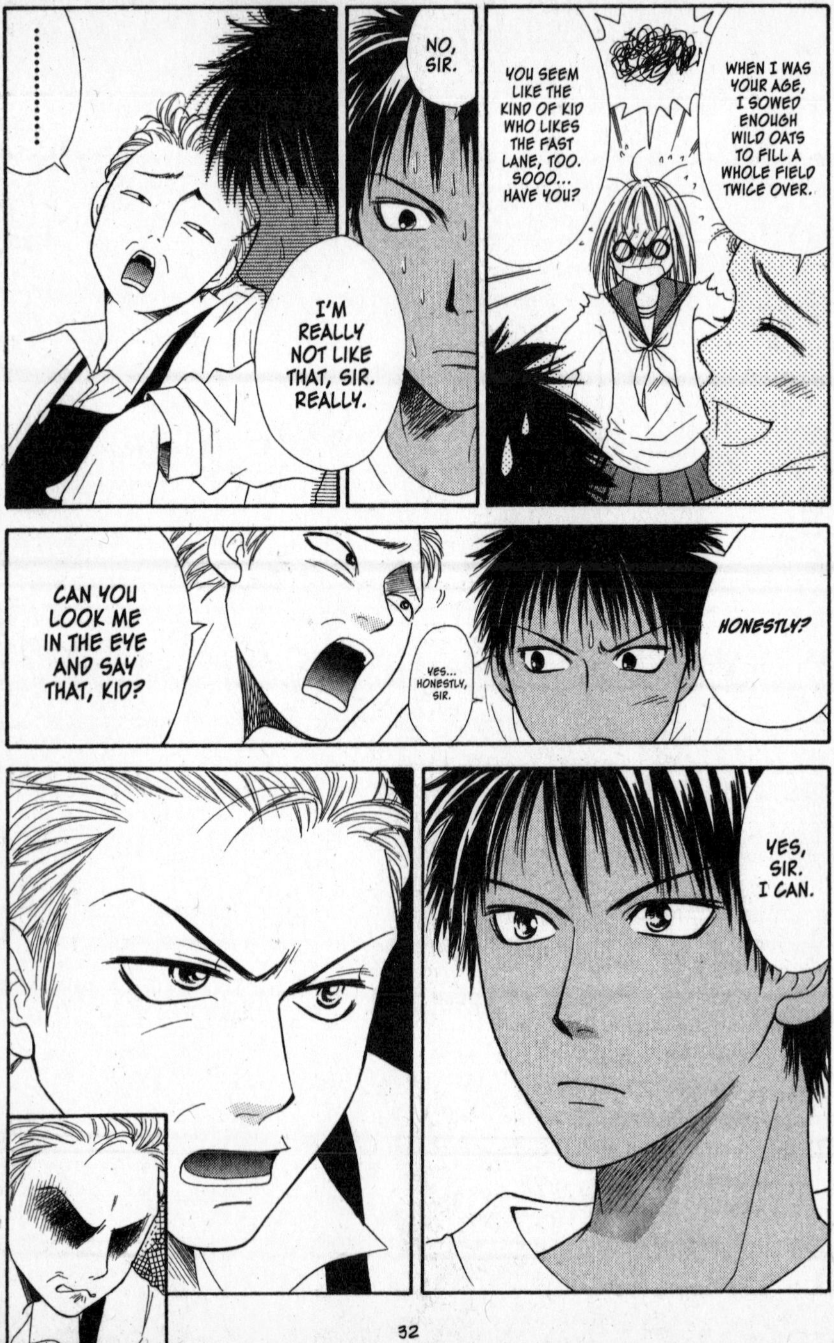
WHEN I WAS YOUR AGE, I SOWED ENOUGH WILD OATS TO FILL A WHOLE FIELD TWICE OVER.
YOU SEEM LIKE THE KIND OF KID WHO LIKES THE FAST LANE, TOO. SOOO... HAVE YOU?
NO, SIR.
I'M REALLY NOT LIKE THAT, SIR. REALLY.
....
HONESTLY?
YES... HONESTLY, SIR.
CAN YOU LOOK ME IN THE EYE AND SAY THAT, KID?
YES, SIR. I CAN.

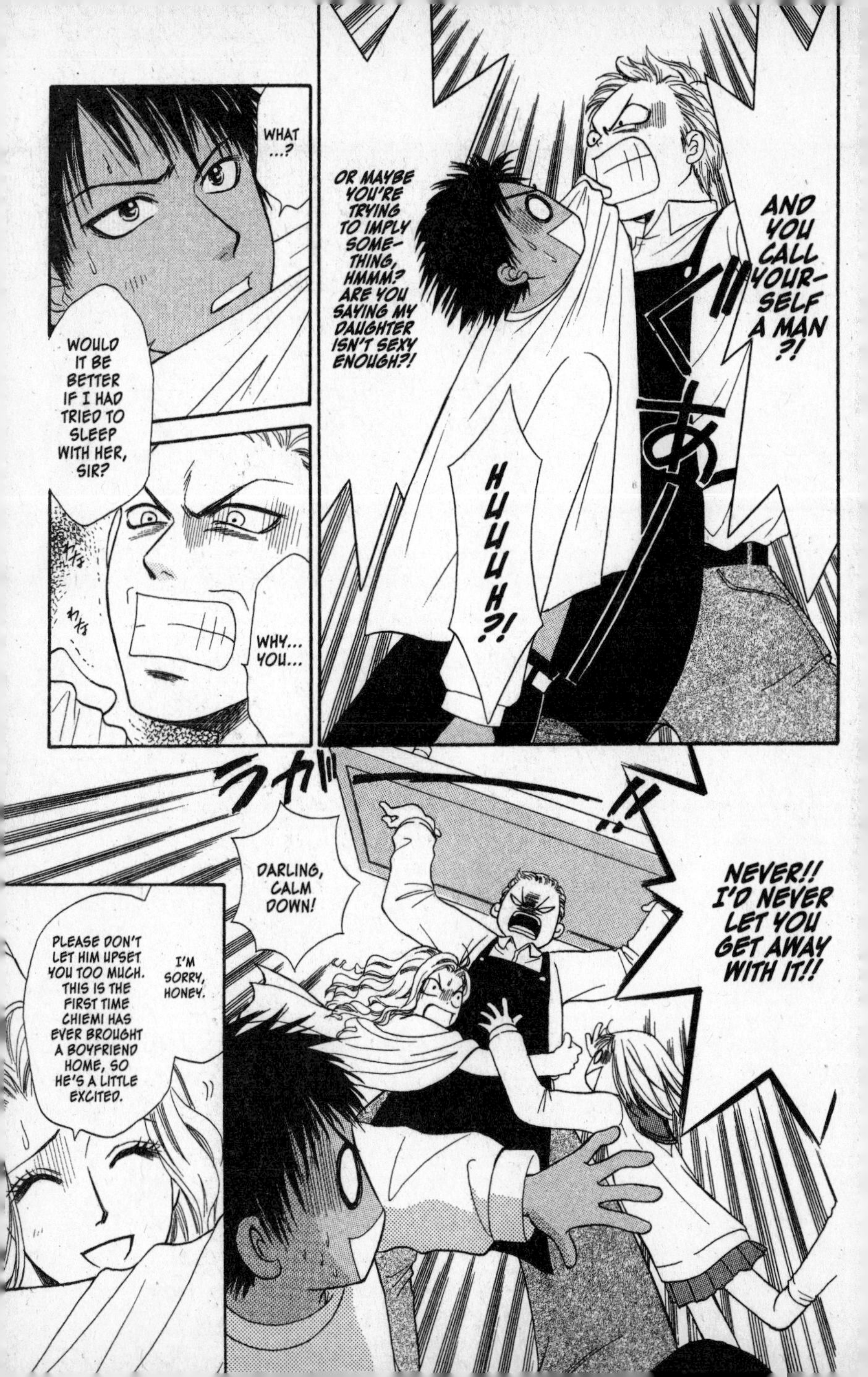

AND YOU CALL YOURSELF A MAN?!
OR MAYBE YOU'RE TRYING TO IMPLY SOMETHING, HMMM? ARE YOU SAYING MY DAUGHTER ISN'T SEXY ENOUGH?!
HUUUUUH?!
WHAT ...?
WOULD IT BE BETTER IF I HAD TRIED TO SLEEP WITH HER, SIR?
WHY... YOU...
NEVER!! I'D NEVER LET YOU GET AWAY WITH IT!!
DARLING, CALM DOWN!
I'M SORRY, HONEY.
PLEASE DON'T LET HIM UPSET YOU TOO MUCH. THIS IS THE FIRST TIME CHIEMI HAS EVER BROUGHT A BOYFRIEND HOME, SO HE'S A LITTLE EXCITED.

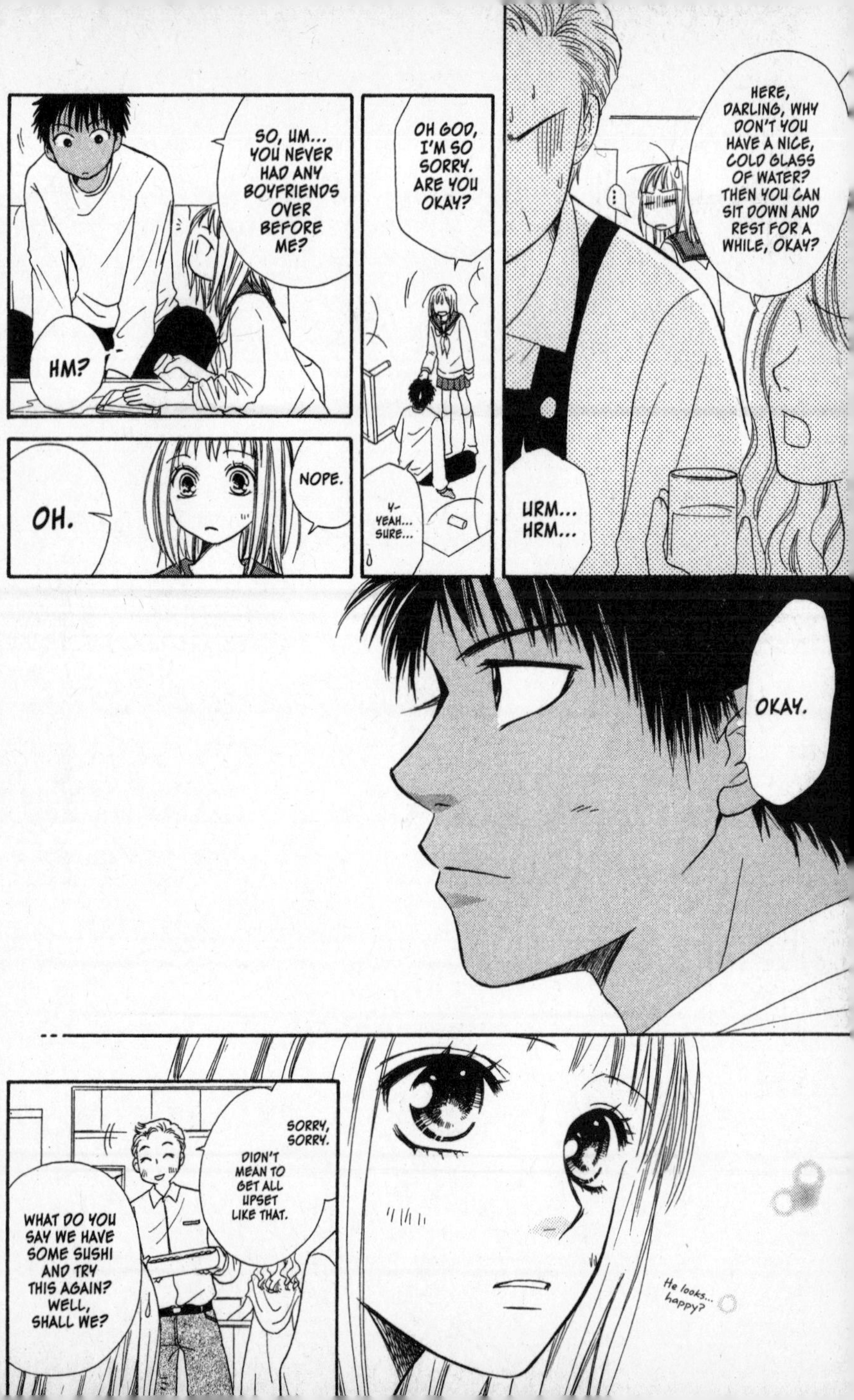
HERE, DARLING, WHY DON'T YOU HAVE A NICE, COLD GLASS OF WATER? THEN YOU CAN SIT DOWN AND REST FOR A WHILE, OKAY?
URM... HRM...
OH GOD, I'M SO SORRY. ARE YOU OKAY?
Y-YEAH... SURE...
SO, UM... YOU NEVER HAD ANY BOYFRIENDS OVER BEFORE ME?
HM?
NOPE.
OH.
OKAY.
He looks... happy?
SORRY, SORRY.
DIDN'T MEAN TO GET ALL UPSET LIKE THAT.
WHAT DO YOU SAY WE HAVE SOME SUSHI AND TRY THIS AGAIN? WELL, SHALL WE?

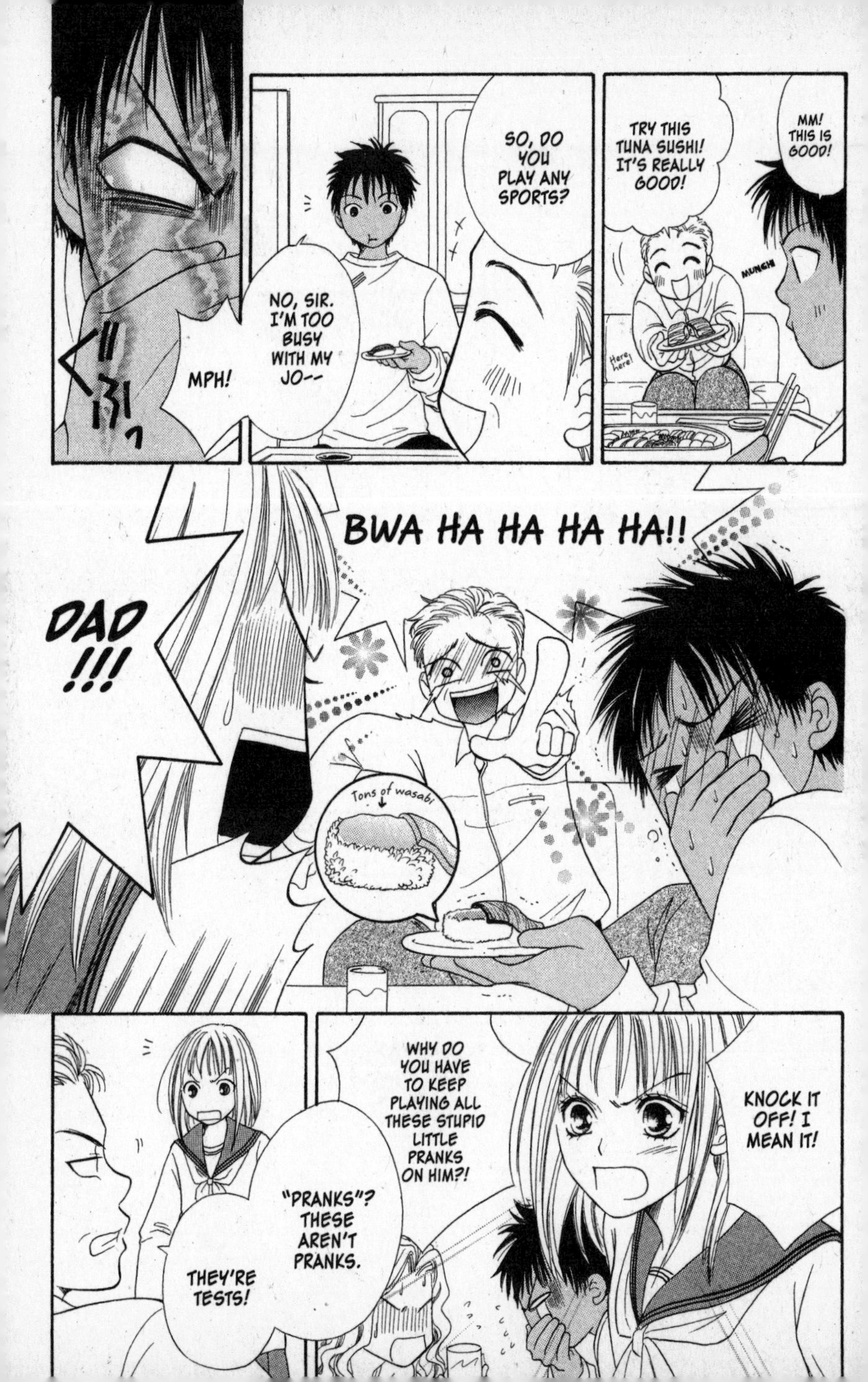
MM! THIS IS GOOD!
TRY THIS TUNA SUSHI! IT'S REALLY GOOD!
MUNCH
Here, here!
SO, DO YOU PLAY ANY SPORTS?
NO, SIR. I'M TOO BUSY WITH MY JO--
MPH!
BWA HA HA HA HA!!
DAD!!!
Tons of wasabi
KNOCK IT OFF! I MEAN IT!
WHY DO YOU HAVE TO KEEP PLAYING ALL THESE STUPID LITTLE PRANKS ON HIM?!
"PRANKS"? THESE AREN'T PRANKS.
THEY'RE TESTS!

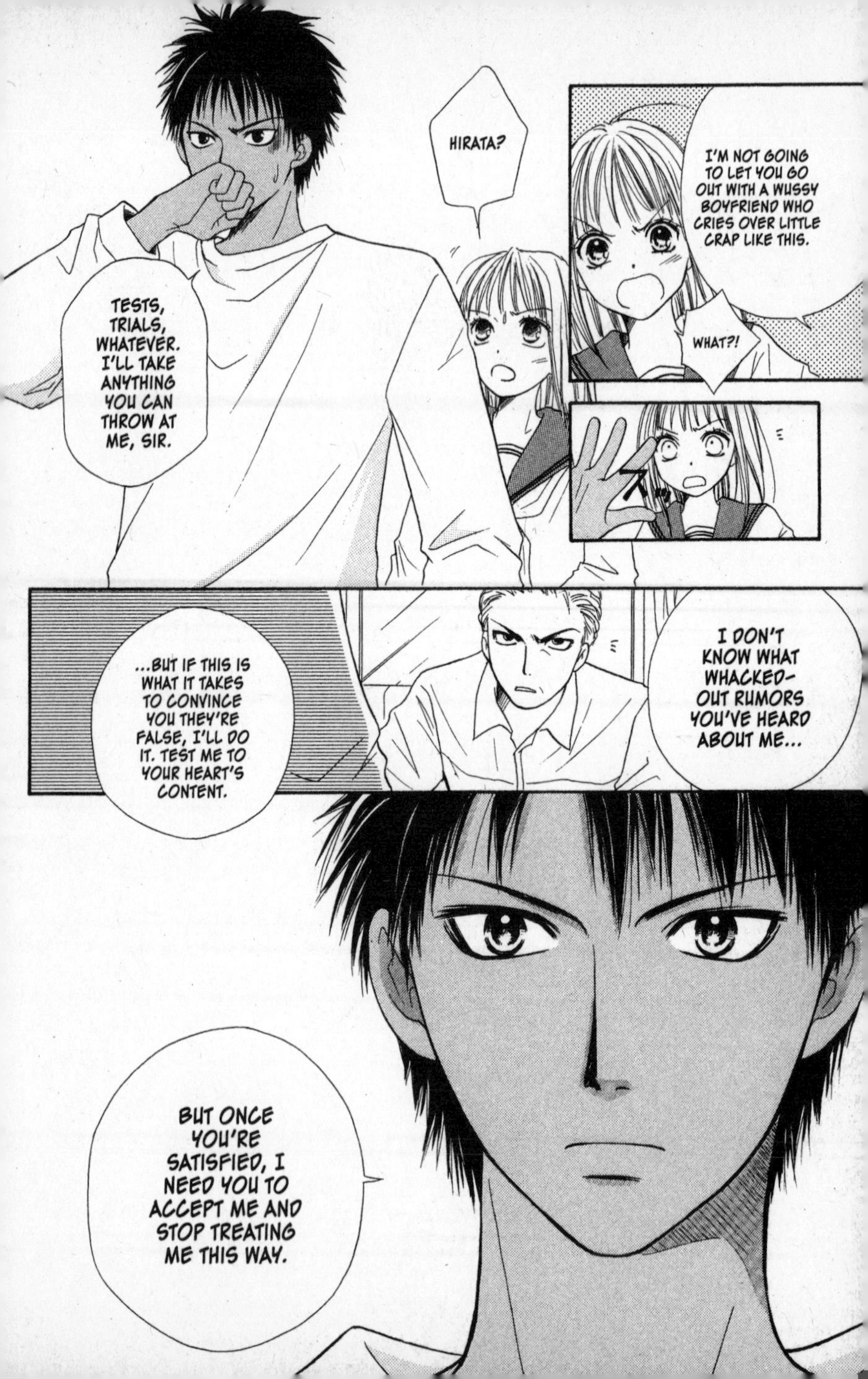
I'M NOT GOING TO LET YOU GO OUT WITH A WUSSY BOYFRIEND WHO CRIES OVER LITTLE CRAP LIKE THIS.
WHAT?!
HIRATA?
TESTS, TRIALS, WHATEVER. I'LL TAKE ANYTHING YOU CAN THROW AT ME, SIR.
I DON'T KNOW WHAT WHACKED-OUT RUMORS YOU'VE HEARD ABOUT ME...
...BUT IF THIS IS WHAT IT TAKES TO CONVINCE YOU THEY'RE FALSE, I'LL DO IT. TEST ME TO YOUR HEART'S CONTENT.
BUT ONCE YOU'RE SATISFIED, I NEED YOU TO ACCEPT ME AND STOP TREATING ME THIS WAY.

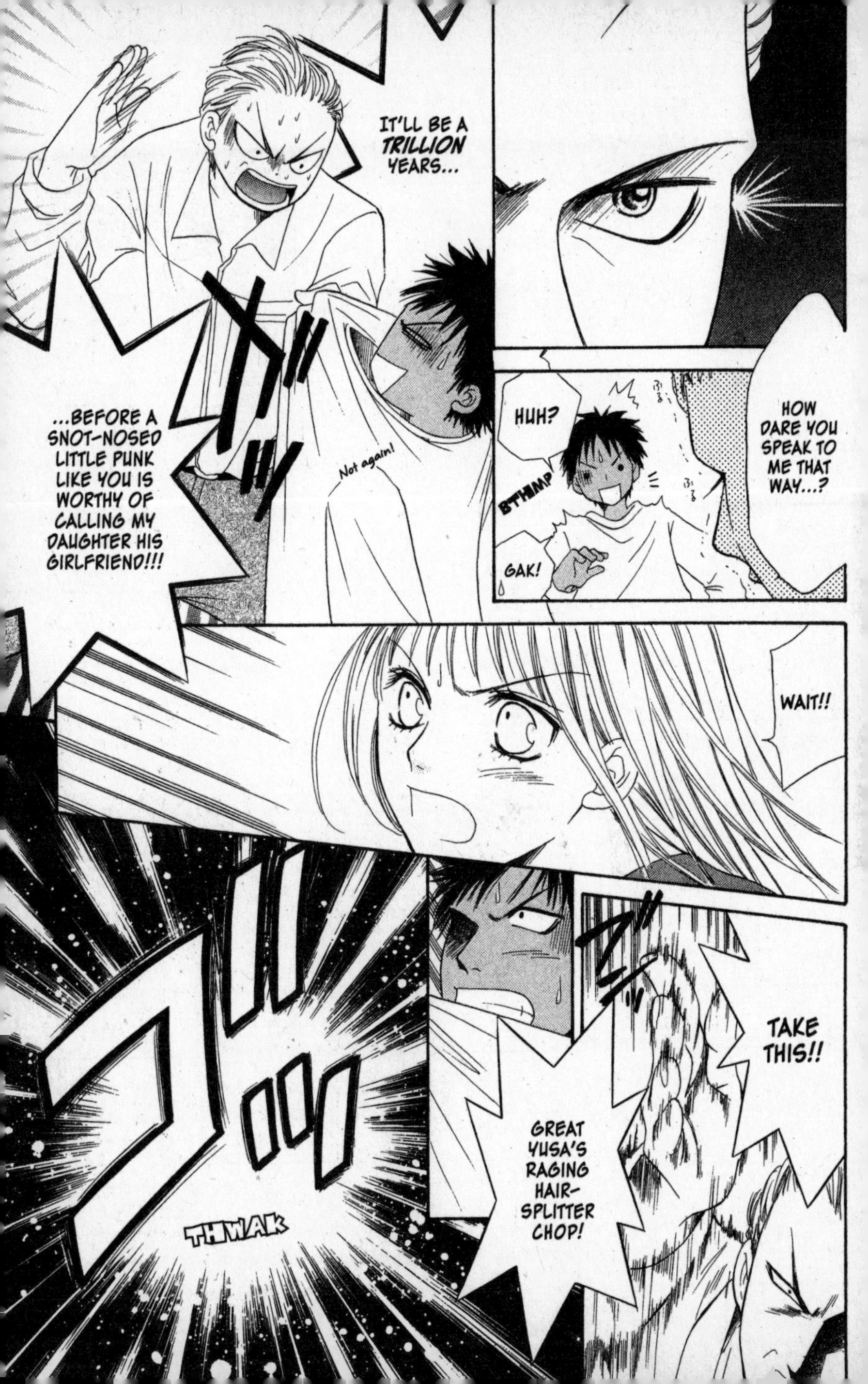
HOW DARE YOU SPEAK TO ME THAT WAY...?
HUH?
BTHMP
GAK!
IT'LL BE A TRILLION YEARS...
...BEFORE A SNOT-NOSED LITTLE PUNK LIKE YOU IS WORTHY OF CALLING MY DAUGHTER HIS GIRLFRIEND!!!
Not again!
WAIT!!
TAKE THIS!!
GREAT YUSA'S RAGING HAIR-SPLITTER CHOP!
THWAK

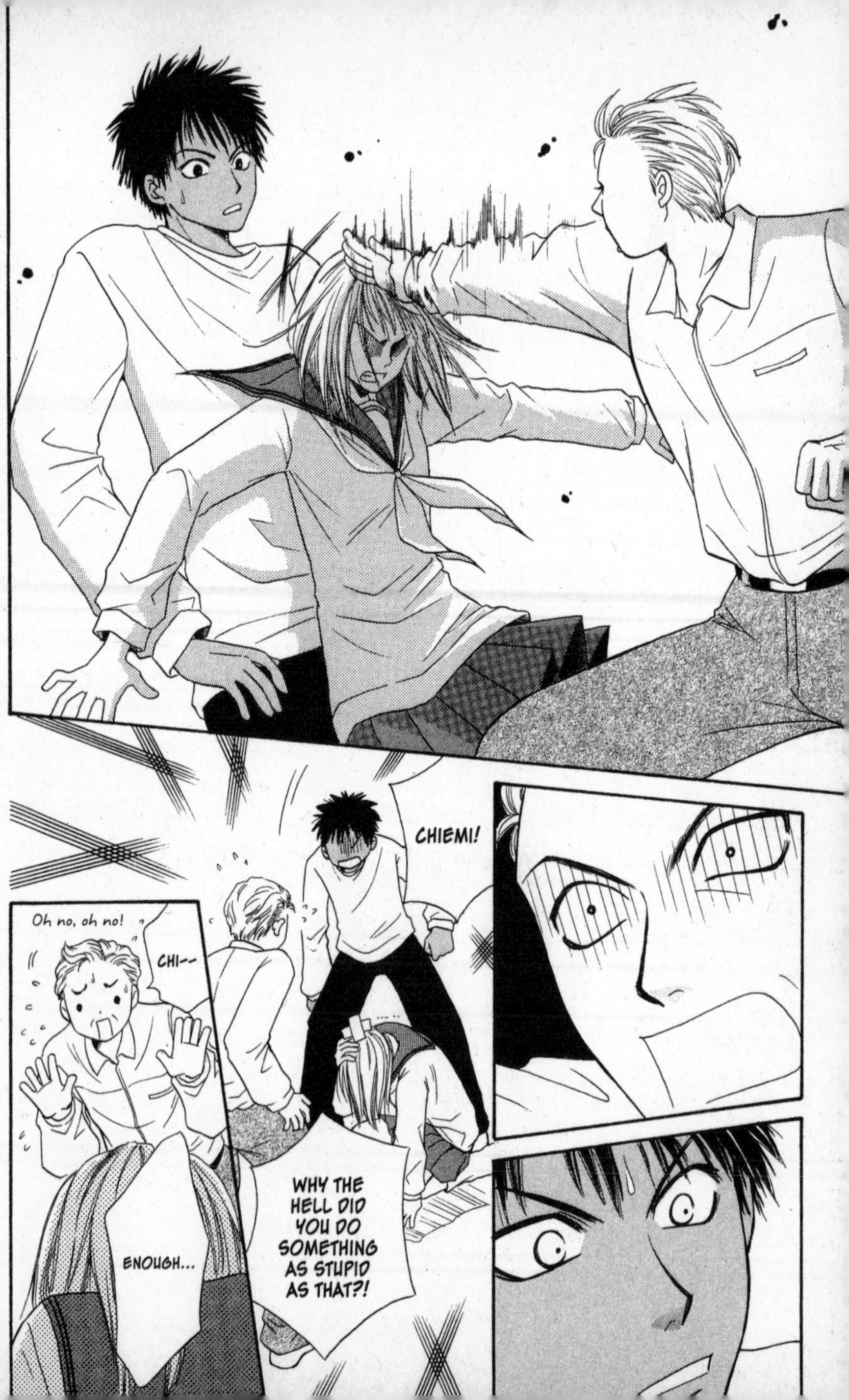
CHIEMI!
CHI--
Oh no, oh no!
WHY THE HELL DID YOU DO SOMETHING AS STUPID AS THAT?!
ENOUGH...

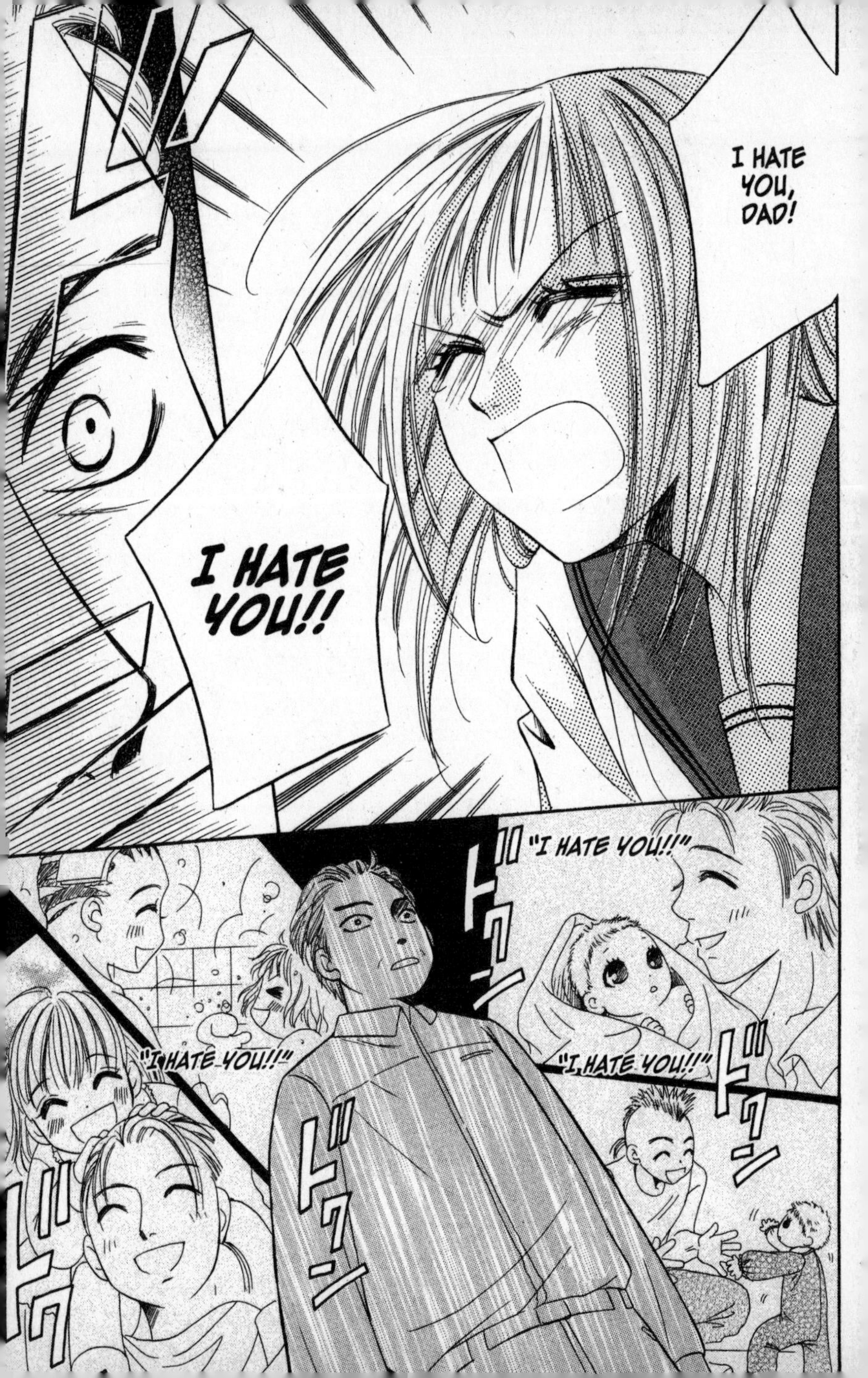
I HATE YOU, DAD!
I HATE YOU!!
"I HATE YOU!!"
ドクン
"I HATE YOU!!"
ドクン
ドクン
"I HATE YOU!!"
ドク

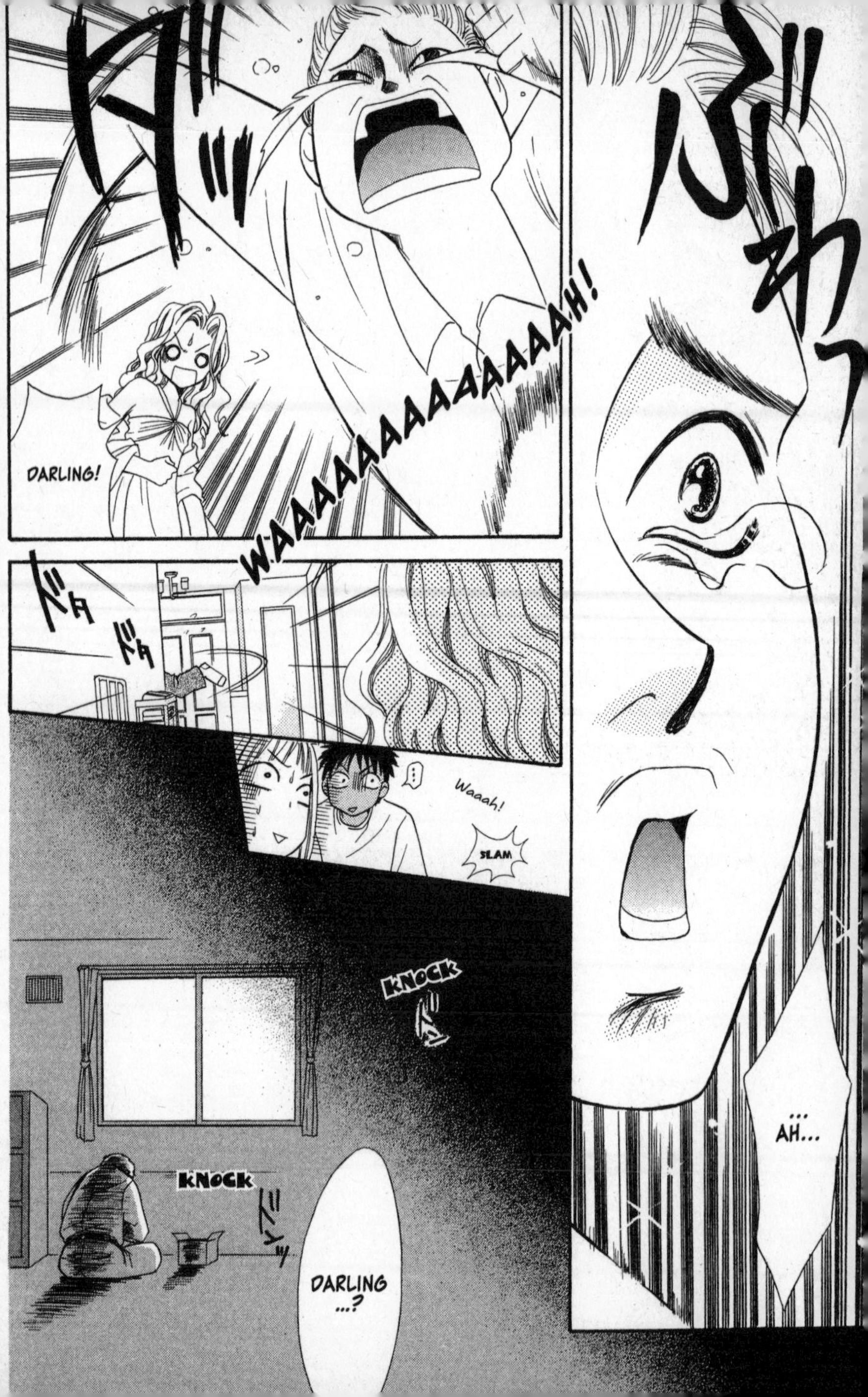
...AH...
WAAAAAAAAAAAAAH!
DARLING!
Waaah!
SLAM
KNOCK
KNOCK
DARLING ...?

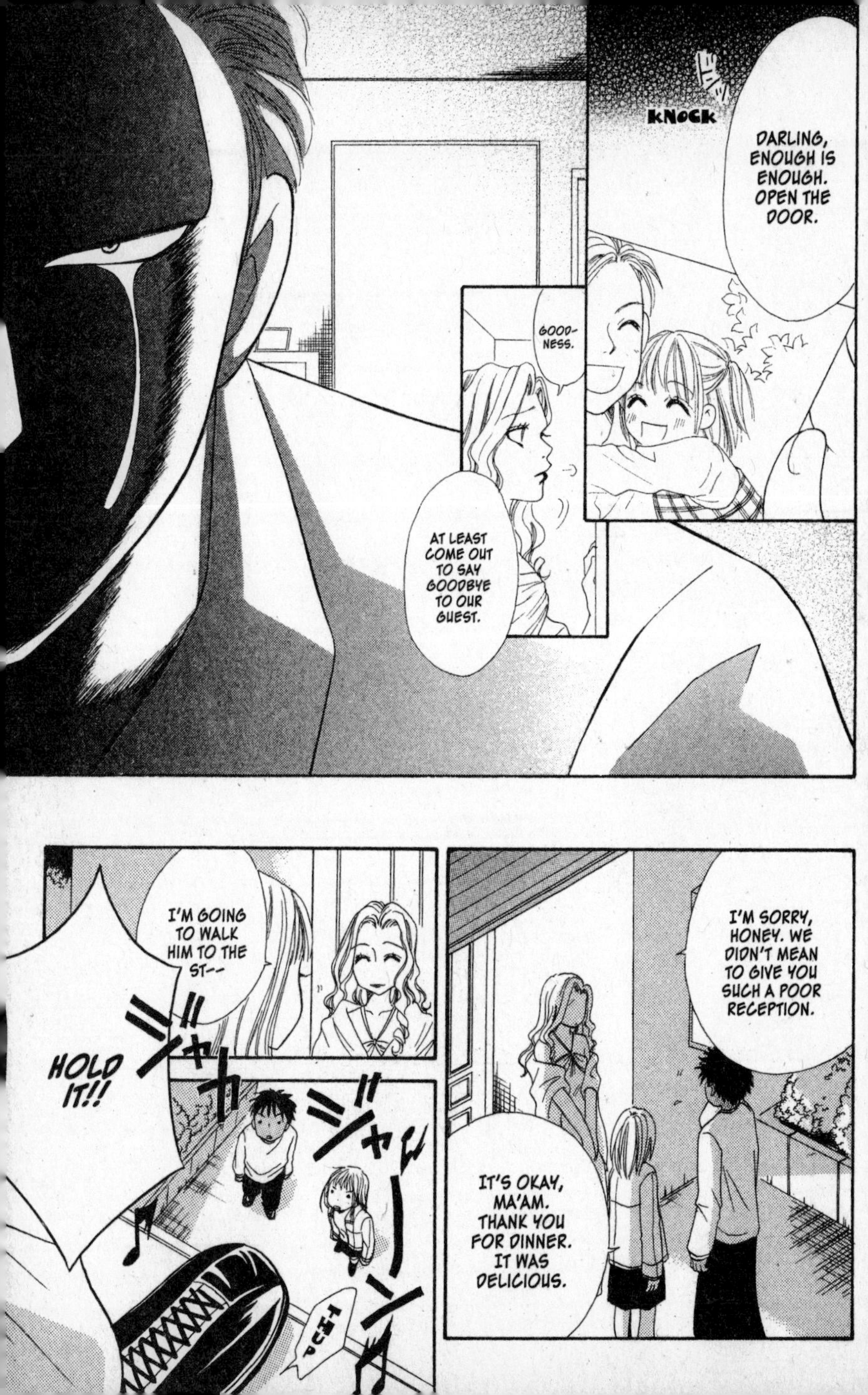
KNOCK
DARLING, ENOUGH IS ENOUGH. OPEN THE DOOR.
GOOD-NESS.
AT LEAST COME OUT TO SAY GOODBYE TO OUR GUEST.
I'M SORRY, HONEY. WE DIDN'T MEAN TO GIVE YOU SUCH A POOR RECEPTION.
IT'S OKAY, MA'AM. THANK YOU FOR DINNER. IT WAS DELICIOUS.
I'M GOING TO WALK HIM TO THE ST--
HOLD IT!!
THUD

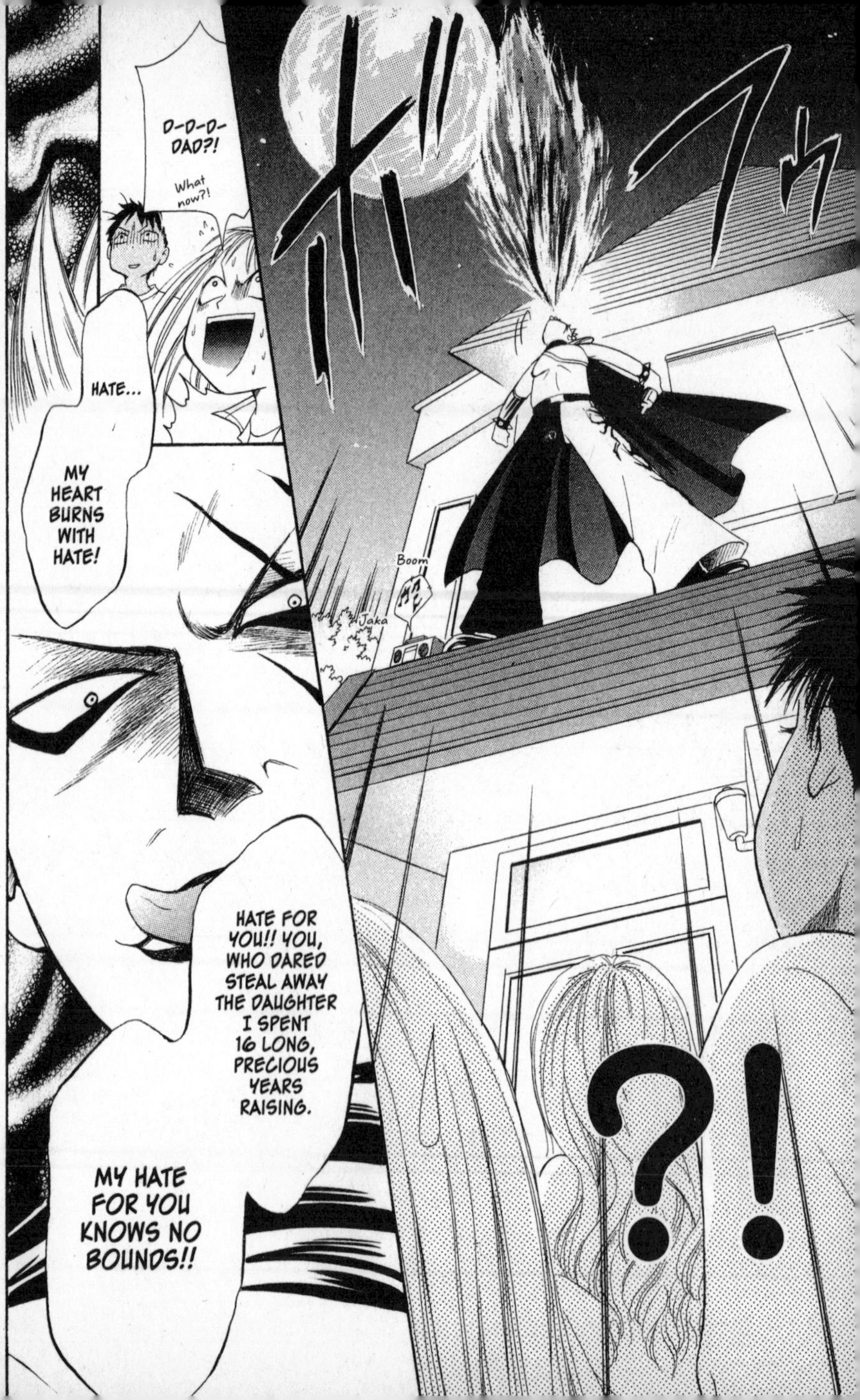
Boom
Jaka
?!
D-D-D-DAD?!
What now?!
HATE...
MY HEART BURNS WITH HATE!
HATE FOR YOU!! YOU, WHO DARED STEAL AWAY THE DAUGHTER I SPENT 16 LONG, PRECIOUS YEARS RAISING.
MY HATE FOR YOU KNOWS NO BOUNDS!!

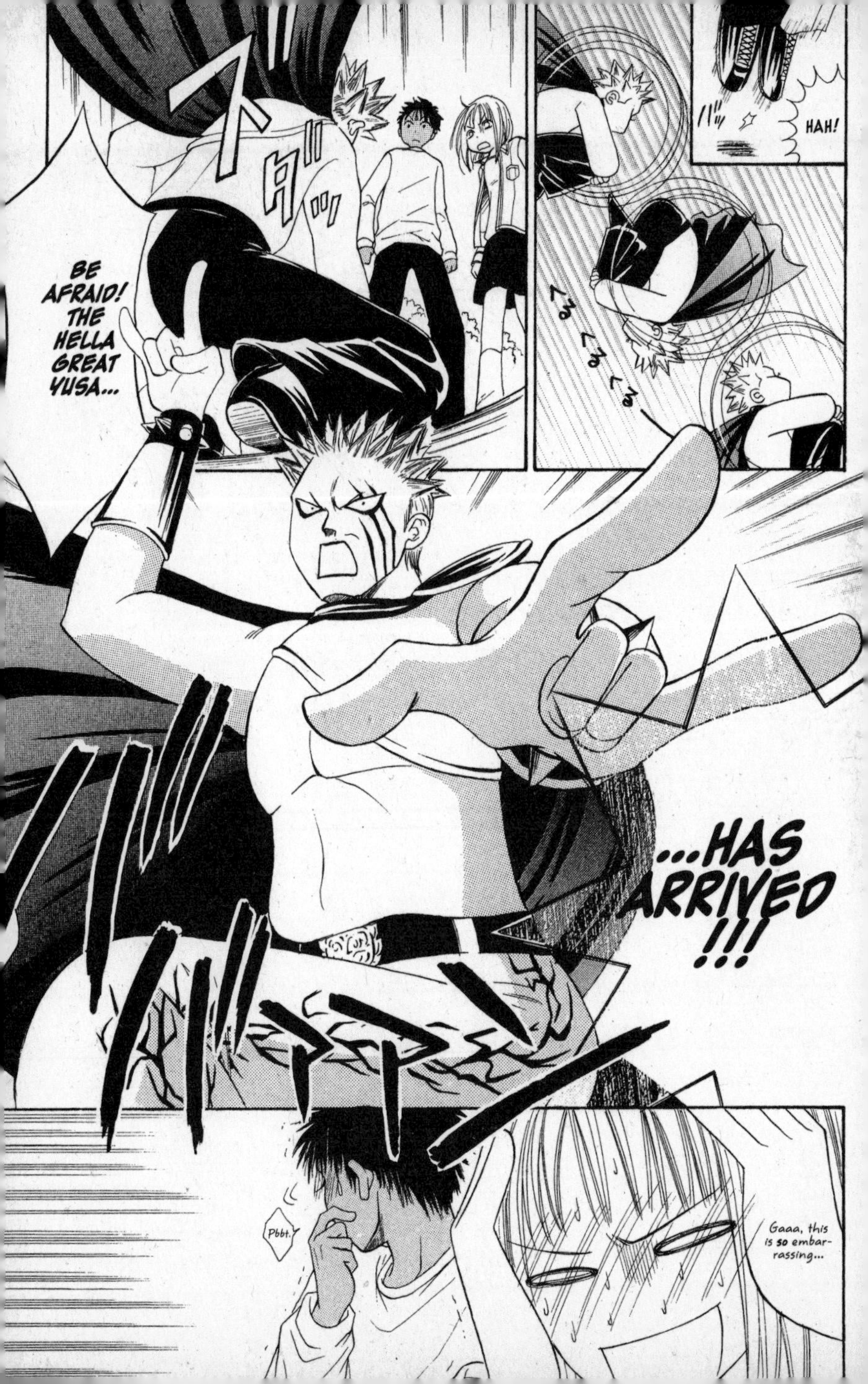
HAH!
BE AFRAID! THE HELLA GREAT YUSA...
...HAS ARRIVED!!!
Gaaa, this is so embar-rassing...
Pbbt.

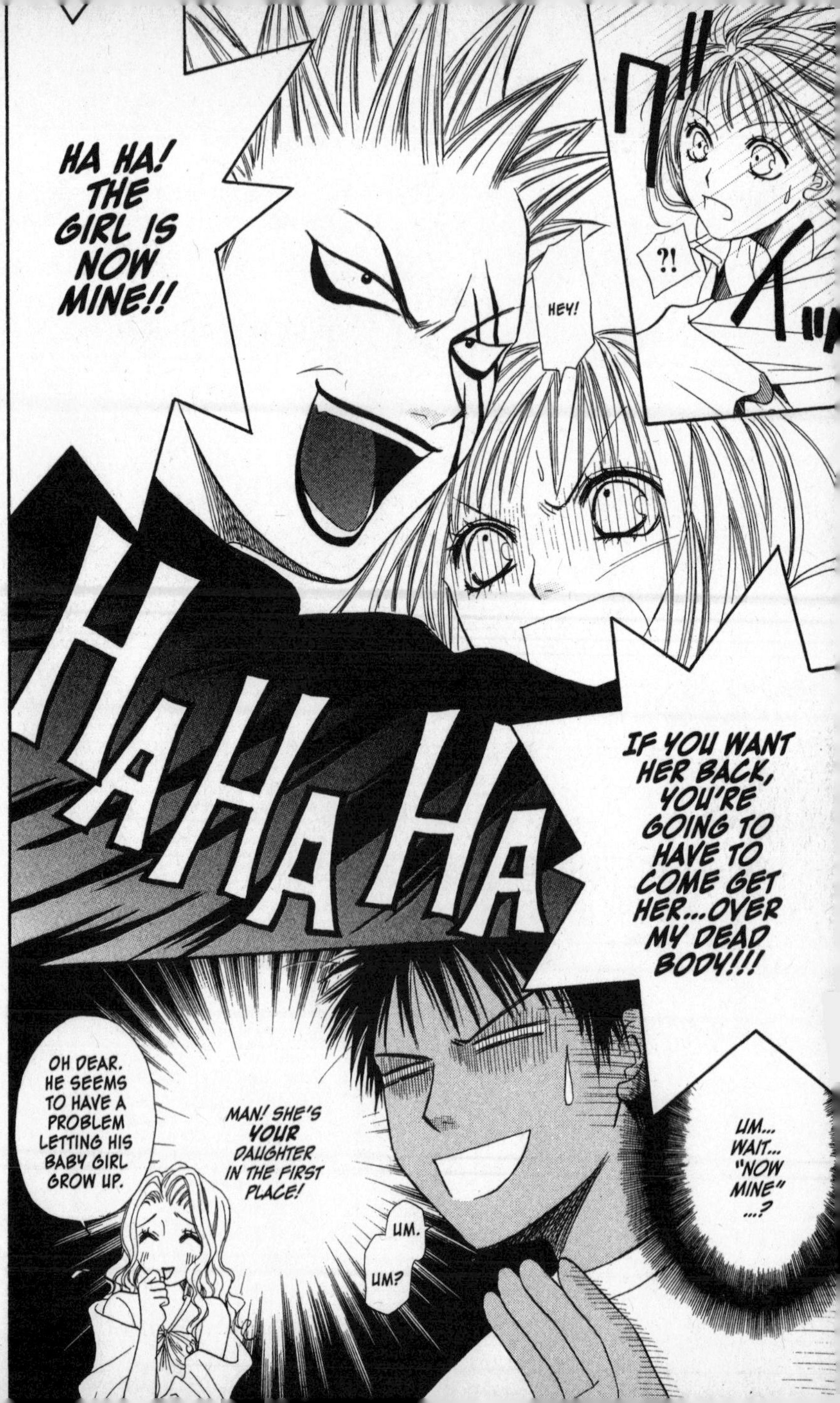
?!
HA HA! THE GIRL IS NOW MINE!!
HEY!
HAHAHAHA
IF YOU WANT HER BACK, YOU'RE GOING TO HAVE TO COME GET HER...OVER MY DEAD BODY!!!
UM... WAIT... "NOW MINE" ...?
MAN! SHE'S YOUR DAUGHTER IN THE FIRST PLACE!
UM.
UM?
OH DEAR. HE SEEMS TO HAVE A PROBLEM LETTING HIS BABY GIRL GROW UP.

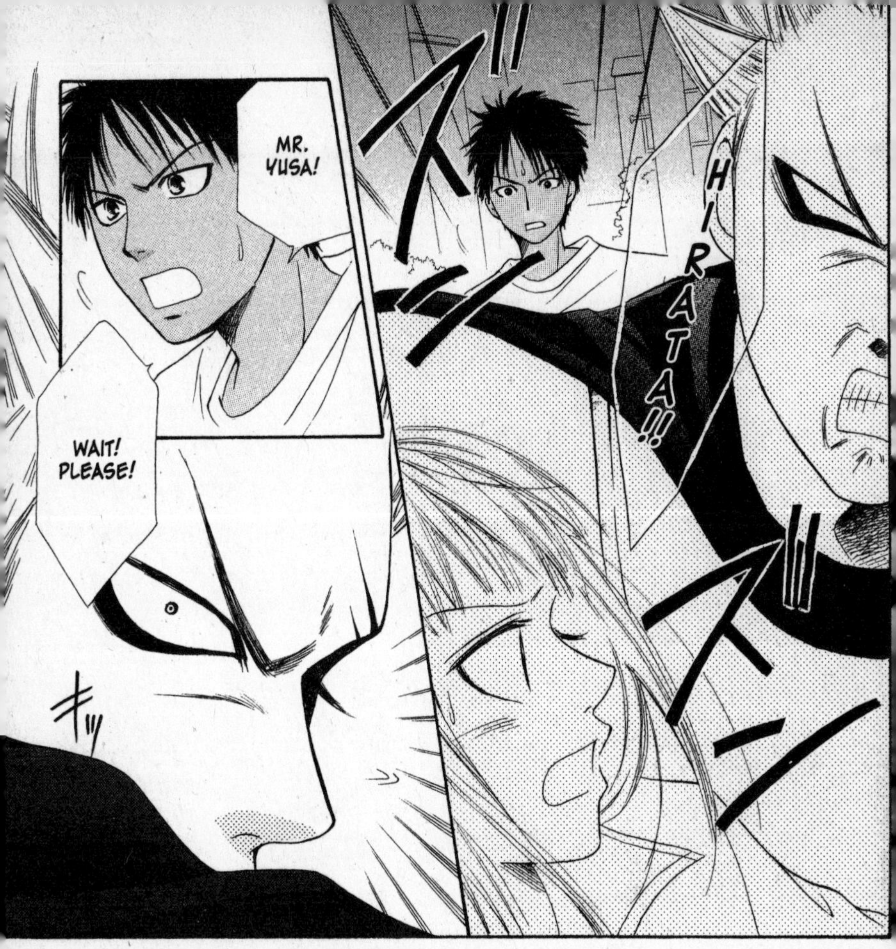
HIRATA!!
MR. YUSA!
WAIT! PLEASE!

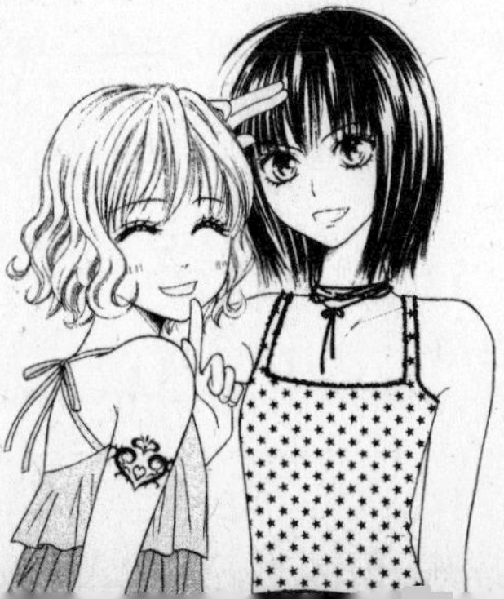

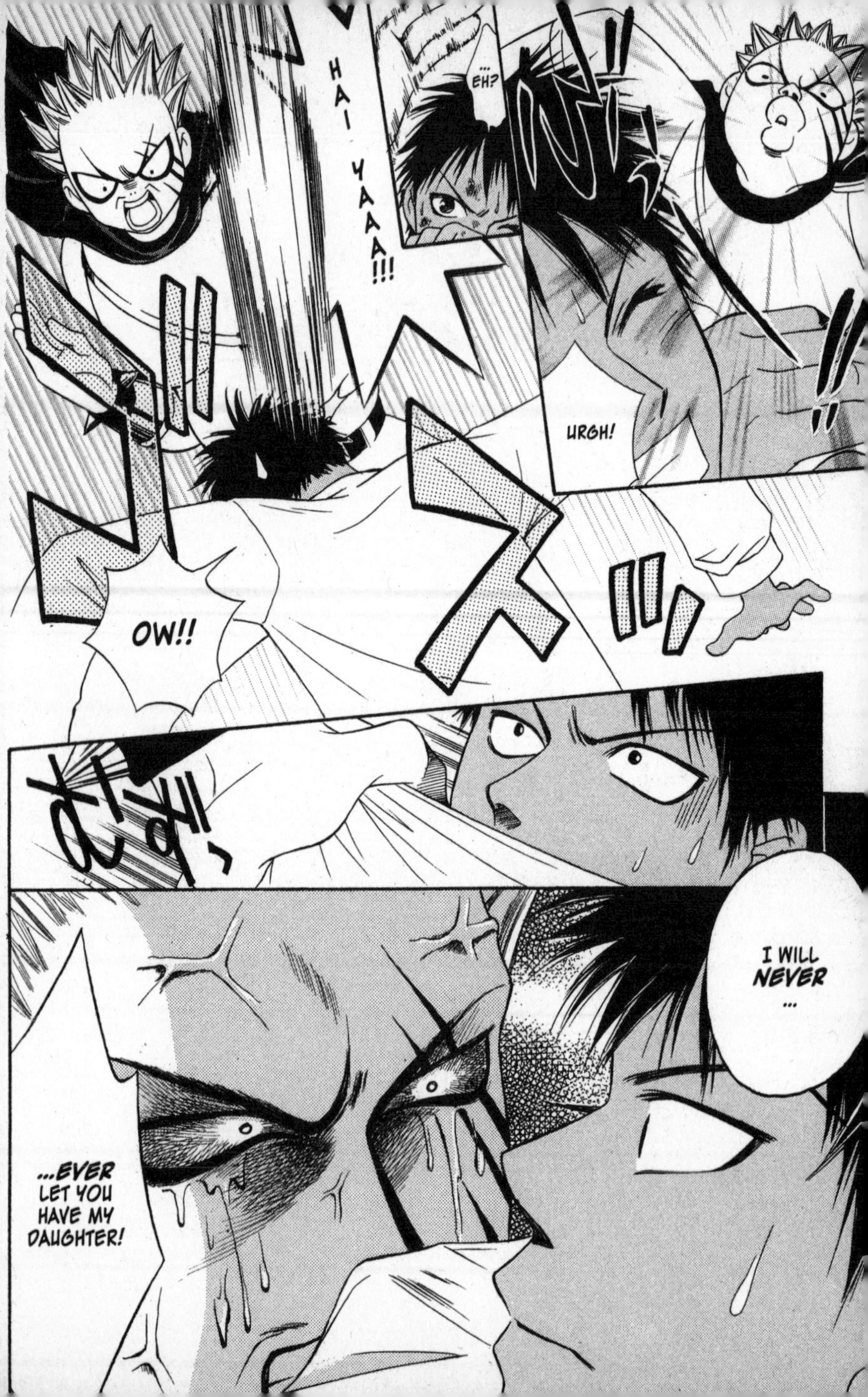
URGH!
...EH?
HAI YAAA!!!
OW!!
I WILL NEVER ...
...EVER LET YOU HAVE MY DAUGHTER!

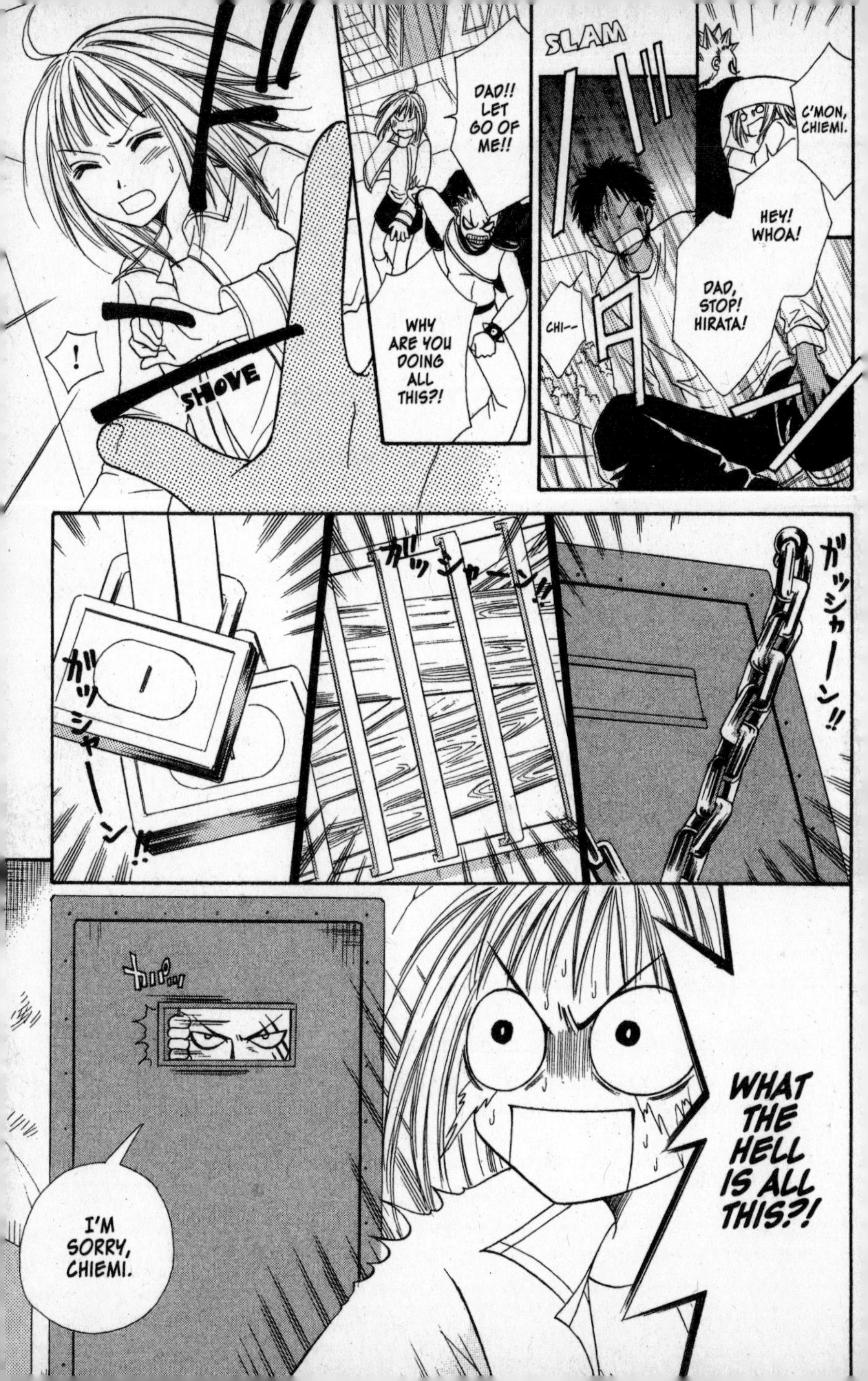
SLAM
C'MON, CHIEMI.
HEY! WHOA!
DAD, STOP! HIRATA!
CHI--
DAD!! LET GO OF ME!!
WHY ARE YOU DOING ALL THIS?!
!
SHOVE
ガッシャーン!!
ガッシャーン!!
ガッシャーン!!
WHAT THE HELL IS ALL THIS?!
カパッ
I'M SORRY, CHIEMI.

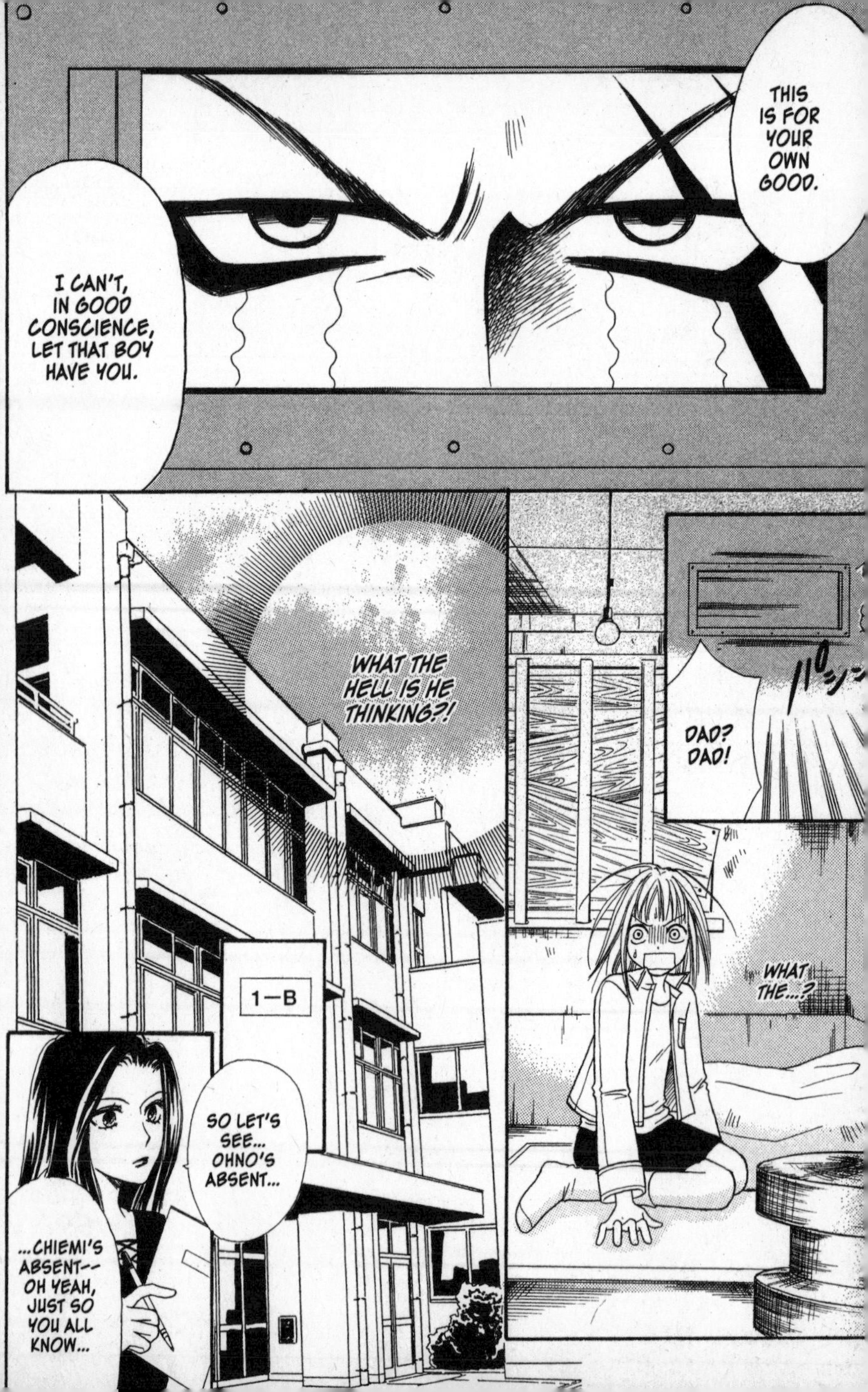
THIS IS FOR YOUR OWN GOOD.
I CAN'T, IN GOOD CONSCIENCE, LET THAT BOY HAVE YOU.
DAD? DAD!
WHAT THE...?
WHAT THE HELL IS HE THINKING?!
1—B
SO LET'S SEE... OHNO'S ABSENT...
...CHIEMI'S ABSENT-- OH YEAH, JUST SO YOU ALL KNOW...

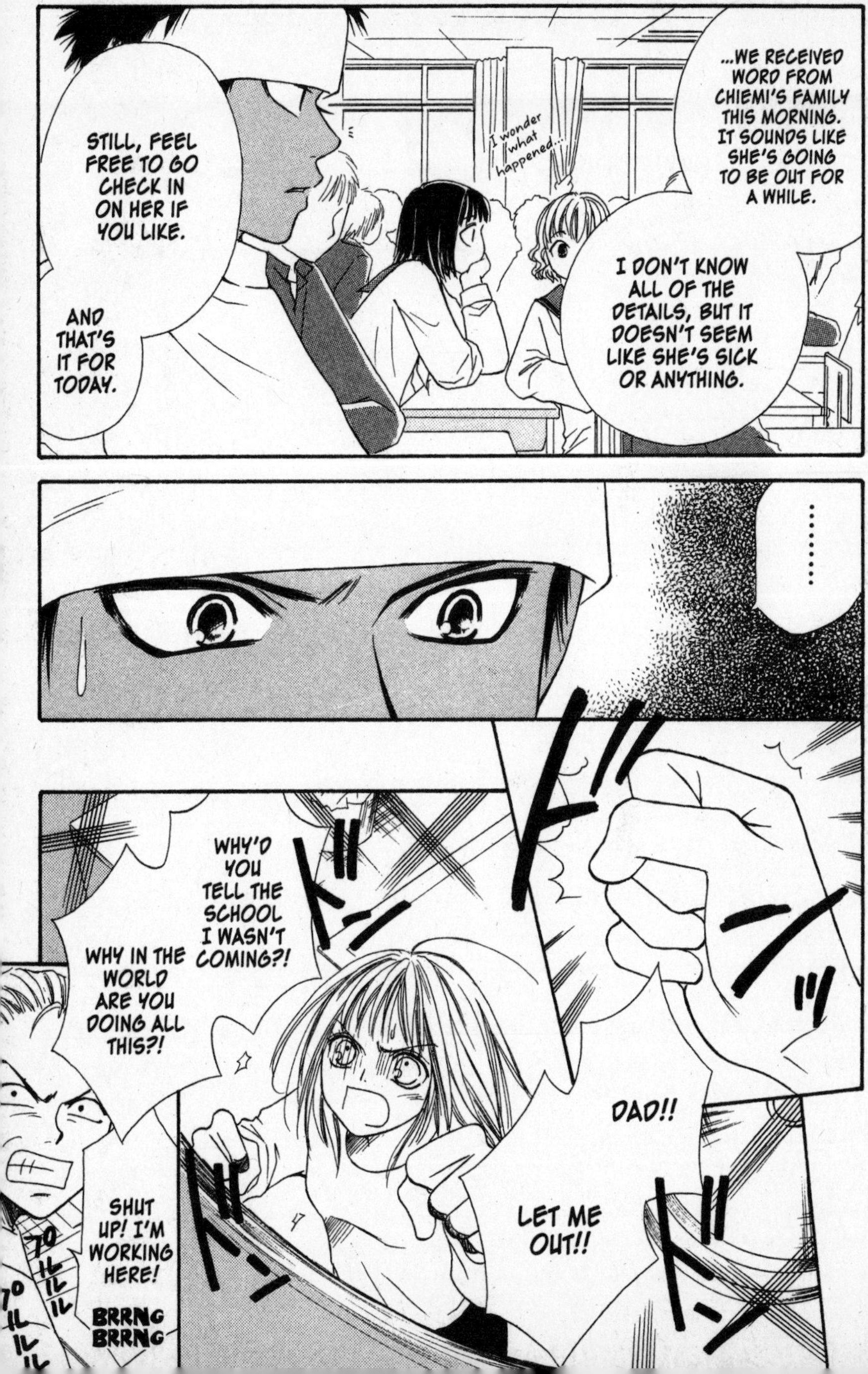
...WE RECEIVED WORD FROM CHIEMI'S FAMILY THIS MORNING. IT SOUNDS LIKE SHE'S GOING TO BE OUT FOR A WHILE.
I DON'T KNOW ALL OF THE DETAILS, BUT IT DOESN'T SEEM LIKE SHE'S SICK OR ANYTHING.
I wonder what happened...
STILL, FEEL FREE TO GO CHECK IN ON HER IF YOU LIKE.
AND THAT'S IT FOR TODAY.
......
DAD!!
LET ME OUT!!
WHY'D YOU TELL THE SCHOOL I WASN'T COMING?!
WHY IN THE WORLD ARE YOU DOING ALL THIS?!
SHUT UP! I'M WORKING HERE!
BRRNG BRRNG

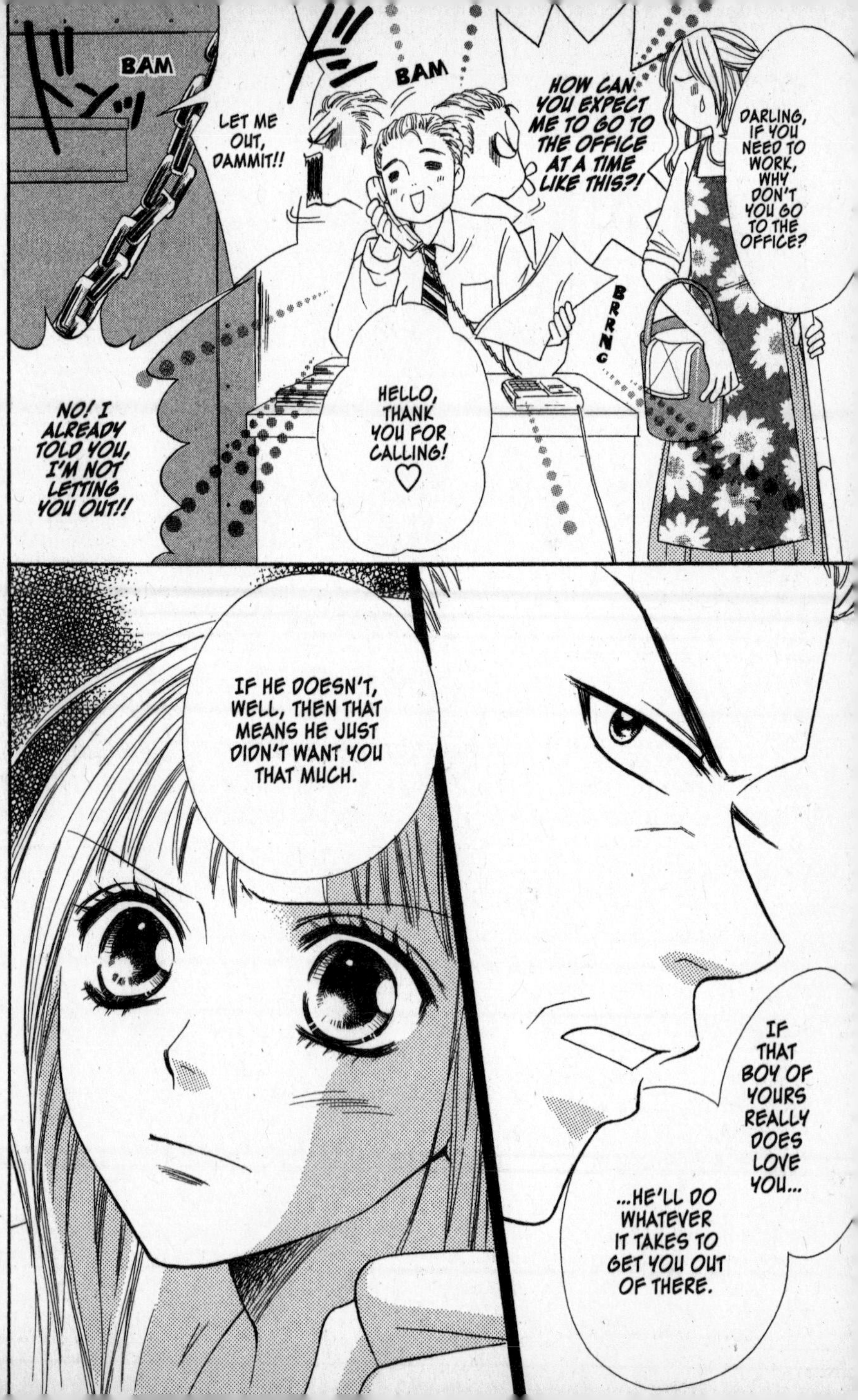
DARLING, IF YOU NEED TO WORK, WHY DON'T YOU GO TO THE OFFICE?
HOW CAN YOU EXPECT ME TO GO TO THE OFFICE AT A TIME LIKE THIS?!
BAM
LET ME OUT, DAMMIT!!
BAM
BRRNG
HELLO, THANK YOU FOR CALLING! ♡
NO! I ALREADY TOLD YOU, I'M NOT LETTING YOU OUT!!
IF THAT BOY OF YOURS REALLY DOES LOVE YOU...
...HE'LL DO WHATEVER IT TAKES TO GET YOU OUT OF THERE.
IF HE DOESN'T, WELL, THEN THAT MEANS HE JUST DIDN'T WANT YOU THAT MUCH.

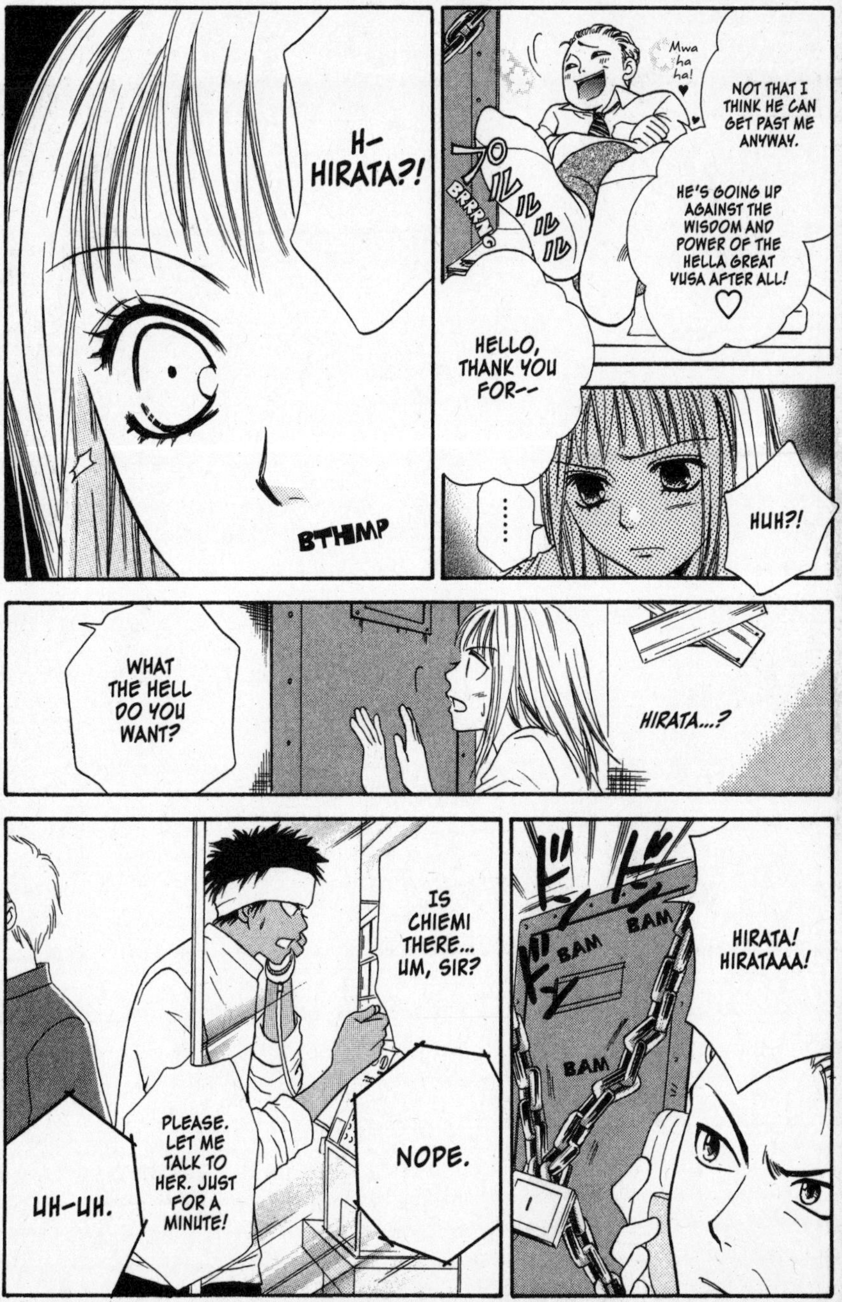
Mwa ha ha! ♥
NOT THAT I THINK HE CAN GET PAST ME ANYWAY.
HE'S GOING UP AGAINST THE WISDOM AND POWER OF THE HELLA GREAT YUSA AFTER ALL! ♡
BRRRNG
HELLO, THANK YOU FOR--
......
HUH?!
H- HIRATA?!
BTHMP
HIRATA...?
WHAT THE HELL DO YOU WANT?
HIRATA! HIRATAAA!
BAM
BAM
BAM
IS CHIEMI THERE... UM, SIR?
NOPE.
PLEASE. LET ME TALK TO HER. JUST FOR A MINUTE!
UH-UH.

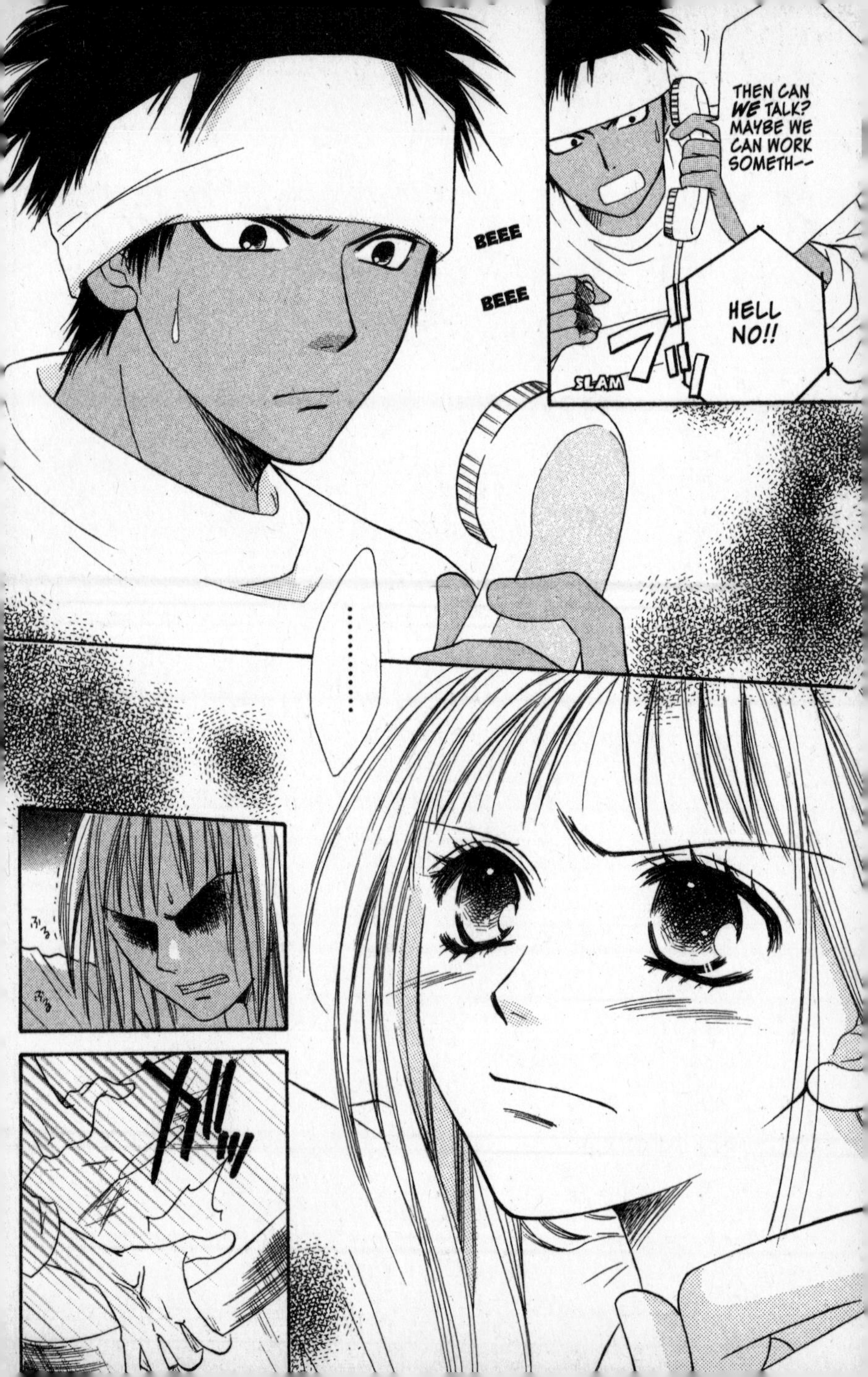
THEN CAN WE TALK? MAYBE WE CAN WORK SOMETH--
HELL NO!!
SLAM
BEEE
BEEE
......

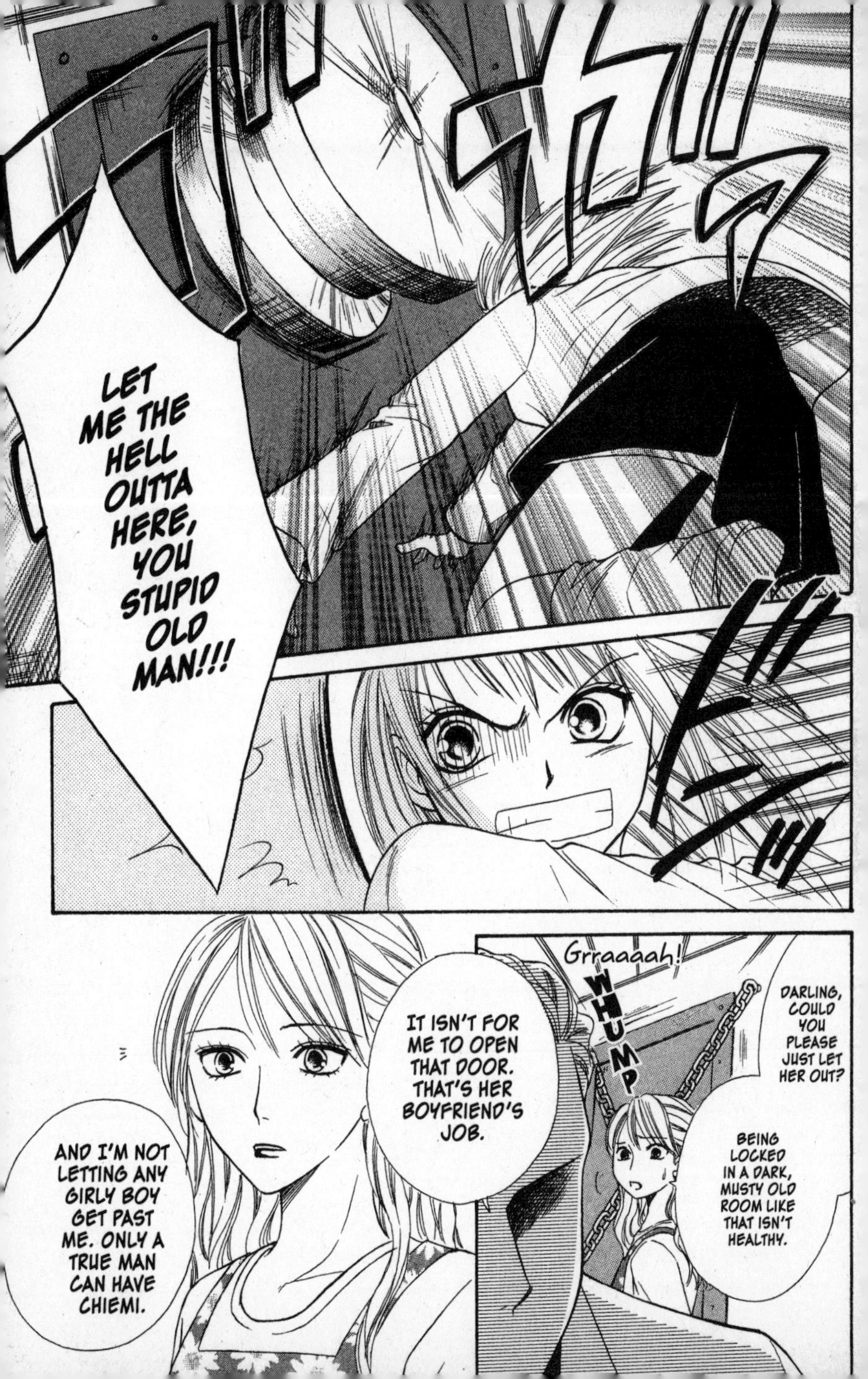
LET ME THE HELL OUTTA HERE, YOU STUPID OLD MAN!!!
Grraaaah!
WHUMP
DARLING, COULD YOU PLEASE JUST LET HER OUT?
BEING LOCKED IN A DARK, MUSTY OLD ROOM LIKE THAT ISN'T HEALTHY.
IT ISN'T FOR ME TO OPEN THAT DOOR. THAT'S HER BOYFRIEND'S JOB.
AND I'M NOT LETTING ANY GIRLY BOY GET PAST ME. ONLY A TRUE MAN CAN HAVE CHIEMI.

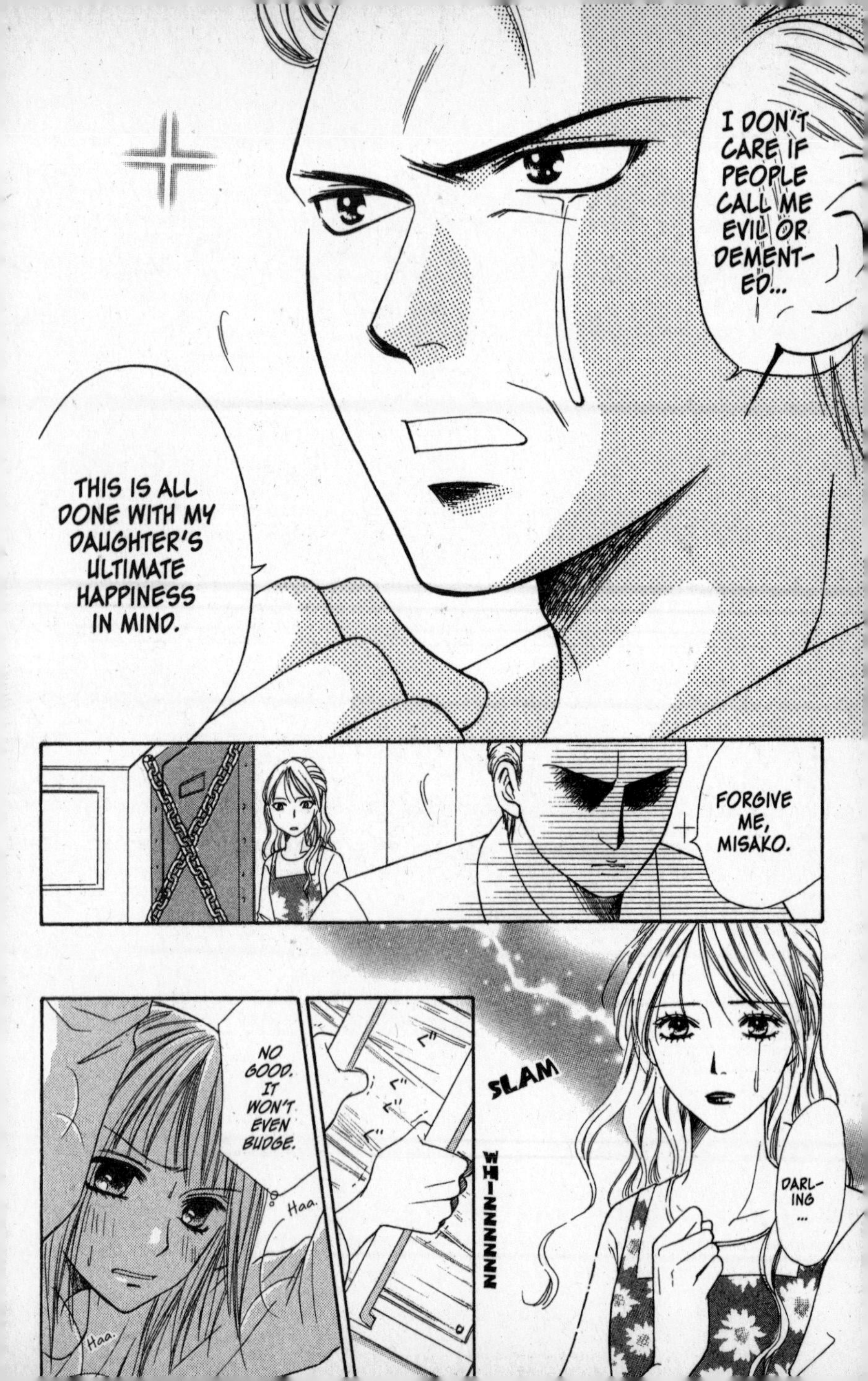
I DON'T CARE IF PEOPLE CALL ME EVIL OR DEMENT-ED...
THIS IS ALL DONE WITH MY DAUGHTER'S ULTIMATE HAPPINESS IN MIND.
FORGIVE ME, MISAKO.
DARL-ING ...
SLAM
WHIZZZZZZZ
NO GOOD. IT WON'T EVEN BUDGE.
Haa.
Haa.

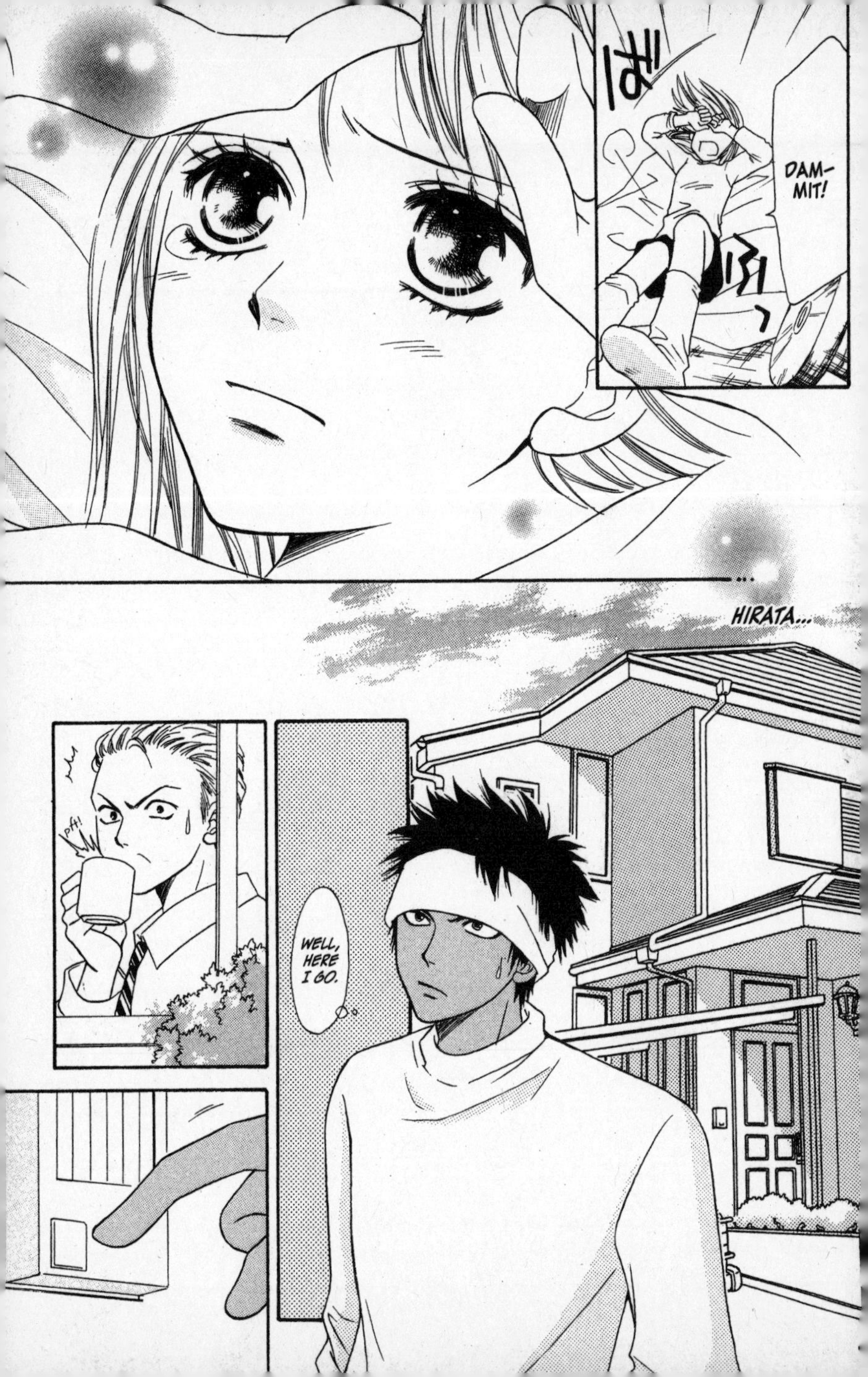
DAM-MIT!
...
HIRATA...
WELL, HERE I GO.
pft!

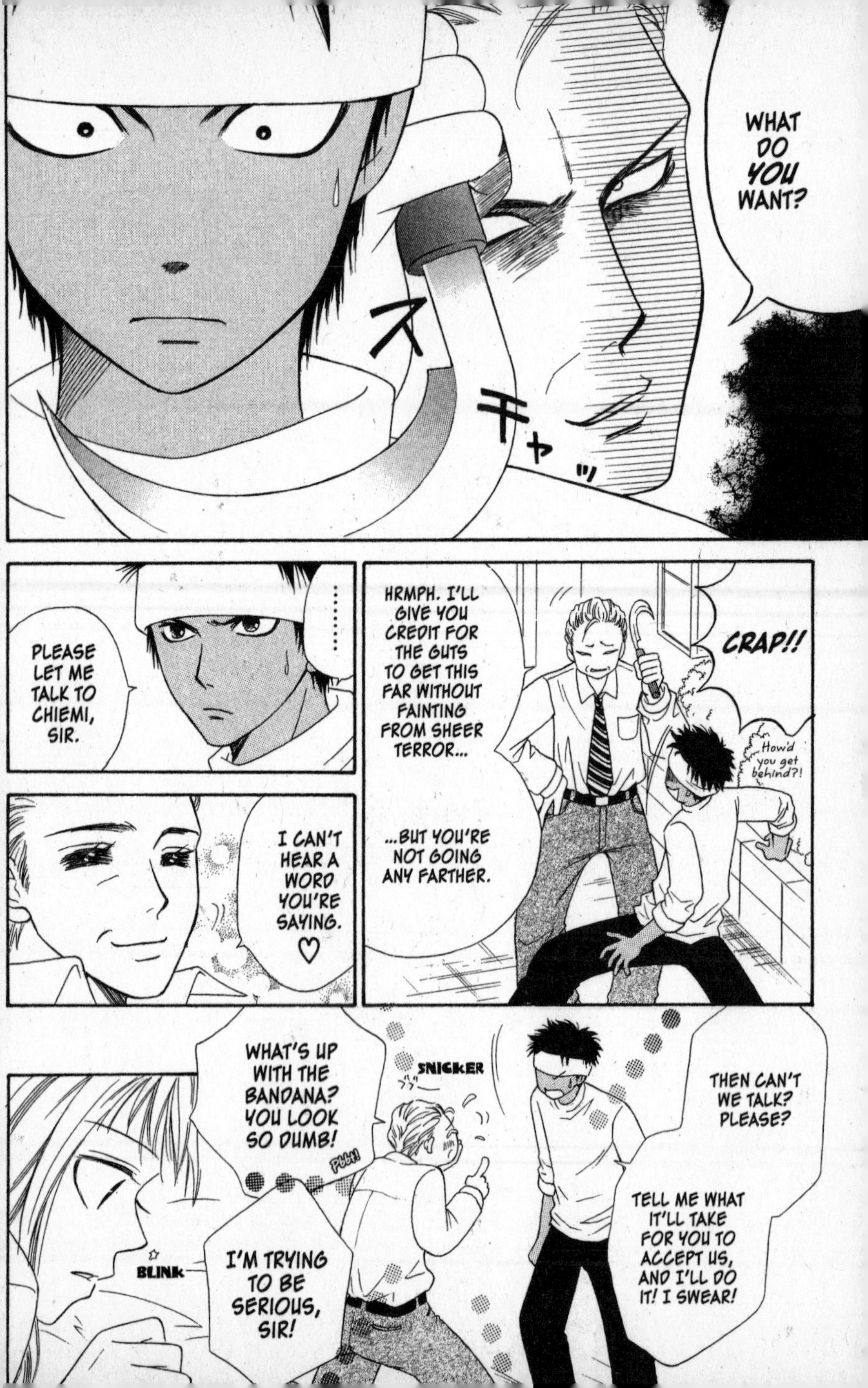
WHAT DO YOU WANT?
スチャッ
CRAP!!
How'd you get behind?!
HRMPH. I'LL GIVE YOU CREDIT FOR THE GUTS TO GET THIS FAR WITHOUT FAINTING FROM SHEER TERROR...
...BUT YOU'RE NOT GOING ANY FARTHER.
......
PLEASE LET ME TALK TO CHIEMI, SIR.
I CAN'T HEAR A WORD YOU'RE SAYING. ♡
THEN CAN'T WE TALK? PLEASE?
TELL ME WHAT IT'LL TAKE FOR YOU TO ACCEPT US, AND I'LL DO IT! I SWEAR!
SNICKER
WHAT'S UP WITH THE BANDANA? YOU LOOK SO DUMB!
I'M TRYING TO BE SERIOUS, SIR!
BLINK

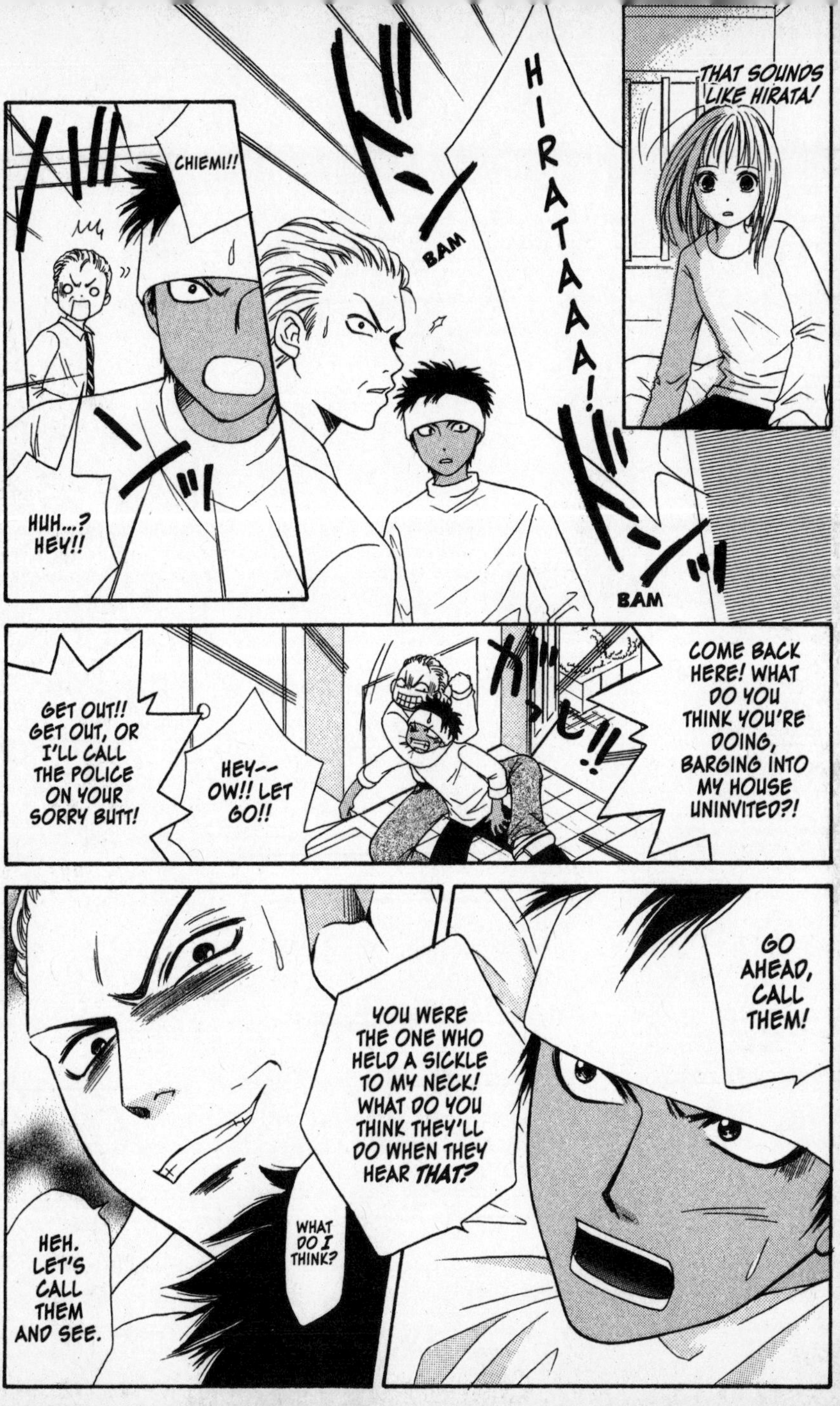
THAT SOUNDS LIKE HIRATA!
HIRATAAA!!
BAM
BAM
CHIEMI!!
HUH...? HEY!!
COME BACK HERE! WHAT DO YOU THINK YOU'RE DOING, BARGING INTO MY HOUSE UNINVITED?!
HEY-- OW!! LET GO!!
GET OUT!! GET OUT, OR I'LL CALL THE POLICE ON YOUR SORRY BUTT!
GO AHEAD, CALL THEM!
YOU WERE THE ONE WHO HELD A SICKLE TO MY NECK! WHAT DO YOU THINK THEY'LL DO WHEN THEY HEAR *THAT?*
WHAT DO I THINK?
HEH. LET'S CALL THEM AND SEE.

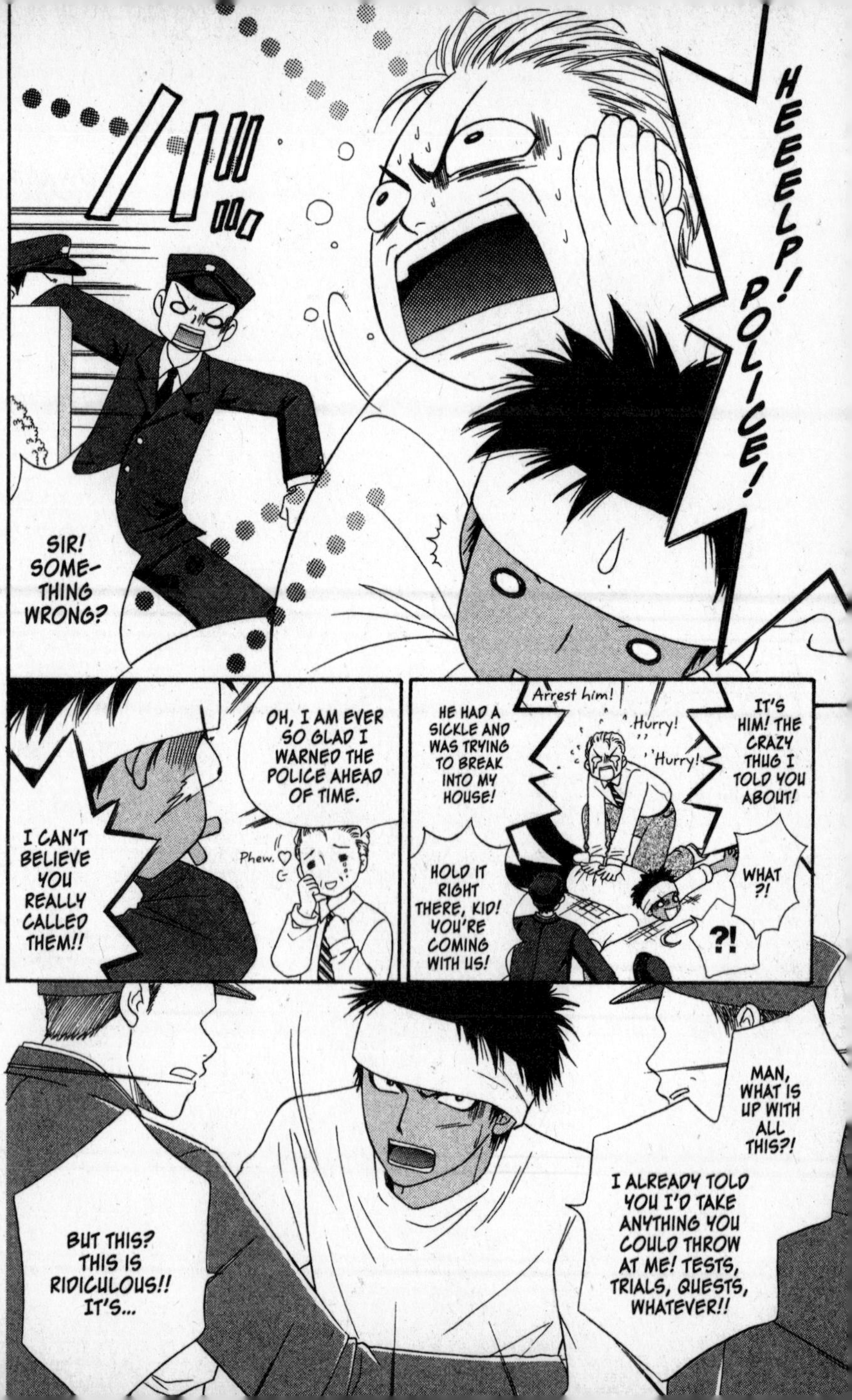
HEEELP! POLICE!
SIR! SOMETHING WRONG?
IT'S HIM! THE CRAZY THUG I TOLD YOU ABOUT!
Arrest him!
Hurry!
Hurry!
HE HAD A SICKLE AND WAS TRYING TO BREAK INTO MY HOUSE!
WHAT ?!
HOLD IT RIGHT THERE, KID! YOU'RE COMING WITH US!
?!
OH, I AM EVER SO GLAD I WARNED THE POLICE AHEAD OF TIME.
Phew. ♡
I CAN'T BELIEVE YOU REALLY CALLED THEM!!
MAN, WHAT IS UP WITH ALL THIS?!
I ALREADY TOLD YOU I'D TAKE ANYTHING YOU COULD THROW AT ME! TESTS, TRIALS, QUESTS, WHATEVER!!
BUT THIS? THIS IS RIDICULOUS!! IT'S...

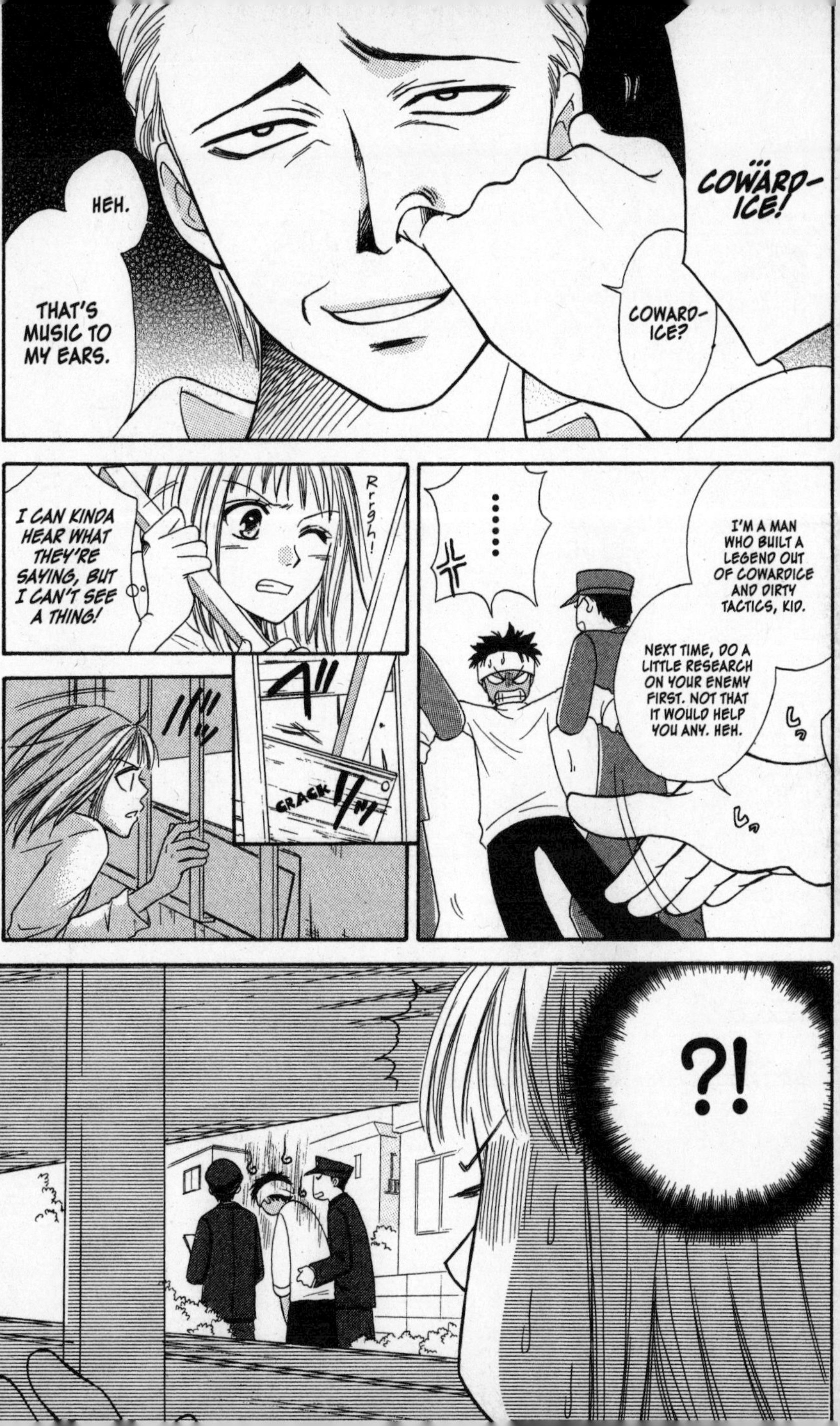
COWÄRD-ICE!
COWARD-ICE?
HEH.
THAT'S MUSIC TO MY EARS.
I'M A MAN WHO BUILT A LEGEND OUT OF COWARDICE AND DIRTY TACTICS, KID.
NEXT TIME, DO A LITTLE RESEARCH ON YOUR ENEMY FIRST. NOT THAT IT WOULD HELP YOU ANY. HEH.
......
Rrrgh!
I CAN KINDA HEAR WHAT THEY'RE SAYING, BUT I CAN'T SEE A THING!
CRACK
?!

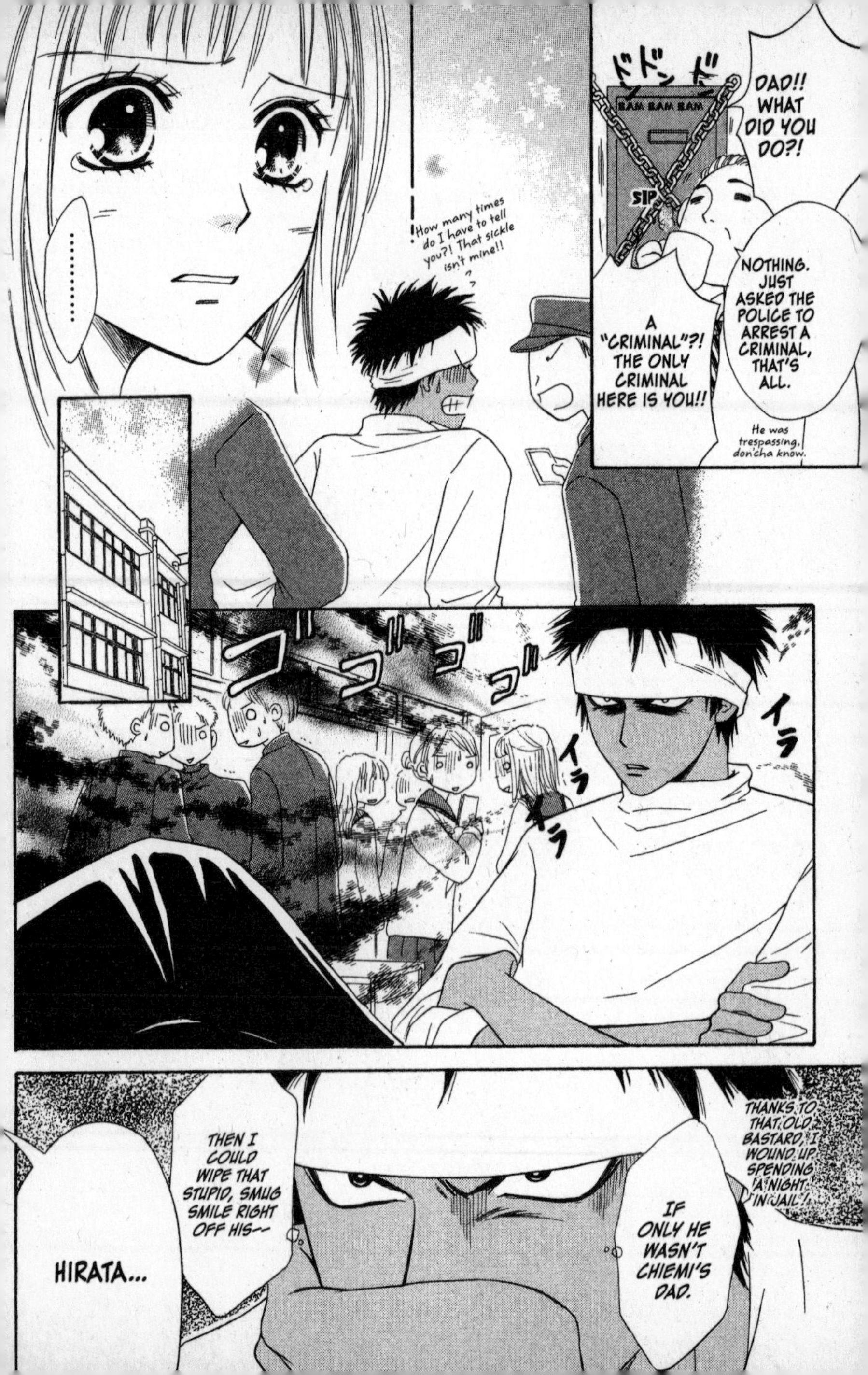
BAM BAM BAM
DAD!! WHAT DID YOU DO?!
SIP
NOTHING. JUST ASKED THE POLICE TO ARREST A CRIMINAL, THAT'S ALL.
A "CRIMINAL"?! THE ONLY CRIMINAL HERE IS YOU!!
He was trespassing, don'cha know.
How many times do I have to tell you?! That sickle isn't mine!!
......
イラ
イラ
イラ
THANKS TO THAT OLD BASTARD, I WOUND UP SPENDING A NIGHT IN JAIL!
IF ONLY HE WASN'T CHIEMI'S DAD.
THEN I COULD WIPE THAT STUPID, SMUG SMILE RIGHT OFF HIS--
HIRATA...

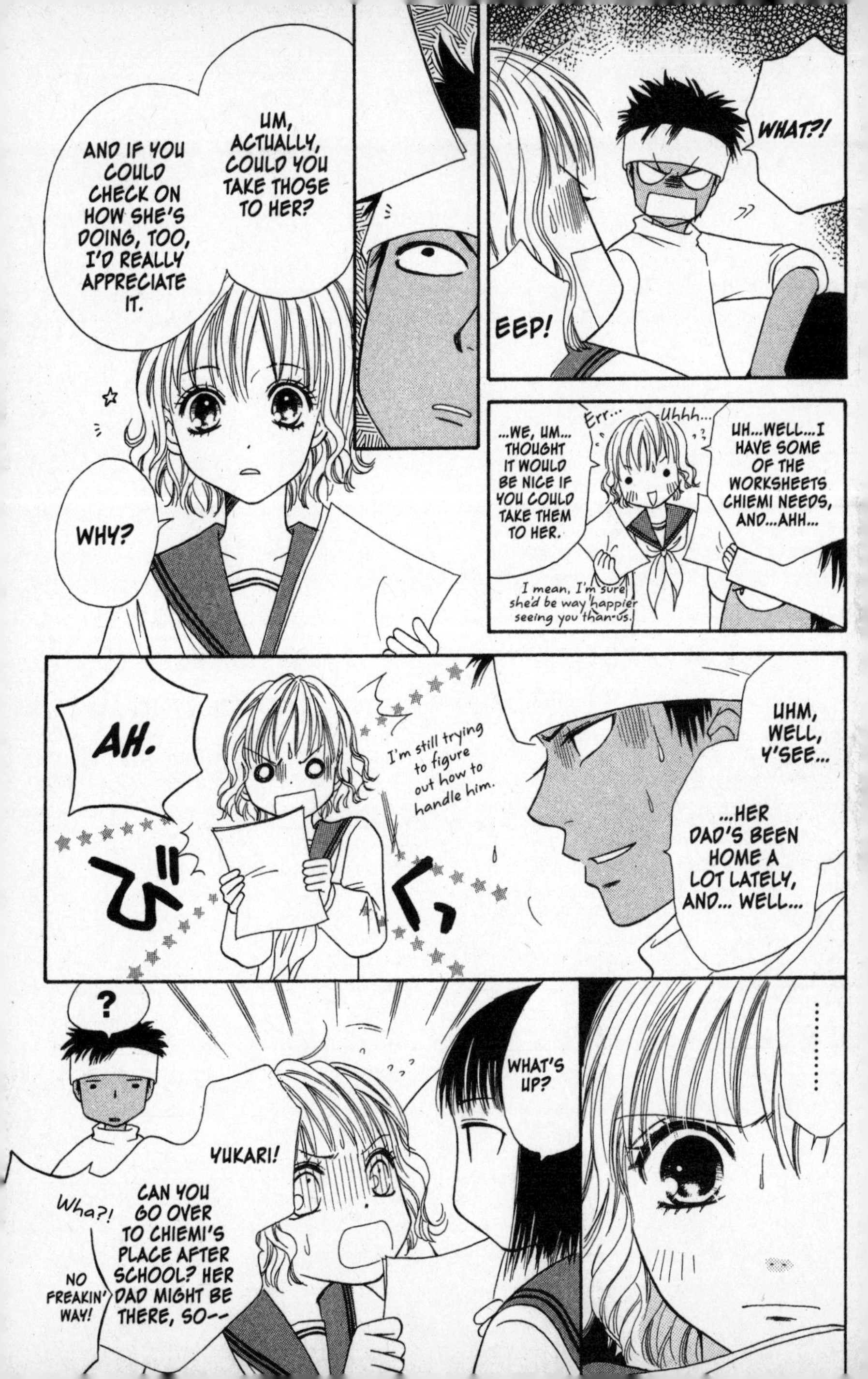
UM, ACTUALLY, COULD YOU TAKE THOSE TO HER?
AND IF YOU COULD CHECK ON HOW SHE'S DOING, TOO, I'D REALLY APPRECIATE IT.
WHY?
WHAT?!
EEP!
Err... Uhhh...
UH...WELL...I HAVE SOME OF THE WORKSHEETS CHIEMI NEEDS, AND...AHH...
...WE, UM... THOUGHT IT WOULD BE NICE IF YOU COULD TAKE THEM TO HER.
I mean, I'm sure she'd be way happier seeing you than us.
UHM, WELL, Y'SEE...
...HER DAD'S BEEN HOME A LOT LATELY, AND... WELL...
AH.
I'm still trying to figure out how to handle him.
び
くっ
……
WHAT'S UP?
YUKARI!
CAN YOU GO OVER TO CHIEMI'S PLACE AFTER SCHOOL? HER DAD MIGHT BE THERE, SO--
Wha?!
NO FREAKIN' WAY!
?

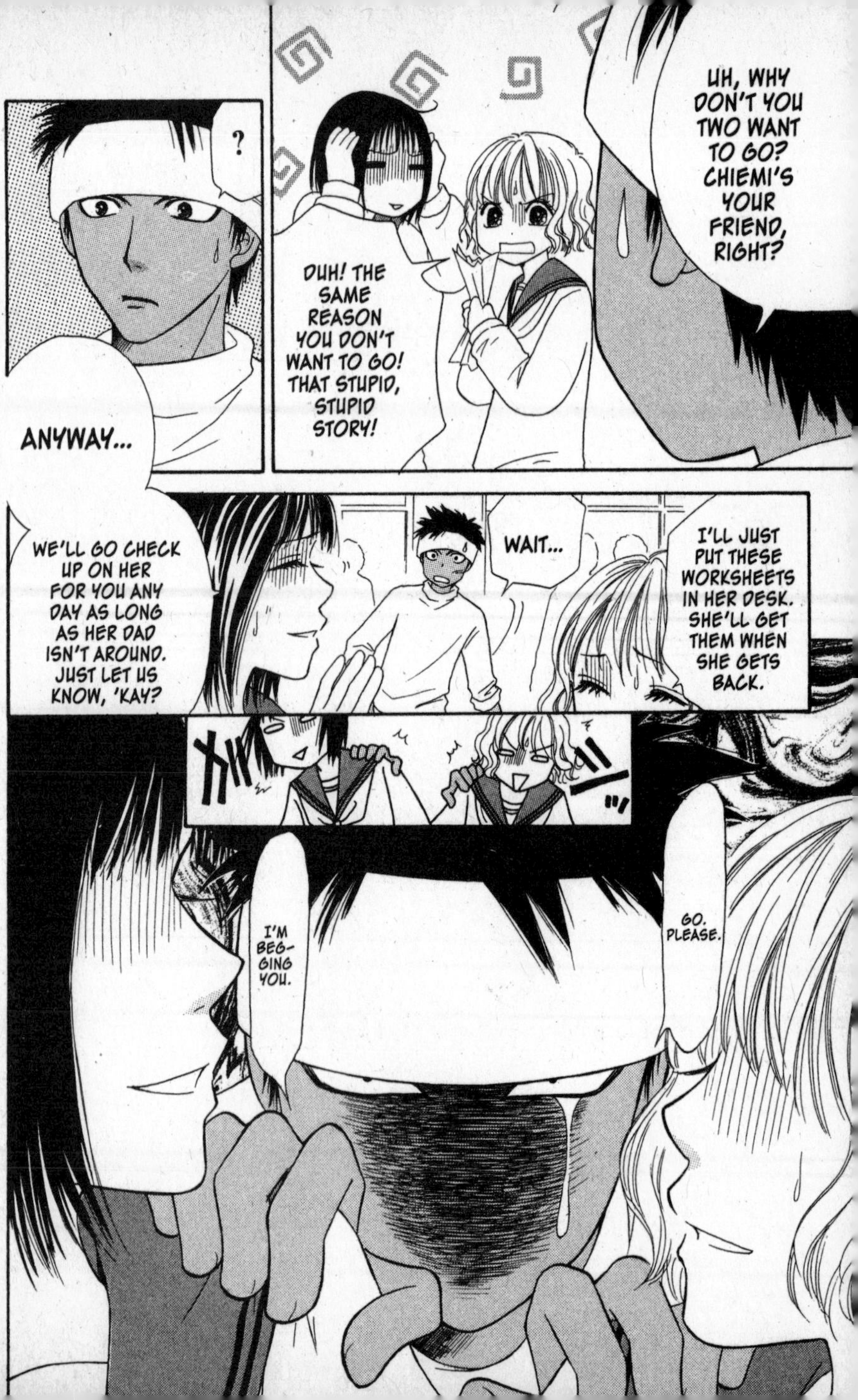
UH, WHY DON'T YOU TWO WANT TO GO? CHIEMI'S YOUR FRIEND, RIGHT?
DUH! THE SAME REASON YOU DON'T WANT TO GO! THAT STUPID, STUPID STORY!
?
ANYWAY...
I'LL JUST PUT THESE WORKSHEETS IN HER DESK. SHE'LL GET THEM WHEN SHE GETS BACK.
WAIT...
WE'LL GO CHECK UP ON HER FOR YOU ANY DAY AS LONG AS HER DAD ISN'T AROUND. JUST LET US KNOW, 'KAY?
GO. PLEASE.
I'M BEG-GING YOU.

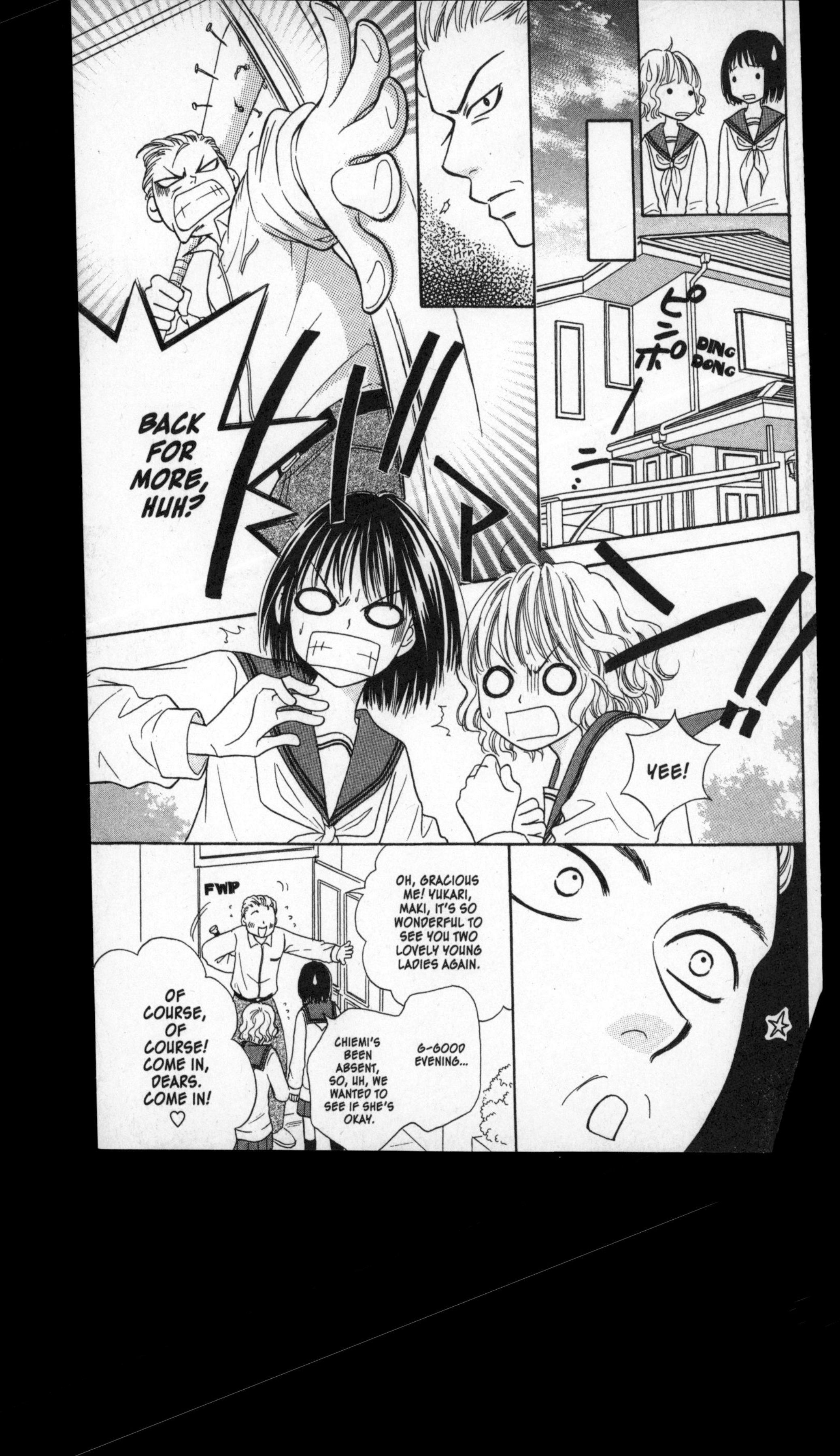
DING DONG
Hrn?
BACK FOR MORE, HUH?
YEE!
OH, GRACIOUS ME! YUKARI, MAKI, IT'S SO WONDERFUL TO SEE YOU TWO LOVELY YOUNG LADIES AGAIN.
G-GOOD EVENING...
CHIEMI'S BEEN ABSENT, SO, UH, WE WANTED TO SEE IF SHE'S OKAY.
FWP
OF COURSE, OF COURSE! COME IN, DEARS. COME IN! ♡

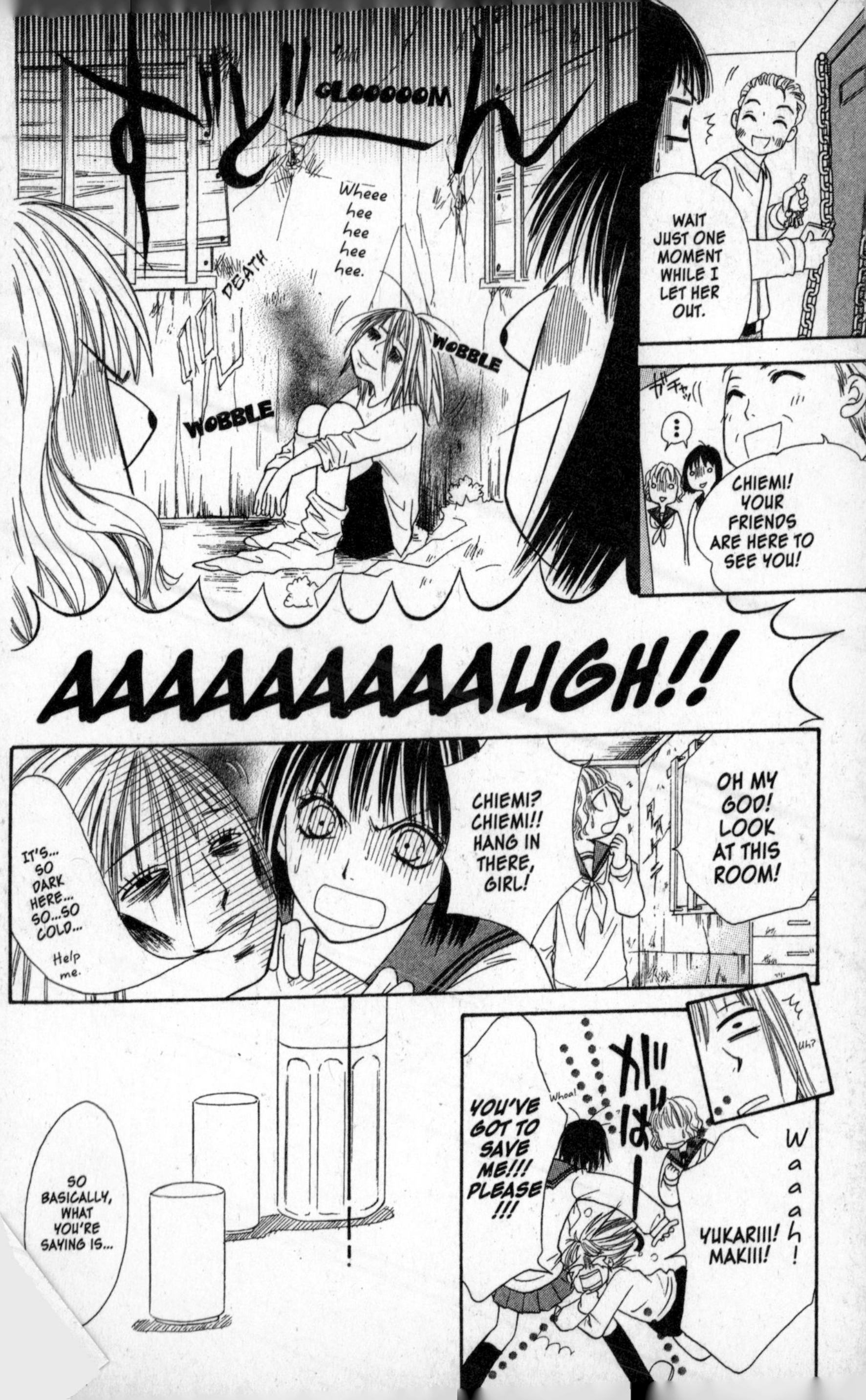
WAIT JUST ONE MOMENT WHILE I LET HER OUT.
CHIEMI! YOUR FRIENDS ARE HERE TO SEE YOU!
GLOOOOOOM
Wheee hee hee hee hee.
DEATH
WOBBLE
WOBBLE
AAAAAAAAAUGH!!
OH MY GOD! LOOK AT THIS ROOM!
CHIEMI? CHIEMI!! HANG IN THERE, GIRL!
IT'S... SO DARK HERE... SO... COLD...
Help me.
Uh?
Waaaah!
YUKARIII! MAKIII!
Whoa!
YOU'VE GOT TO SAVE ME!!! PLEASE!!!
SO BASICALLY, WHAT YOU'RE SAYING IS...

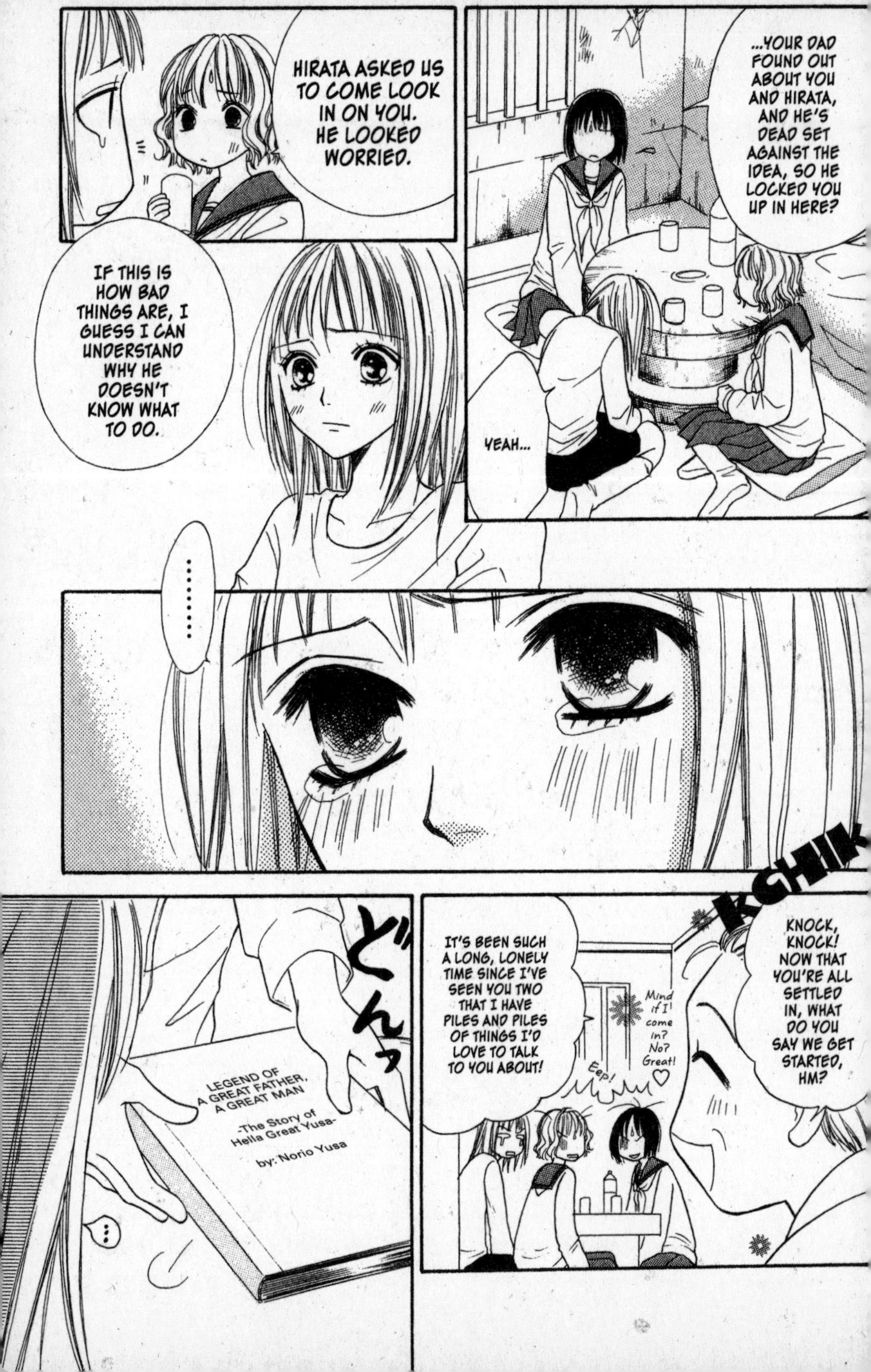
...YOUR DAD FOUND OUT ABOUT YOU AND HIRATA, AND HE'S DEAD SET AGAINST THE IDEA, SO HE LOCKED YOU UP IN HERE?
YEAH...
HIRATA ASKED US TO COME LOOK IN ON YOU. HE LOOKED WORRIED.
IF THIS IS HOW BAD THINGS ARE, I GUESS I CAN UNDERSTAND WHY HE DOESN'T KNOW WHAT TO DO.
......
KCHIK
KNOCK, KNOCK! NOW THAT YOU'RE ALL SETTLED IN, WHAT DO YOU SAY WE GET STARTED, HM?
Mind if I come in? No? Great! ♡
IT'S BEEN SUCH A LONG, LONELY TIME SINCE I'VE SEEN YOU TWO THAT I HAVE PILES AND PILES OF THINGS I'D LOVE TO TALK TO YOU ABOUT!
Eep!
どんっ
LEGEND OF A GREAT FATHER, A GREAT MAN
-The Story of Hella Great Yusa-
by: Norio Yusa
...

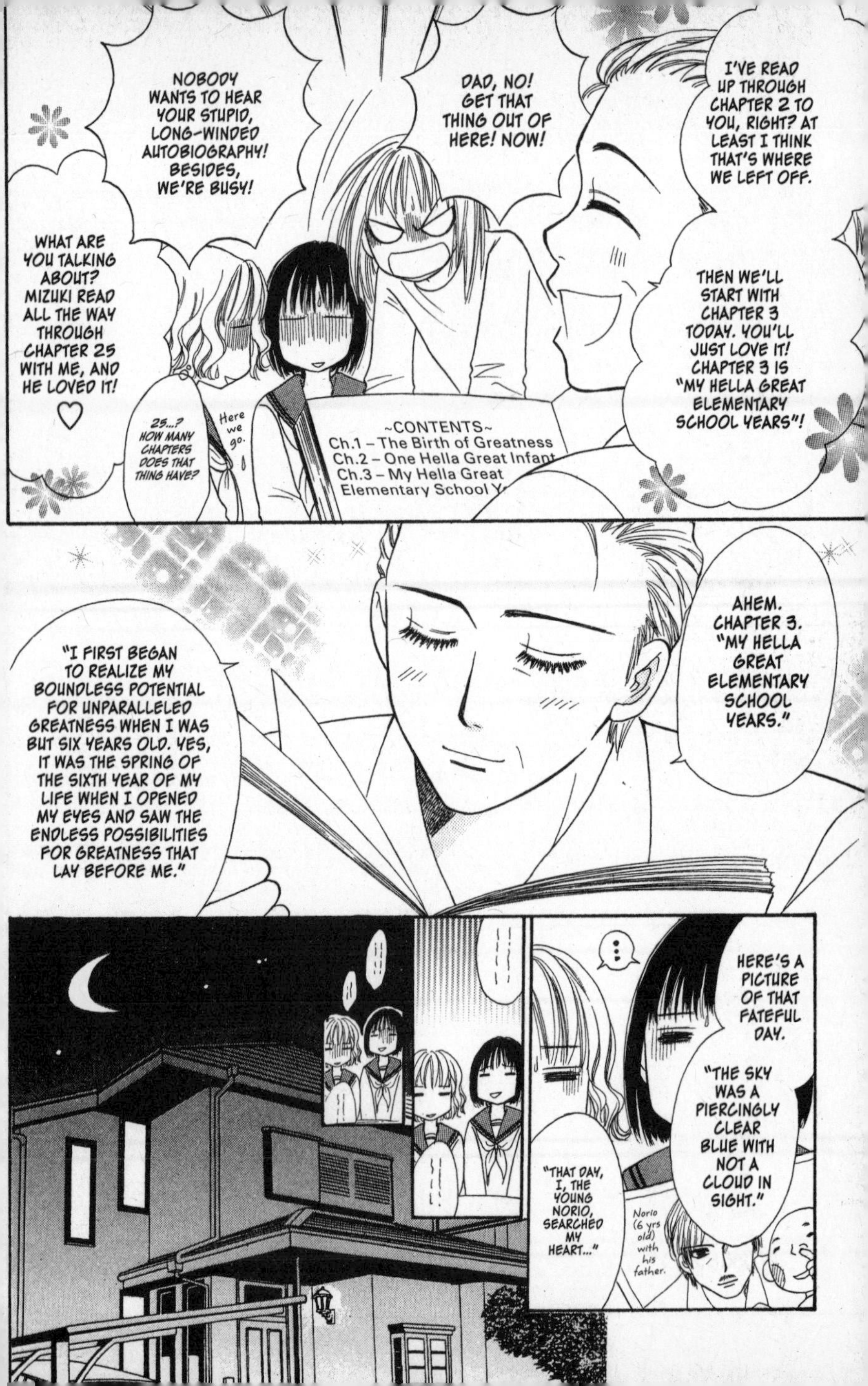
I'VE READ UP THROUGH CHAPTER 2 TO YOU, RIGHT? AT LEAST I THINK THAT'S WHERE WE LEFT OFF.
THEN WE'LL START WITH CHAPTER 3 TODAY. YOU'LL JUST LOVE IT! CHAPTER 3 IS "MY HELLA GREAT ELEMENTARY SCHOOL YEARS"!
DAD, NO! GET THAT THING OUT OF HERE! NOW!
NOBODY WANTS TO HEAR YOUR STUPID, LONG-WINDED AUTOBIOGRAPHY! BESIDES, WE'RE BUSY!
WHAT ARE YOU TALKING ABOUT? MIZUKI READ ALL THE WAY THROUGH CHAPTER 25 WITH ME, AND HE LOVED IT! ♡
Here we go.
25...? HOW MANY CHAPTERS DOES THAT THING HAVE?
~CONTENTS~
Ch.1 – The Birth of Greatness
Ch.2 – One Hella Great Infant
Ch.3 – My Hella Great Elementary School Y
AHEM. CHAPTER 3. "MY HELLA GREAT ELEMENTARY SCHOOL YEARS."
"I FIRST BEGAN TO REALIZE MY BOUNDLESS POTENTIAL FOR UNPARALLELED GREATNESS WHEN I WAS BUT SIX YEARS OLD. YES, IT WAS THE SPRING OF THE SIXTH YEAR OF MY LIFE WHEN I OPENED MY EYES AND SAW THE ENDLESS POSSIBILITIES FOR GREATNESS THAT LAY BEFORE ME."
...
HERE'S A PICTURE OF THAT FATEFUL DAY.
"THE SKY WAS A PIERCINGLY CLEAR BLUE WITH NOT A CLOUD IN SIGHT."
"THAT DAY, I, THE YOUNG NORIO, SEARCHED MY HEART..."
Norio (6 yrs old) with his father.
!!
!!

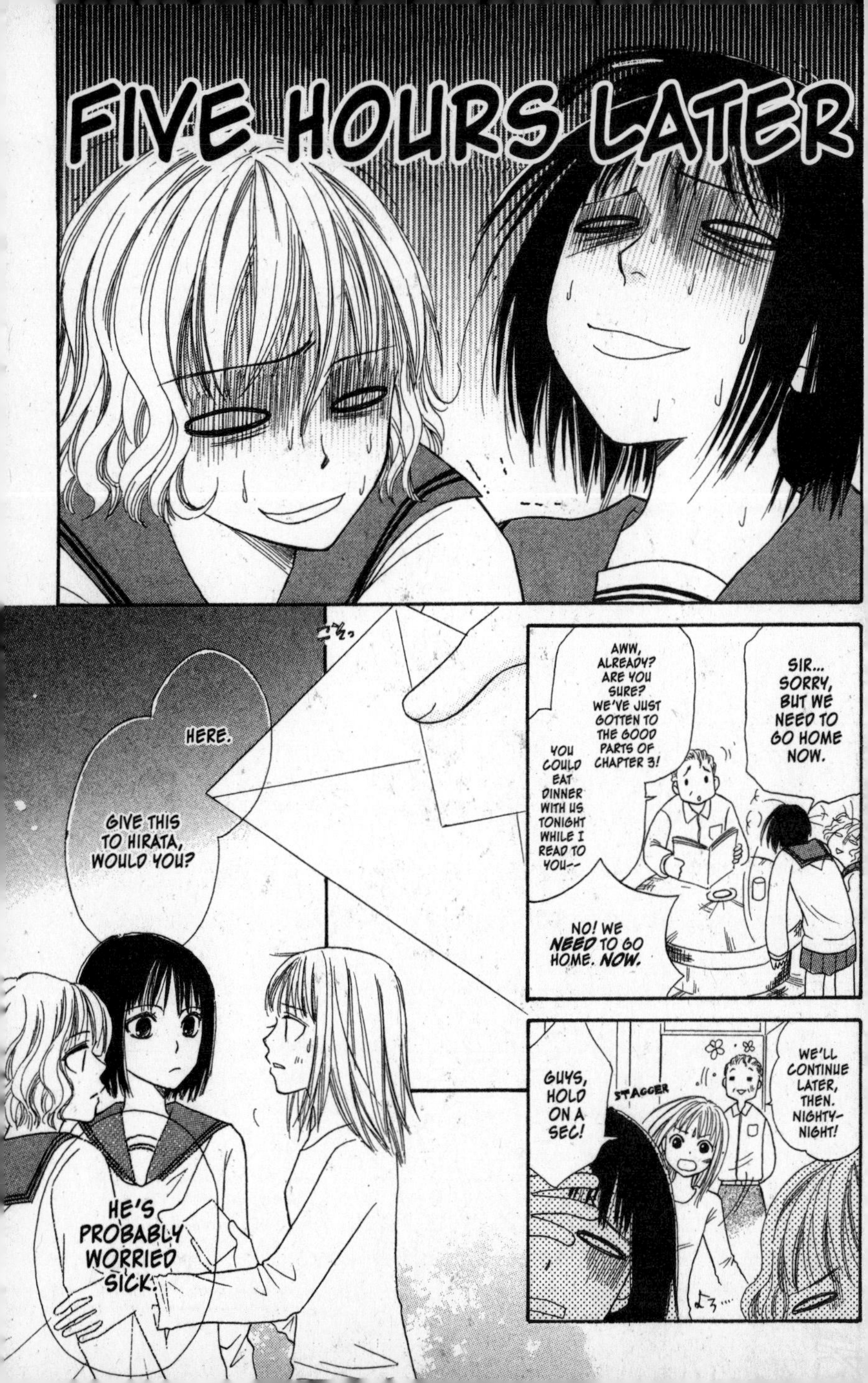
FIVE HOURS LATER
SIR... SORRY, BUT WE NEED TO GO HOME NOW.
AWW, ALREADY? ARE YOU SURE? WE'VE JUST GOTTEN TO THE GOOD PARTS OF CHAPTER 3!
YOU COULD EAT DINNER WITH US TONIGHT WHILE I READ TO YOU--
NO! WE NEED TO GO HOME. NOW.
WE'LL CONTINUE LATER, THEN. NIGHTY-NIGHT!
STAGGER
GUYS, HOLD ON A SEC!
HERE.
GIVE THIS TO HIRATA, WOULD YOU?
HE'S PROBABLY WORRIED SICK.

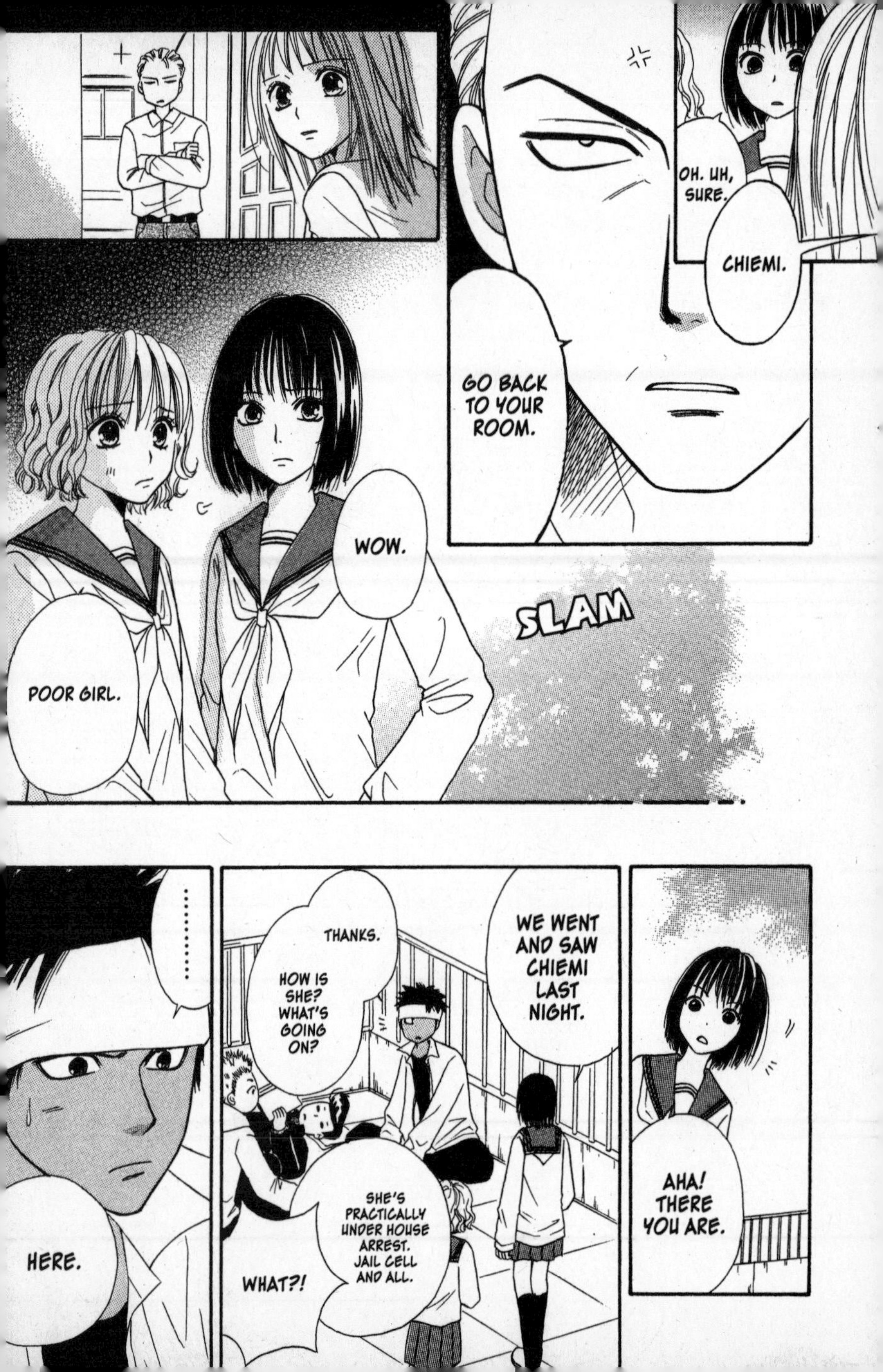
OH. UH, SURE.
CHIEMI.
GO BACK TO YOUR ROOM.
SLAM
WOW.
POOR GIRL.
AHA! THERE YOU ARE.
WE WENT AND SAW CHIEMI LAST NIGHT.
THANKS.
HOW IS SHE? WHAT'S GOING ON?
SHE'S PRACTICALLY UNDER HOUSE ARREST. JAIL CELL AND ALL.
WHAT?!
......
HERE.

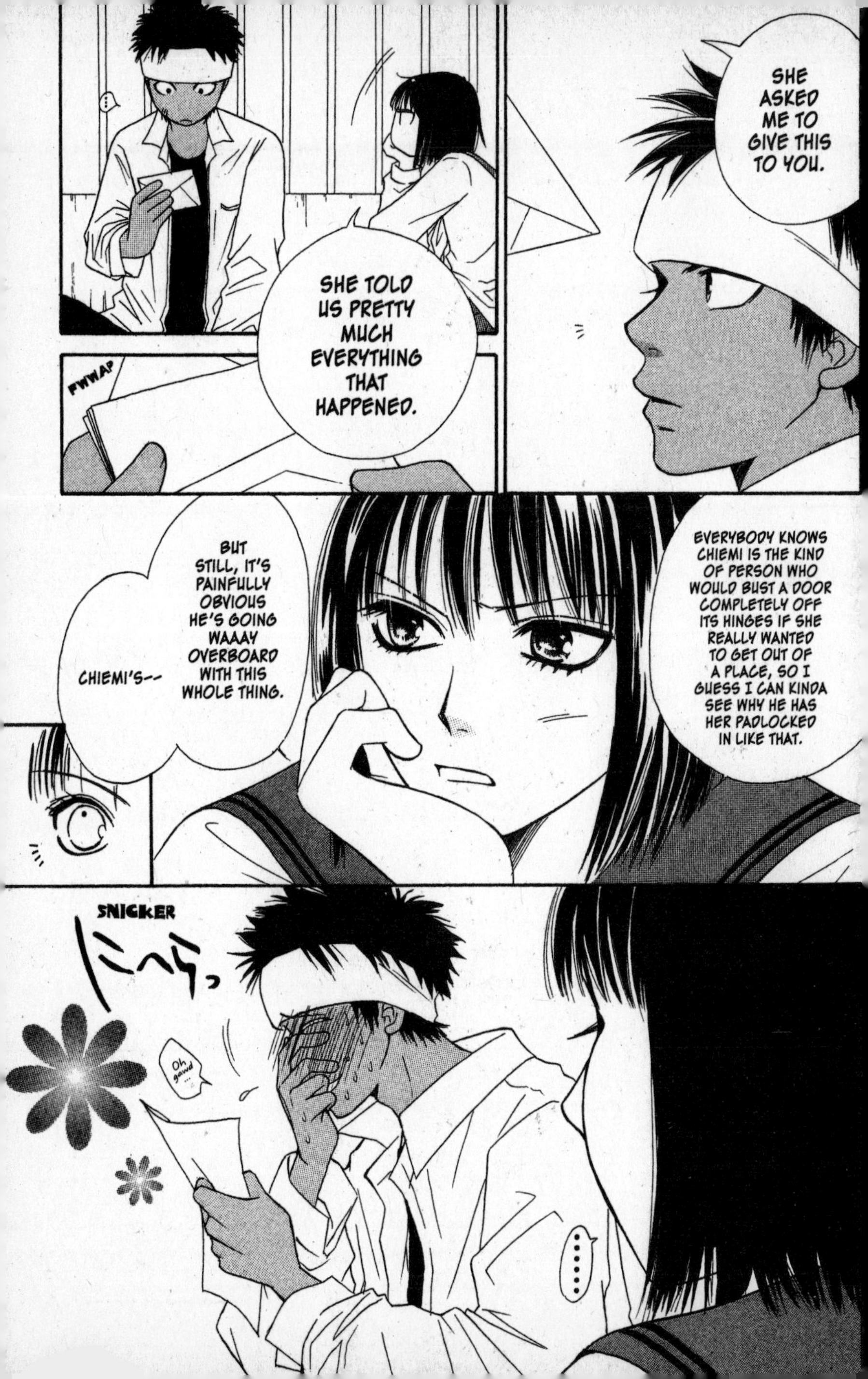
SHE ASKED ME TO GIVE THIS TO YOU.
...
FWWAP
SHE TOLD US PRETTY MUCH EVERYTHING THAT HAPPENED.
EVERYBODY KNOWS CHIEMI IS THE KIND OF PERSON WHO WOULD BUST A DOOR COMPLETELY OFF ITS HINGES IF SHE REALLY WANTED TO GET OUT OF A PLACE, SO I GUESS I CAN KINDA SEE WHY HE HAS HER PADLOCKED IN LIKE THAT.
BUT STILL, IT'S PAINFULLY OBVIOUS HE'S GOING WAAAY OVERBOARD WITH THIS WHOLE THING.
CHIEMI'S--
SNICKER
にへらっ
Oh gawd ...
......

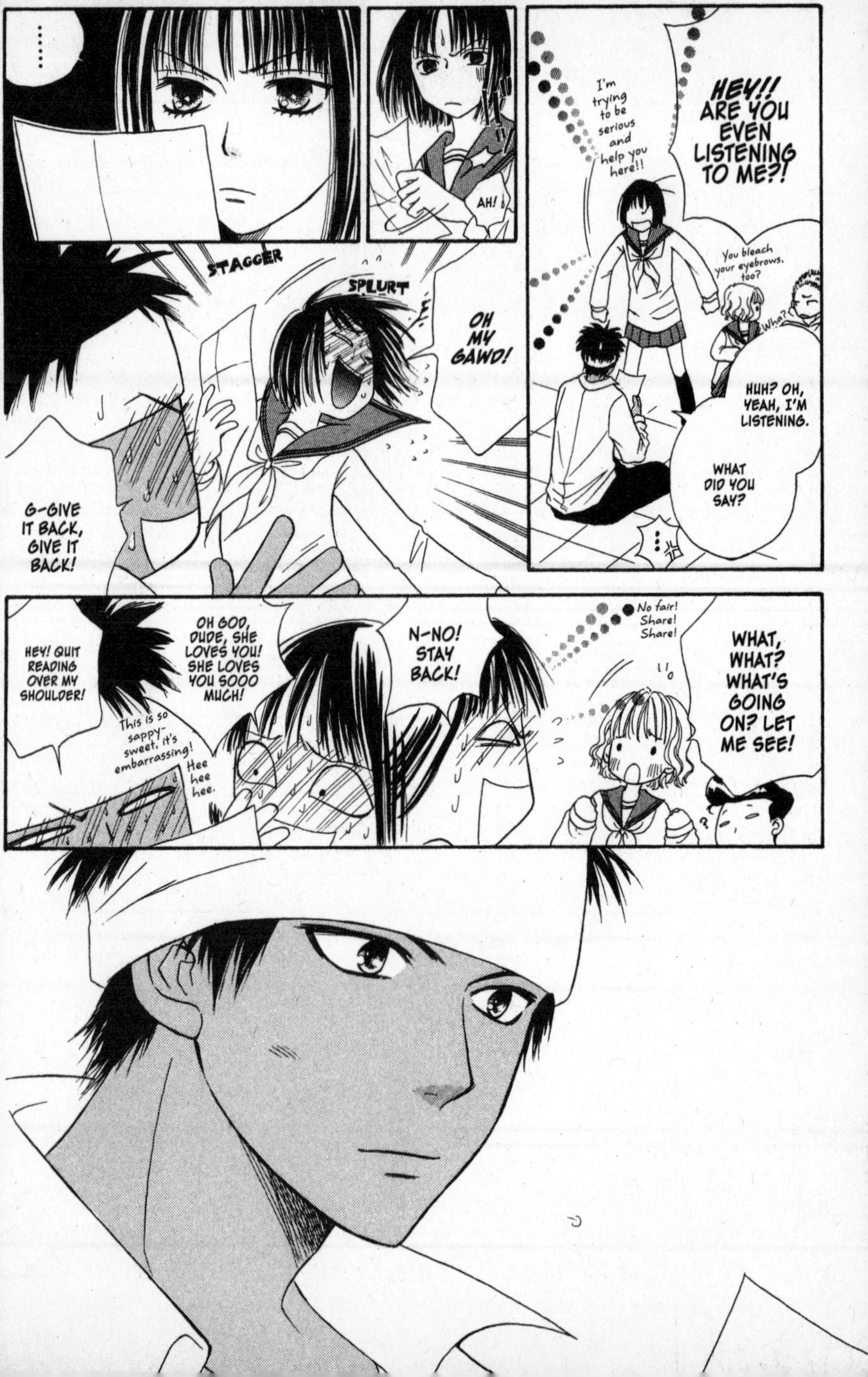
HEY!! ARE YOU EVEN LISTENING TO ME?!
I'm trying to be serious and help you here!!
You bleach your eyebrows, too?
Wha?
HUH? OH, YEAH, I'M LISTENING.
WHAT DID YOU SAY?
...
AH!
......
STAGGER
SPLURT
OH MY GAWD!
G-GIVE IT BACK, GIVE IT BACK!
WHAT, WHAT? WHAT'S GOING ON? LET ME SEE!
No fair! Share! Share!
N-NO! STAY BACK!
OH GOD, DUDE, SHE LOVES YOU! SHE LOVES YOU SOOO MUCH!
HEY! QUIT READING OVER MY SHOULDER!
This is so sappy-sweet, it's embarrassing!
Hee hee hee.

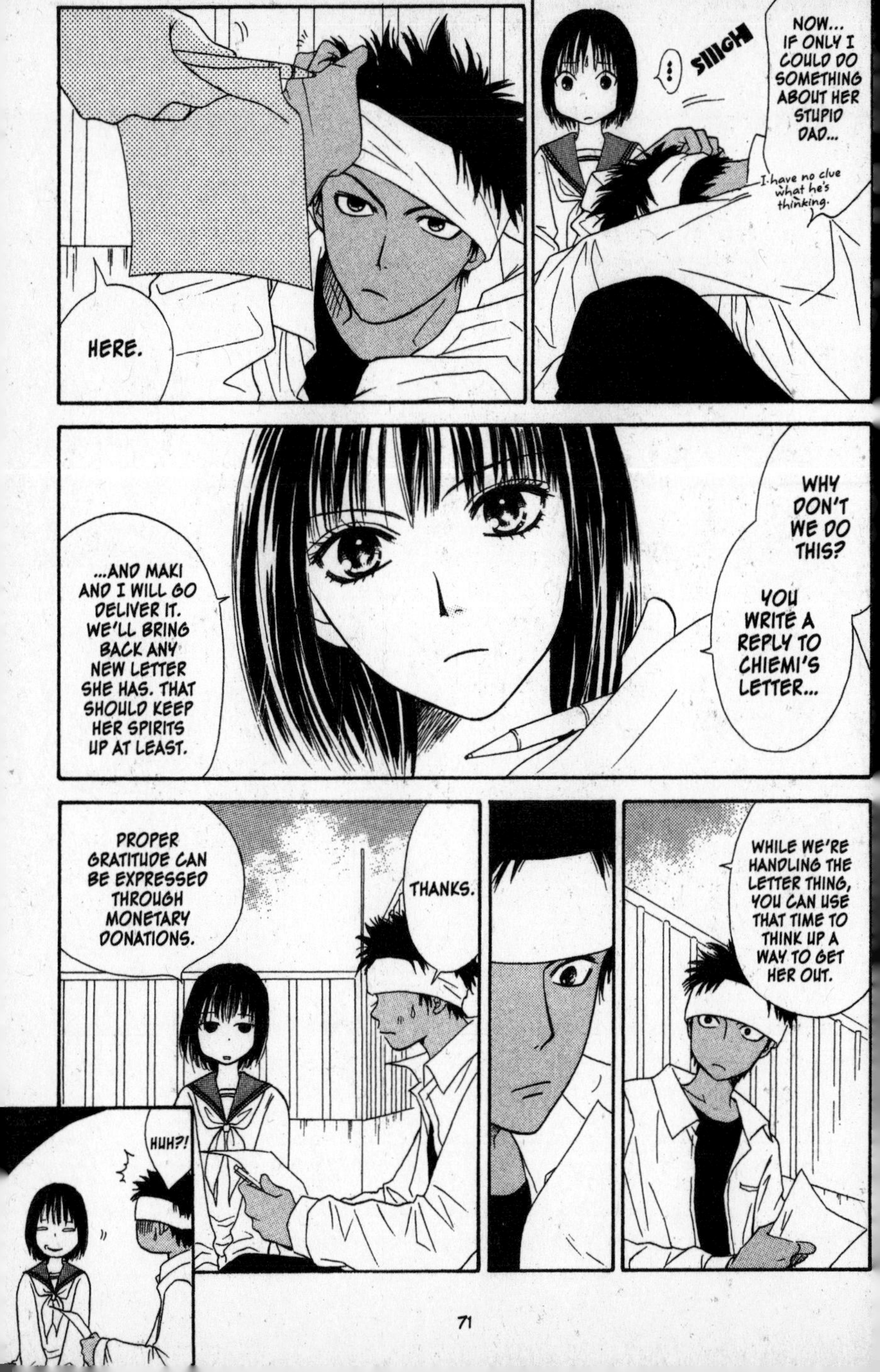
NOW... IF ONLY I COULD DO SOMETHING ABOUT HER STUPID DAD...
I have no clue what he's thinking.
SIIIGH
...
HERE.
WHY DON'T WE DO THIS?
YOU WRITE A REPLY TO CHIEMI'S LETTER...
...AND MAKI AND I WILL GO DELIVER IT. WE'LL BRING BACK ANY NEW LETTER SHE HAS. THAT SHOULD KEEP HER SPIRITS UP AT LEAST.
WHILE WE'RE HANDLING THE LETTER THING, YOU CAN USE THAT TIME TO THINK UP A WAY TO GET HER OUT.
THANKS.
PROPER GRATITUDE CAN BE EXPRESSED THROUGH MONETARY DONATIONS.
HUH?!

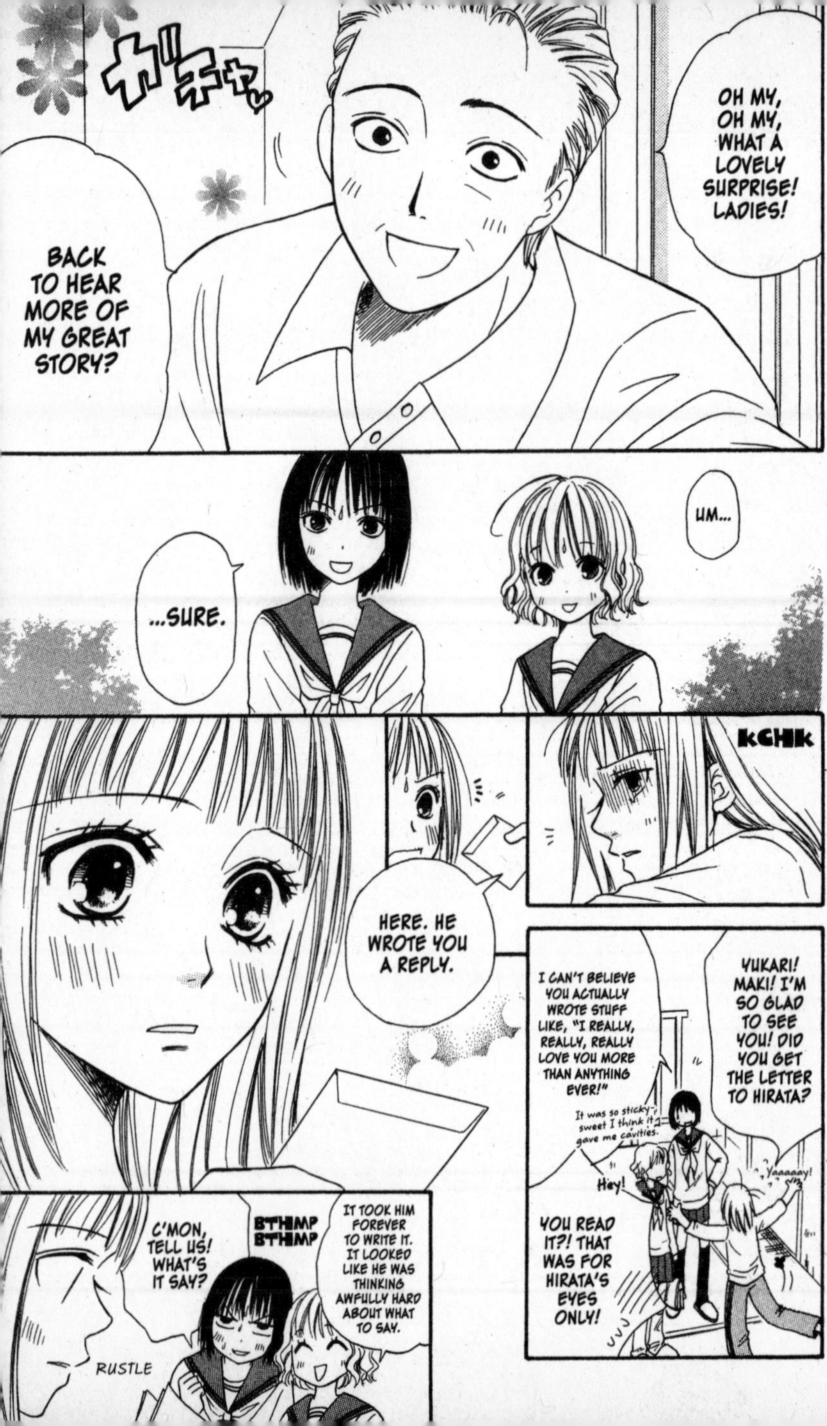
OH MY, OH MY, WHAT A LOVELY SURPRISE! LADIES!
ガチャ
BACK TO HEAR MORE OF MY GREAT STORY?
UM...
...SURE.
kCHK
HERE. HE WROTE YOU A REPLY.
YUKARI! MAKI! I'M SO GLAD TO SEE YOU! DID YOU GET THE LETTER TO HIRATA?
Yaaaaay!
I CAN'T BELIEVE YOU ACTUALLY WROTE STUFF LIKE, "I REALLY, REALLY, REALLY LOVE YOU MORE THAN ANYTHING EVER!"
It was so sticky-sweet I think it gave me cavities.
Hey!
YOU READ IT?! THAT WAS FOR HIRATA'S EYES ONLY!
IT TOOK HIM FOREVER TO WRITE IT. IT LOOKED LIKE HE WAS THINKING AWFULLY HARD ABOUT WHAT TO SAY.
BTHMP BTHMP
C'MON, TELL US! WHAT'S IT SAY?
RUSTLE

I only had paper to write that one.

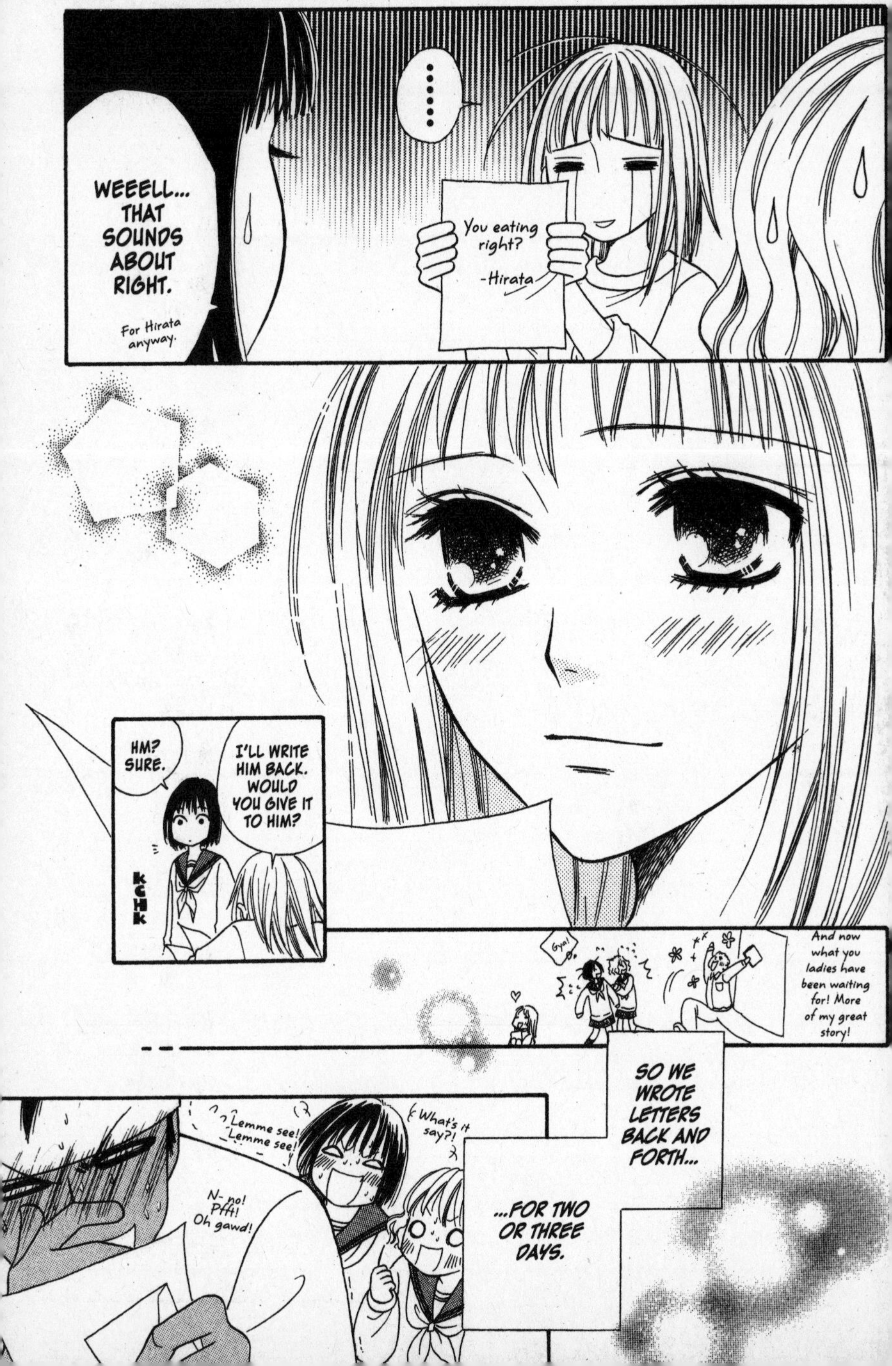
......
You eating right?
-Hirata
WEEELL... THAT SOUNDS ABOUT RIGHT.
For Hirata anyway.
I'LL WRITE HIM BACK. WOULD YOU GIVE IT TO HIM?
HM? SURE.
KCHK
And now what you ladies have been waiting for! More of my great story!
Gya!
SO WE WROTE LETTERS BACK AND FORTH...
...FOR TWO OR THREE DAYS.
What's it say?!
Lemme see! Lemme see!
N-no! Pfft! Oh gawd!

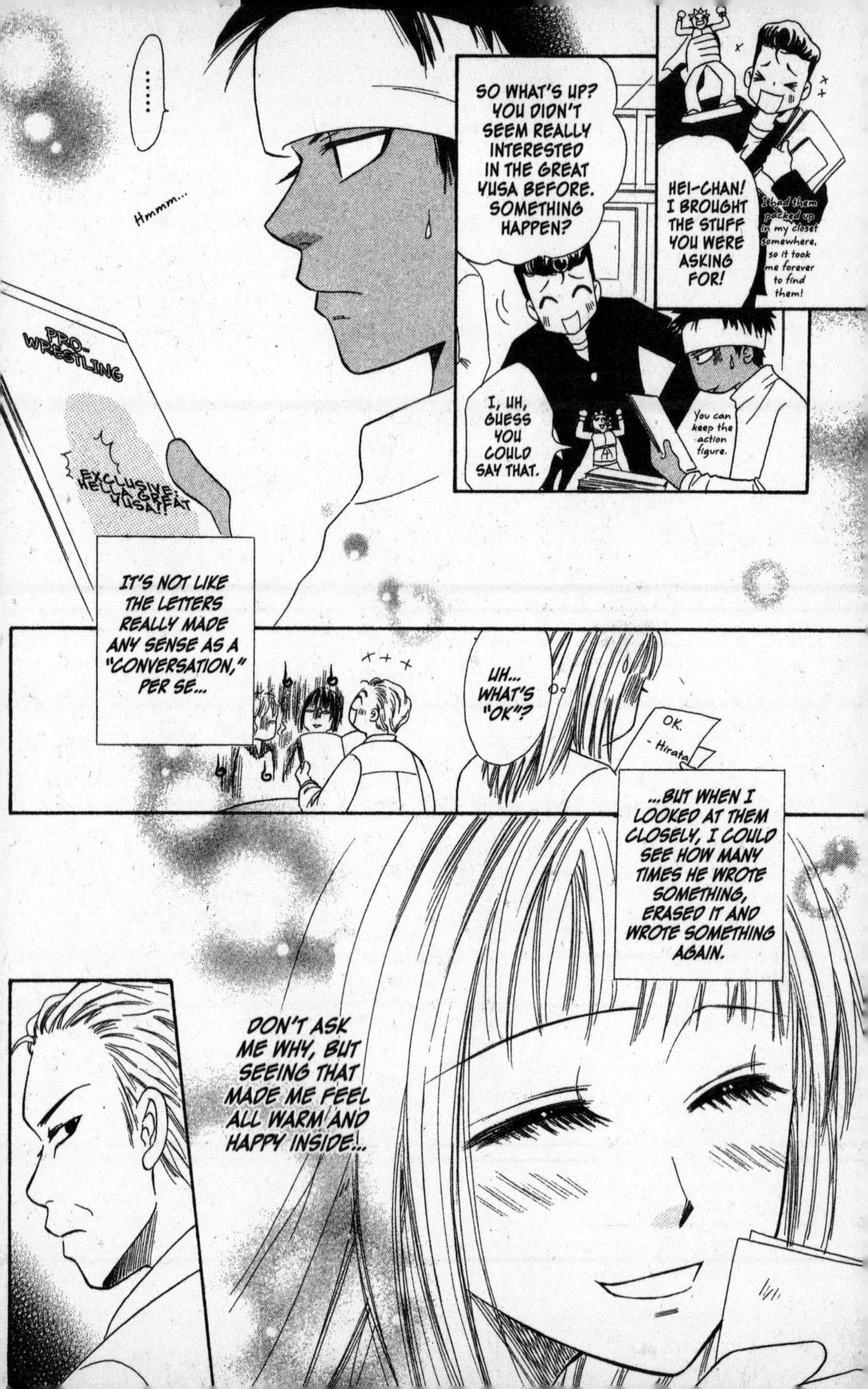
HEI-CHAN! I BROUGHT THE STUFF YOU WERE ASKING FOR!
I had them packed up in my closet somewhere, so it took me forever to find them!
SO WHAT'S UP? YOU DIDN'T SEEM REALLY INTERESTED IN THE GREAT YUSA BEFORE. SOMETHING HAPPEN?
You can keep the action figure.
I, UH, GUESS YOU COULD SAY THAT.
......
Hmmm...
PRO-WRESTLING
EXCLUSIVE: HELLA GREAT YUSA!
IT'S NOT LIKE THE LETTERS REALLY MADE ANY SENSE AS A "CONVERSATION," PER SE...
OK.
- Hirata
UH... WHAT'S "OK"?
...BUT WHEN I LOOKED AT THEM CLOSELY, I COULD SEE HOW MANY TIMES HE WROTE SOMETHING, ERASED IT AND WROTE SOMETHING AGAIN.
DON'T ASK ME WHY, BUT SEEING THAT MADE ME FEEL ALL WARM AND HAPPY INSIDE...

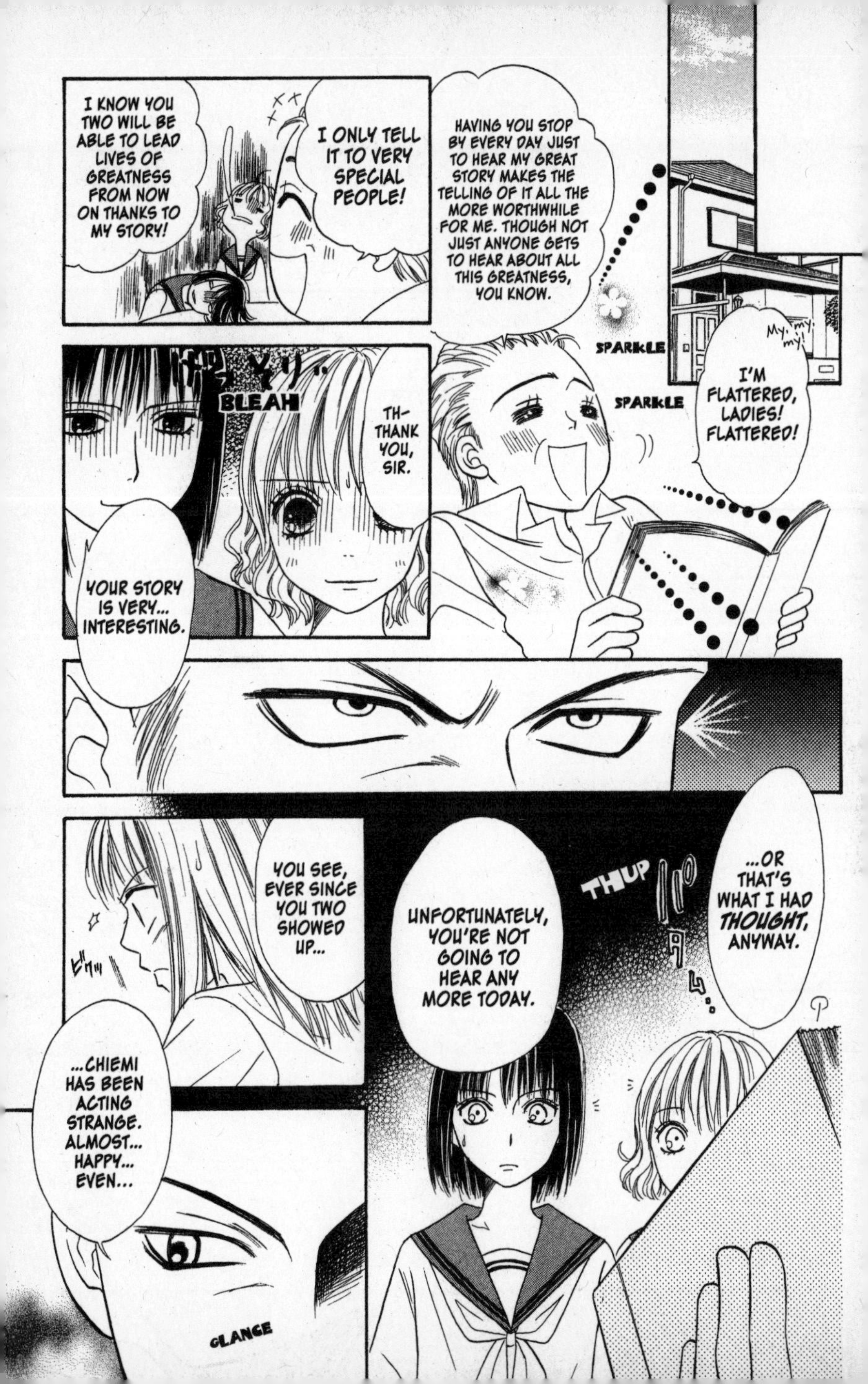
My, my, my!
I'M FLATTERED, LADIES! FLATTERED!
SPARKLE
SPARKLE
HAVING YOU STOP BY EVERY DAY JUST TO HEAR MY GREAT STORY MAKES THE TELLING OF IT ALL THE MORE WORTHWHILE FOR ME. THOUGH NOT JUST ANYONE GETS TO HEAR ABOUT ALL THIS GREATNESS, YOU KNOW.
I ONLY TELL IT TO VERY SPECIAL PEOPLE!
I KNOW YOU TWO WILL BE ABLE TO LEAD LIVES OF GREATNESS FROM NOW ON THANKS TO MY STORY!
TH-THANK YOU, SIR.
BLEAH
YOUR STORY IS VERY... INTERESTING.
...OR THAT'S WHAT I HAD THOUGHT, ANYWAY.
THUP
UNFORTUNATELY, YOU'RE NOT GOING TO HEAR ANY MORE TODAY.
YOU SEE, EVER SINCE YOU TWO SHOWED UP...
...CHIEMI HAS BEEN ACTING STRANGE. ALMOST... HAPPY... EVEN...
GLANCE

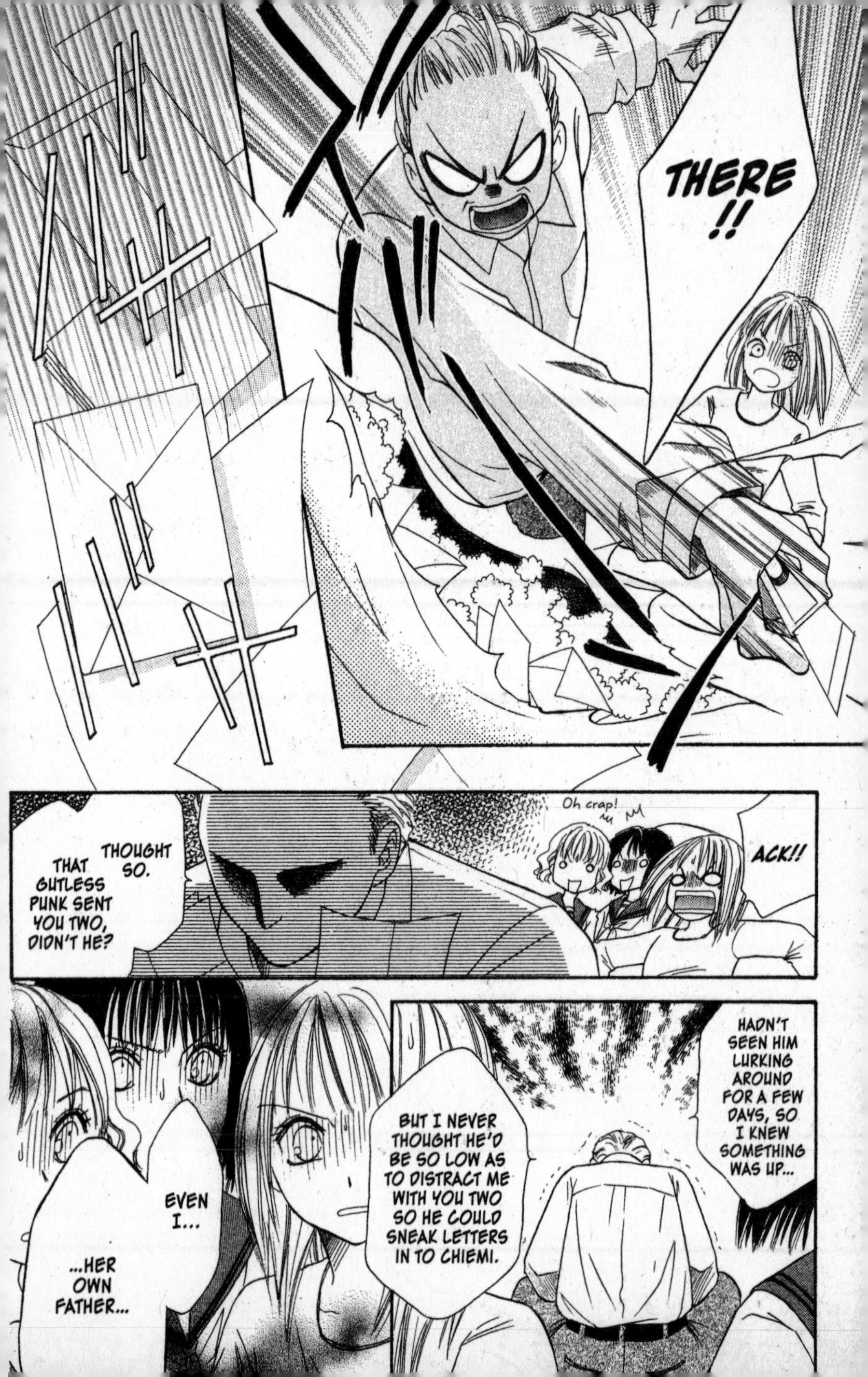
THERE !!
ACK!!
Oh crap!
THOUGHT SO.
THAT GUTLESS PUNK SENT YOU TWO, DIDN'T HE?
HADN'T SEEN HIM LURKING AROUND FOR A FEW DAYS, SO I KNEW SOMETHING WAS UP...
BUT I NEVER THOUGHT HE'D BE SO LOW AS TO DISTRACT ME WITH YOU TWO SO HE COULD SNEAK LETTERS IN TO CHIEMI.
EVEN I...
...HER OWN FATHER...

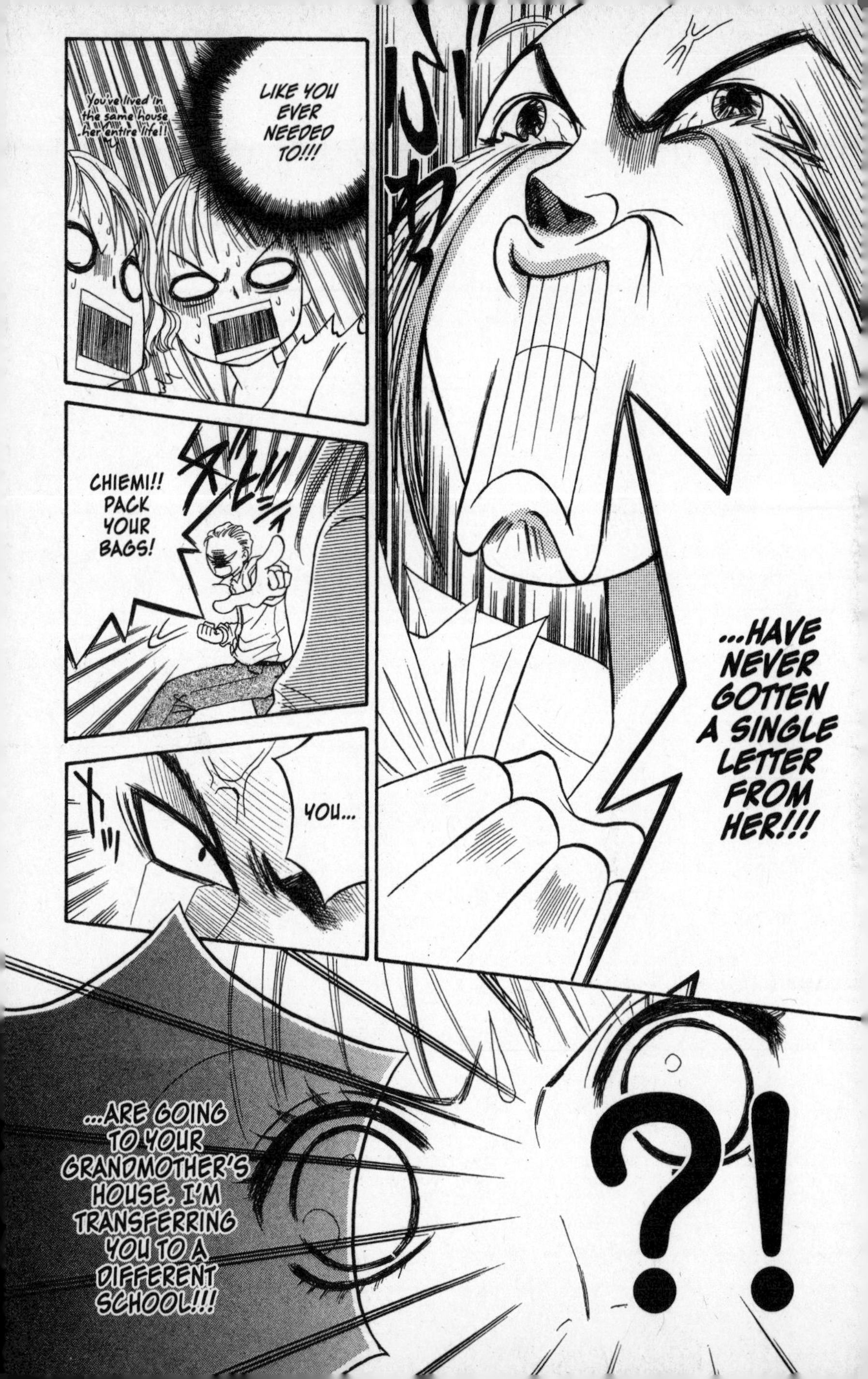

...HAVE NEVER GOTTEN A SINGLE LETTER FROM HER!!!
LIKE YOU EVER NEEDED TO!!!
You've lived in the same house her entire life!!
CHIEMI!! PACK YOUR BAGS!
YOU...
?!
...ARE GOING TO YOUR GRANDMOTHER'S HOUSE. I'M TRANSFERRING YOU TO A DIFFERENT SCHOOL!!!

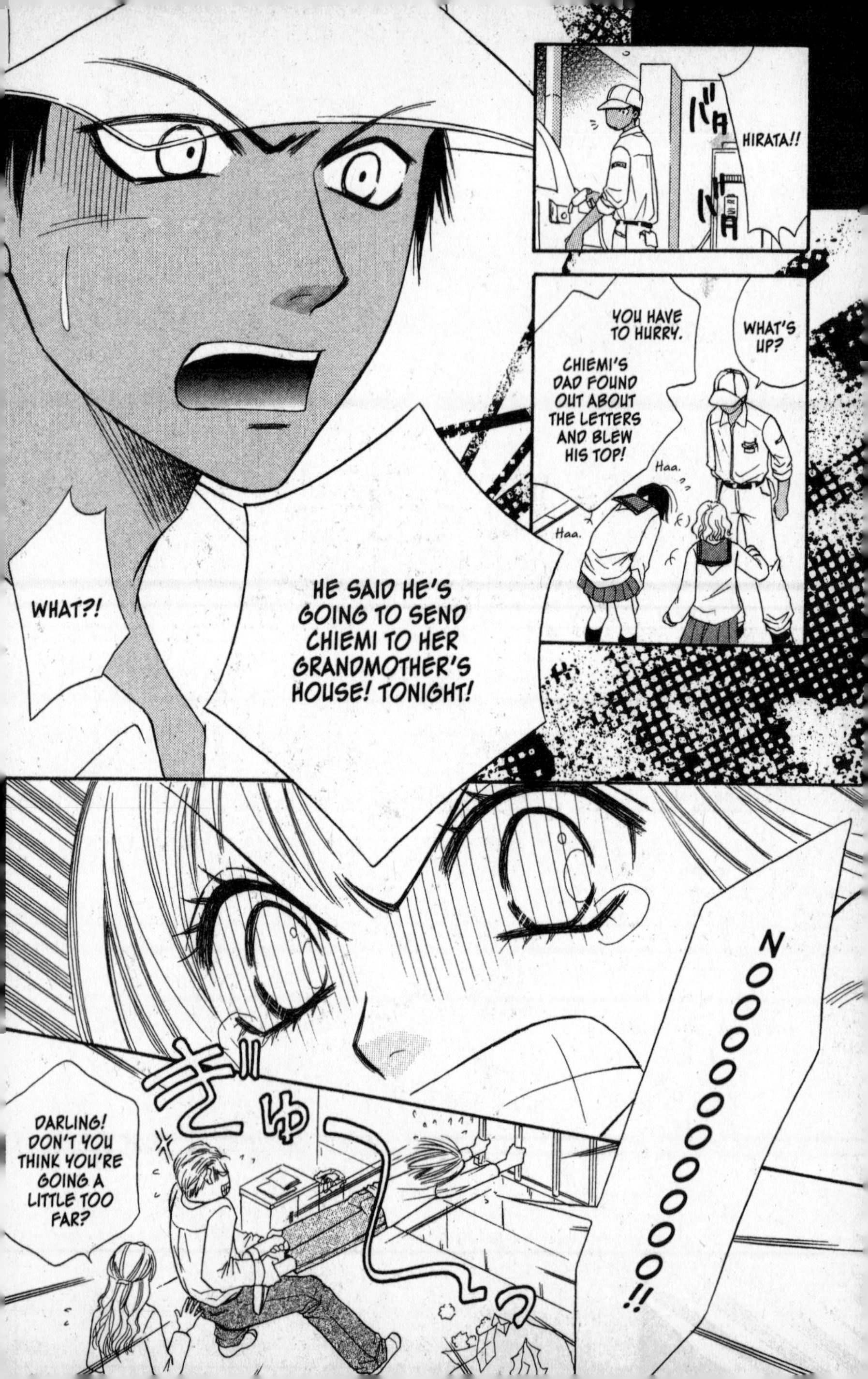
バタ
バタ
HIRATA!!
WHAT'S UP?
YOU HAVE TO HURRY.
CHIEMI'S DAD FOUND OUT ABOUT THE LETTERS AND BLEW HIS TOP!
Haa.
Haa.
HE SAID HE'S GOING TO SEND CHIEMI TO HER GRANDMOTHER'S HOUSE! TONIGHT!
WHAT?!
NOOOOOOOOOOOOOO!!
DARLING! DON'T YOU THINK YOU'RE GOING A LITTLE TOO FAR?

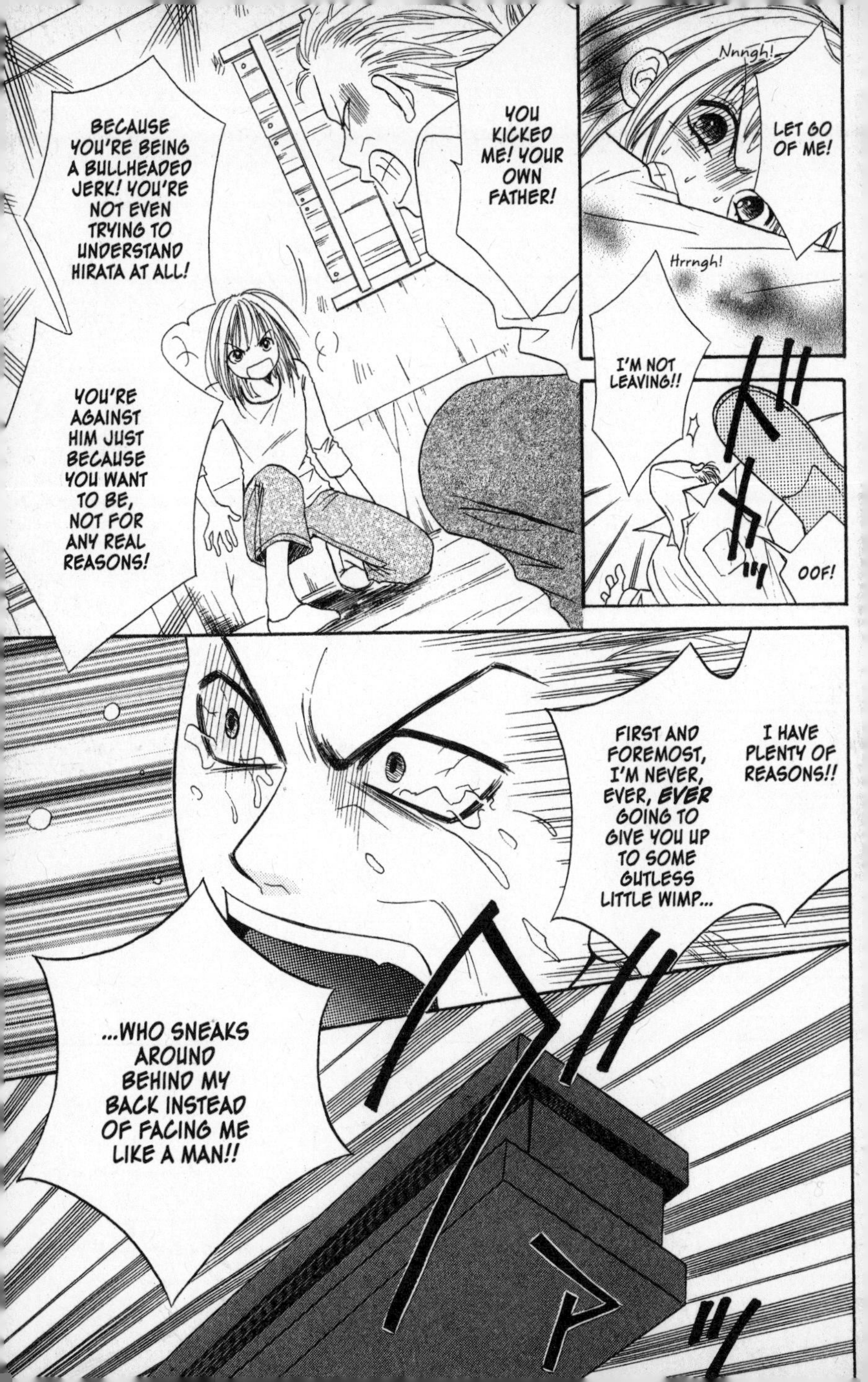
Nnngh!
LET GO OF ME!
Hrrngh!
I'M NOT LEAVING!!
OOF!
YOU KICKED ME! YOUR OWN FATHER!
BECAUSE YOU'RE BEING A BULLHEADED JERK! YOU'RE NOT EVEN TRYING TO UNDERSTAND HIRATA AT ALL!
YOU'RE AGAINST HIM JUST BECAUSE YOU WANT TO BE, NOT FOR ANY REAL REASONS!
I HAVE PLENTY OF REASONS!!
FIRST AND FOREMOST, I'M NEVER, EVER, ***EVER*** GOING TO GIVE YOU UP TO SOME GUTLESS LITTLE WIMP...
...WHO SNEAKS AROUND BEHIND MY BACK INSTEAD OF FACING ME LIKE A MAN!!

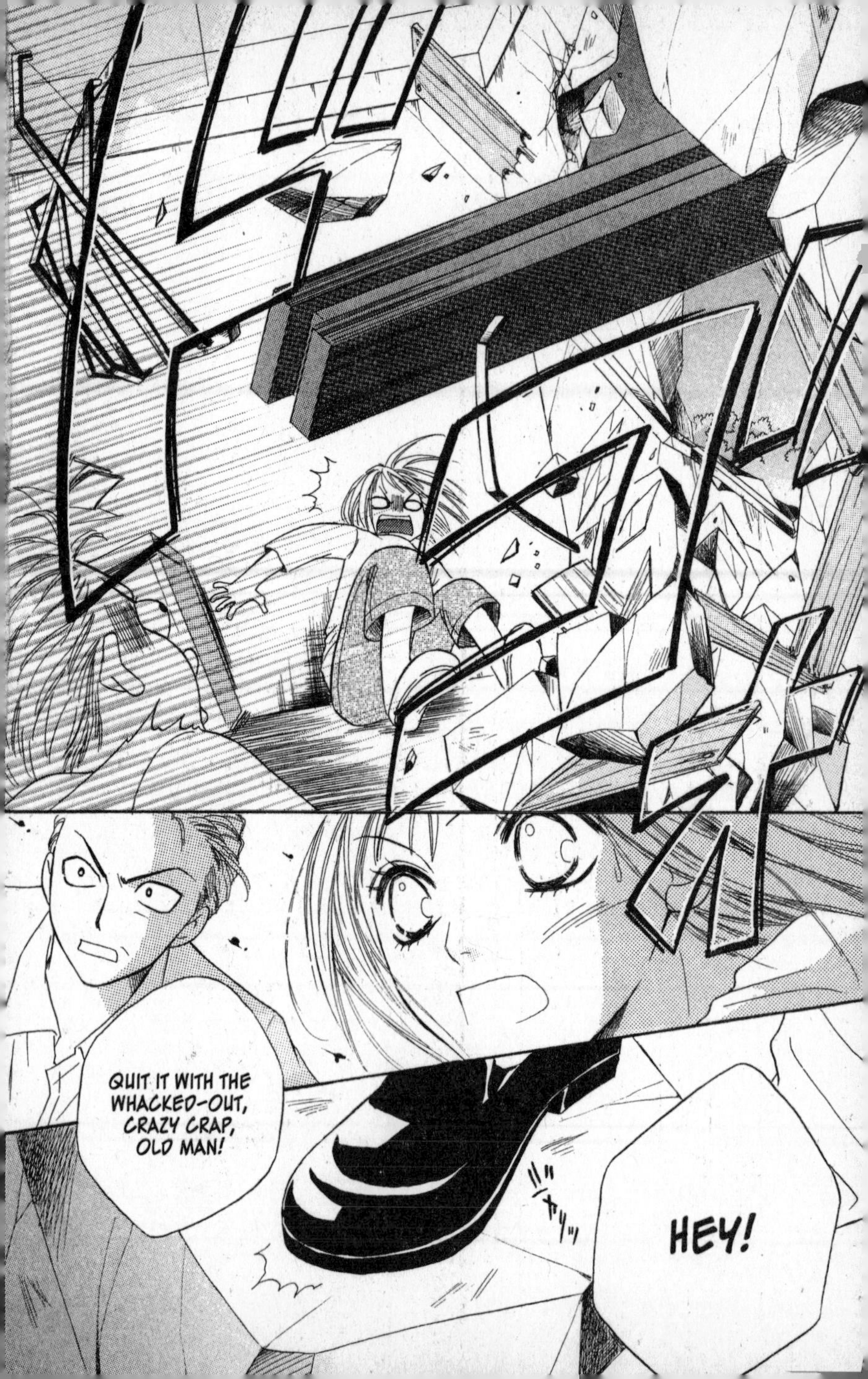
HEY!
QUIT IT WITH THE WHACKED-OUT, CRAZY CRAP, OLD MAN!

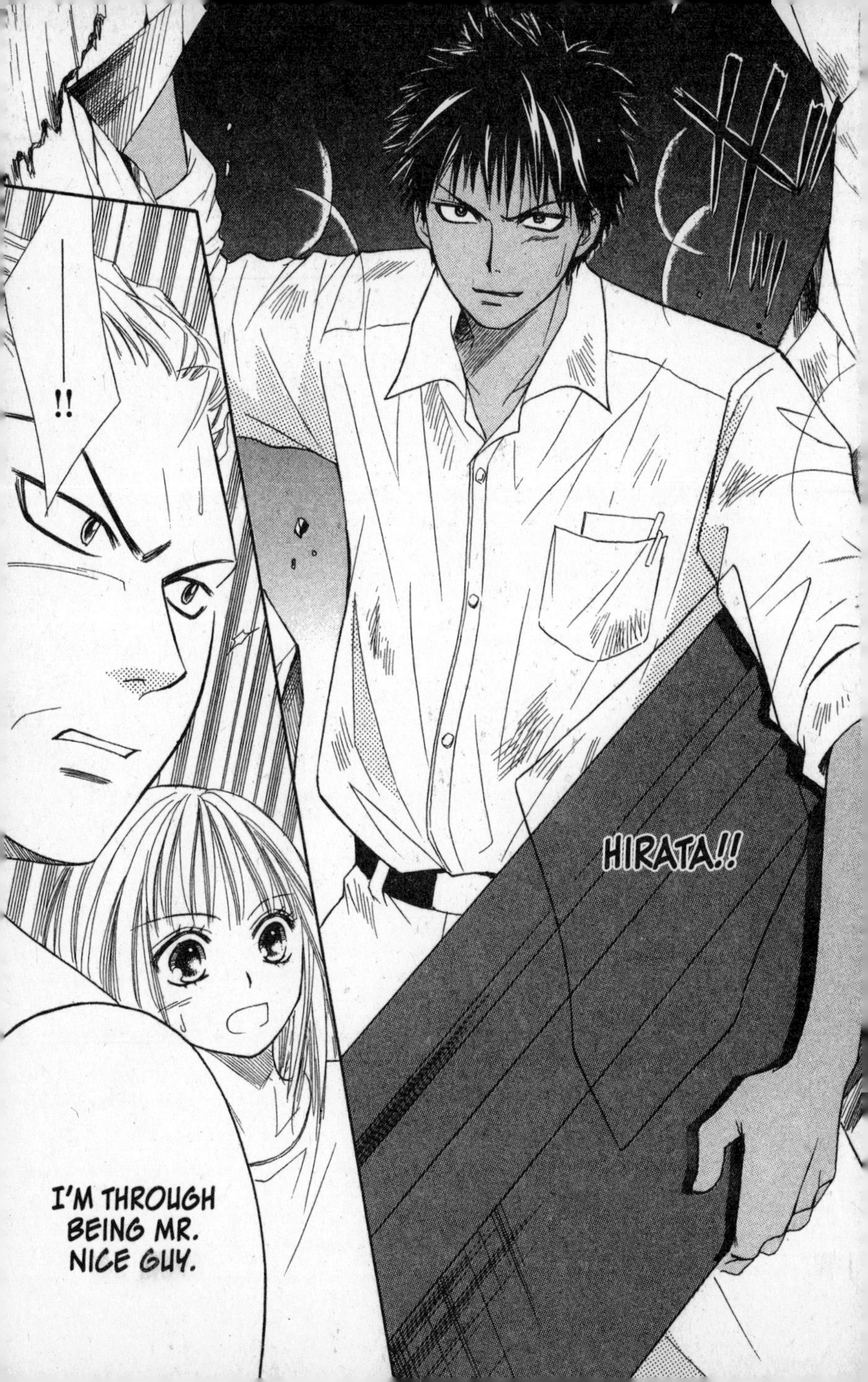
!!
HIRATA!!
I'M THROUGH BEING MR. NICE GUY.

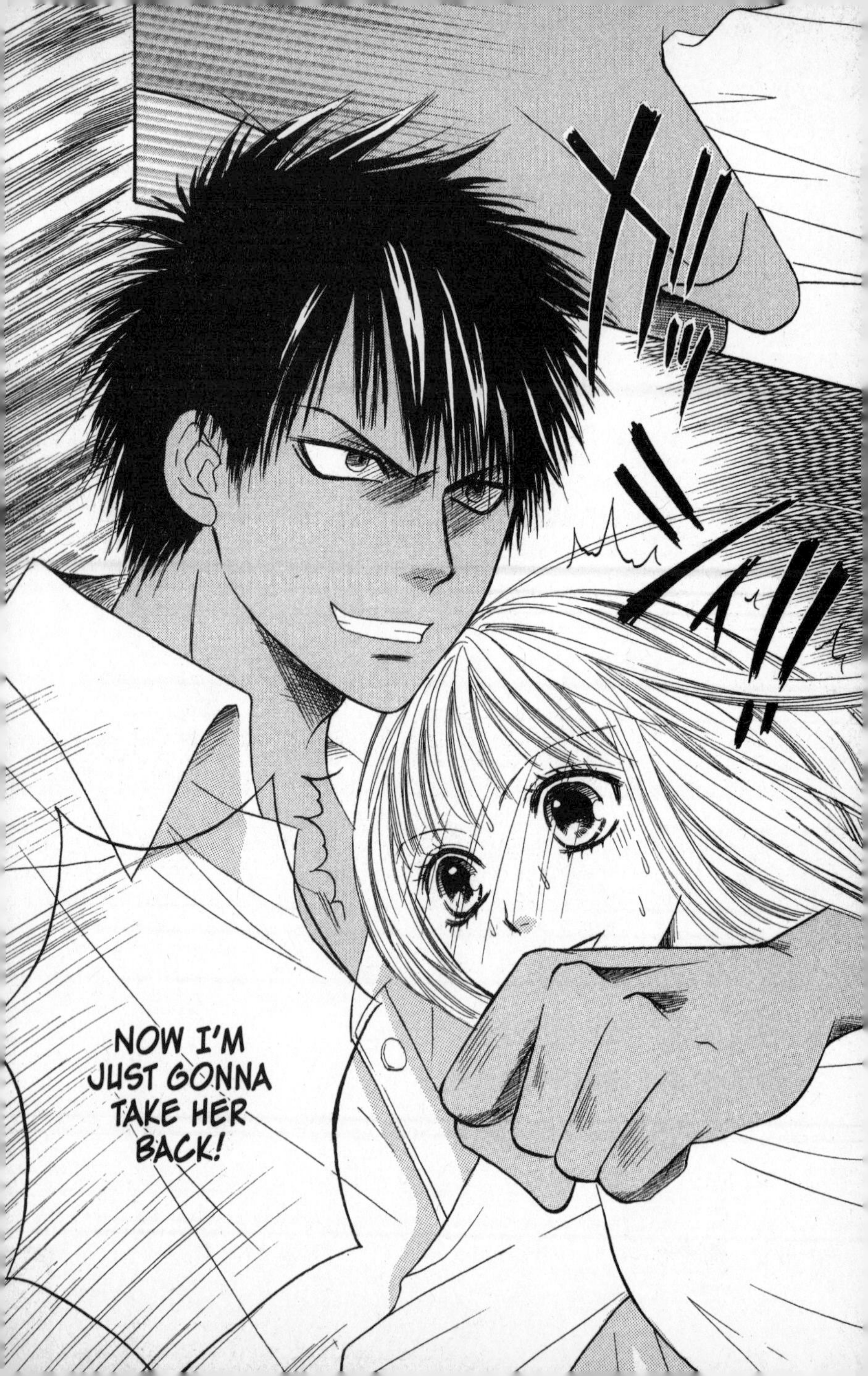
NOW I'M JUST GONNA TAKE HER BACK!

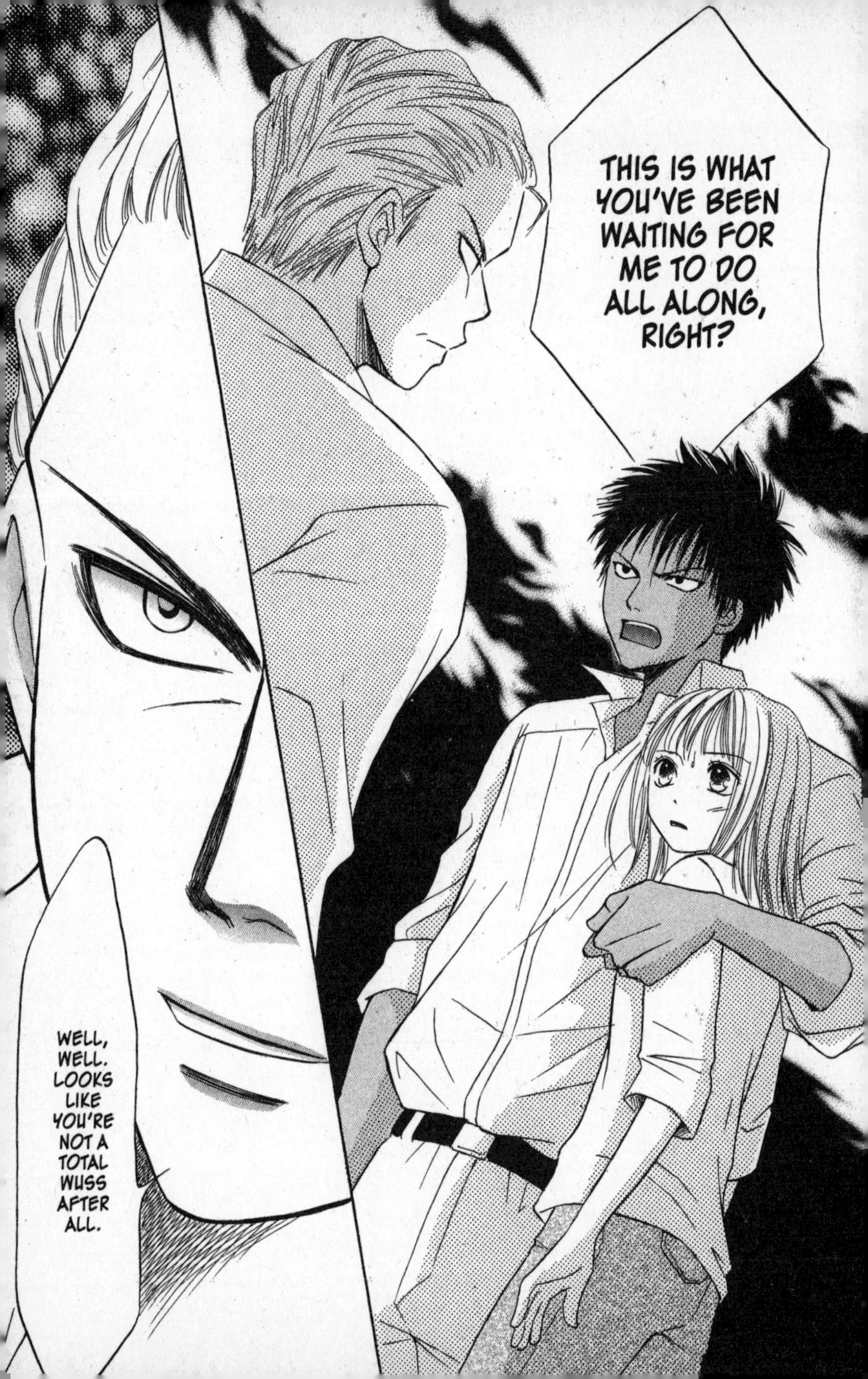
THIS IS WHAT YOU'VE BEEN WAITING FOR ME TO DO ALL ALONG, RIGHT?
WELL, WELL. LOOKS LIKE YOU'RE NOT A TOTAL WUSS AFTER ALL.

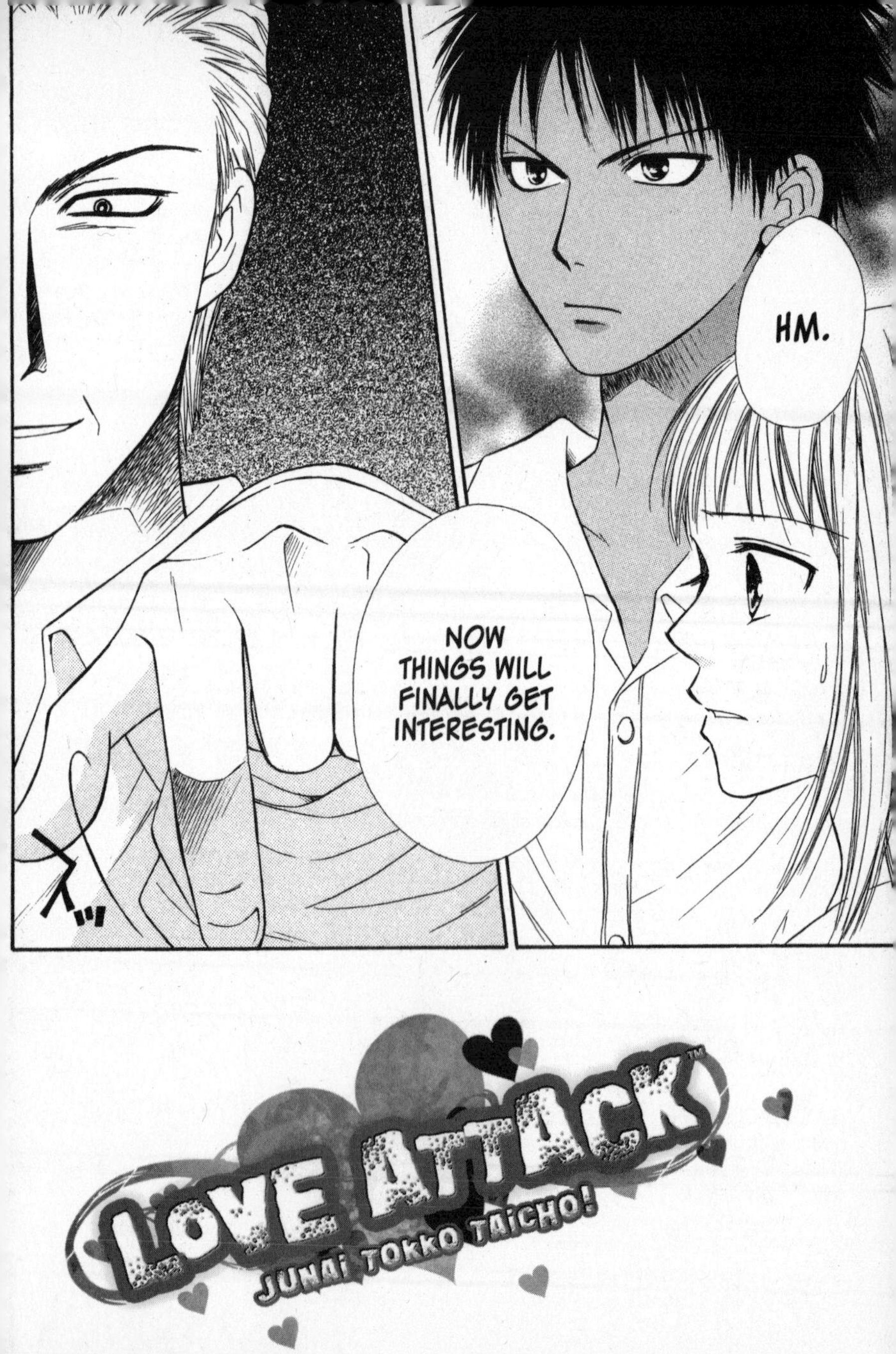
HM.
NOW THINGS WILL FINALLY GET INTERESTING.

LOVE ATTACK™
JUNAI TOKKO TAICHO!

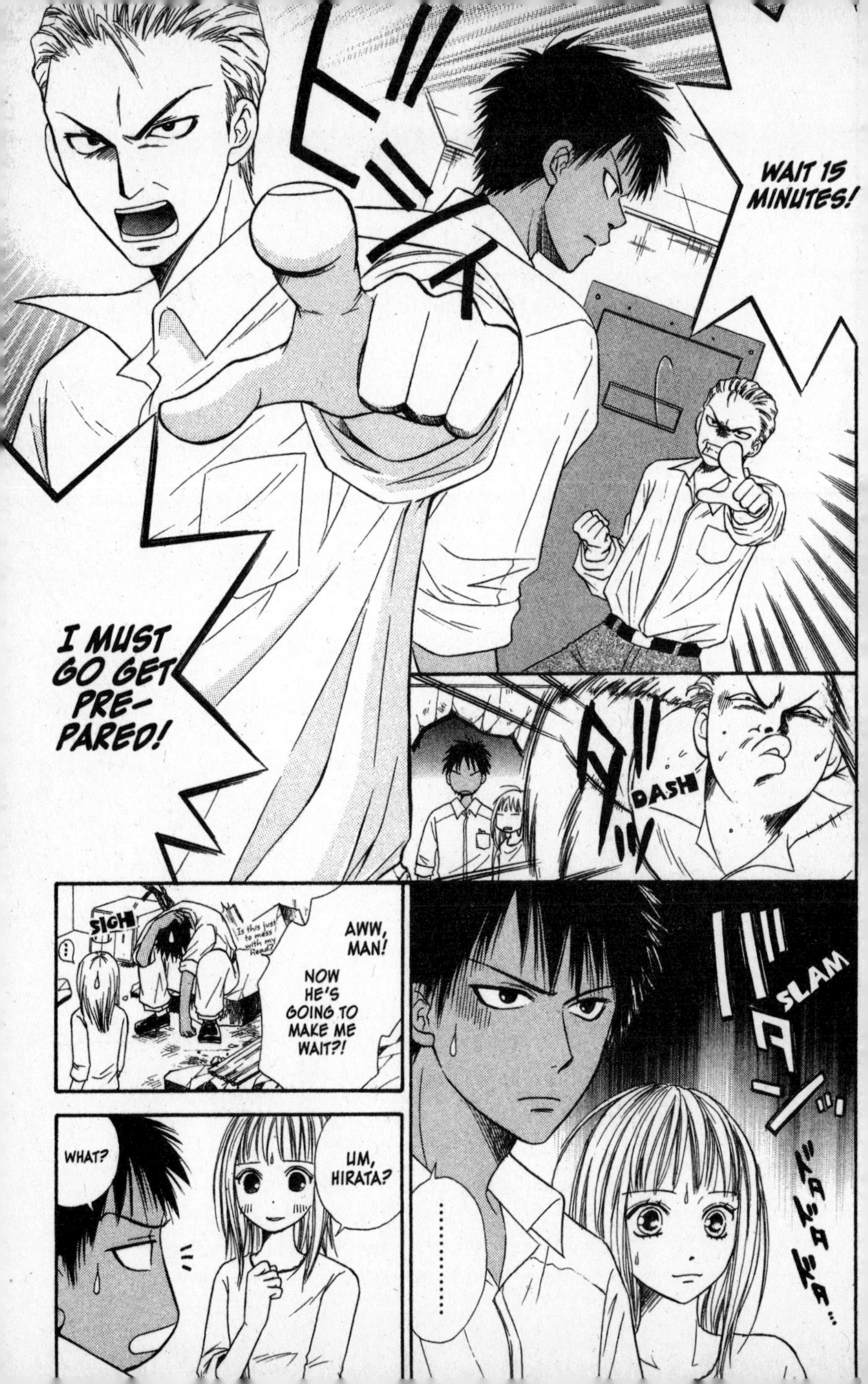
WAIT 15 MINUTES!
I MUST GO GET PRE-PARED!
DASH
SLAM
......
AWW, MAN!
NOW HE'S GOING TO MAKE ME WAIT?!
SIGH
Is this just to mess with my head?!
UM, HIRATA?
WHAT?

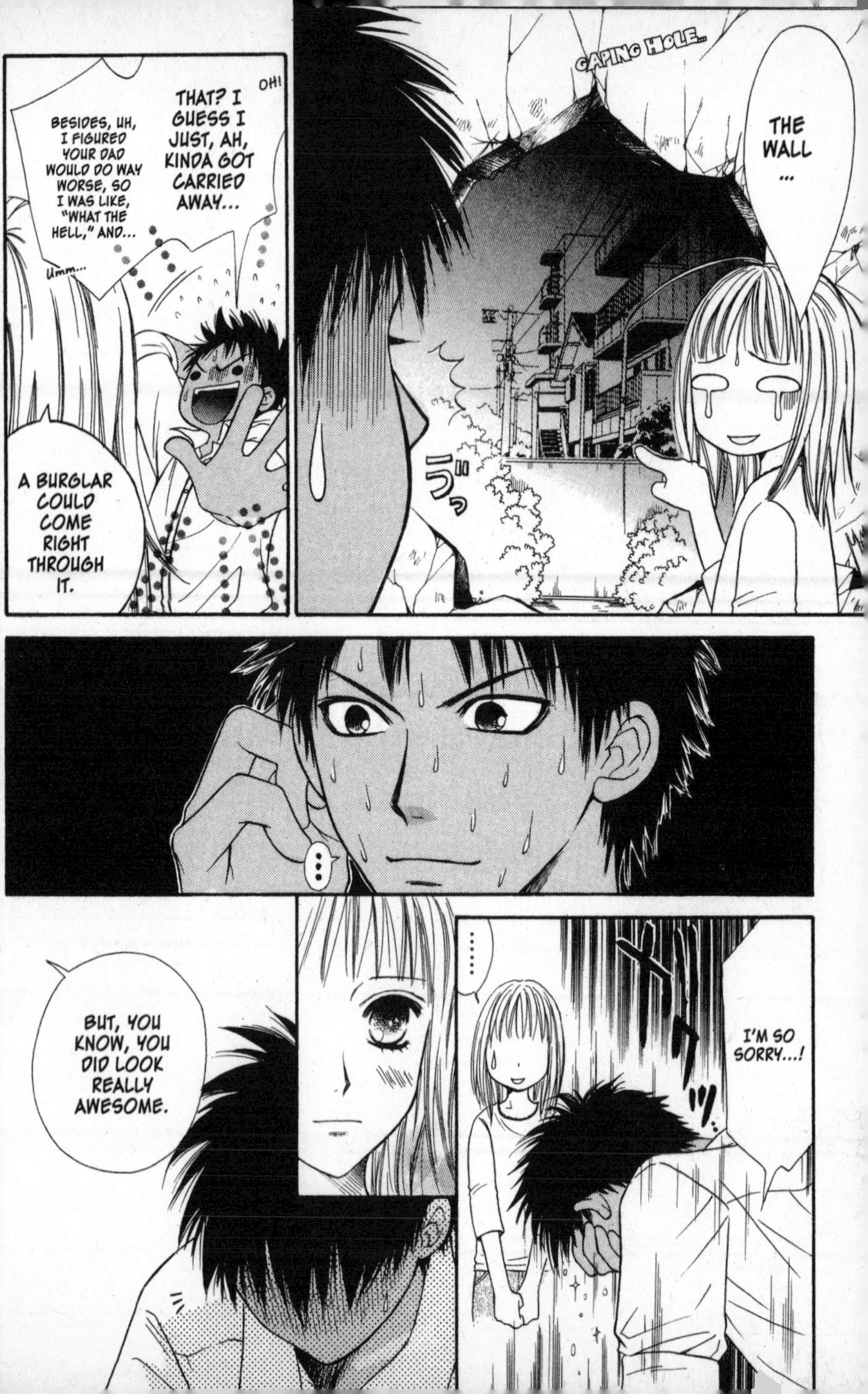
GAPING HOLE...
THE WALL ...
うっ
OH!
THAT? I GUESS I JUST, AH, KINDA GOT CARRIED AWAY...
BESIDES, UH, I FIGURED YOUR DAD WOULD DO WAY WORSE, SO I WAS LIKE, "WHAT THE HELL," AND...
Umm...
A BURGLAR COULD COME RIGHT THROUGH IT.
...
......
I'M SO SORRY...!
BUT, YOU KNOW, YOU DID LOOK REALLY AWESOME.

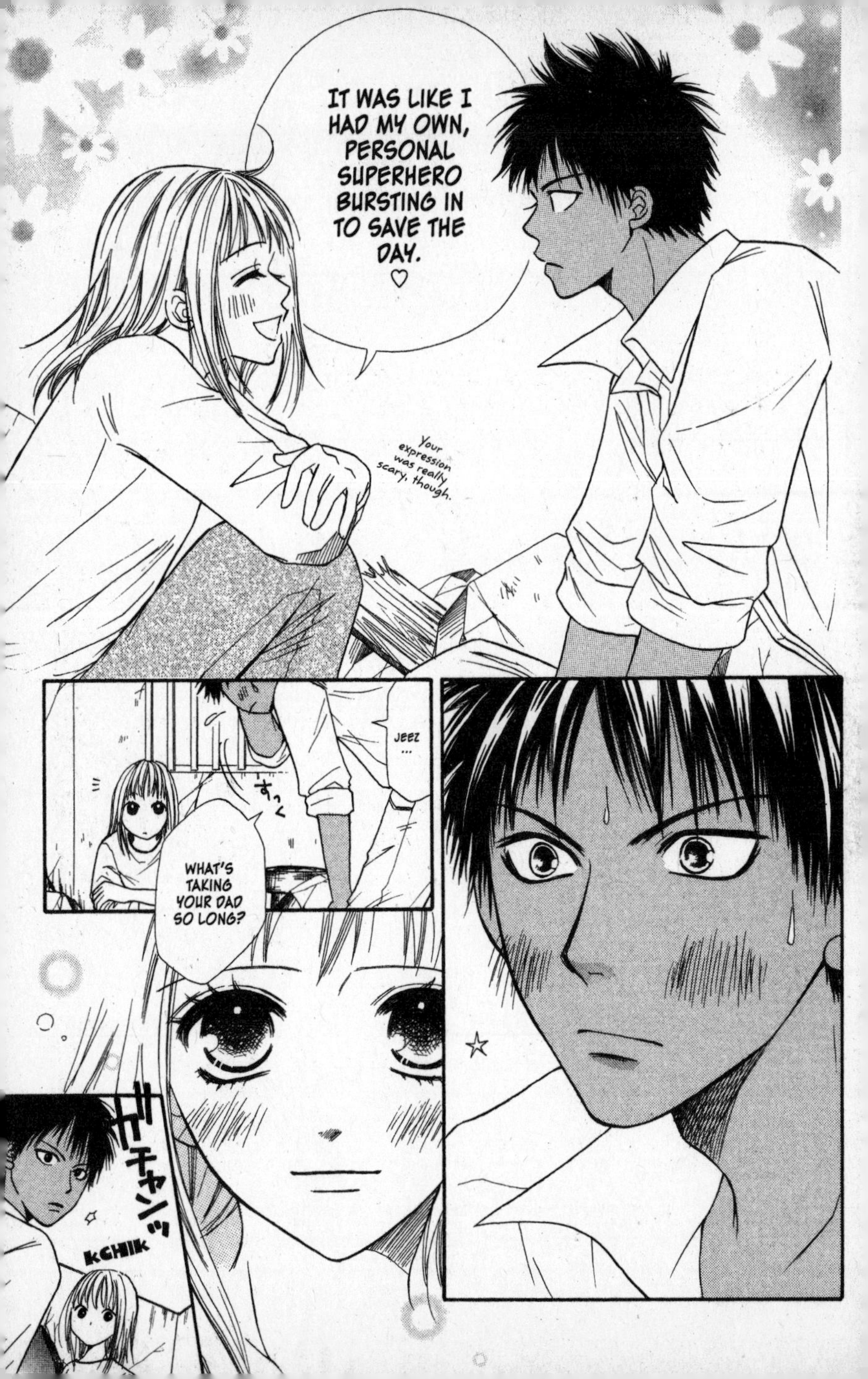
IT WAS LIKE I HAD MY OWN, PERSONAL SUPERHERO BURSTING IN TO SAVE THE DAY. ♡
Your expression was really scary, though.
JEEZ ...
すっく
WHAT'S TAKING YOUR DAD SO LONG?
ガチャンッ
KCHIK

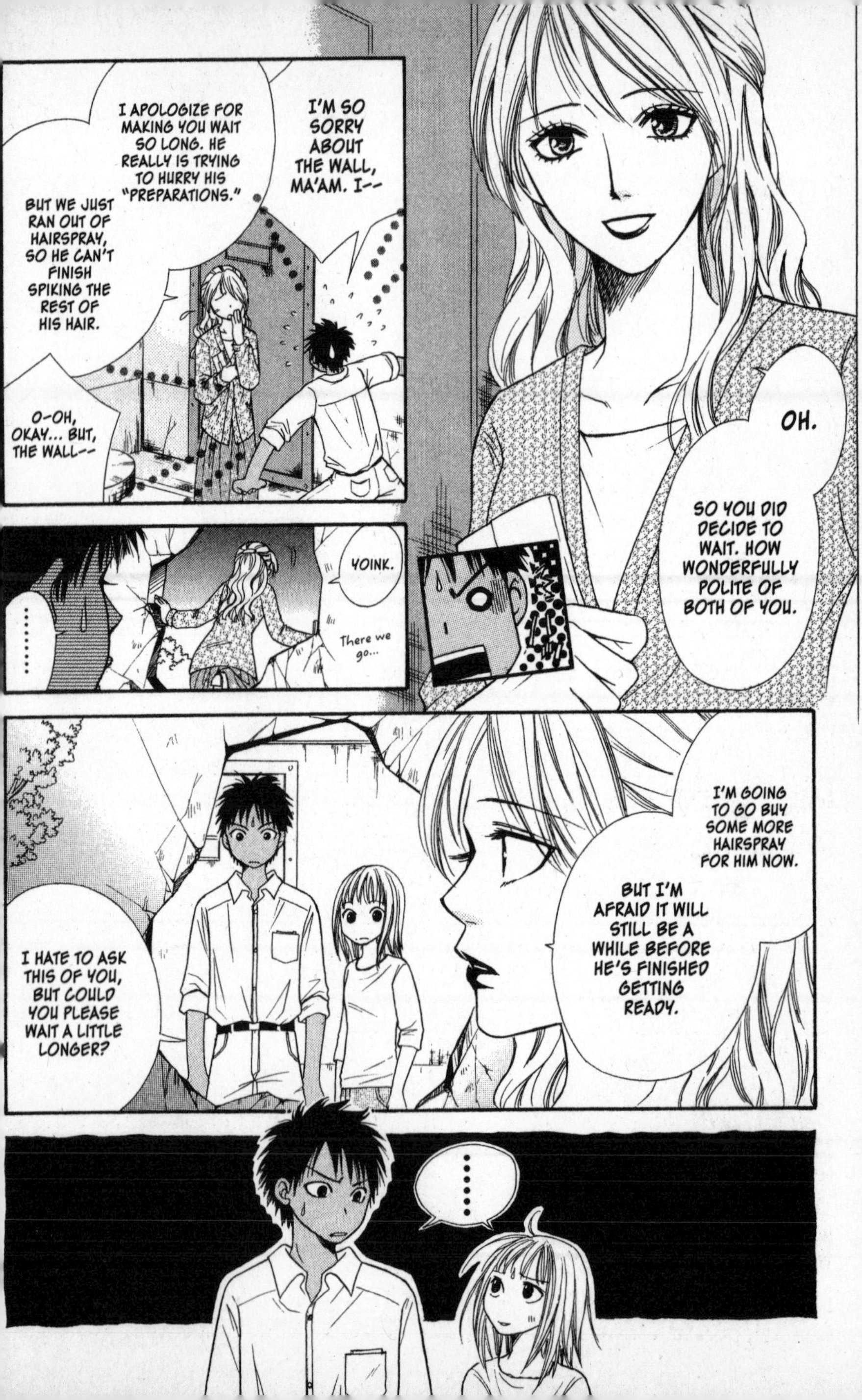
OH.
SO YOU DID DECIDE TO WAIT. HOW WONDERFULLY POLITE OF BOTH OF YOU.
I'M SO SORRY ABOUT THE WALL, MA'AM. I--
I APOLOGIZE FOR MAKING YOU WAIT SO LONG. HE REALLY IS TRYING TO HURRY HIS "PREPARATIONS."
BUT WE JUST RAN OUT OF HAIRSPRAY, SO HE CAN'T FINISH SPIKING THE REST OF HIS HAIR.
O-OH, OKAY... BUT, THE WALL--
YOINK.
There we go...
......
I'M GOING TO GO BUY SOME MORE HAIRSPRAY FOR HIM NOW.
BUT I'M AFRAID IT WILL STILL BE A WHILE BEFORE HE'S FINISHED GETTING READY.
I HATE TO ASK THIS OF YOU, BUT COULD YOU PLEASE WAIT A LITTLE LONGER?
......

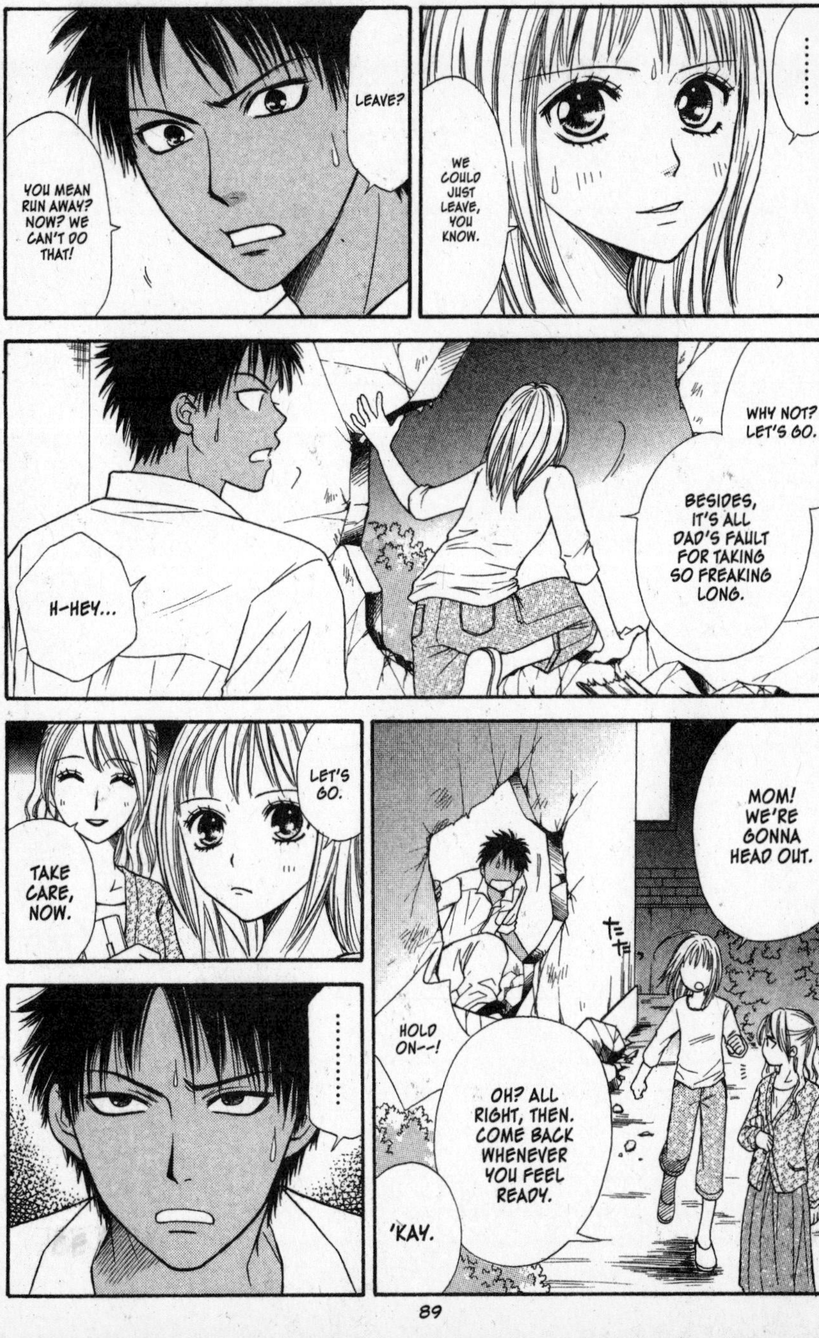
……
WE COULD JUST LEAVE, YOU KNOW.
LEAVE?
YOU MEAN RUN AWAY? NOW? WE CAN'T DO THAT!
WHY NOT? LET'S GO.
BESIDES, IT'S ALL DAD'S FAULT FOR TAKING SO FREAKING LONG.
H-HEY...
MOM! WE'RE GONNA HEAD OUT.
タタ
HOLD ON--!
OH? ALL RIGHT, THEN. COME BACK WHENEVER YOU FEEL READY.
'KAY.
LET'S GO.
TAKE CARE, NOW.
……

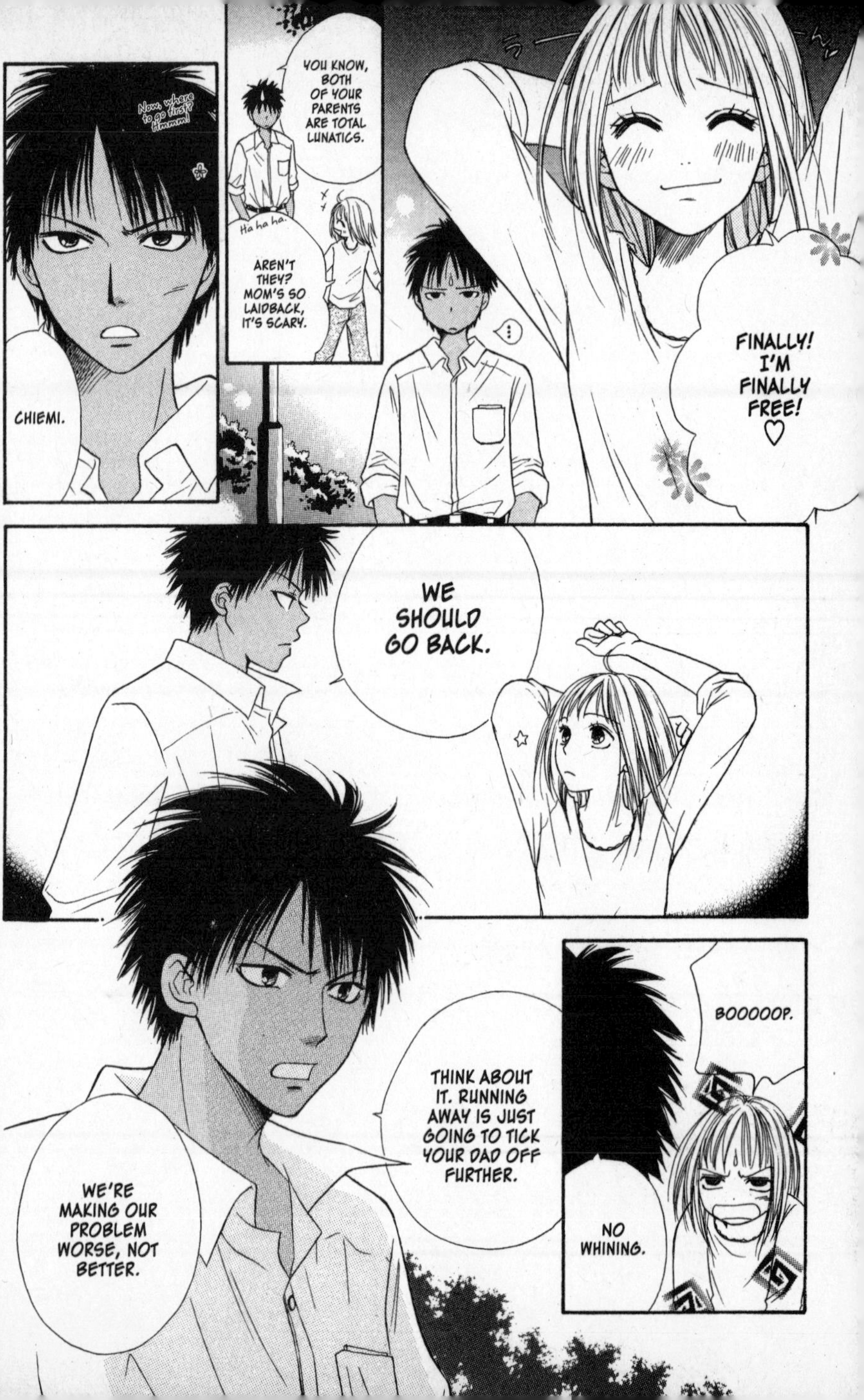
FINALLY! I'M FINALLY FREE! ♡
…
YOU KNOW, BOTH OF YOUR PARENTS ARE TOTAL LUNATICS.
Ha ha ha.
AREN'T THEY? MOM'S SO LAIDBACK, IT'S SCARY.
Now, where to go first? Hmmm!
CHIEMI.
WE SHOULD GO BACK.
BOOOOOP.
NO WHINING.
THINK ABOUT IT. RUNNING AWAY IS JUST GOING TO TICK YOUR DAD OFF FURTHER.
WE'RE MAKING OUR PROBLEM WORSE, NOT BETTER.

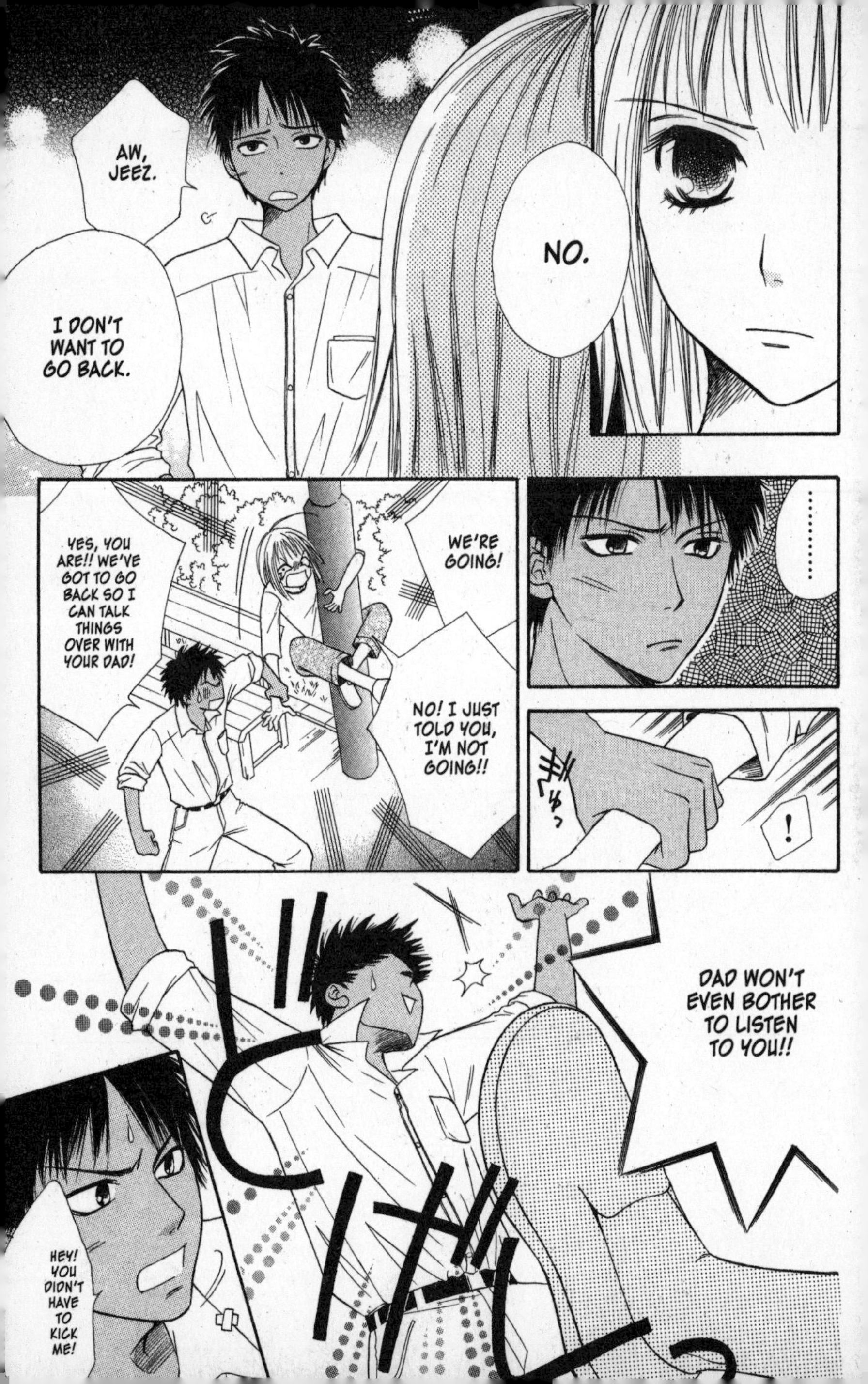
NO.
AW, JEEZ.
I DON'T WANT TO GO BACK.
......
!
ぎゅっ
WE'RE GOING!
NO! I JUST TOLD YOU, I'M NOT GOING!!
YES, YOU ARE!! WE'VE GOT TO GO BACK SO I CAN TALK THINGS OVER WITH YOUR DAD!
DAD WON'T EVEN BOTHER TO LISTEN TO YOU!!
HEY! YOU DIDN'T HAVE TO KICK ME!

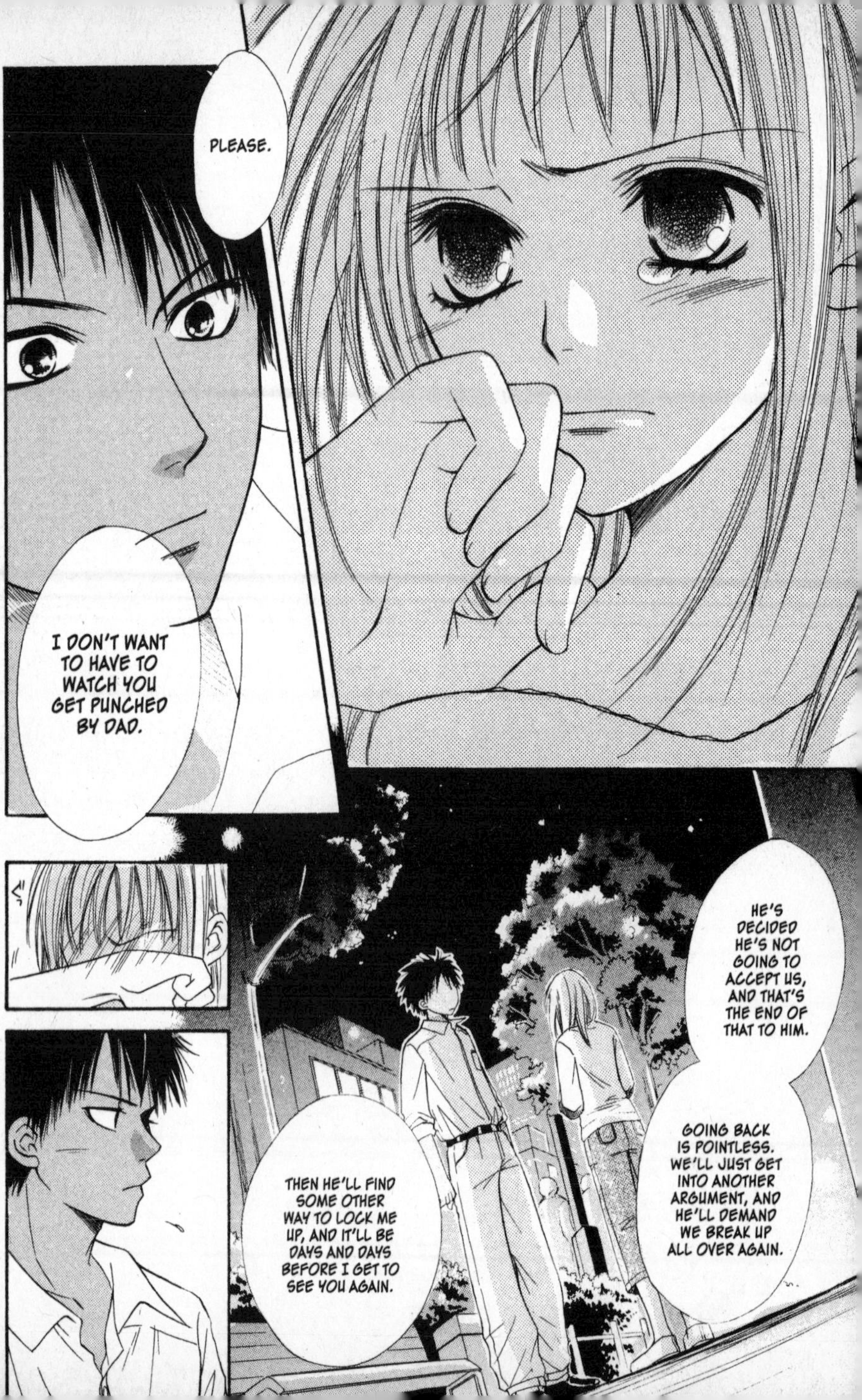
PLEASE.
I DON'T WANT TO HAVE TO WATCH YOU GET PUNCHED BY DAD.
HE'S DECIDED HE'S NOT GOING TO ACCEPT US, AND THAT'S THE END OF THAT TO HIM.
GOING BACK IS POINTLESS. WE'LL JUST GET INTO ANOTHER ARGUMENT, AND HE'LL DEMAND WE BREAK UP ALL OVER AGAIN.
THEN HE'LL FIND SOME OTHER WAY TO LOCK ME UP, AND IT'LL BE DAYS AND DAYS BEFORE I GET TO SEE YOU AGAIN.

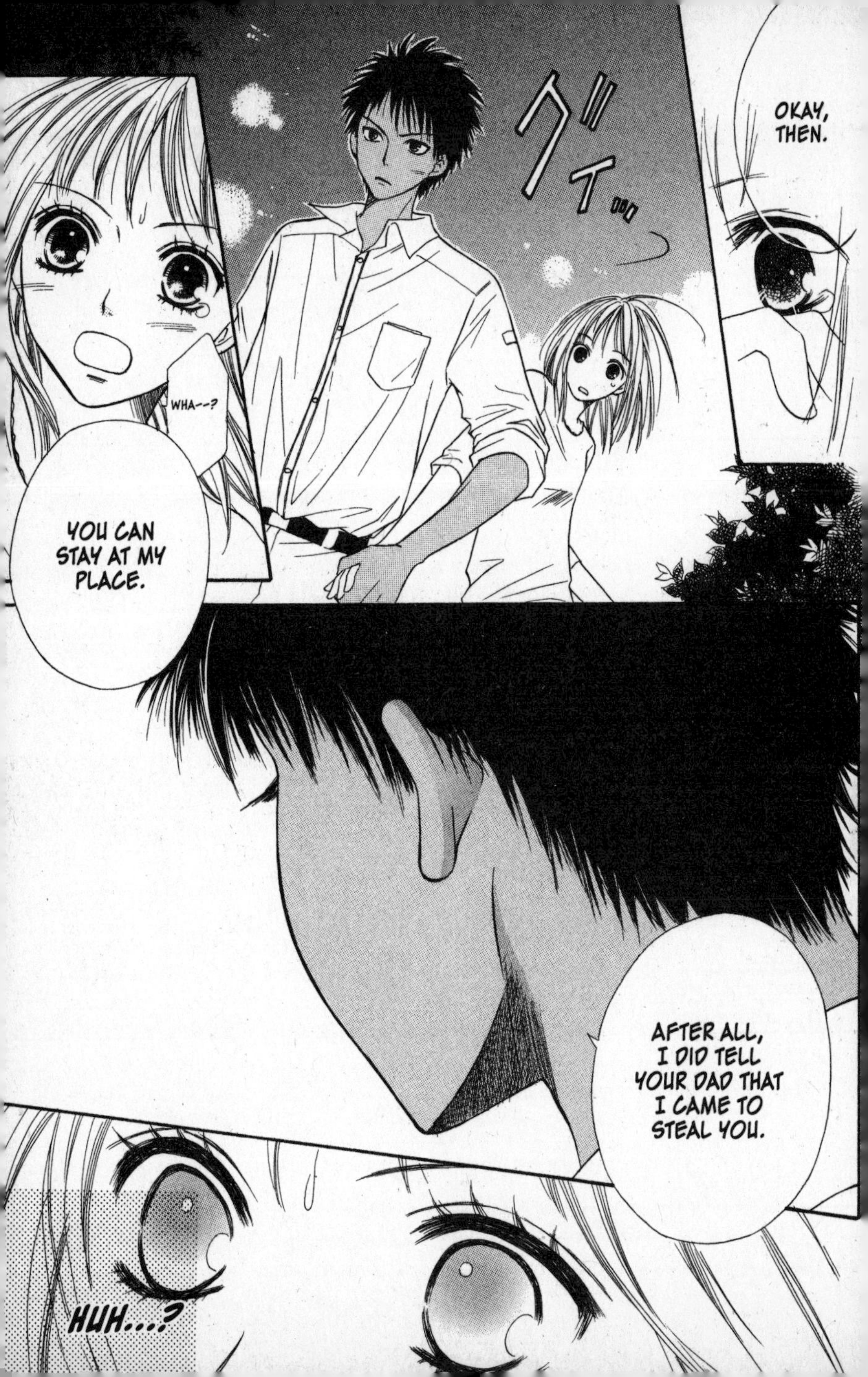
OKAY, THEN.
WHA--?
YOU CAN STAY AT MY PLACE.
AFTER ALL, I DID TELL YOUR DAD THAT I CAME TO STEAL YOU.
HUH...?

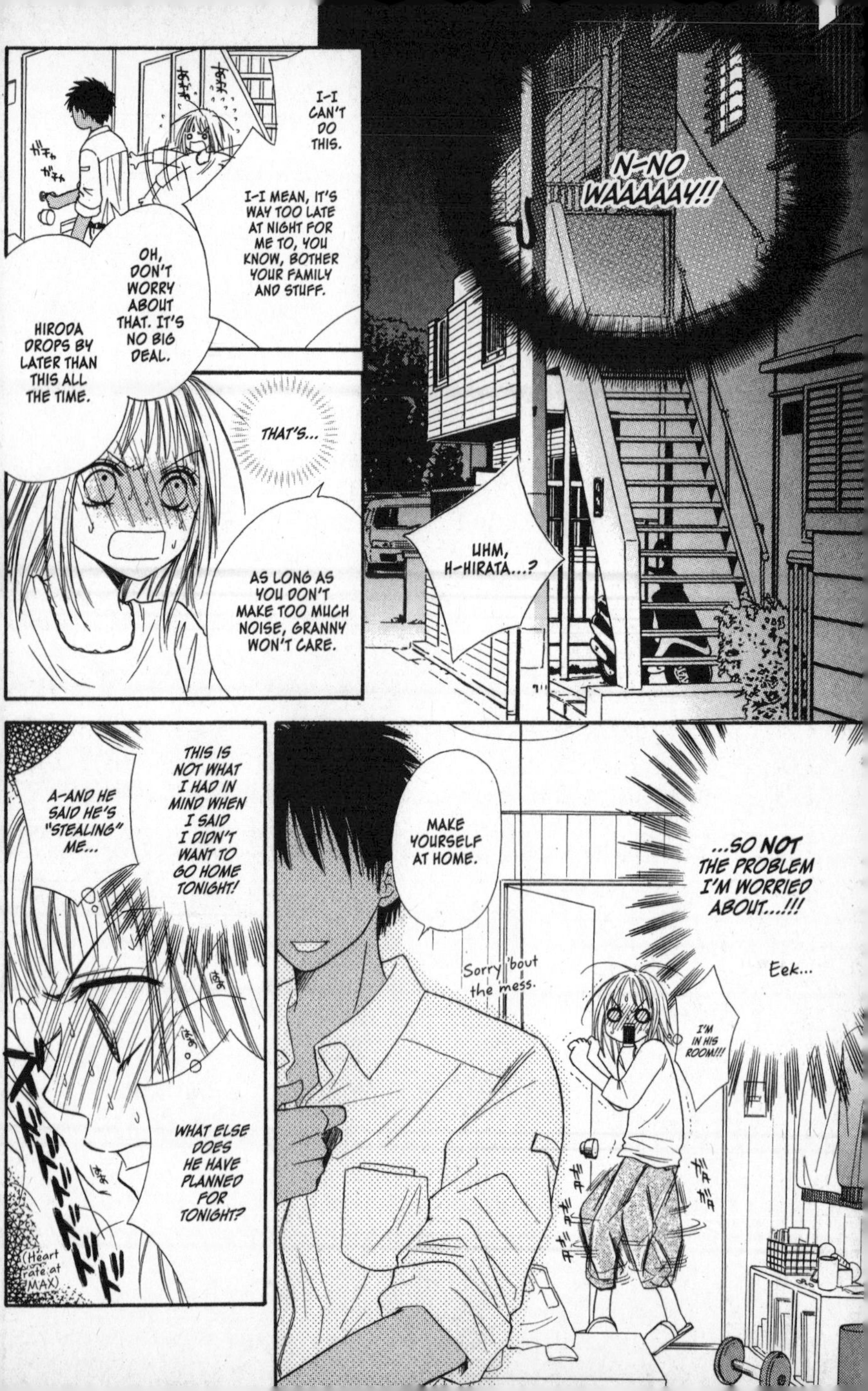
N-NO WAAAAAY!!
UHM, H-HIRATA...?
I-I CAN'T DO THIS.
I-I MEAN, IT'S WAY TOO LATE AT NIGHT FOR ME TO, YOU KNOW, BOTHER YOUR FAMILY AND STUFF.
OH, DON'T WORRY ABOUT THAT. IT'S NO BIG DEAL.
HIRODA DROPS BY LATER THAN THIS ALL THE TIME.
THAT'S...
AS LONG AS YOU DON'T MAKE TOO MUCH NOISE, GRANNY WON'T CARE.
...SO NOT THE PROBLEM I'M WORRIED ABOUT...!!!
MAKE YOURSELF AT HOME.
Eek...
Sorry 'bout the mess.
I'M IN HIS ROOM!!!
THIS IS NOT WHAT I HAD IN MIND WHEN I SAID I DIDN'T WANT TO GO HOME TONIGHT!
A-AND HE SAID HE'S "STEALING" ME...
WHAT ELSE DOES HE HAVE PLANNED FOR TONIGHT?
(Heart rate at MAX)

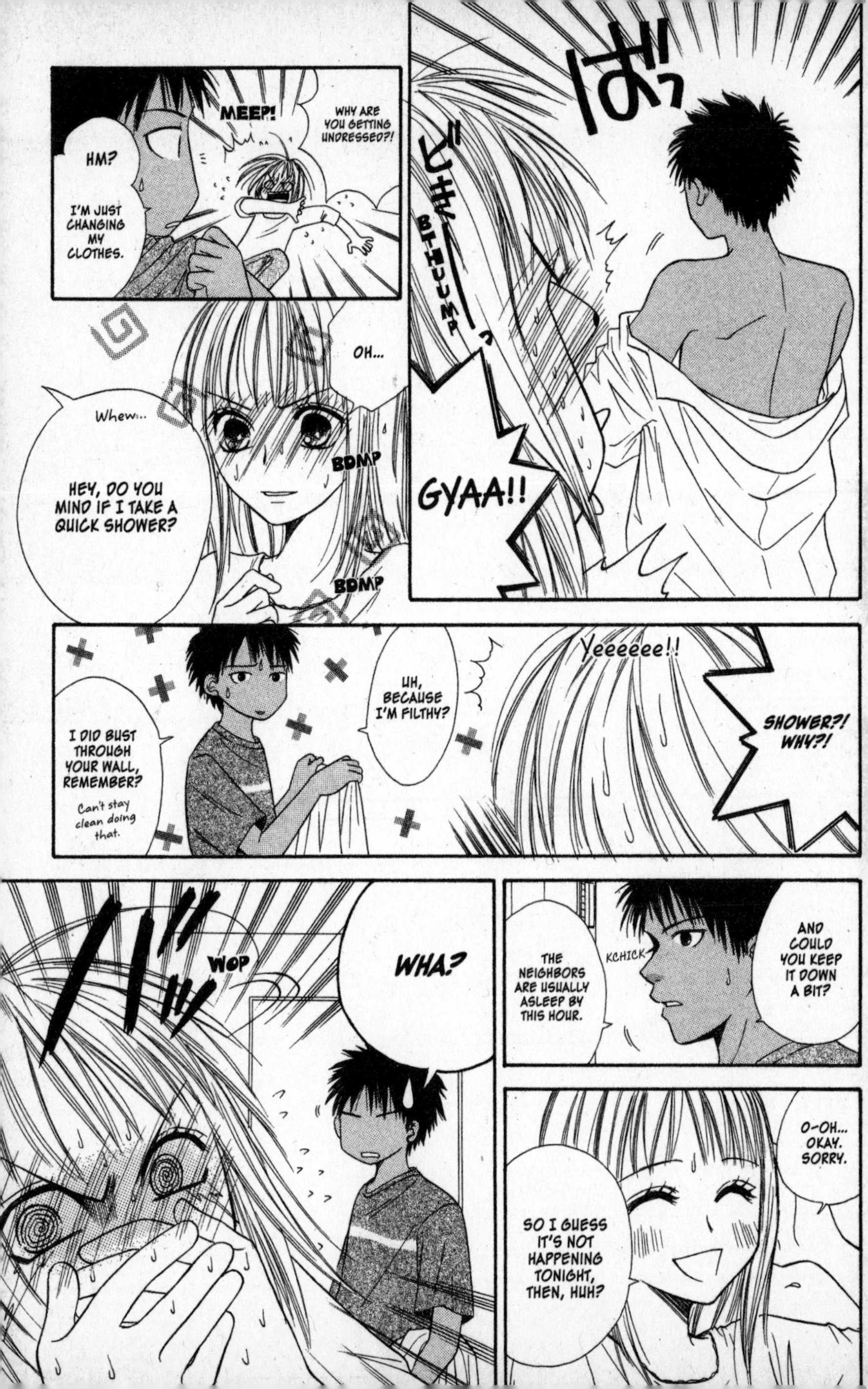
ぱっ
びくっ
BTHUUUMP
GYAA!!
MEEP!
WHY ARE YOU GETTING UNDRESSED?!
HM?
I'M JUST CHANGING MY CLOTHES.
OH...
BDMP
Whew...
HEY, DO YOU MIND IF I TAKE A QUICK SHOWER?
BDMP
Yeeeeee!!
SHOWER?! WHY?!
UH, BECAUSE I'M FILTHY?
I DID BUST THROUGH YOUR WALL, REMEMBER?
Can't stay clean doing that.
AND COULD YOU KEEP IT DOWN A BIT?
KCHICK
THE NEIGHBORS ARE USUALLY ASLEEP BY THIS HOUR.
O-OH... OKAY. SORRY.
SO I GUESS IT'S NOT HAPPENING TONIGHT, THEN, HUH?
WHA?
WOP

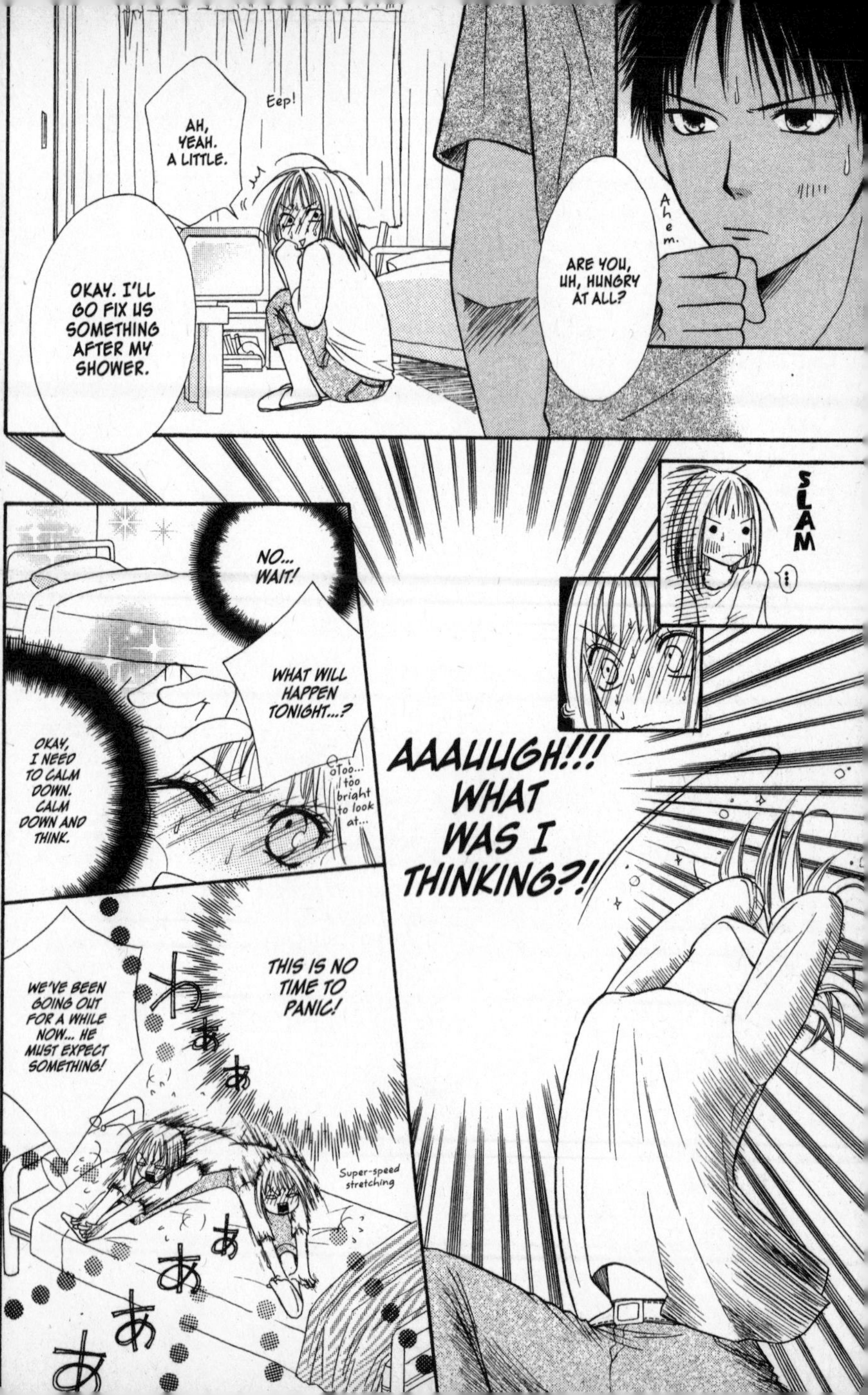

Ahem.
ARE YOU, UH, HUNGRY AT ALL?
Eep!
AH, YEAH. A LITTLE.
OKAY. I'LL GO FIX US SOMETHING AFTER MY SHOWER.
SLAM
...
AAAUUGH!!! WHAT WAS I THINKING?!
NO... WAIT!
WHAT WILL HAPPEN TONIGHT...?
Too... too bright to look at...
OKAY, I NEED TO CALM DOWN. CALM DOWN AND THINK.
THIS IS NO TIME TO PANIC!
WE'VE BEEN GOING OUT FOR A WHILE NOW... HE MUST EXPECT SOMETHING!
わああああああ
Super-speed stretching

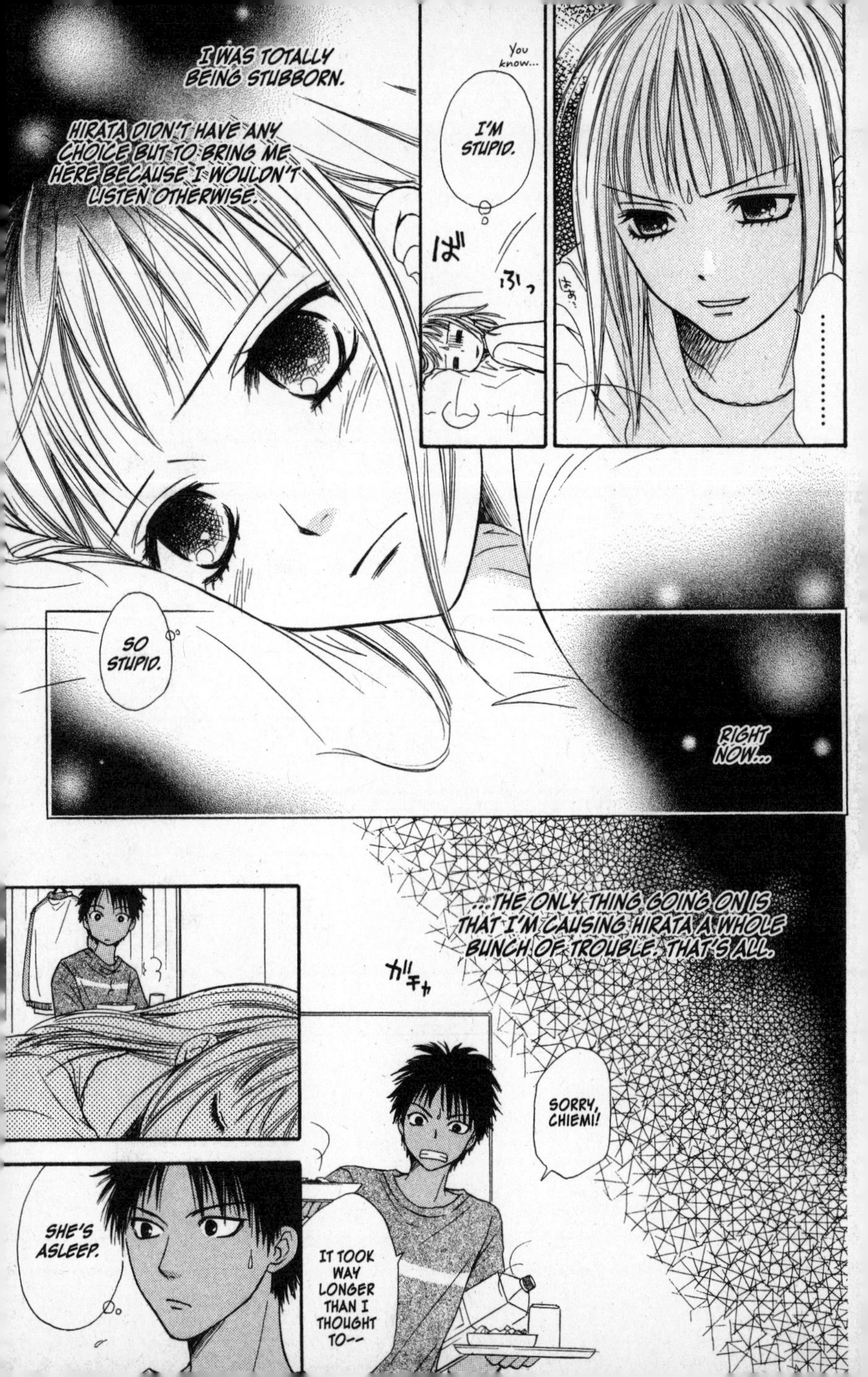

はあ…
......
You know...
I'M STUPID.
ば
ふっ
I WAS TOTALLY BEING STUBBORN.
HIRATA DIDN'T HAVE ANY CHOICE BUT TO BRING ME HERE BECAUSE I WOULDN'T LISTEN OTHERWISE.
SO STUPID.
RIGHT NOW...
...THE ONLY THING GOING ON IS THAT I'M CAUSING HIRATA A WHOLE BUNCH OF TROUBLE. THAT'S ALL.
ガチャ
SORRY, CHIEMI!
IT TOOK WAY LONGER THAN I THOUGHT TO--
SHE'S ASLEEP.

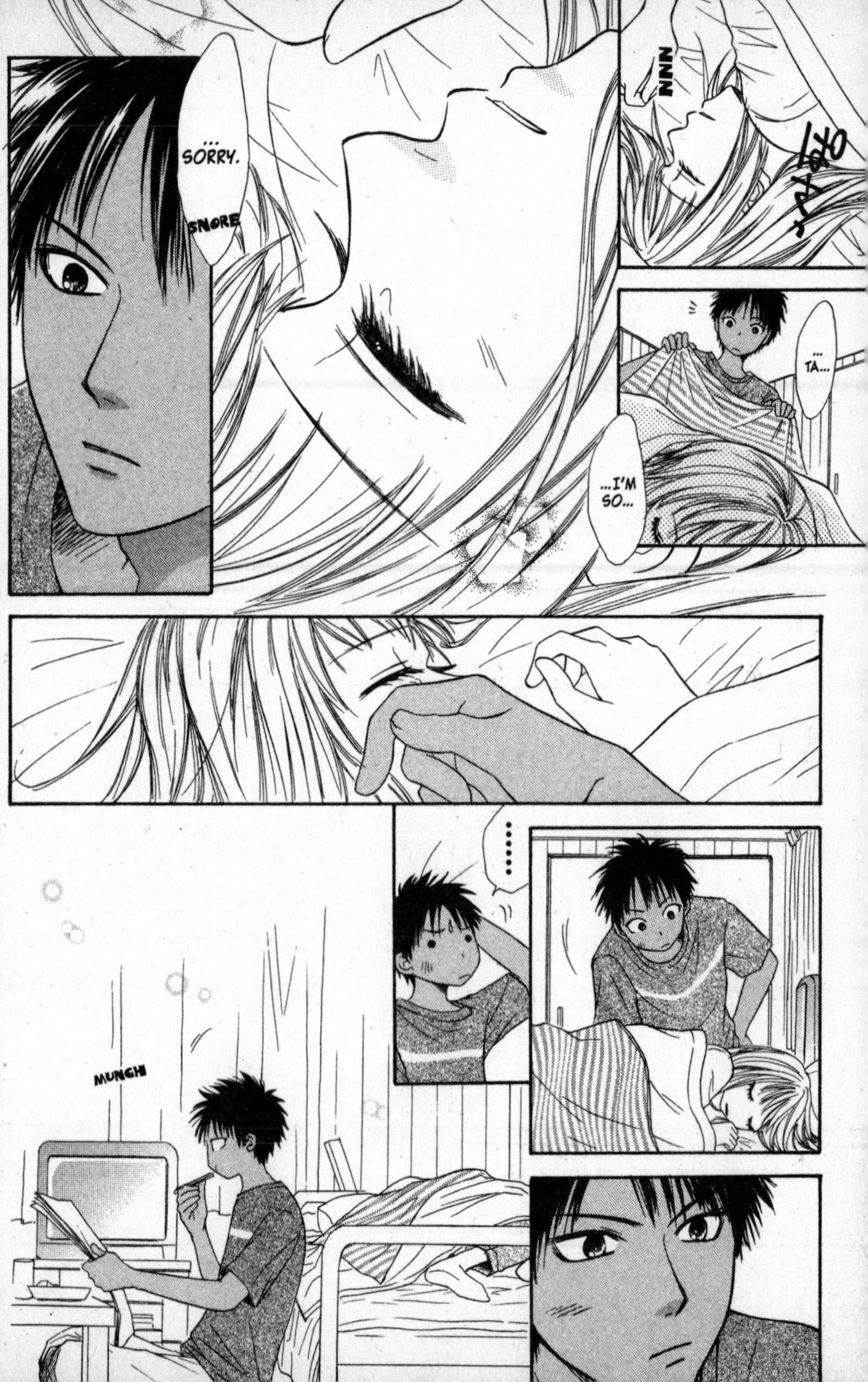
NNN
... TA...
...I'M SO...
... SORRY.
SNORE
......
MUNCH

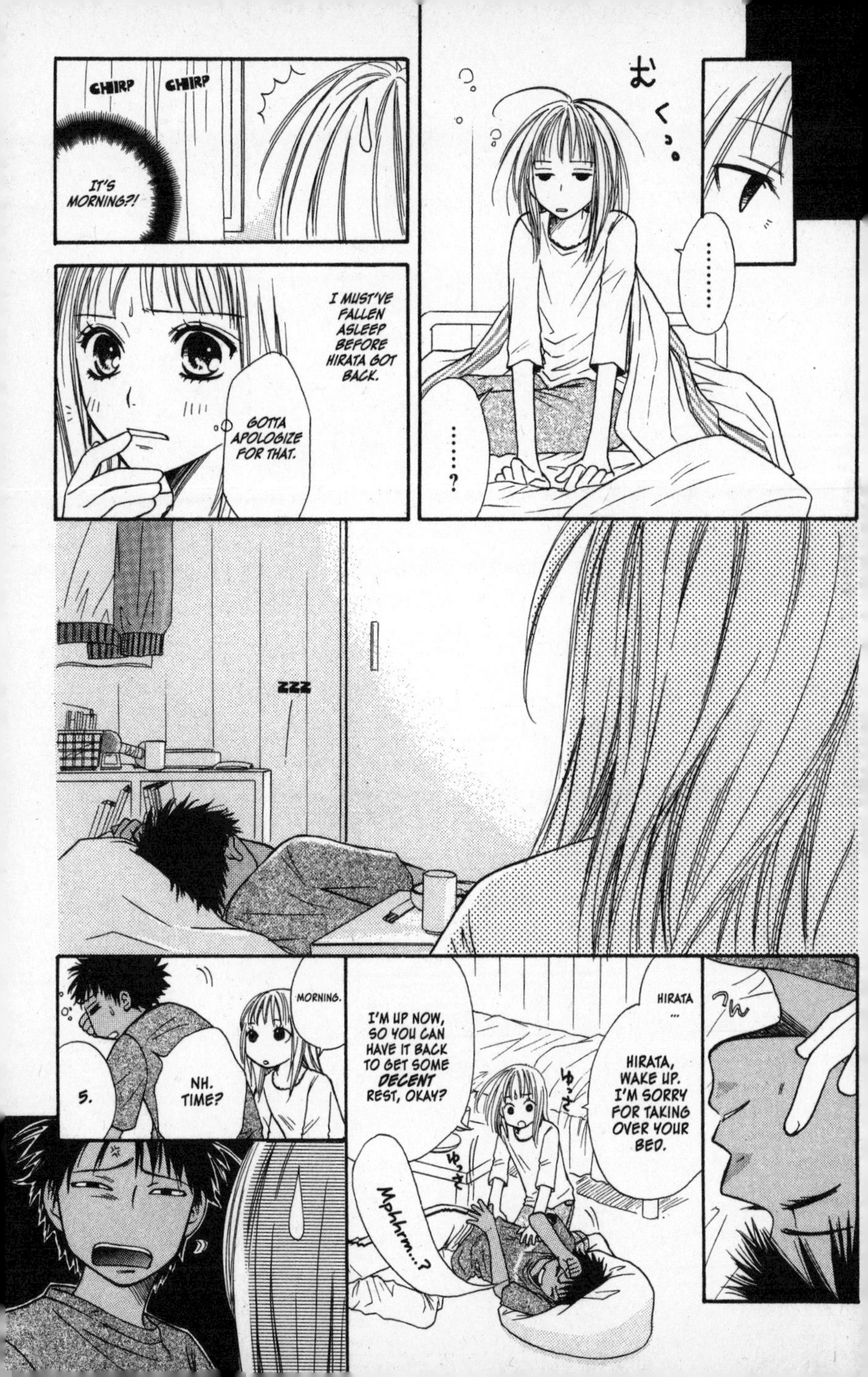

......
むくっ
......?
CHIRP
CHIRP
IT'S MORNING?!
I MUST'VE FALLEN ASLEEP BEFORE HIRATA GOT BACK.
GOTTA APOLOGIZE FOR THAT.
ZZZ
HIRATA ...
HIRATA, WAKE UP. I'M SORRY FOR TAKING OVER YOUR BED.
I'M UP NOW, SO YOU CAN HAVE IT BACK TO GET SOME DECENT REST, OKAY?
Mphhrm...?
MORNING.
NH. TIME?
5.

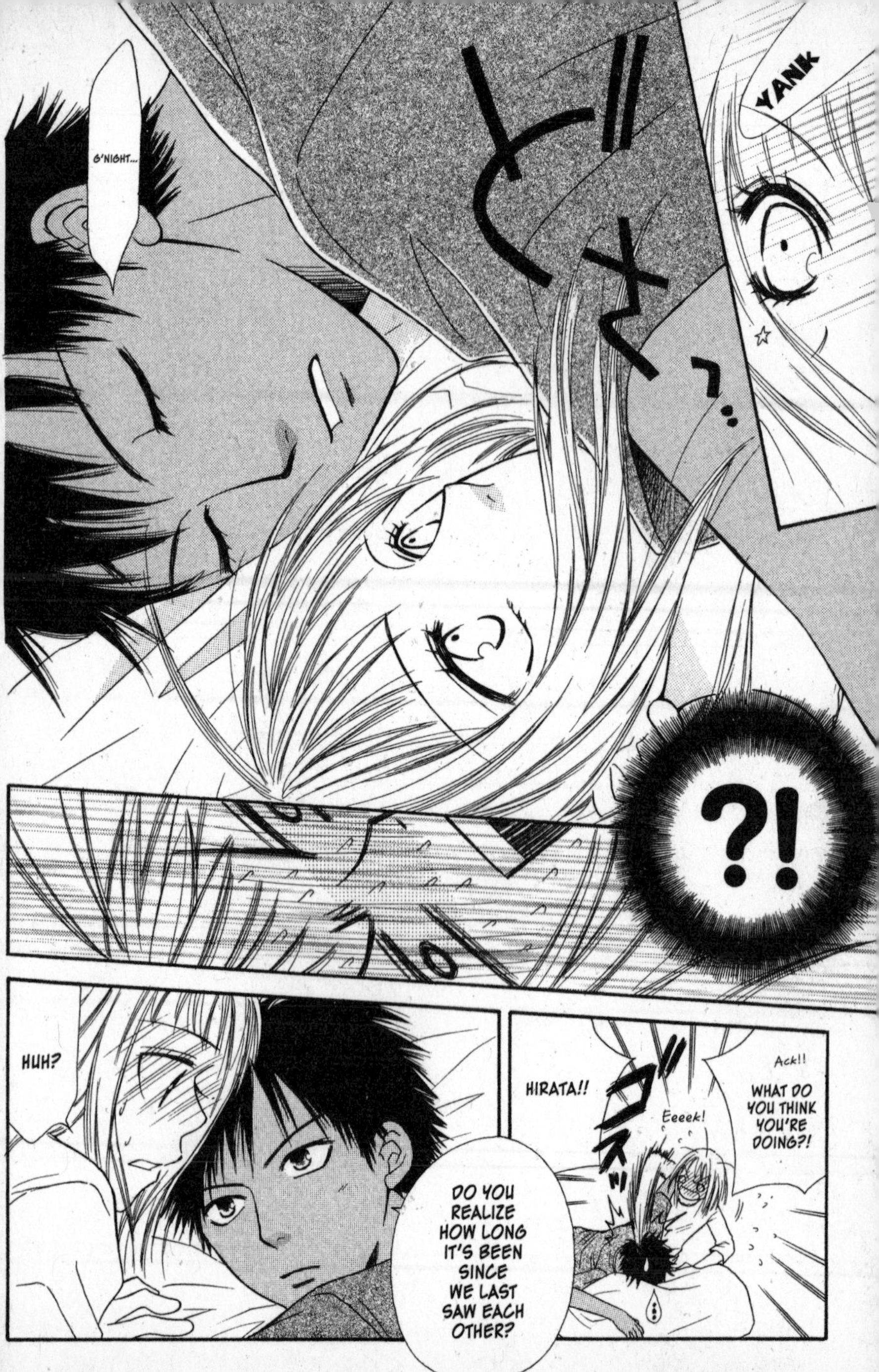
YANK
G'NIGHT...
?!
Ack!!
WHAT DO YOU THINK YOU'RE DOING?!
HIRATA!!
Eeeek!
HUH?
DO YOU REALIZE HOW LONG IT'S BEEN SINCE WE LAST SAW EACH OTHER?

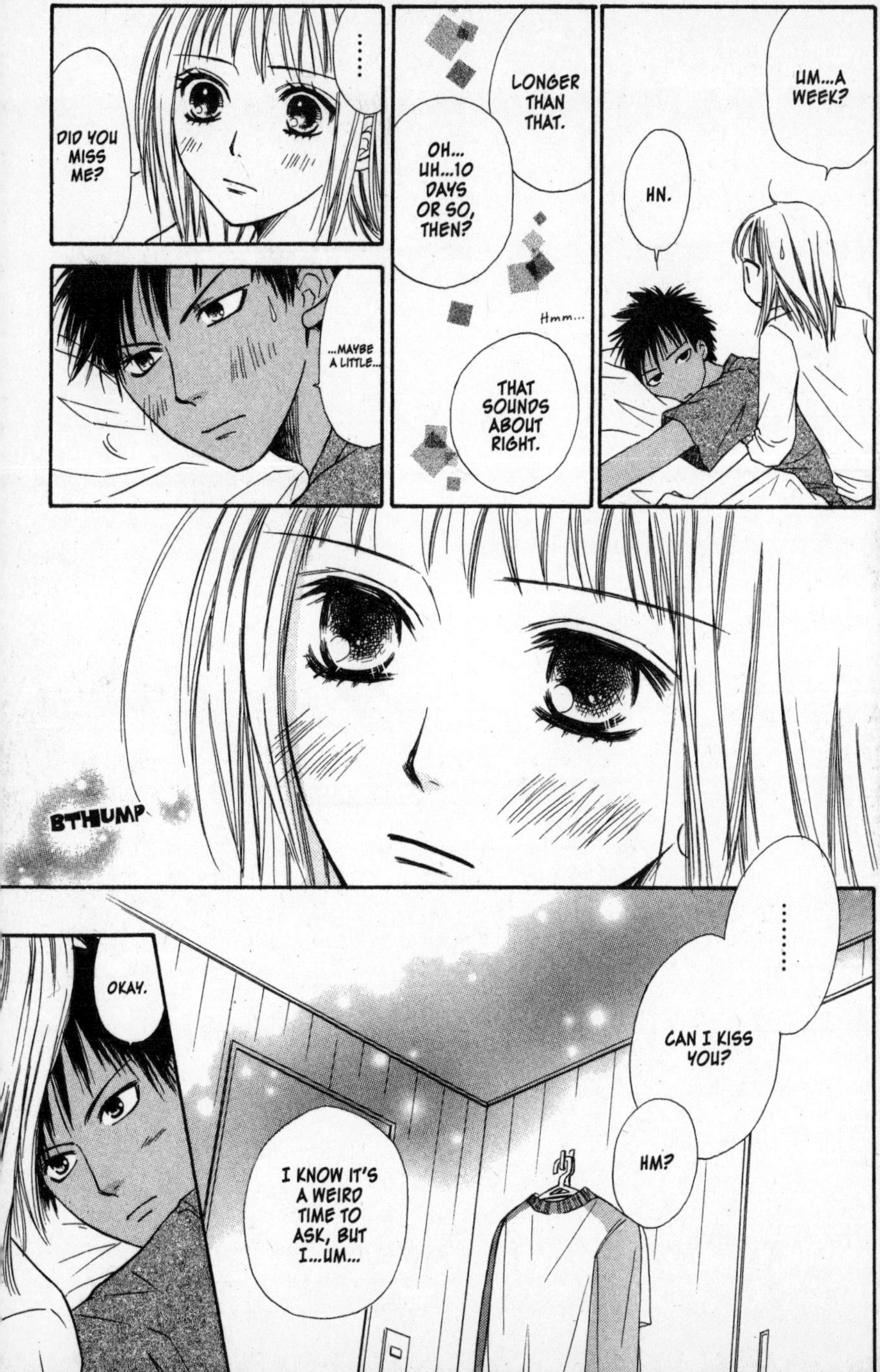
UM...A WEEK?
HN.
LONGER THAN THAT.
OH... UH...10 DAYS OR SO, THEN?
Hmm...
THAT SOUNDS ABOUT RIGHT.
......
DID YOU MISS ME?
...MAYBE A LITTLE...
BTHUMP
......
CAN I KISS YOU?
HM?
I KNOW IT'S A WEIRD TIME TO ASK, BUT I...UM...
OKAY.

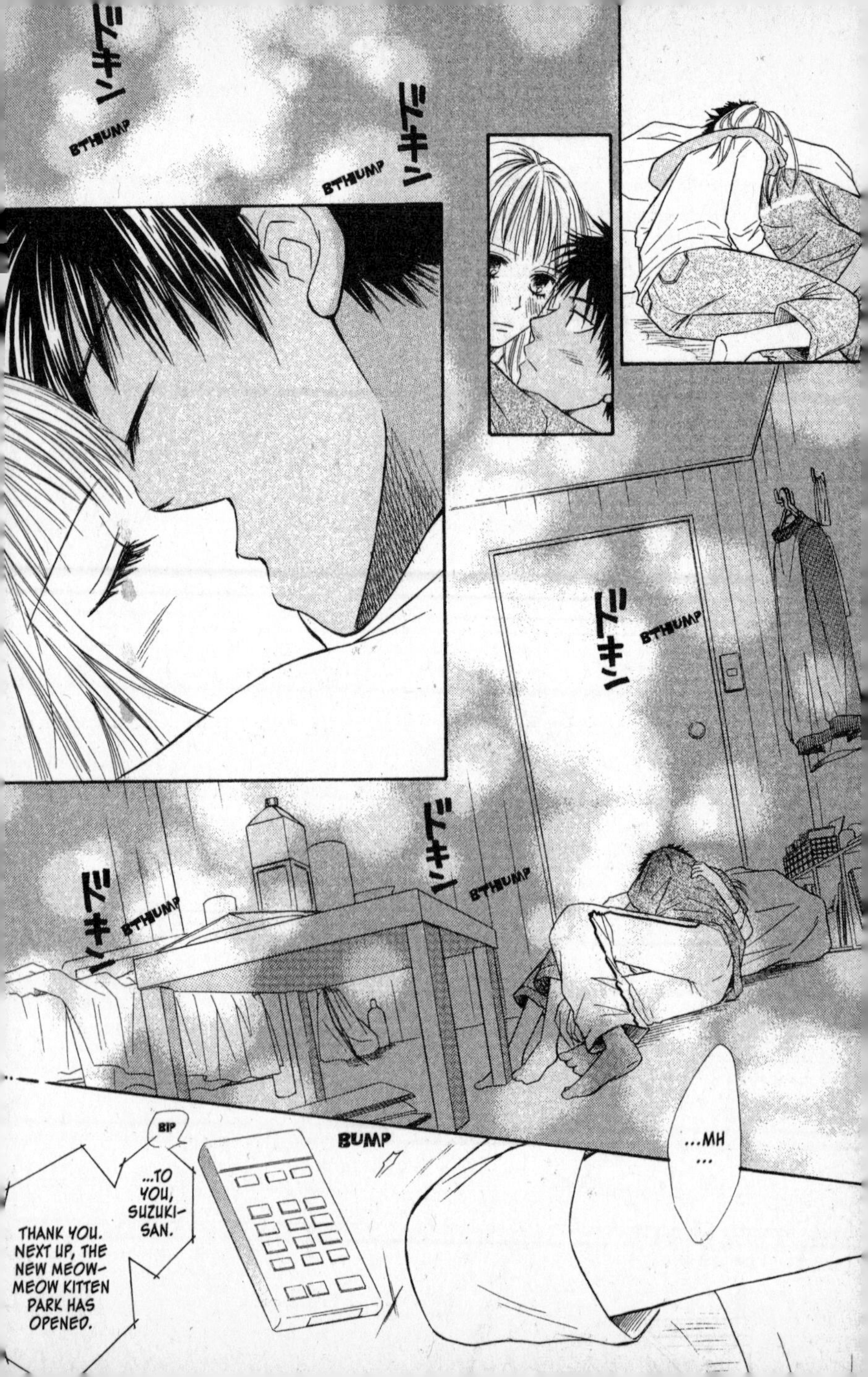

ドキン
BTHUMP
ドキン
BTHUMP
ドキン
BTHUMP
ドキン
BTHUMP
ドキン
BTHUMP
...MH ...
BUMP
BIP
...TO YOU, SUZUKI-SAN.
THANK YOU. NEXT UP, THE NEW MEOW-MEOW KITTEN PARK HAS OPENED.

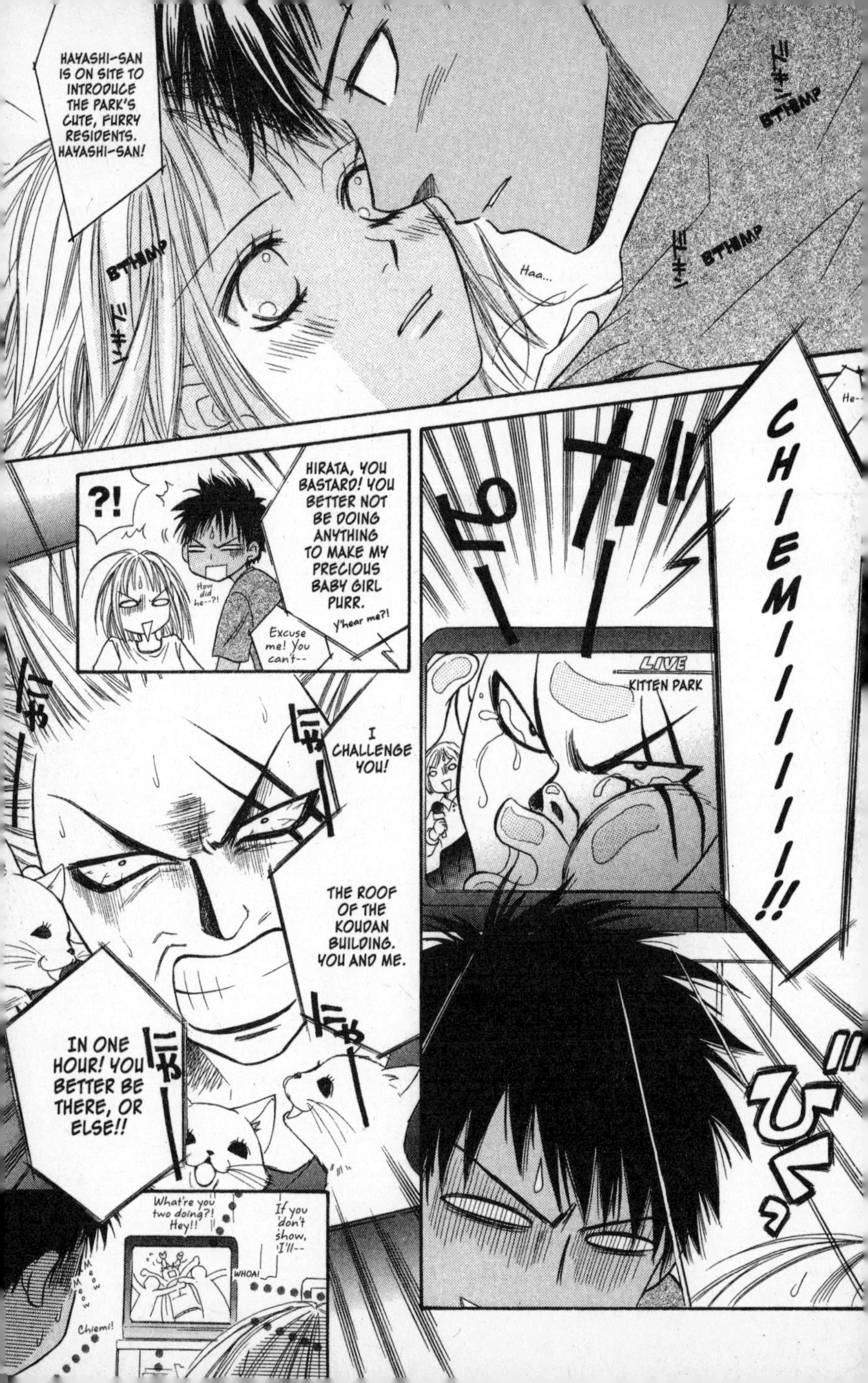

BTHMP
BTHMP
Haa...
BTHMP
HAYASHI-SAN IS ON SITE TO INTRODUCE THE PARK'S CUTE, FURRY RESIDENTS. HAYASHI-SAN!
He--
CHIEMIIIIIIIII!!
LIVE
KITTEN PARK
HIRATA, YOU BASTARD! YOU BETTER NOT BE DOING ANYTHING TO MAKE MY PRECIOUS BABY GIRL PURR.
y'hear me?!
?!
How did he--?!
Excuse me! You can't--
I CHALLENGE YOU!
THE ROOF OF THE KOUDAN BUILDING. YOU AND ME.
IN ONE HOUR! YOU BETTER BE THERE, OR ELSE!!
If you don't show, I'll--
What're you two doing?! Hey!!
WHOA!
Meow Meow
Chiemi!

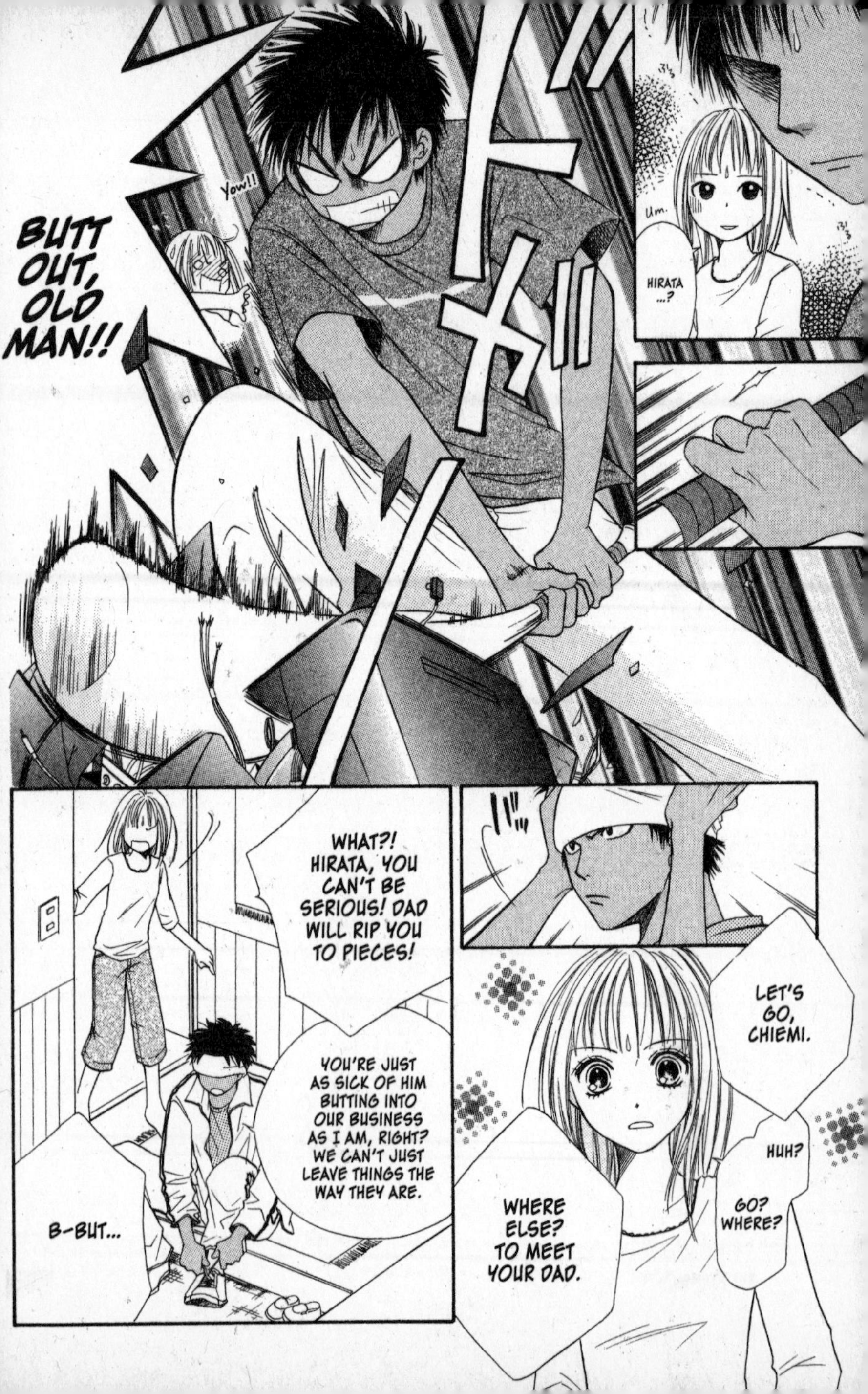
Um.
HIRATA ...?
Yow!!
BUTT OUT, OLD MAN!!
LET'S GO, CHIEMI.
HUH?
GO? WHERE?
WHERE ELSE? TO MEET YOUR DAD.
WHAT?! HIRATA, YOU CAN'T BE SERIOUS! DAD WILL RIP YOU TO PIECES!
YOU'RE JUST AS SICK OF HIM BUTTING INTO OUR BUSINESS AS I AM, RIGHT? WE CAN'T JUST LEAVE THINGS THE WAY THEY ARE.
B-BUT...

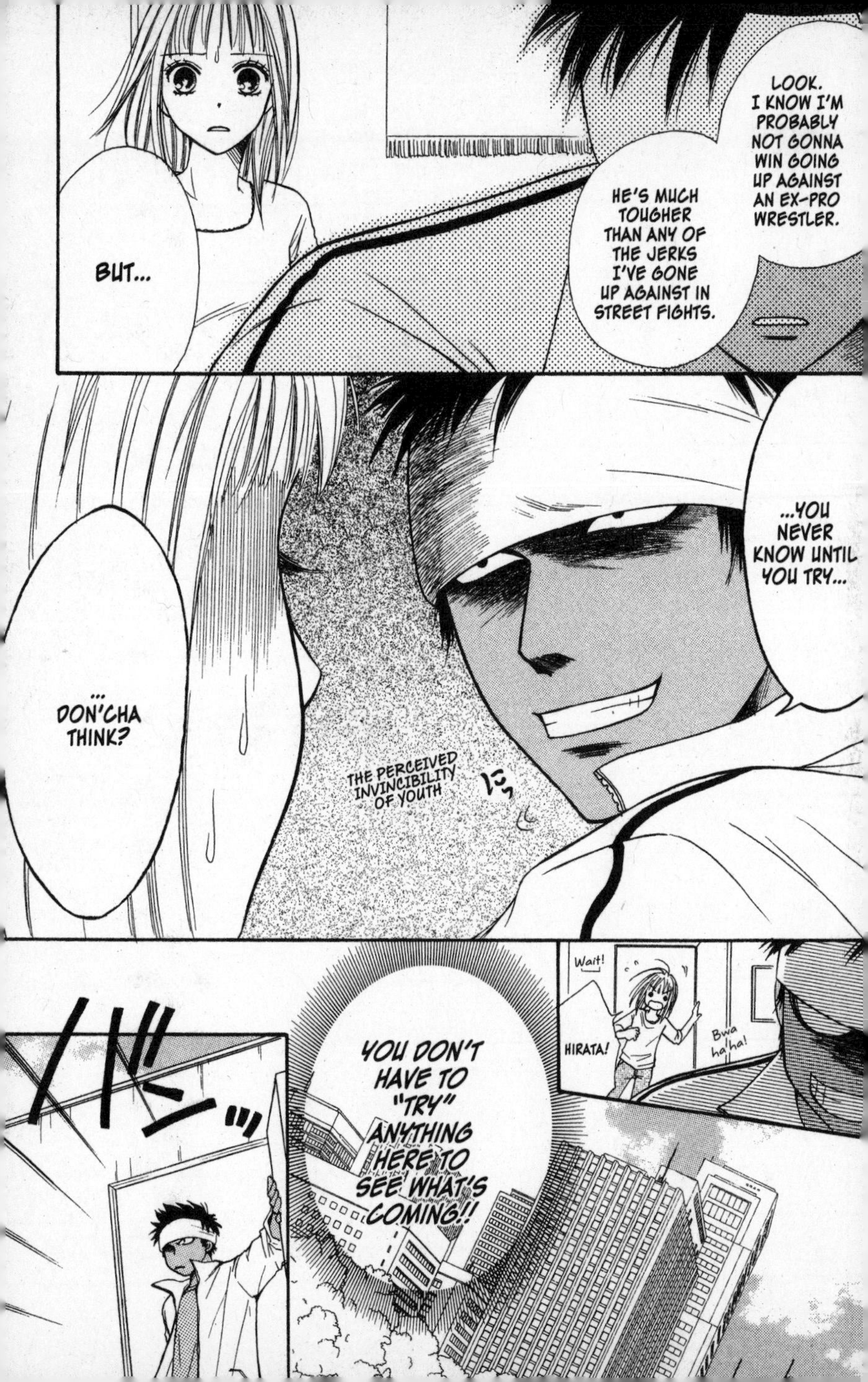
LOOK. I KNOW I'M PROBABLY NOT GONNA WIN GOING UP AGAINST AN EX-PRO WRESTLER.
HE'S MUCH TOUGHER THAN ANY OF THE JERKS I'VE GONE UP AGAINST IN STREET FIGHTS.
BUT...
...YOU NEVER KNOW UNTIL YOU TRY...
...DON'CHA THINK?
THE PERCEIVED INVINCIBILITY OF YOUTH
Bwa ha ha!
Wait!
HIRATA!
YOU DON'T HAVE TO "TRY" ANYTHING HERE TO SEE WHAT'S COMING!!

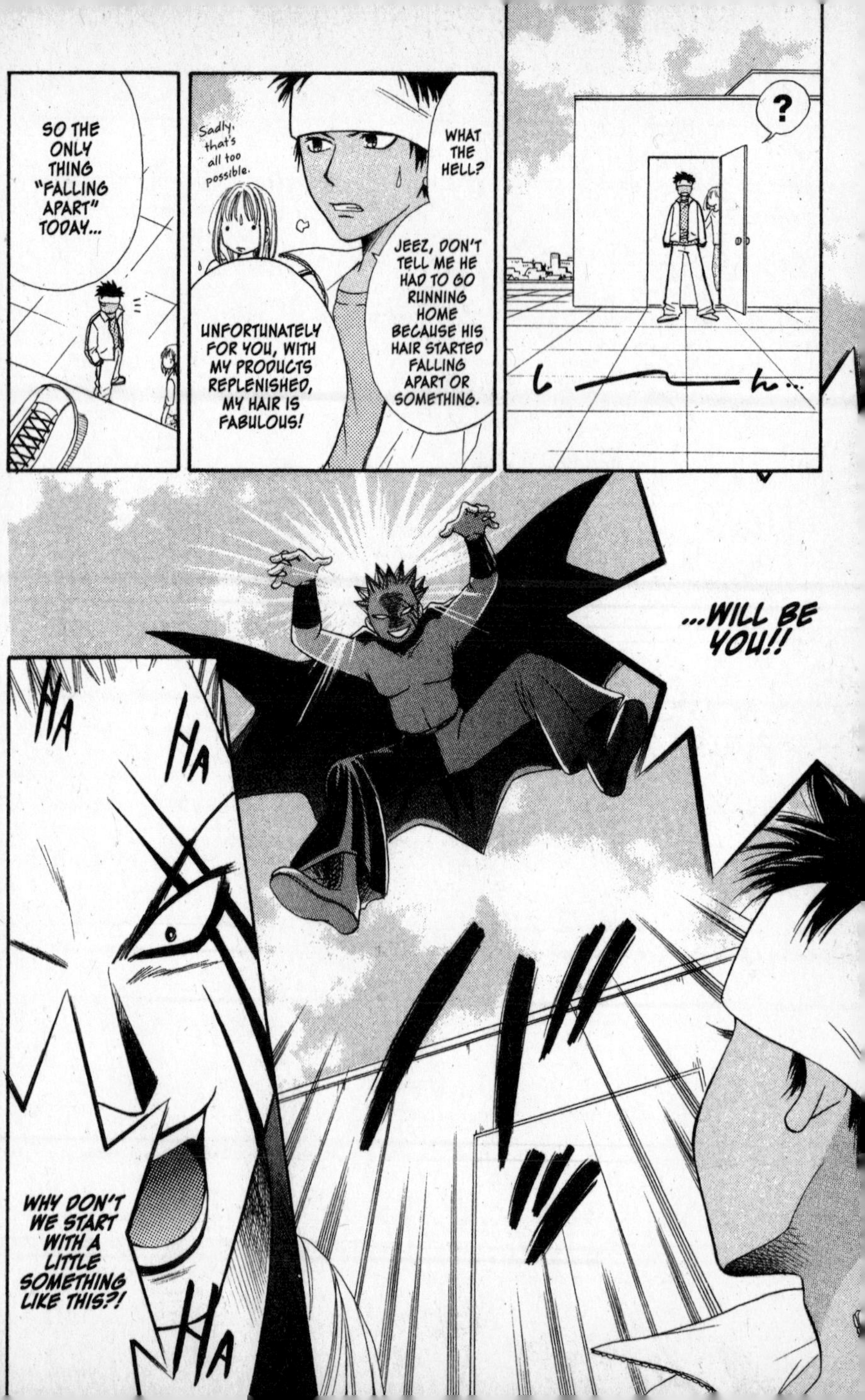
?
WHAT THE HELL?
JEEZ, DON'T TELL ME HE HAD TO GO RUNNING HOME BECAUSE HIS HAIR STARTED FALLING APART OR SOMETHING.
Sadly, that's all too possible.
UNFORTUNATELY FOR YOU, WITH MY PRODUCTS REPLENISHED, MY HAIR IS FABULOUS!
SO THE ONLY THING "FALLING APART" TODAY...
...WILL BE YOU!!
HA
HA
WHY DON'T WE START WITH A LITTLE SOMETHING LIKE THIS?!
HA
HA

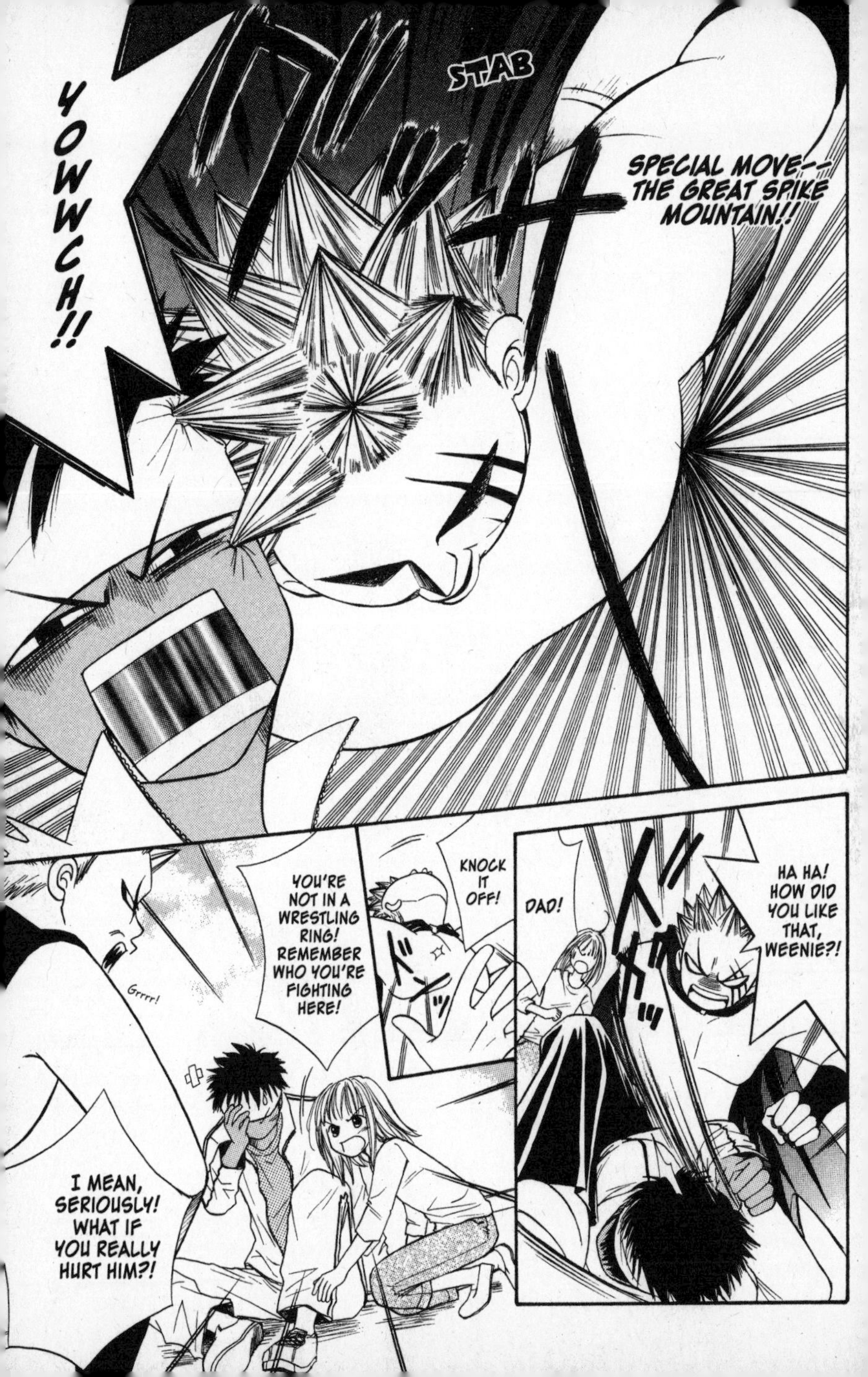
STAB
SPECIAL MOVE--THE GREAT SPIKE MOUNTAIN!!
YOWWCH!!
HA HA! HOW DID YOU LIKE THAT, WEENIE?!
DAD!
KNOCK IT OFF!
YOU'RE NOT IN A WRESTLING RING! REMEMBER WHO YOU'RE FIGHTING HERE!
Grrrr!
I MEAN, SERIOUSLY! WHAT IF YOU REALLY HURT HIM?!

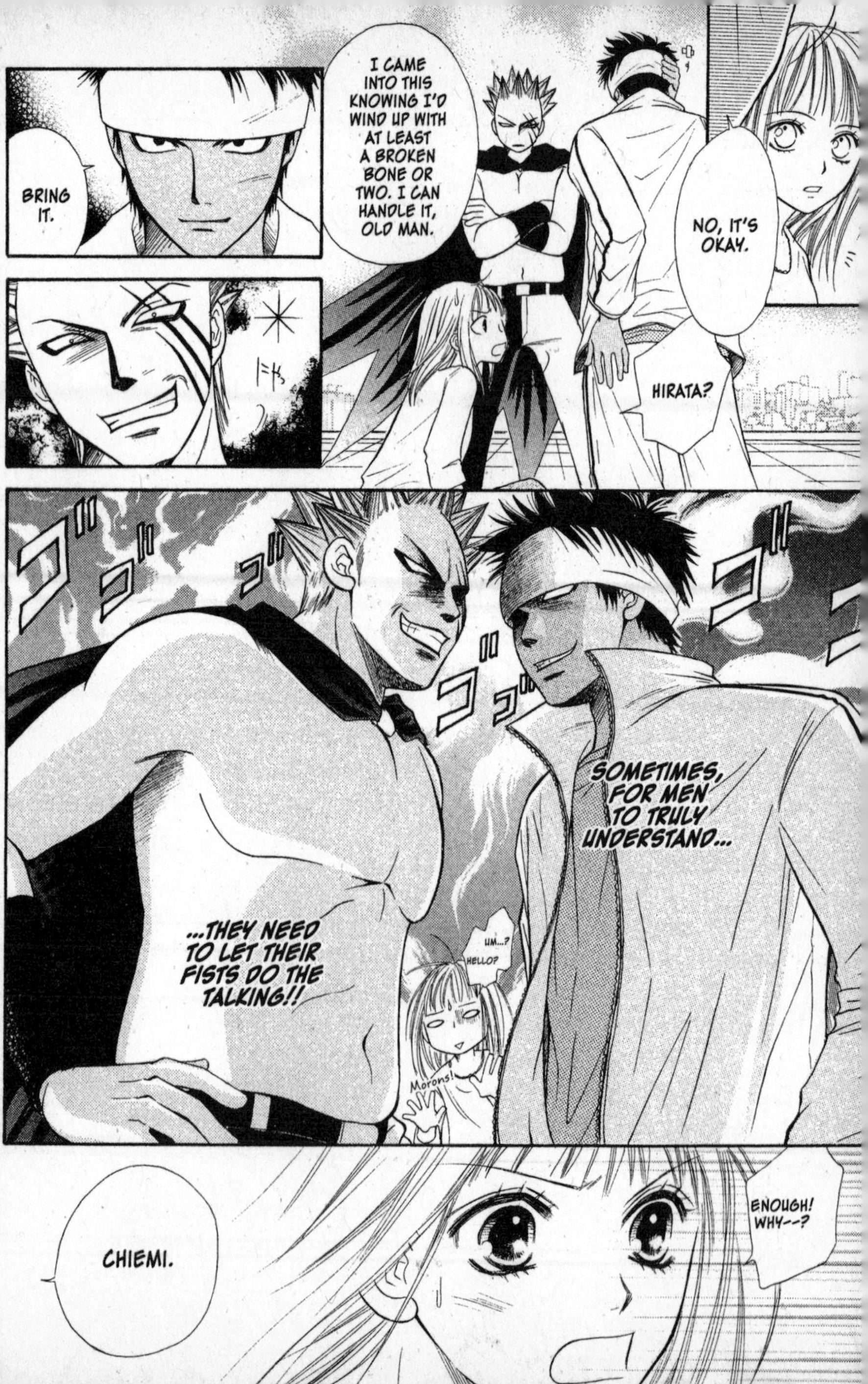
NO, IT'S OKAY.
I CAME INTO THIS KNOWING I'D WIND UP WITH AT LEAST A BROKEN BONE OR TWO. I CAN HANDLE IT, OLD MAN.
HIRATA?
BRING IT.
SOMETIMES, FOR MEN TO TRULY UNDERSTAND...
...THEY NEED TO LET THEIR FISTS DO THE TALKING!!
UM...?
HELLO?
Morons!
ENOUGH! WHY--?
CHIEMI.

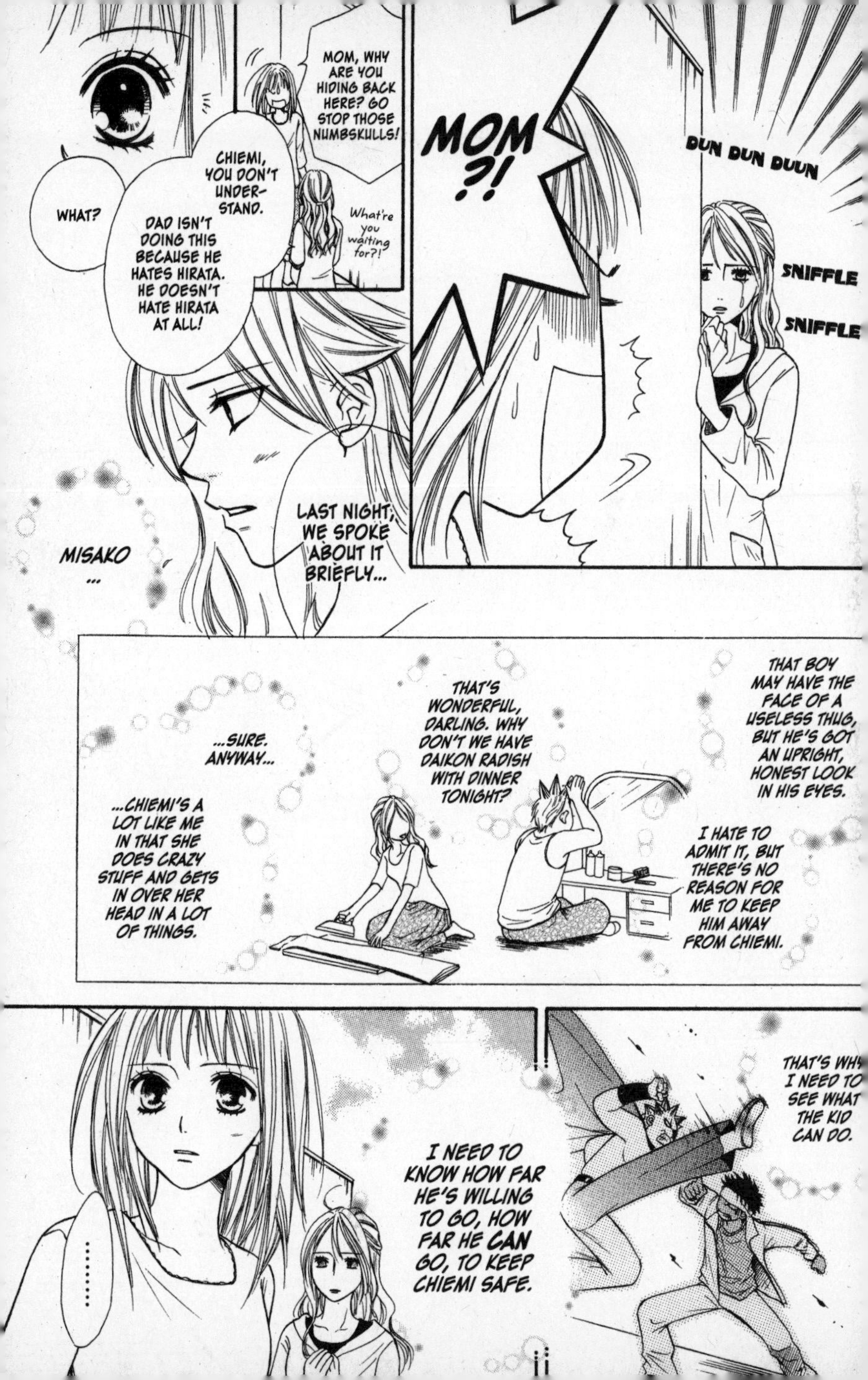
DUN DUN DUUN
SNIFFLE
SNIFFLE
MOM ?!
MOM, WHY ARE YOU HIDING BACK HERE? GO STOP THOSE NUMBSKULLS!
What're you waiting for?!
CHIEMI, YOU DON'T UNDER-STAND.
DAD ISN'T DOING THIS BECAUSE HE HATES HIRATA. HE DOESN'T HATE HIRATA AT ALL!
WHAT?
LAST NIGHT, WE SPOKE ABOUT IT BRIEFLY...
MISAKO ...
THAT BOY MAY HAVE THE FACE OF A USELESS THUG, BUT HE'S GOT AN UPRIGHT, HONEST LOOK IN HIS EYES.
I HATE TO ADMIT IT, BUT THERE'S NO REASON FOR ME TO KEEP HIM AWAY FROM CHIEMI.
THAT'S WONDERFUL, DARLING. WHY DON'T WE HAVE DAIKON RADISH WITH DINNER TONIGHT?
...SURE. ANYWAY...
...CHIEMI'S A LOT LIKE ME IN THAT SHE DOES CRAZY STUFF AND GETS IN OVER HER HEAD IN A LOT OF THINGS.
THAT'S WHY I NEED TO SEE WHAT THE KID CAN DO.
I NEED TO KNOW HOW FAR HE'S WILLING TO GO, HOW FAR HE CAN GO, TO KEEP CHIEMI SAFE.
....

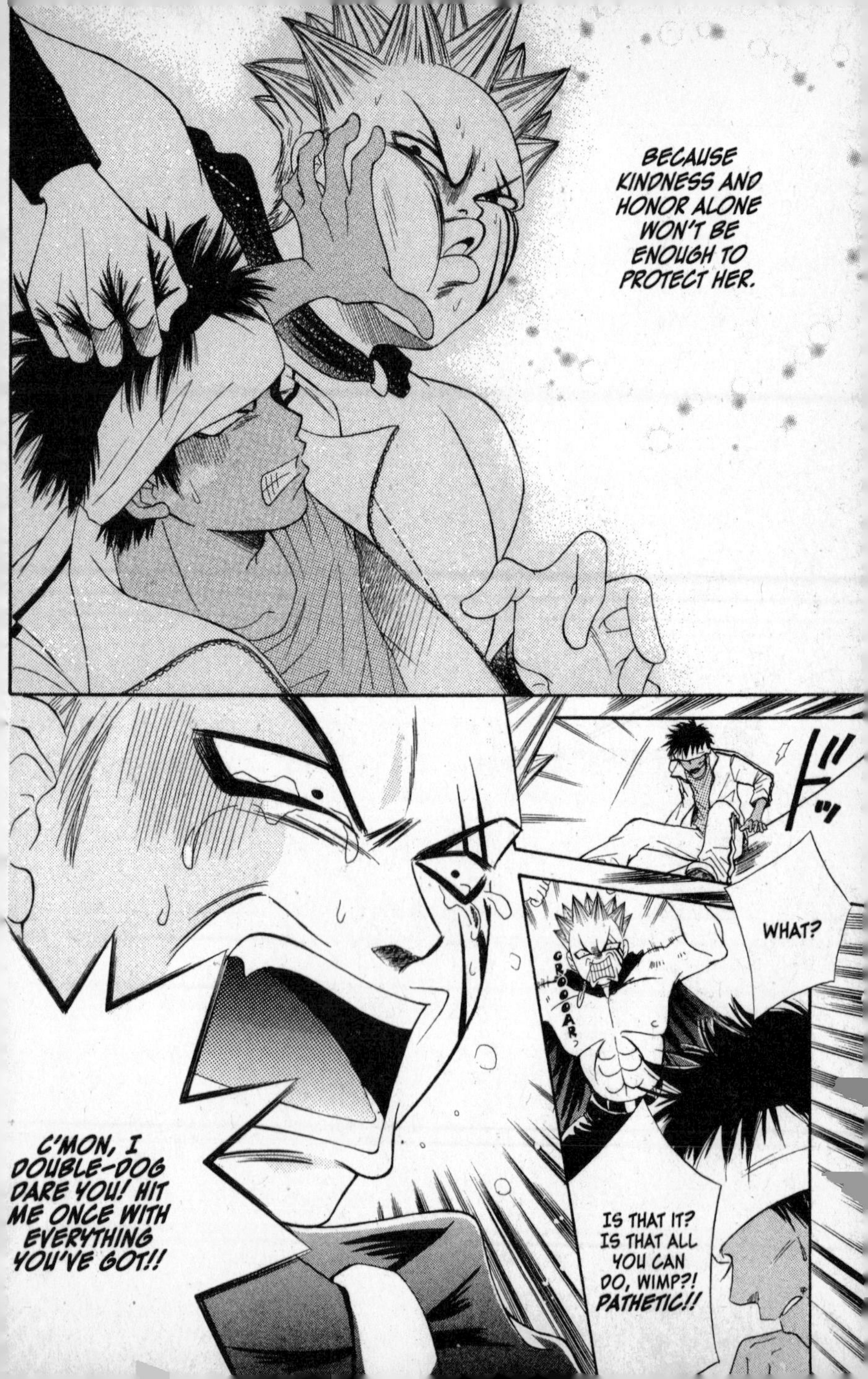
BECAUSE KINDNESS AND HONOR ALONE WON'T BE ENOUGH TO PROTECT HER.
ドッ
WHAT?
GROOOAR
IS THAT IT? IS THAT ALL YOU CAN DO, WIMP?! PATHETIC!!
C'MON, I DOUBLE-DOG DARE YOU! HIT ME ONCE WITH EVERYTHING YOU'VE GOT!!

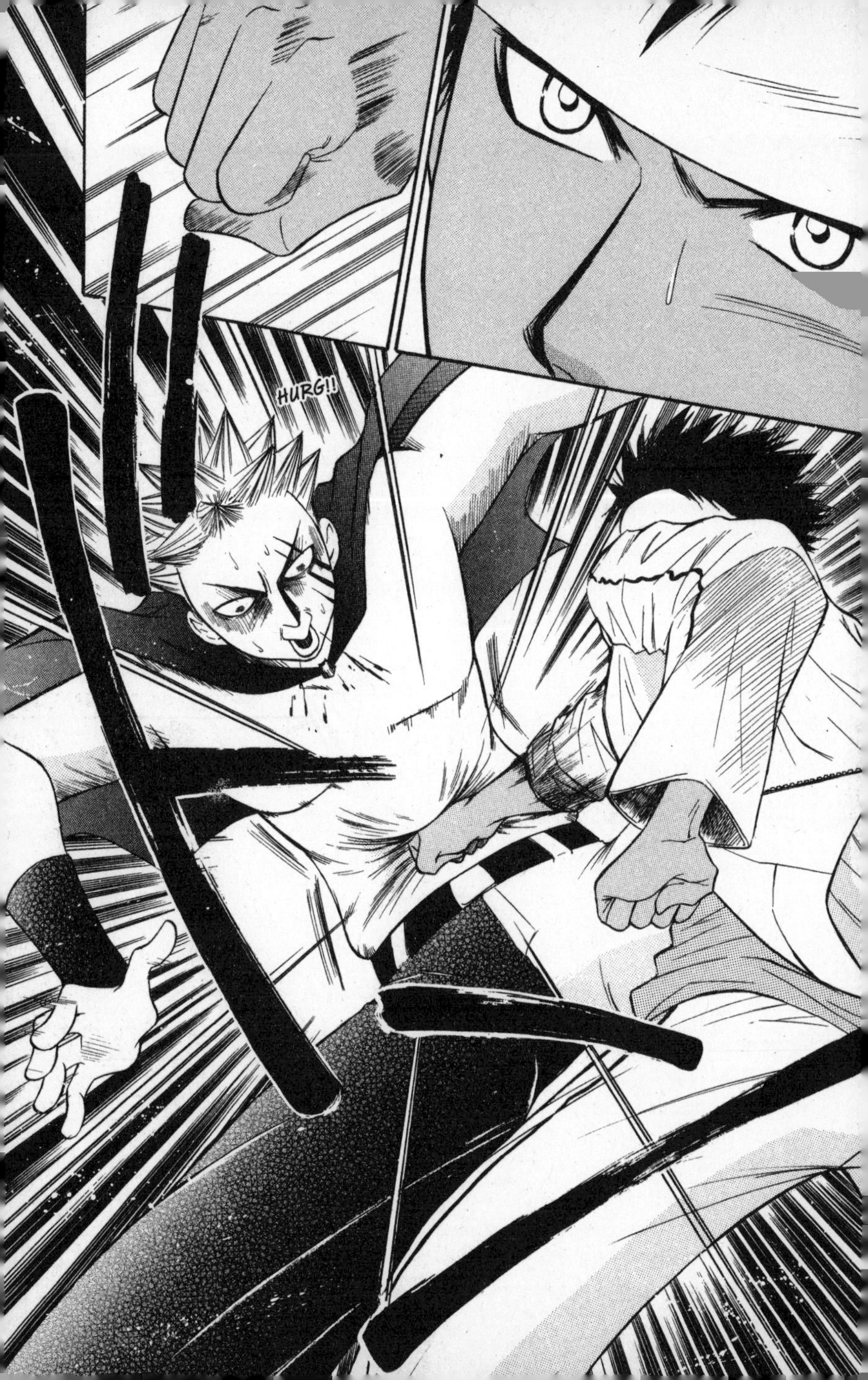
HURG!!

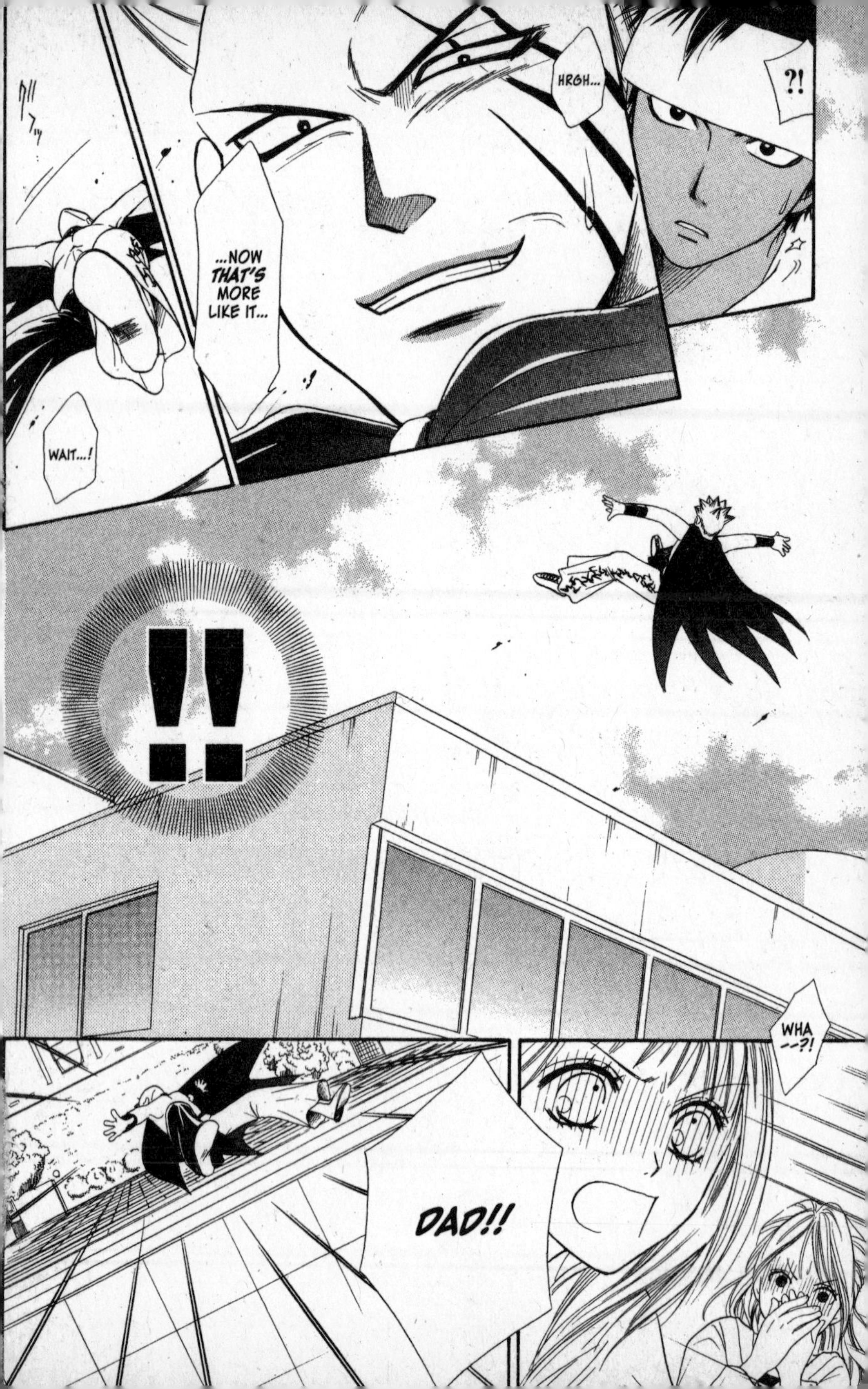
?!
HRGH...
...NOW THAT'S MORE LIKE IT...
WAIT...!
!!
WHA--?!
DAD!!

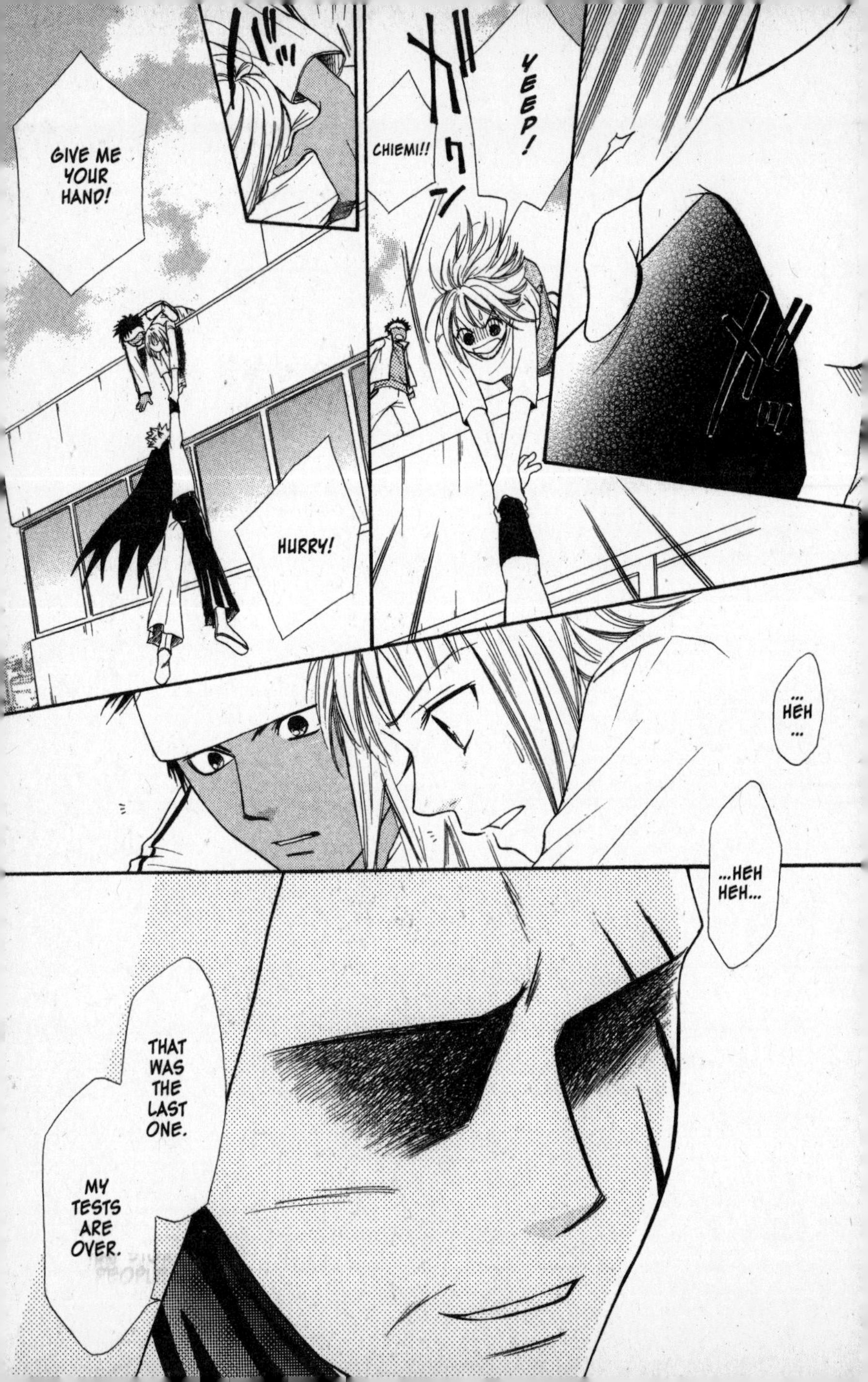

CHIEMI!!
YEEP!
GIVE ME YOUR HAND!
HURRY!
...HEH...
...HEH HEH...
THAT WAS THE LAST ONE.
MY TESTS ARE OVER.

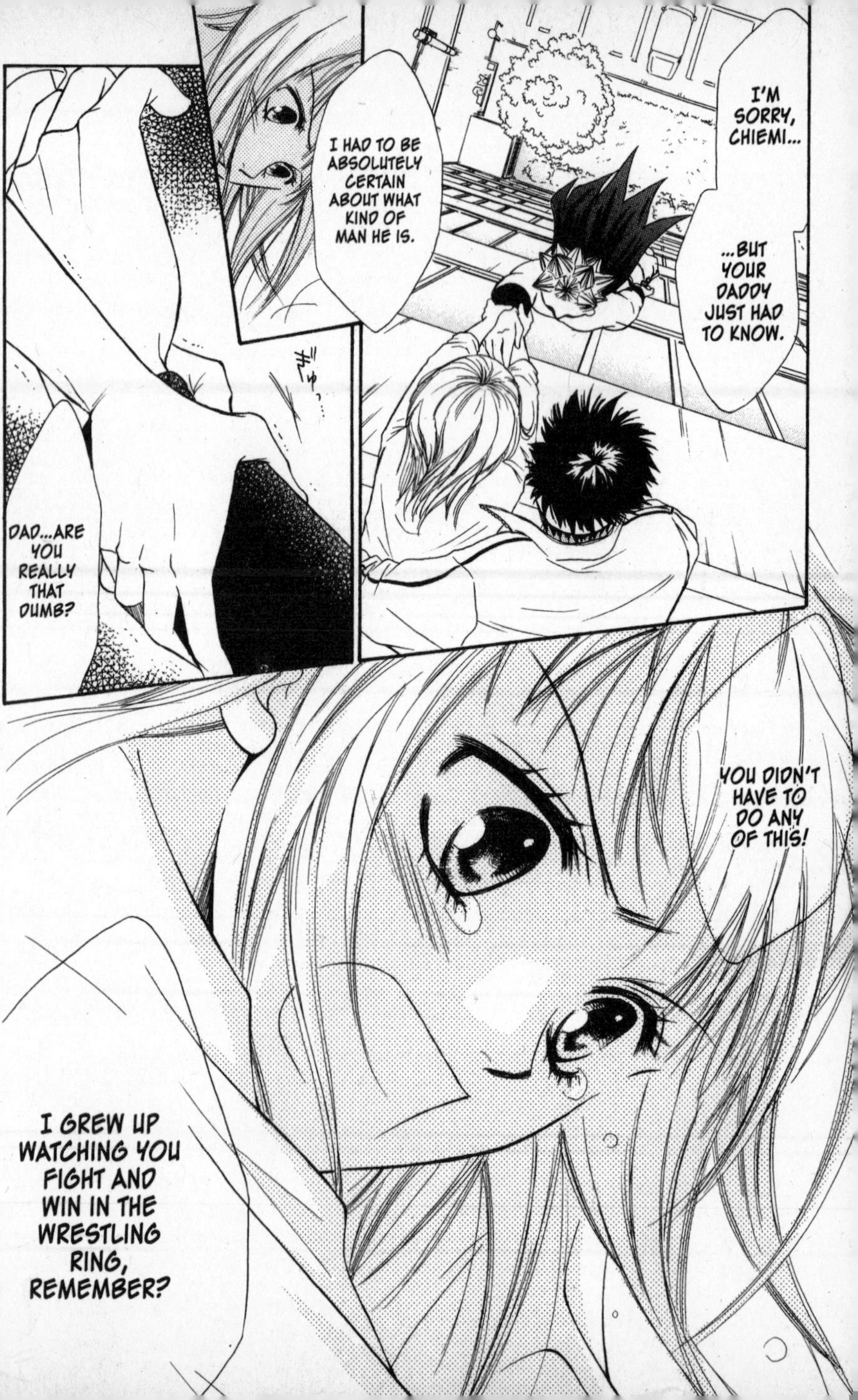
I'M SORRY, CHIEMI...
...BUT YOUR DADDY JUST HAD TO KNOW.
I HAD TO BE ABSOLUTELY CERTAIN ABOUT WHAT KIND OF MAN HE IS.
ぎゅっ…
DAD...ARE YOU REALLY THAT DUMB?
YOU DIDN'T HAVE TO DO ANY OF THIS!
I GREW UP WATCHING YOU FIGHT AND WIN IN THE WRESTLING RING, REMEMBER?

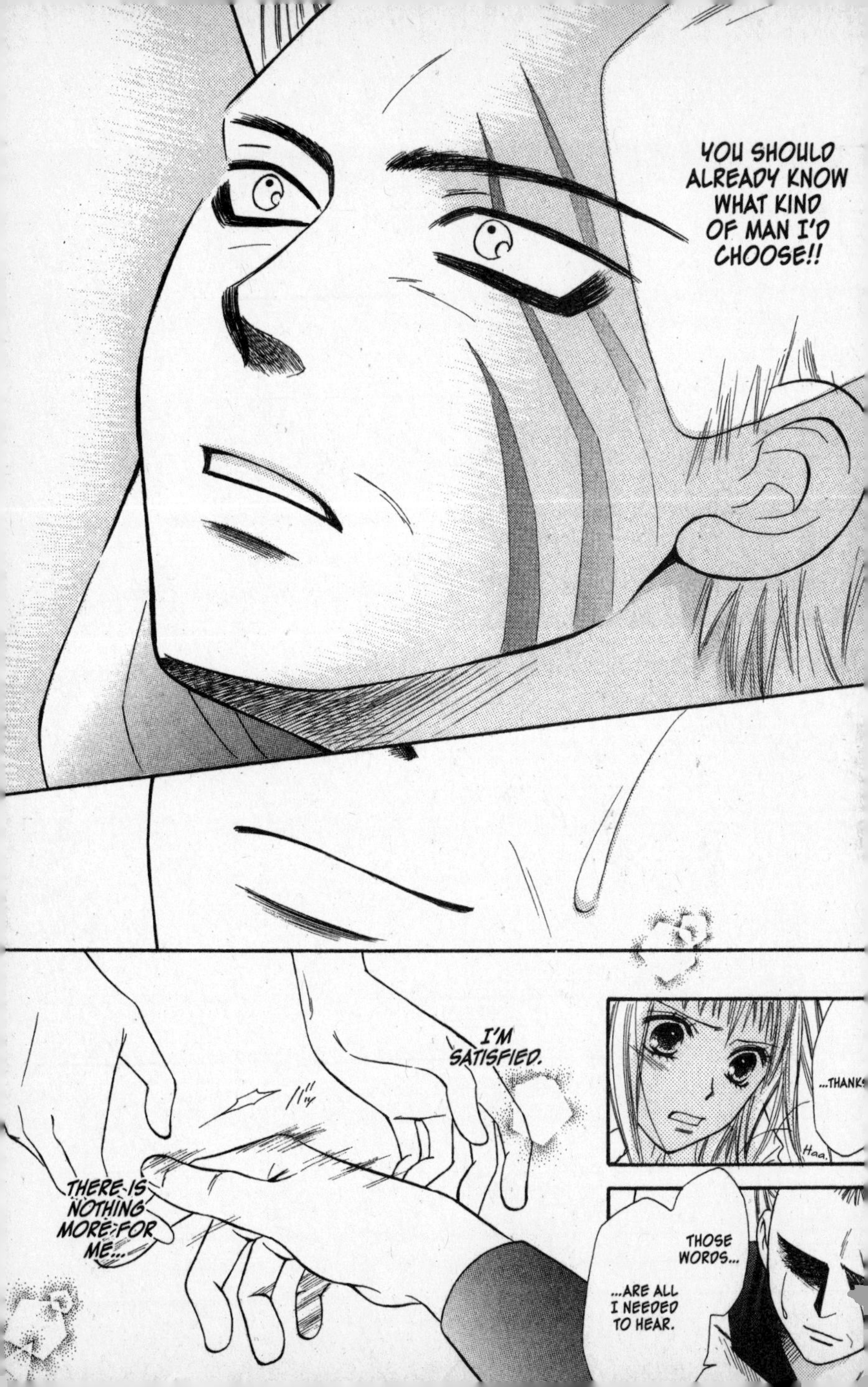
YOU SHOULD ALREADY KNOW WHAT KIND OF MAN I'D CHOOSE!!
...THANKS
Haa.
THOSE WORDS...
...ARE ALL I NEEDED TO HEAR.
I'M SATISFIED.
THERE IS NOTHING MORE FOR ME...

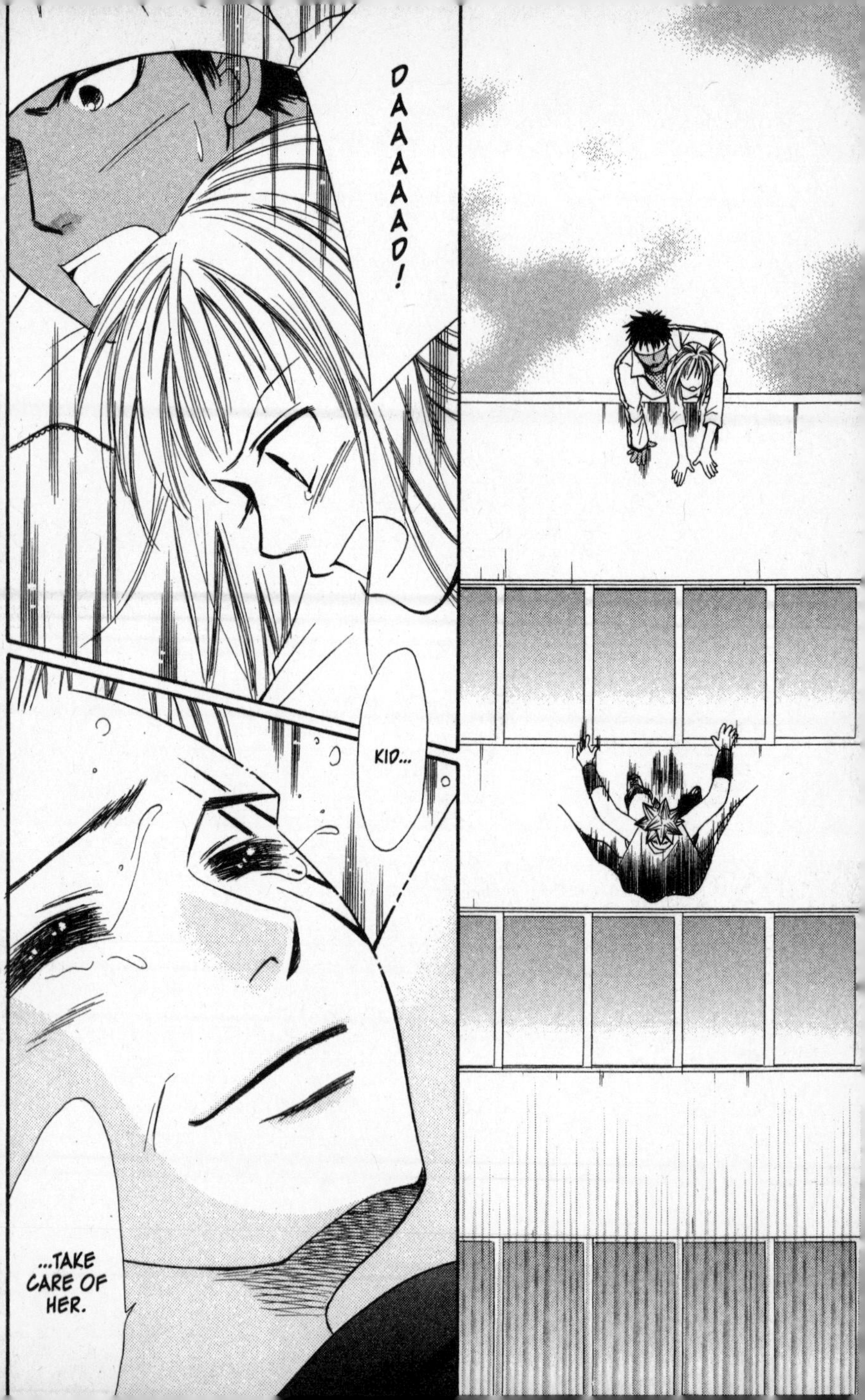
DAAAAAD!
KID...
...TAKE CARE OF HER.

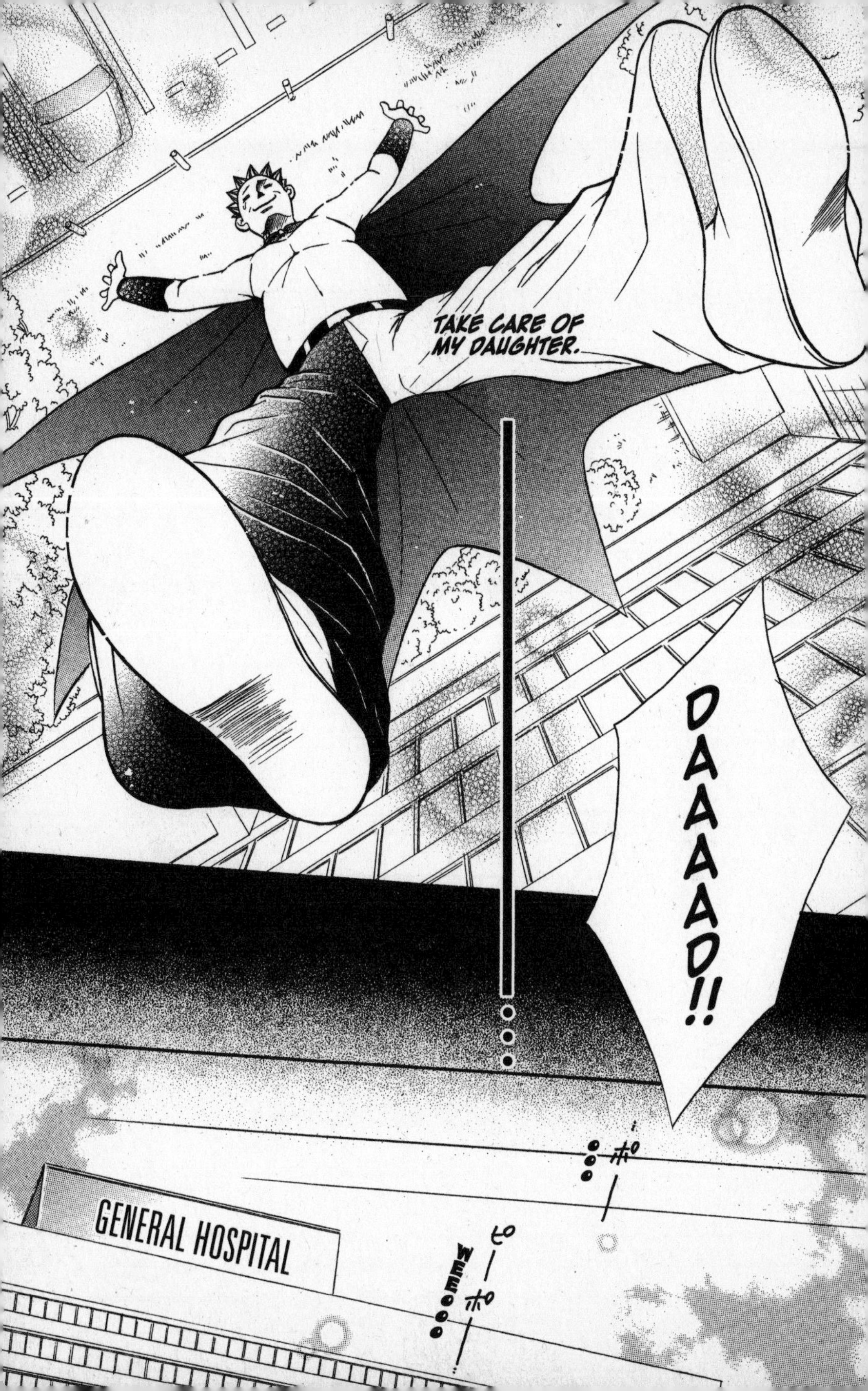
TAKE CARE OF MY DAUGHTER.
—…
DAAAAD!!
GENERAL HOSPITAL
…ポー
ピーポー…
WEEOOO

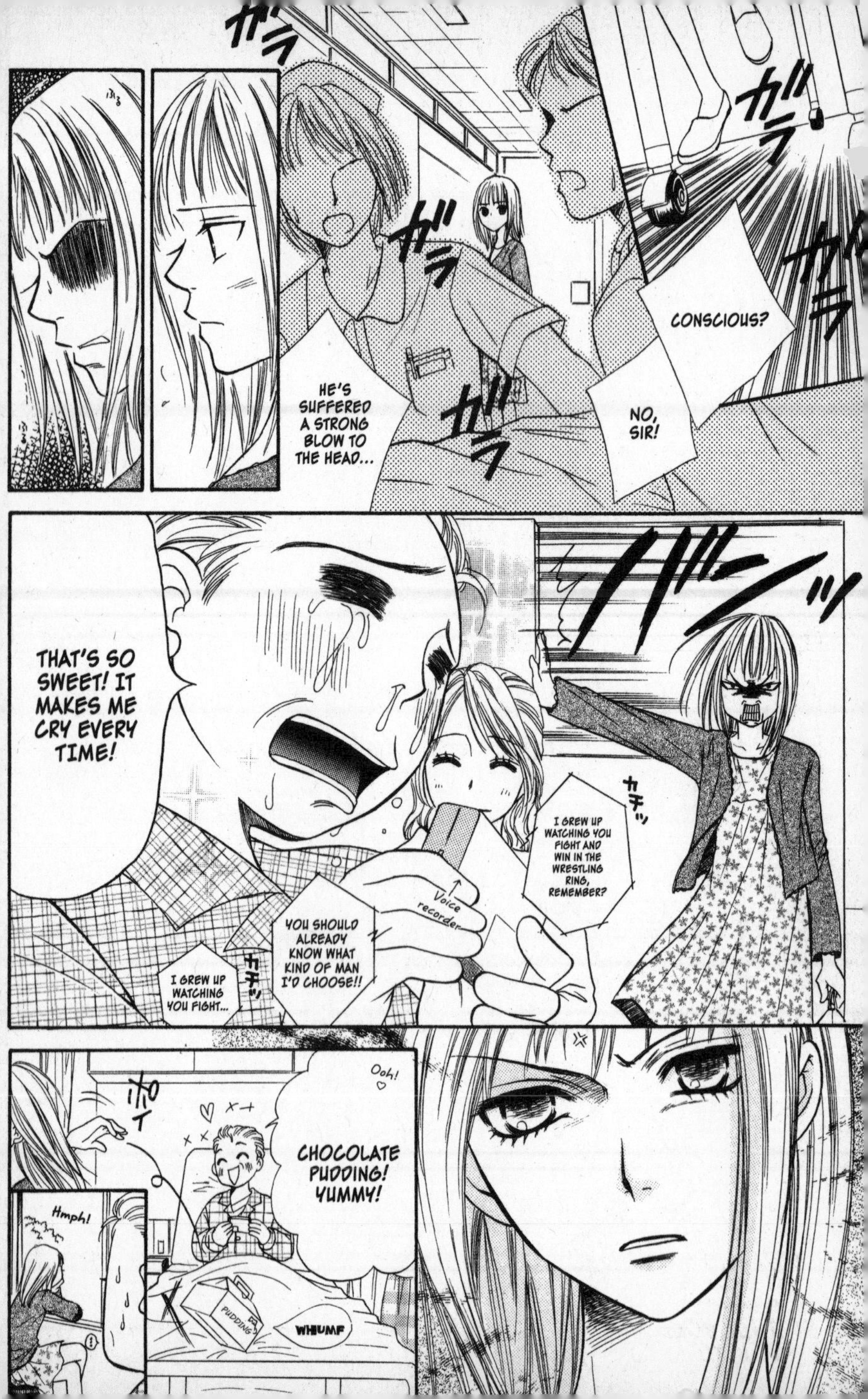
ガラ
ガラ
ガラ
CONSCIOUS?
NO, SIR!
ガラ
ガラ
HE'S SUFFERED A STRONG BLOW TO THE HEAD...
ガーンッ
カチッ
I GREW UP WATCHING YOU FIGHT AND WIN IN THE WRESTLING RING, REMEMBER?
Voice recorder
YOU SHOULD ALREADY KNOW WHAT KIND OF MAN I'D CHOOSE!!
カチッ
I GREW UP WATCHING YOU FIGHT...
THAT'S SO SWEET! IT MAKES ME CRY EVERY TIME!
Ooh! ♡
CHOCOLATE PUDDING! YUMMY!
ポイ
Hmph!
PUDDING
WHUMF

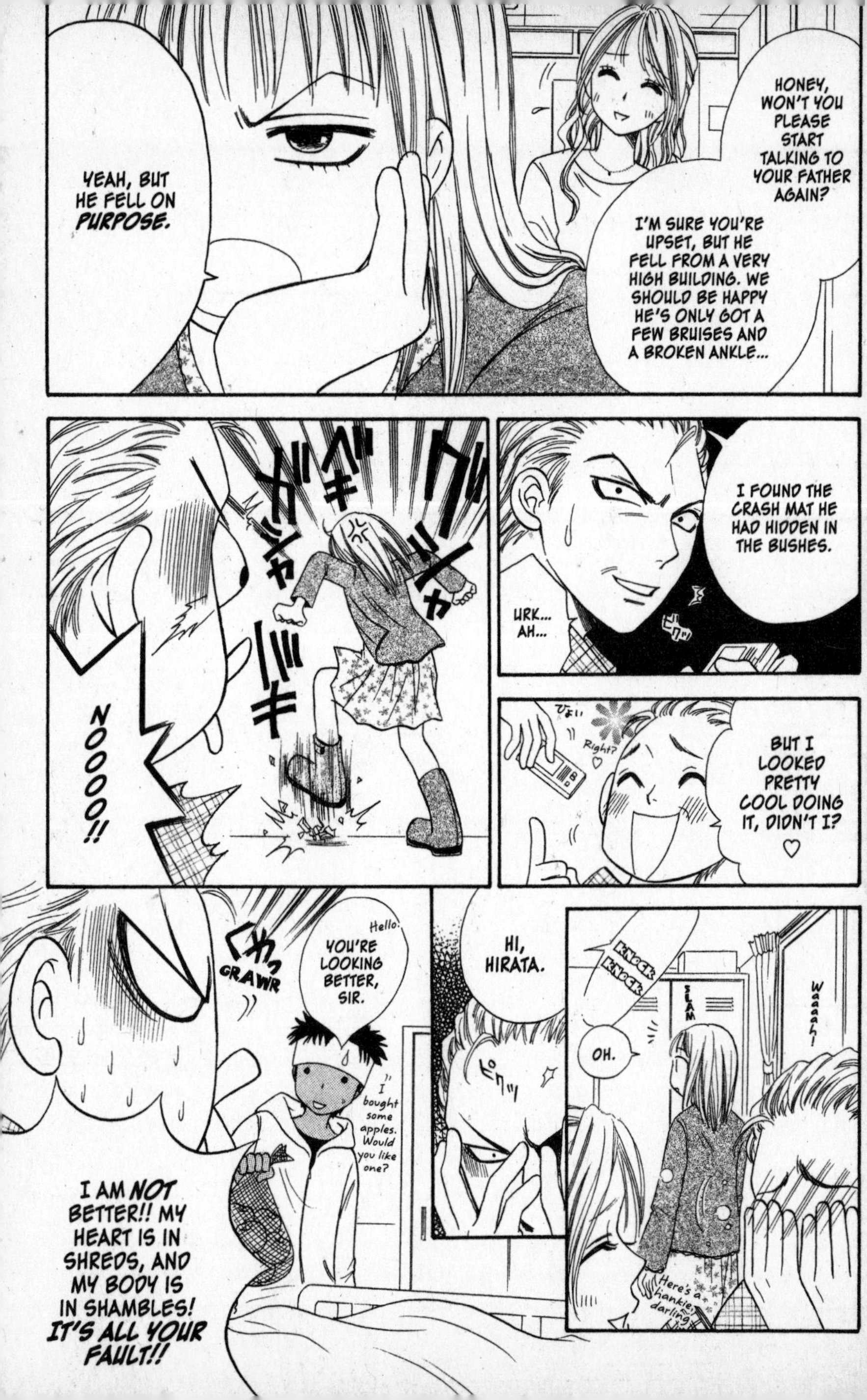
HONEY, WON'T YOU PLEASE START TALKING TO YOUR FATHER AGAIN?
I'M SURE YOU'RE UPSET, BUT HE FELL FROM A VERY HIGH BUILDING. WE SHOULD BE HAPPY HE'S ONLY GOT A FEW BRUISES AND A BROKEN ANKLE...
YEAH, BUT HE FELL ON PURPOSE.
I FOUND THE CRASH MAT HE HAD HIDDEN IN THE BUSHES.
URK... AH...
Right? ♡
BUT I LOOKED PRETTY COOL DOING IT, DIDN'T I? ♡
NOOOOOO!!
Waaaah!
SLAM
KNOCK KNOCK
OH.
Here's a hankie, darling.
HI, HIRATA.
Hello.
YOU'RE LOOKING BETTER, SIR.
I bought some apples. Would you like one?
GRAWR
I AM NOT BETTER!! MY HEART IS IN SHREDS, AND MY BODY IS IN SHAMBLES! IT'S ALL YOUR FAULT!!

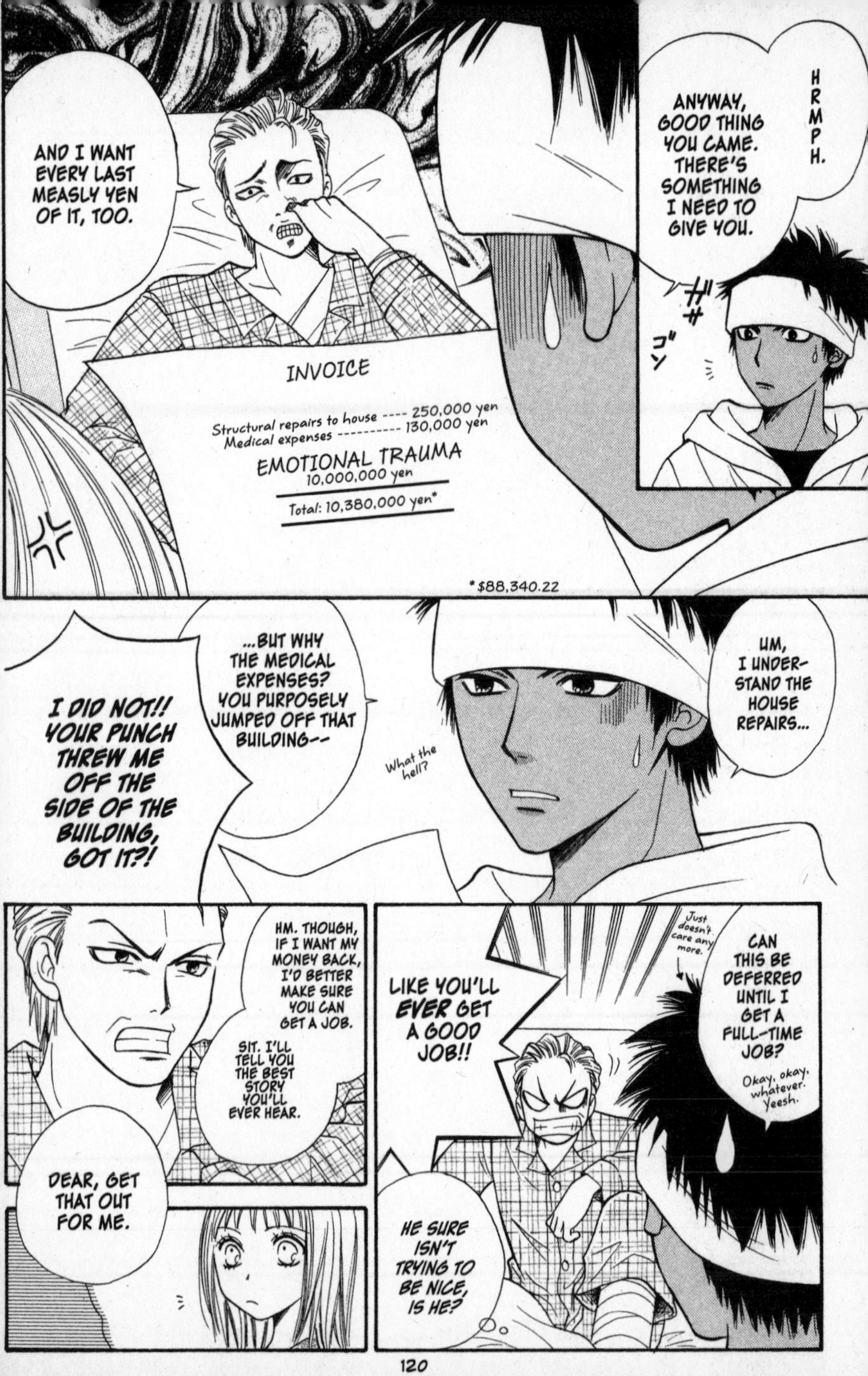
HRMPH.
ANYWAY, GOOD THING YOU CAME. THERE'S SOMETHING I NEED TO GIVE YOU.
INVOICE
Structural repairs to house ---- 250,000 yen
Medical expenses ----------- 130,000 yen
EMOTIONAL TRAUMA
10,000,000 yen
Total: 10,380,000 yen*
AND I WANT EVERY LAST MEASLY YEN OF IT, TOO.
*$88,340.22
UM, I UNDER-STAND THE HOUSE REPAIRS...
What the hell?
...BUT WHY THE MEDICAL EXPENSES? YOU PURPOSELY JUMPED OFF THAT BUILDING--
I DID NOT!! YOUR PUNCH THREW ME OFF THE SIDE OF THE BUILDING, GOT IT?!
Just doesn't care any more.
CAN THIS BE DEFERRED UNTIL I GET A FULL-TIME JOB?
Okay, okay, whatever. Yeesh.
LIKE YOU'LL EVER GET A GOOD JOB!!
HE SURE ISN'T TRYING TO BE NICE, IS HE?
HM. THOUGH, IF I WANT MY MONEY BACK, I'D BETTER MAKE SURE YOU CAN GET A JOB.
SIT. I'LL TELL YOU THE BEST STORY YOU'LL EVER HEAR.
DEAR, GET THAT OUT FOR ME.

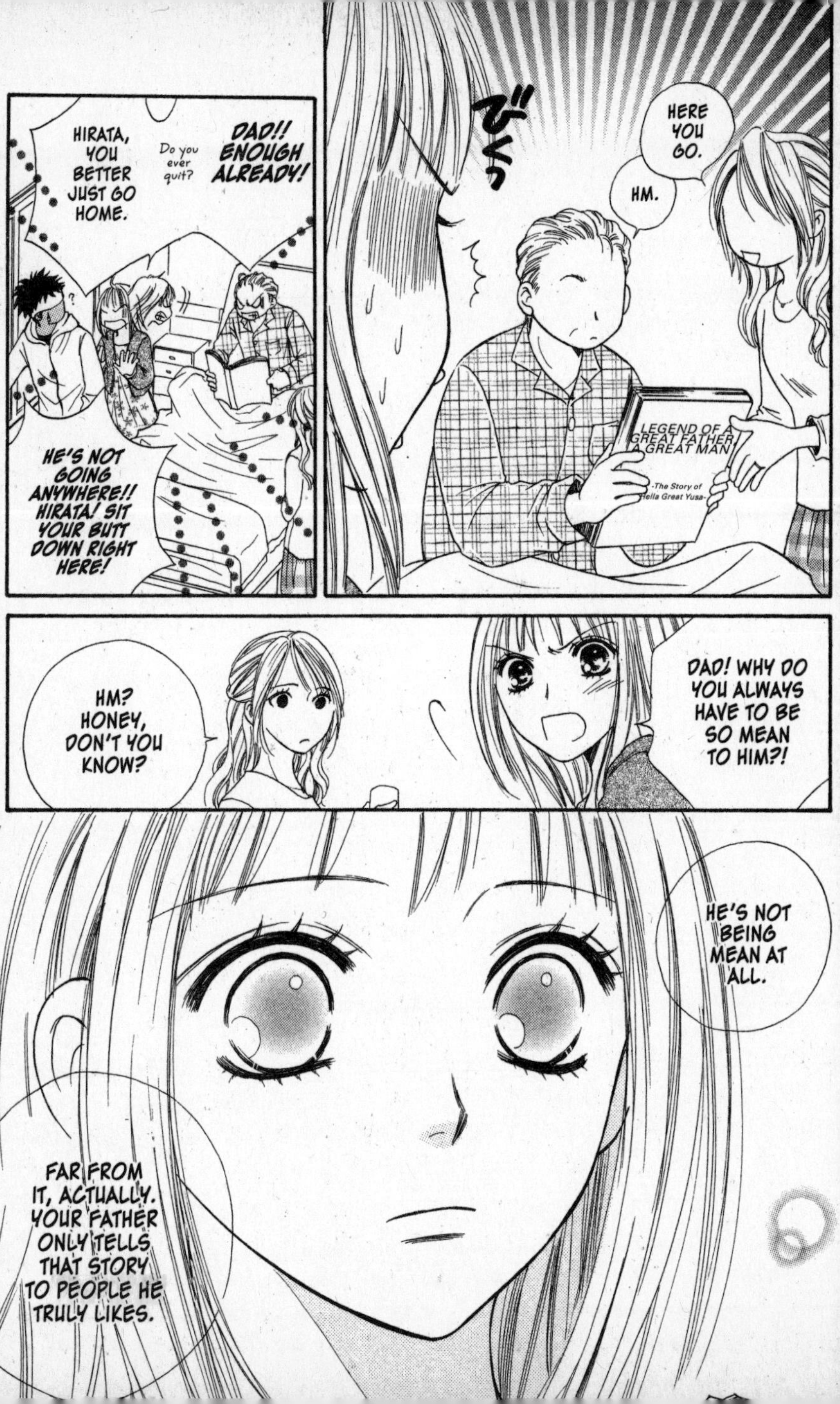
HERE YOU GO.
HM.
びくっ
LEGEND OF A GREAT FATHER A GREAT MAN
-The Story of Hella Great Yusa-
DAD!! ENOUGH ALREADY!
Do you ever quit?
HIRATA, YOU BETTER JUST GO HOME.
HE'S NOT GOING ANYWHERE!! HIRATA! SIT YOUR BUTT DOWN RIGHT HERE!
DAD! WHY DO YOU ALWAYS HAVE TO BE SO MEAN TO HIM?!
HM? HONEY, DON'T YOU KNOW?
HE'S NOT BEING MEAN AT ALL.
FAR FROM IT, ACTUALLY. YOUR FATHER ONLY TELLS THAT STORY TO PEOPLE HE TRULY LIKES.

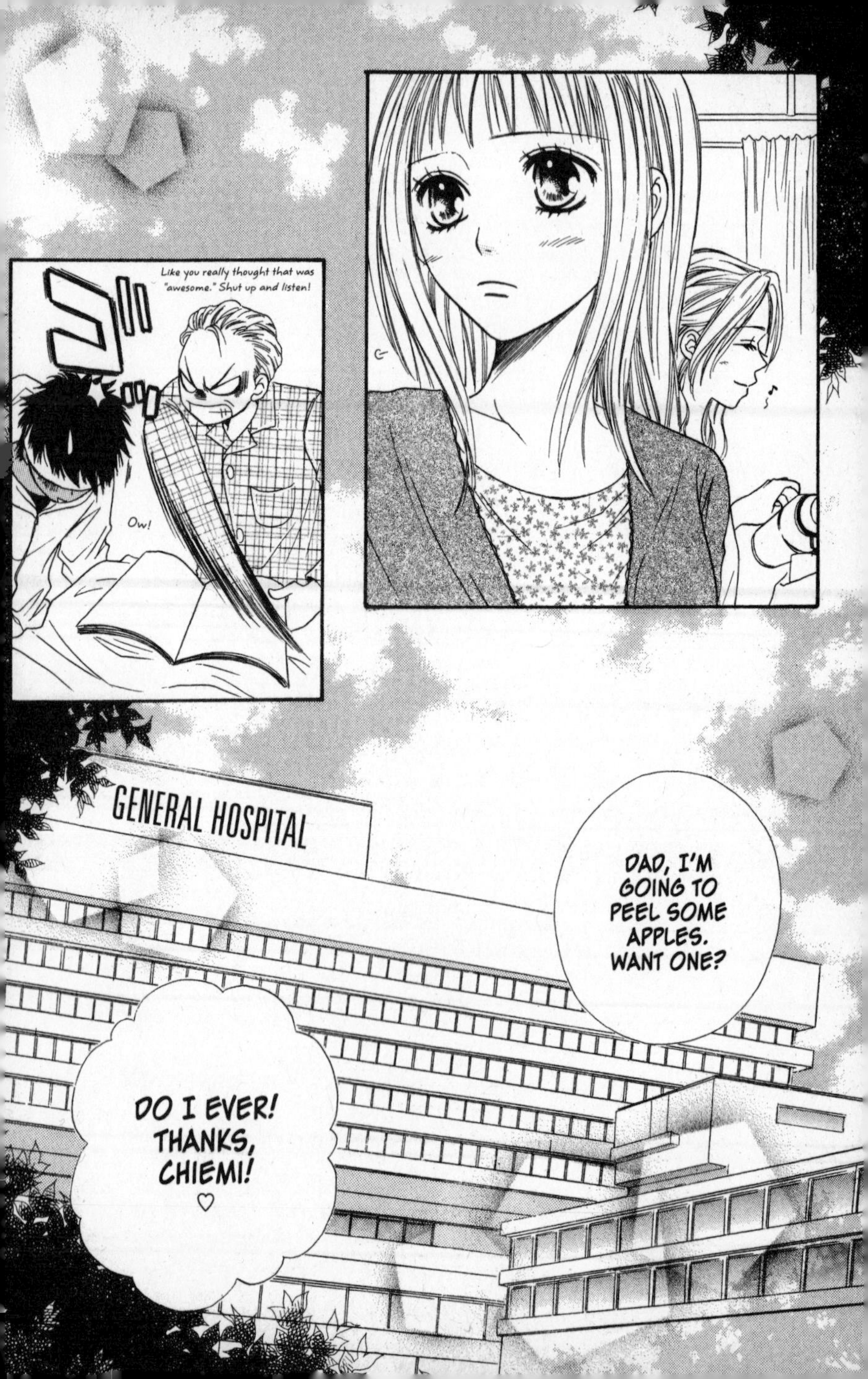
Like you really thought that was "awesome." Shut up and listen!
Ow!
DAD, I'M GOING TO PEEL SOME APPLES. WANT ONE?
GENERAL HOSPITAL
DO I EVER! THANKS, CHIEMI! ♡

Ch. 5 Platonic 'Til the End?!

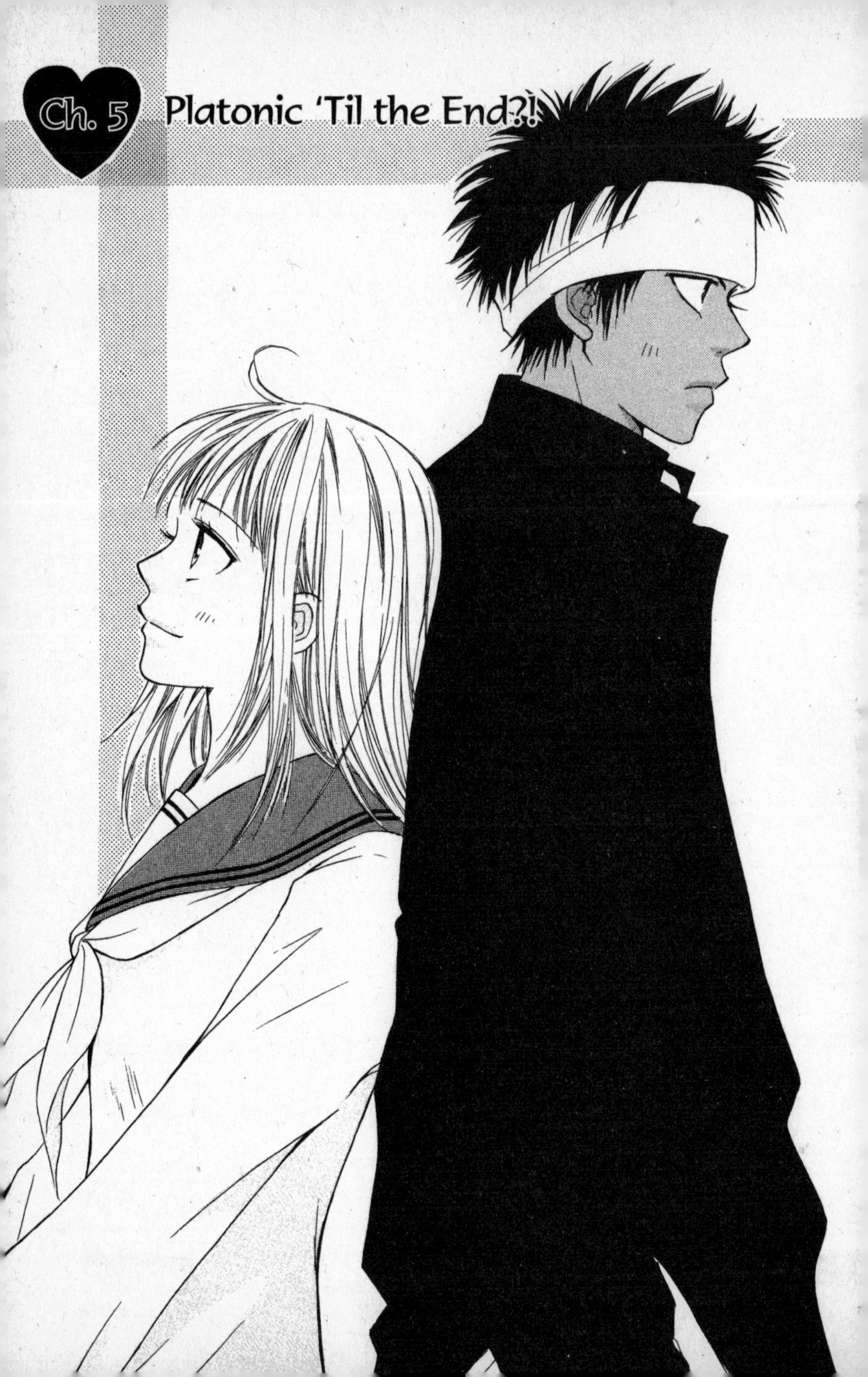

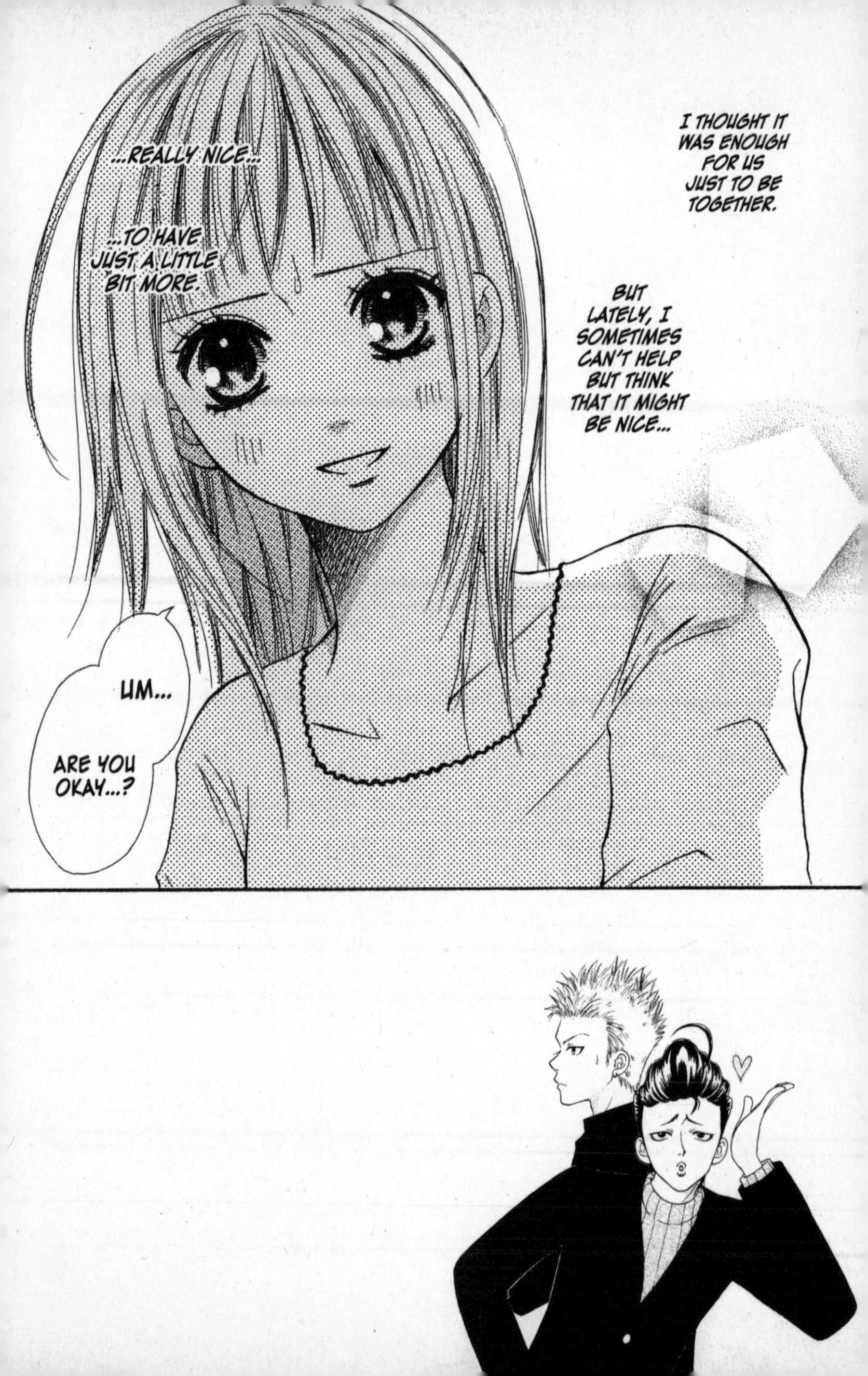
I THOUGHT IT WAS ENOUGH FOR US JUST TO BE TOGETHER.
BUT LATELY, I SOMETIMES CAN'T HELP BUT THINK THAT IT MIGHT BE NICE...
...REALLY NICE...
...TO HAVE JUST A LITTLE BIT MORE.
UM...
ARE YOU OKAY...?

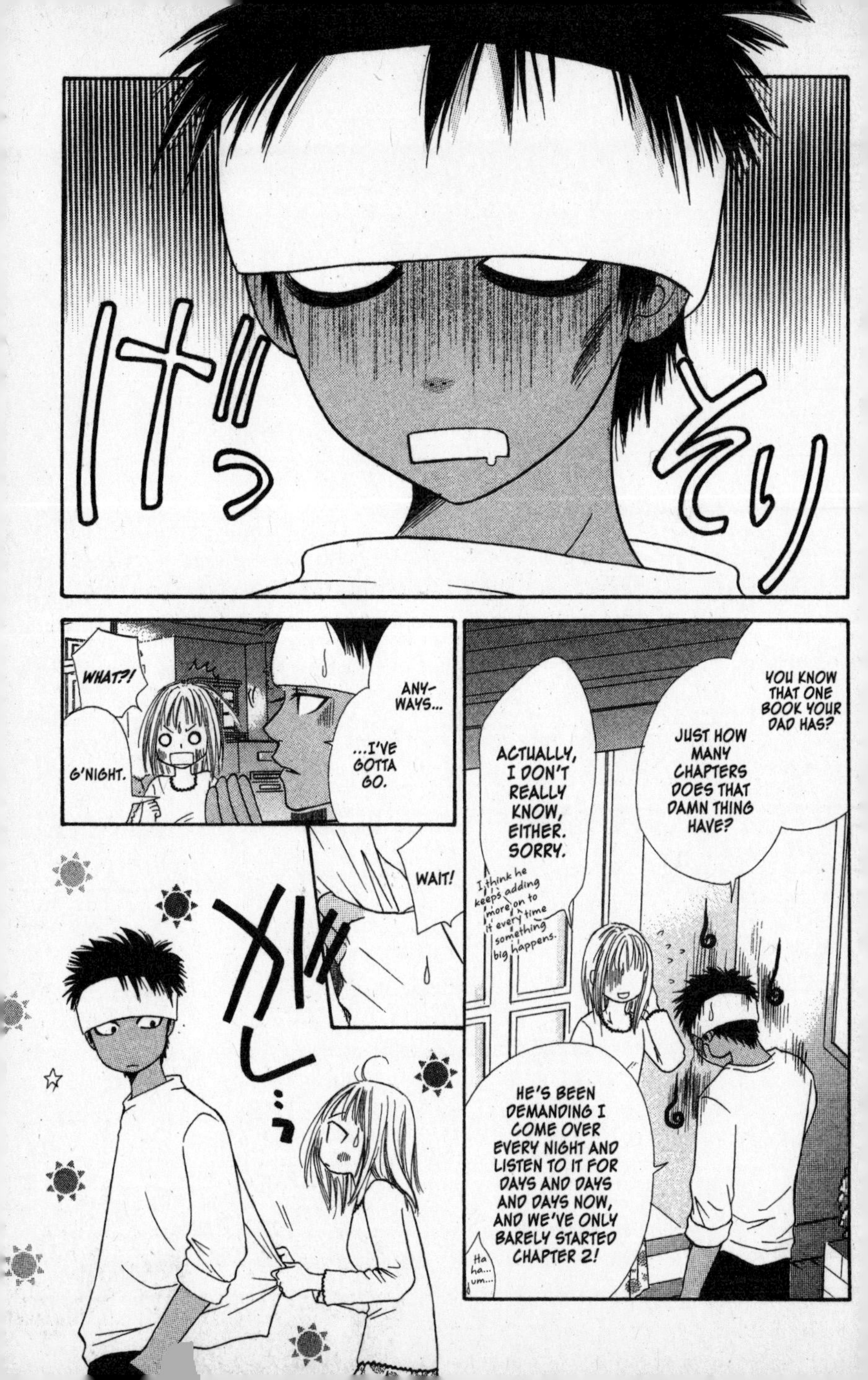
げっそり
YOU KNOW THAT ONE BOOK YOUR DAD HAS?
JUST HOW MANY CHAPTERS DOES THAT DAMN THING HAVE?
ACTUALLY, I DON'T REALLY KNOW, EITHER. SORRY.
I think he keeps adding more on to it every time something big happens.
HE'S BEEN DEMANDING I COME OVER EVERY NIGHT AND LISTEN TO IT FOR DAYS AND DAYS AND DAYS NOW, AND WE'VE ONLY BARELY STARTED CHAPTER 2!
Ha ha... um...
ANY-WAYS...
...I'VE GOTTA GO.
WHAT?!
G'NIGHT.
WAIT!
ガしっ

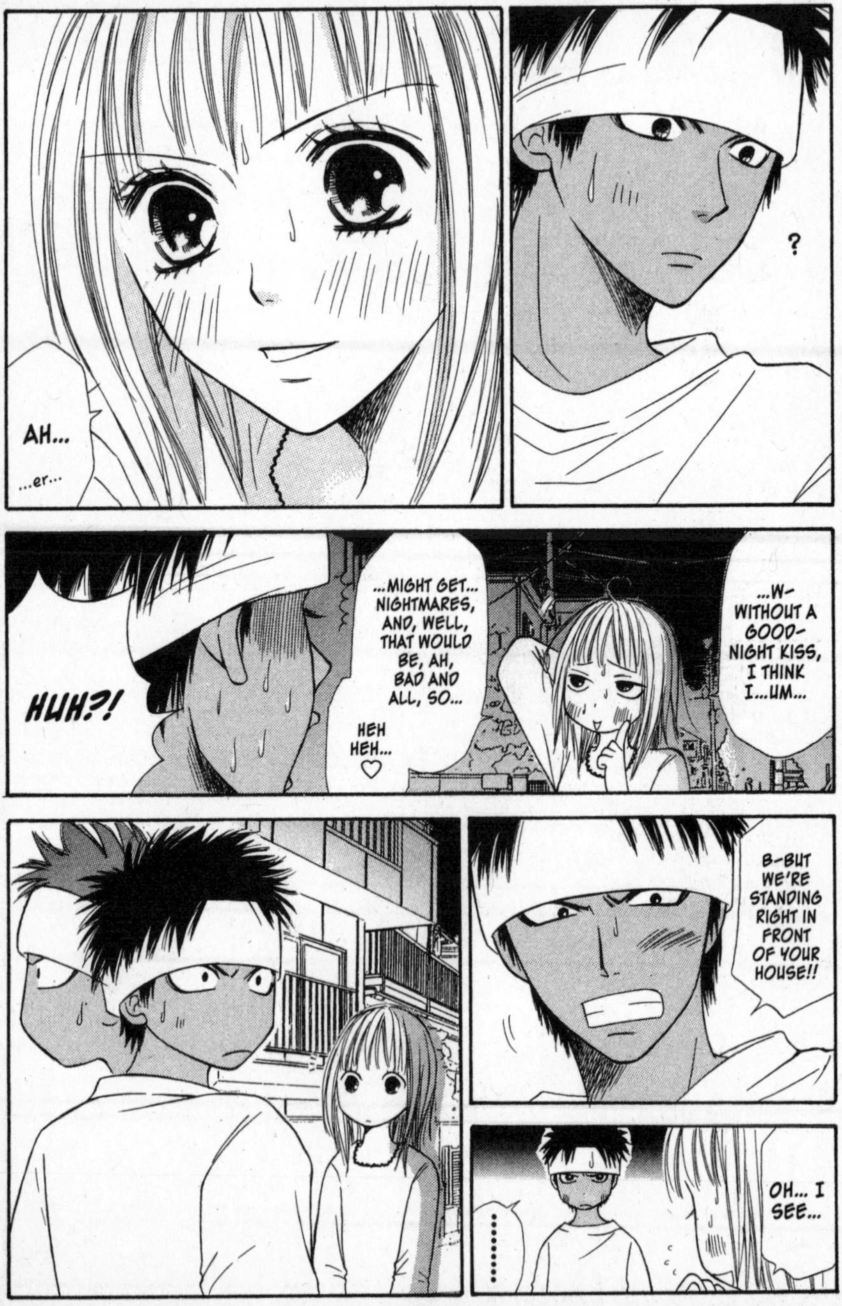
?
AH...
...er...
...W-WITHOUT A GOOD-NIGHT KISS, I THINK I...UM...
...MIGHT GET... NIGHTMARES, AND, WELL, THAT WOULD BE, AH, BAD AND ALL, SO...
HEH HEH... ♡
HUH?!
B-BUT WE'RE STANDING RIGHT IN FRONT OF YOUR HOUSE!!
OH... I SEE...
....

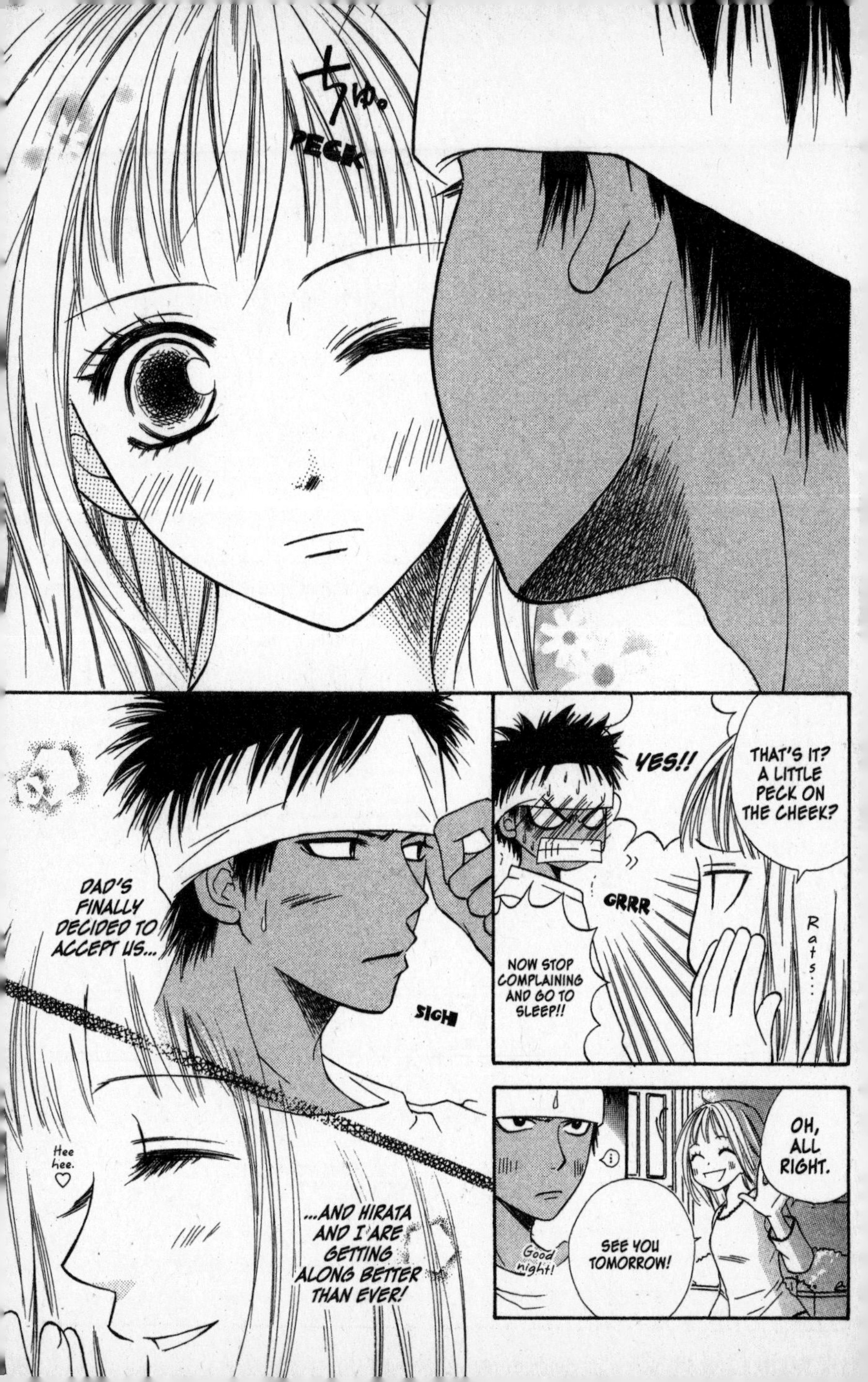
ちゅ。
PECK
THAT'S IT? A LITTLE PECK ON THE CHEEK?
Rats...
YES!!
GRRR
NOW STOP COMPLAINING AND GO TO SLEEP!!
OH, ALL RIGHT.
SEE YOU TOMORROW!
Good night!
DAD'S FINALLY DECIDED TO ACCEPT US...
SIGH
Hee hee. ♡
...AND HIRATA AND I ARE GETTING ALONG BETTER THAN EVER!

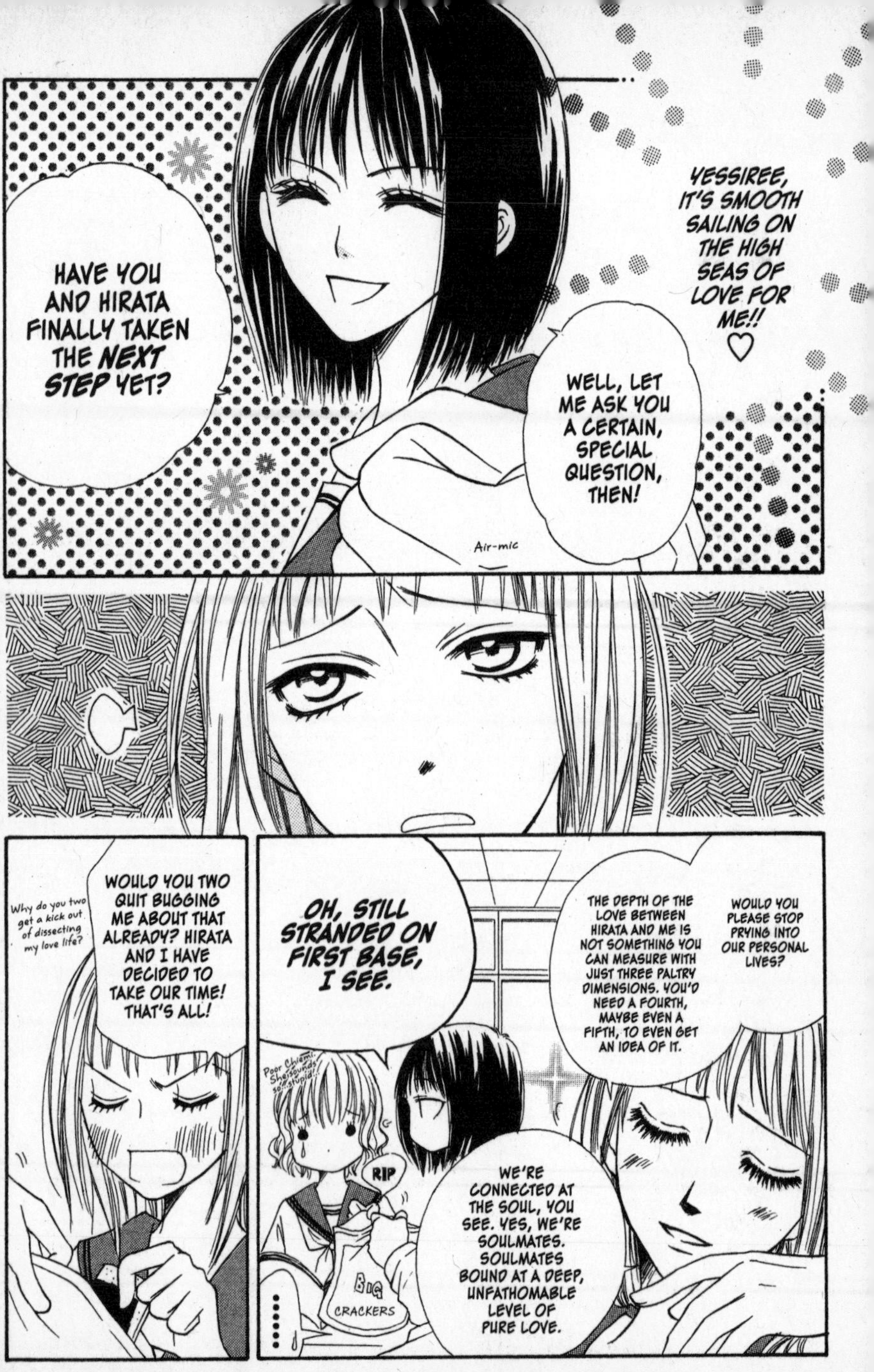
YESSIREE, IT'S SMOOTH SAILING ON THE HIGH SEAS OF LOVE FOR ME!! ♡
WELL, LET ME ASK YOU A CERTAIN, SPECIAL QUESTION, THEN!
HAVE YOU AND HIRATA FINALLY TAKEN THE NEXT STEP YET?
Air-mic
WOULD YOU PLEASE STOP PRYING INTO OUR PERSONAL LIVES?
THE DEPTH OF THE LOVE BETWEEN HIRATA AND ME IS NOT SOMETHING YOU CAN MEASURE WITH JUST THREE PALTRY DIMENSIONS. YOU'D NEED A FOURTH, MAYBE EVEN A FIFTH, TO EVEN GET AN IDEA OF IT.
OH, STILL STRANDED ON FIRST BASE, I SEE.
WE'RE CONNECTED AT THE SOUL, YOU SEE. YES, WE'RE SOULMATES. SOULMATES BOUND AT A DEEP, UNFATHOMABLE LEVEL OF PURE LOVE.
Poor Chiemi. She sounds so... stupid...
RIP
BIG
CRACKERS
......
WOULD YOU TWO QUIT BUGGING ME ABOUT THAT ALREADY? HIRATA AND I HAVE DECIDED TO TAKE OUR TIME! THAT'S ALL!
Why do you two get a kick out of dissecting my love life?

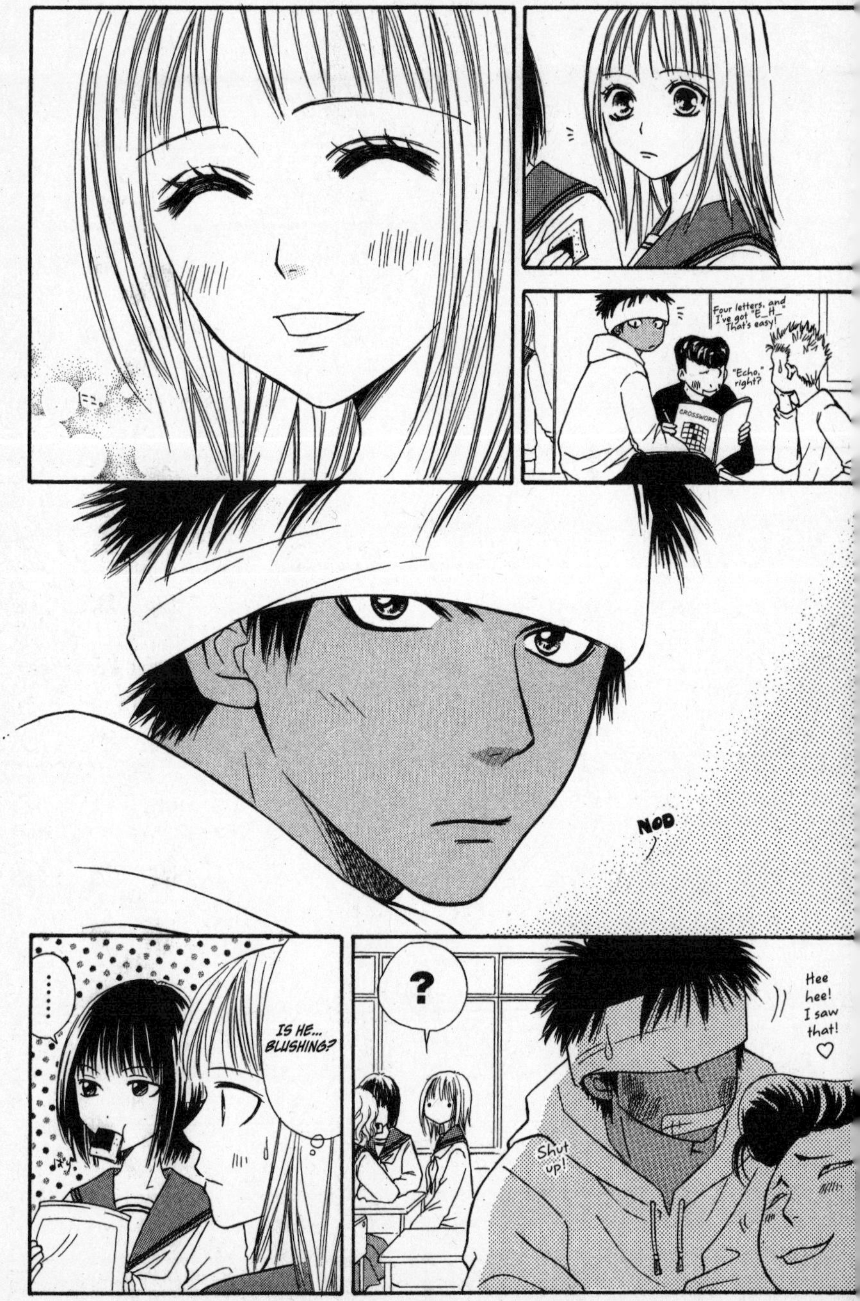

Four letters, and I've got "E_H_" That's easy!
"Echo," right?
CROSSWORD
NOD
Hee hee! I saw that! ♡
Shut up!
?
IS HE... BLUSHING?
......

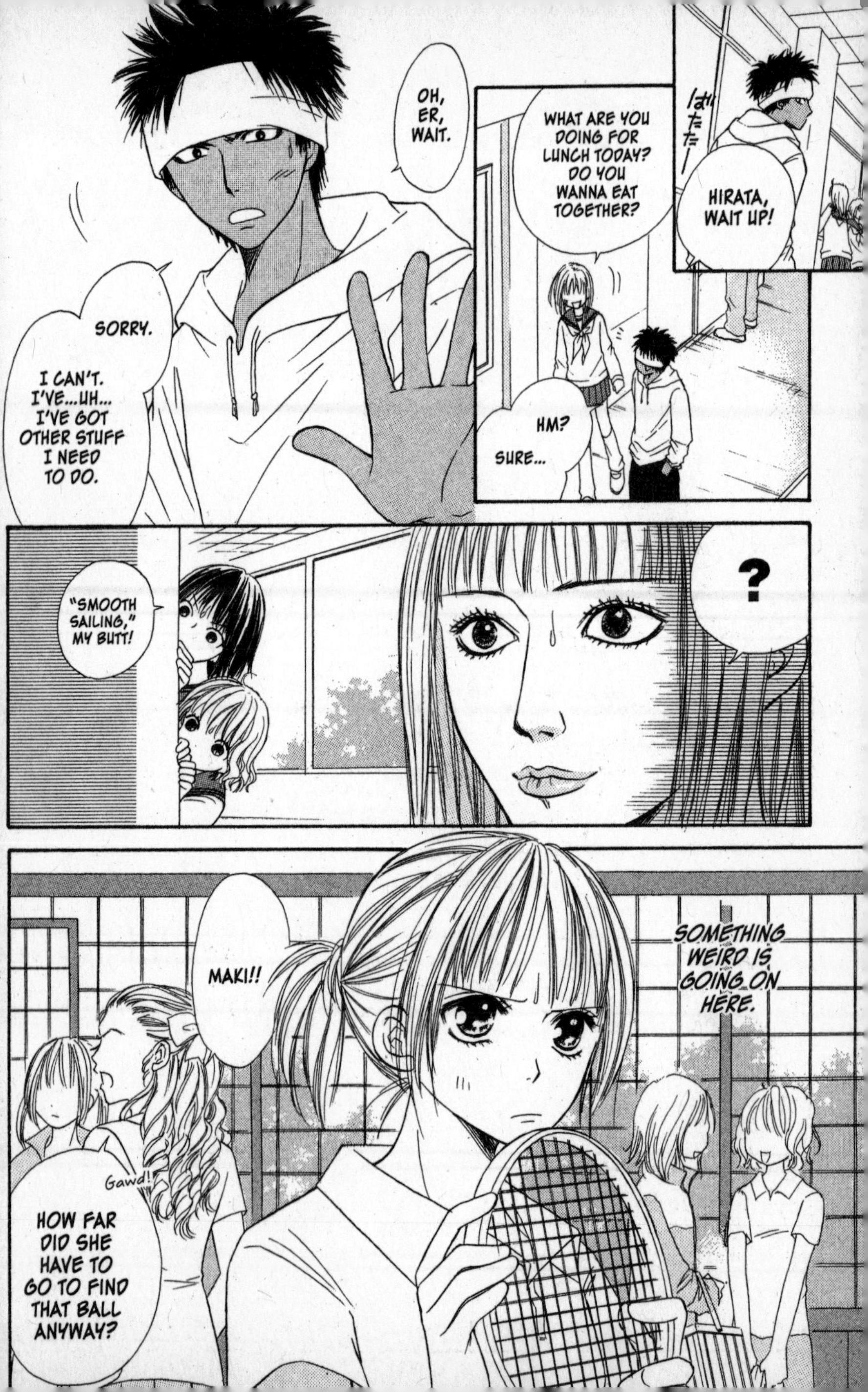
HIRATA, WAIT UP!
WHAT ARE YOU DOING FOR LUNCH TODAY? DO YOU WANNA EAT TOGETHER?
HM?
SURE...
OH, ER, WAIT.
SORRY.
I CAN'T. I'VE...UH... I'VE GOT OTHER STUFF I NEED TO DO.
?
"SMOOTH SAILING," MY BUTT!
SOMETHING WEIRD IS GOING ON HERE.
MAKI!!
Gawd!!
HOW FAR DID SHE HAVE TO GO TO FIND THAT BALL ANYWAY?

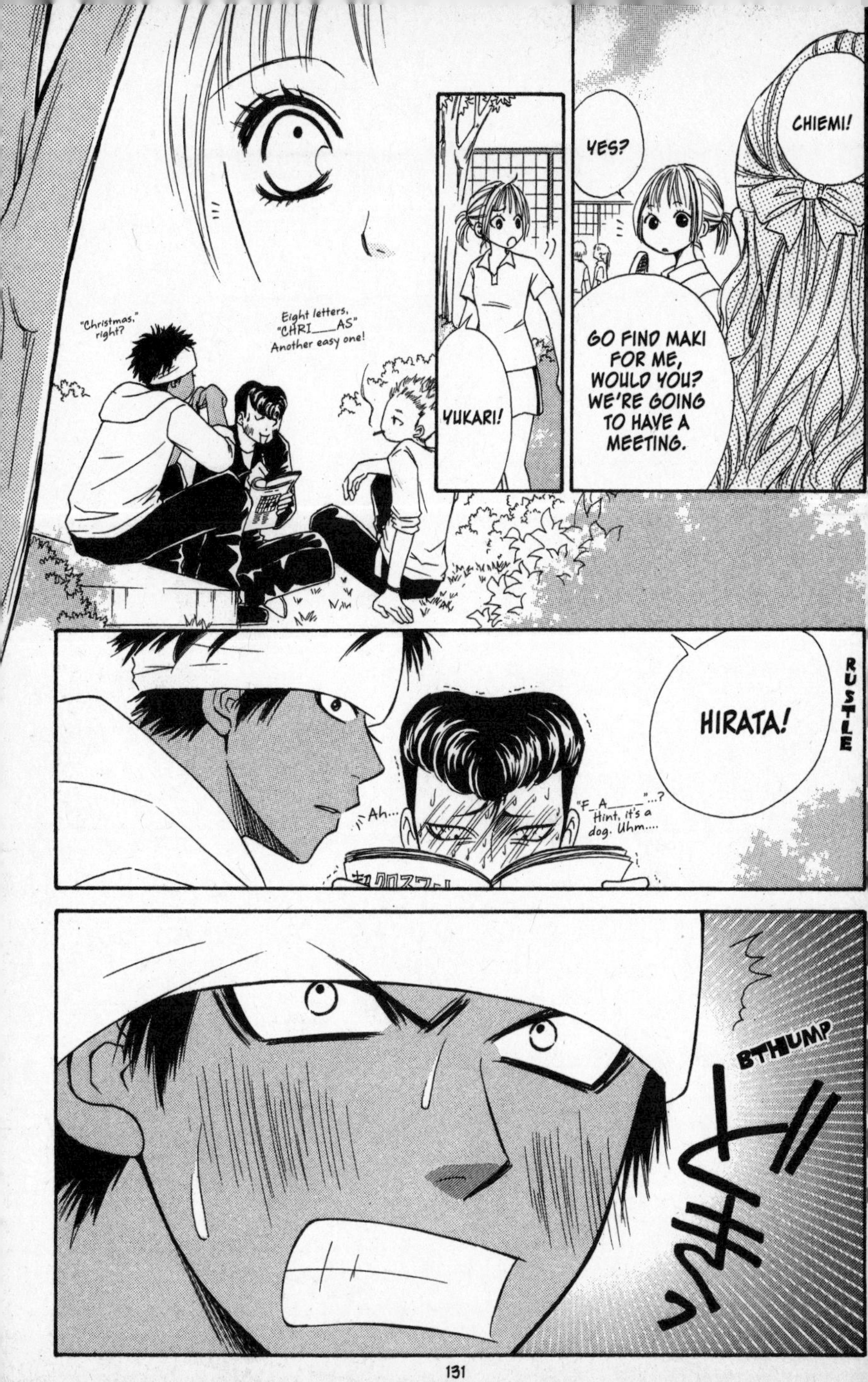

CHIEMI!
YES?
GO FIND MAKI FOR ME, WOULD YOU? WE'RE GOING TO HAVE A MEETING.
YUKARI!
Eight letters, "CHRI___AS" Another easy one!
"Christmas," right?
HIRATA!
RUSTLE
"F_A____"...? Hint, it's a dog. Uhm....
Ah...
BTHUMP

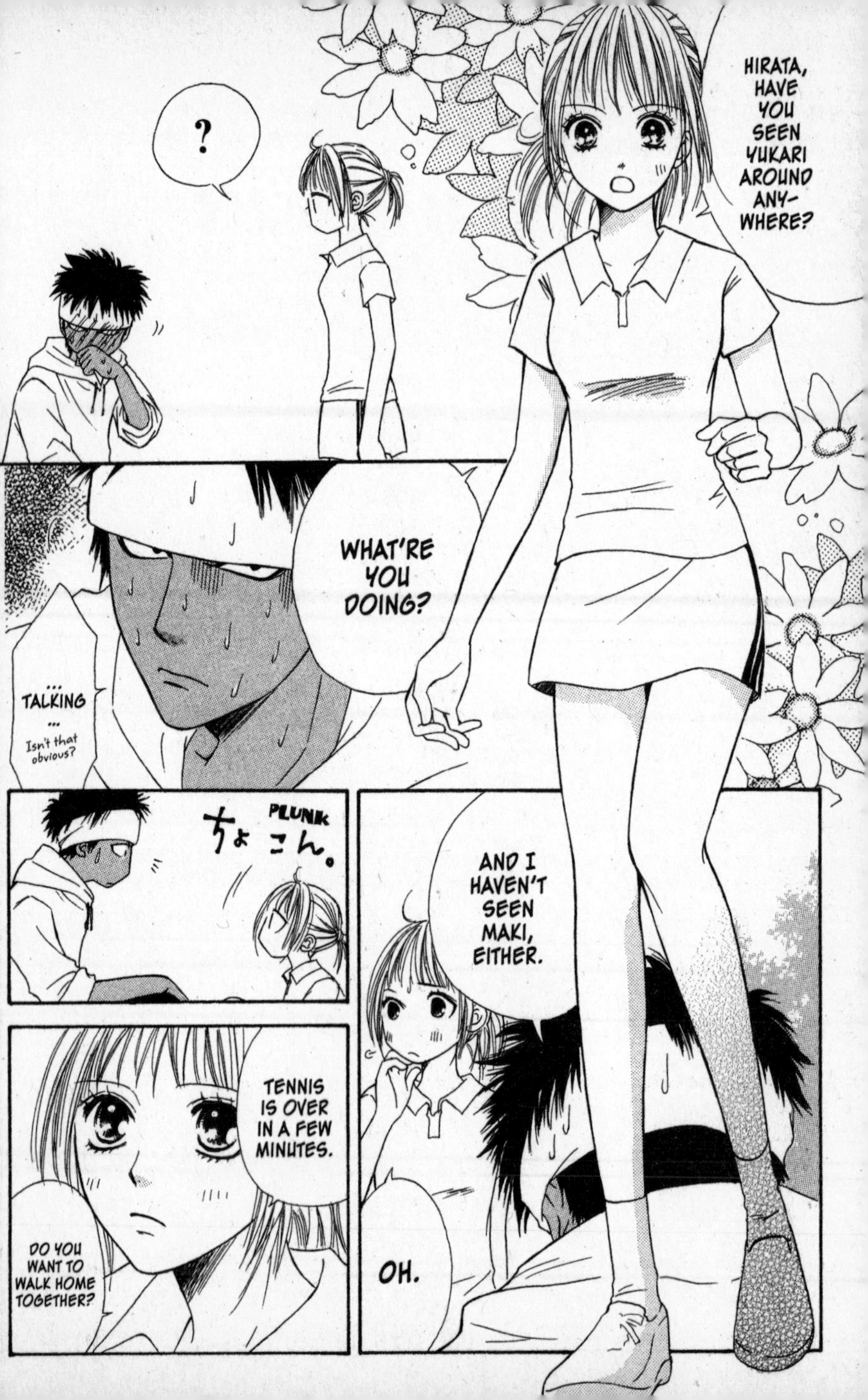
HIRATA, HAVE YOU SEEN YUKARI AROUND ANY-WHERE?
?
WHAT'RE YOU DOING?
... TALKING ... Isn't that obvious?
AND I HAVEN'T SEEN MAKI, EITHER.
OH.
PLUNK
ちょこん。
TENNIS IS OVER IN A FEW MINUTES.
DO YOU WANT TO WALK HOME TOGETHER?

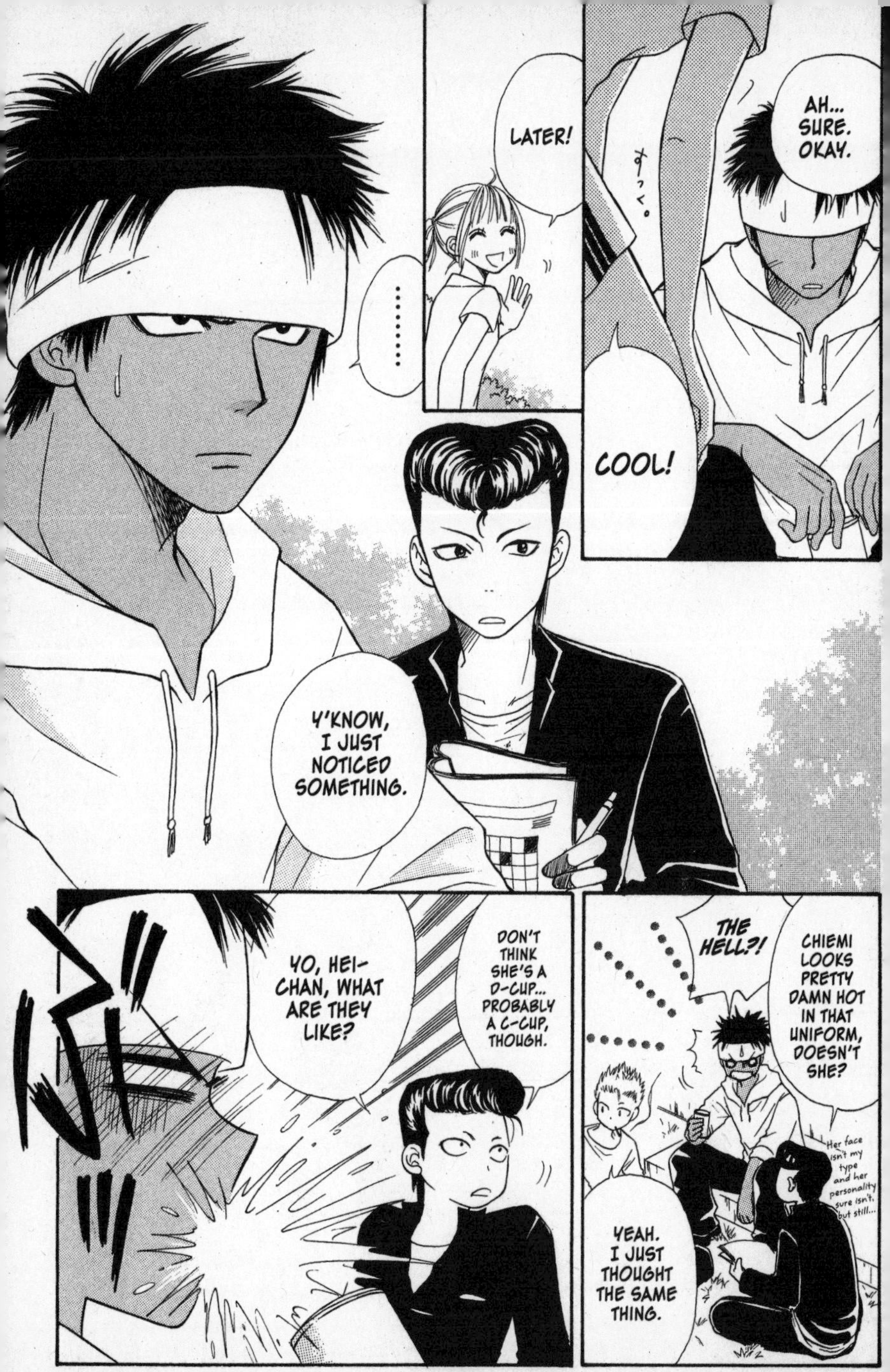
AH... SURE. OKAY.
すっく。
COOL!
LATER!
......
Y'KNOW, I JUST NOTICED SOMETHING.
CHIEMI LOOKS PRETTY DAMN HOT IN THAT UNIFORM, DOESN'T SHE?
THE HELL?!
......
YEAH. I JUST THOUGHT THE SAME THING.
Her face isn't my type and her personality sure isn't, but still...
DON'T THINK SHE'S A D-CUP... PROBABLY A C-CUP, THOUGH.
YO, HEI-CHAN, WHAT ARE THEY LIKE?

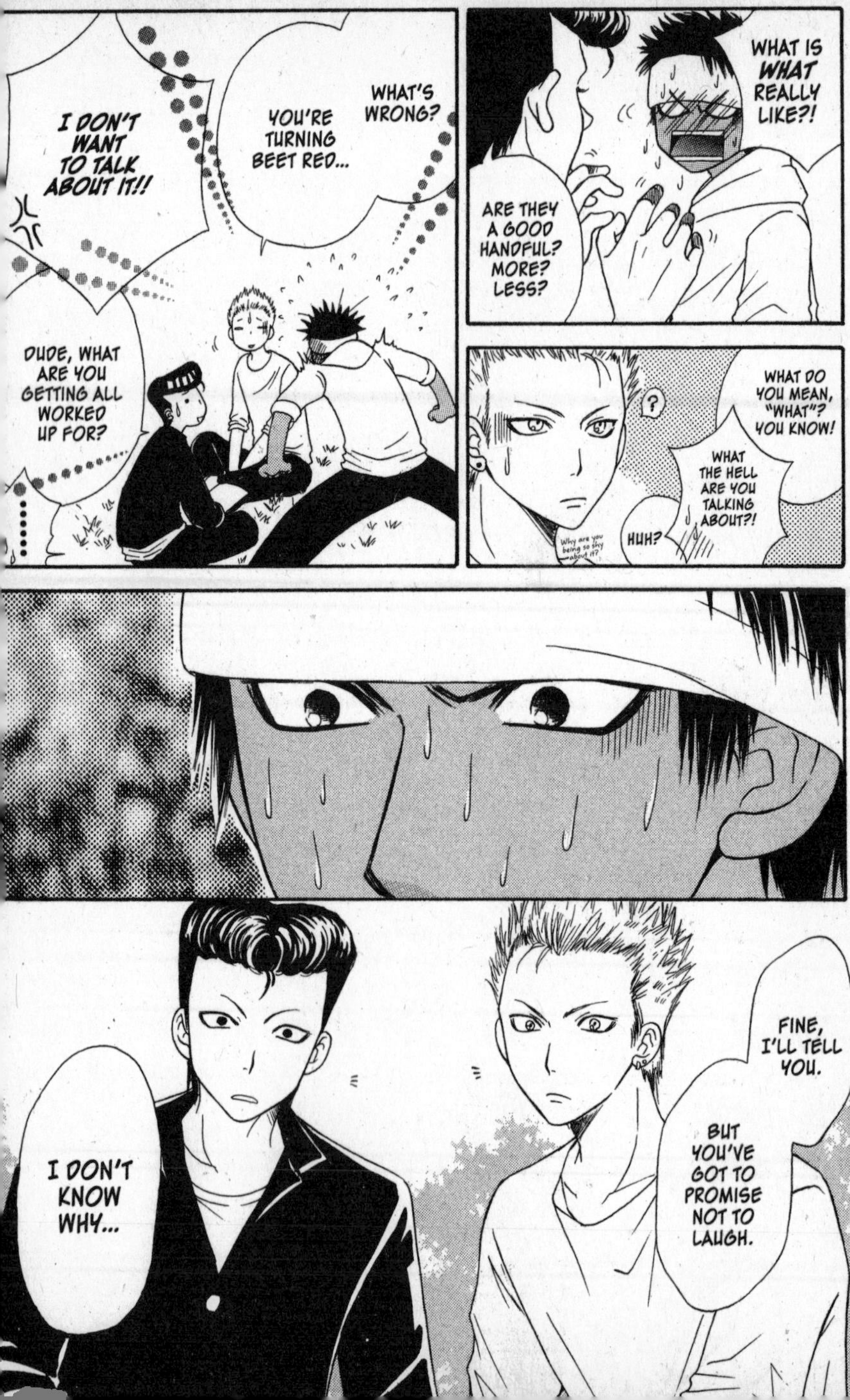
WHAT IS WHAT REALLY LIKE?!
ARE THEY A GOOD HANDFUL? MORE? LESS?
WHAT DO YOU MEAN, "WHAT"? YOU KNOW!
WHAT THE HELL ARE YOU TALKING ABOUT?!
HUH?
Why are you being so shy about it?
WHAT'S WRONG?
YOU'RE TURNING BEET RED...
I DON'T WANT TO TALK ABOUT IT!!
DUDE, WHAT ARE YOU GETTING ALL WORKED UP FOR?
FINE, I'LL TELL YOU.
BUT YOU'VE GOT TO PROMISE NOT TO LAUGH.
I DON'T KNOW WHY...

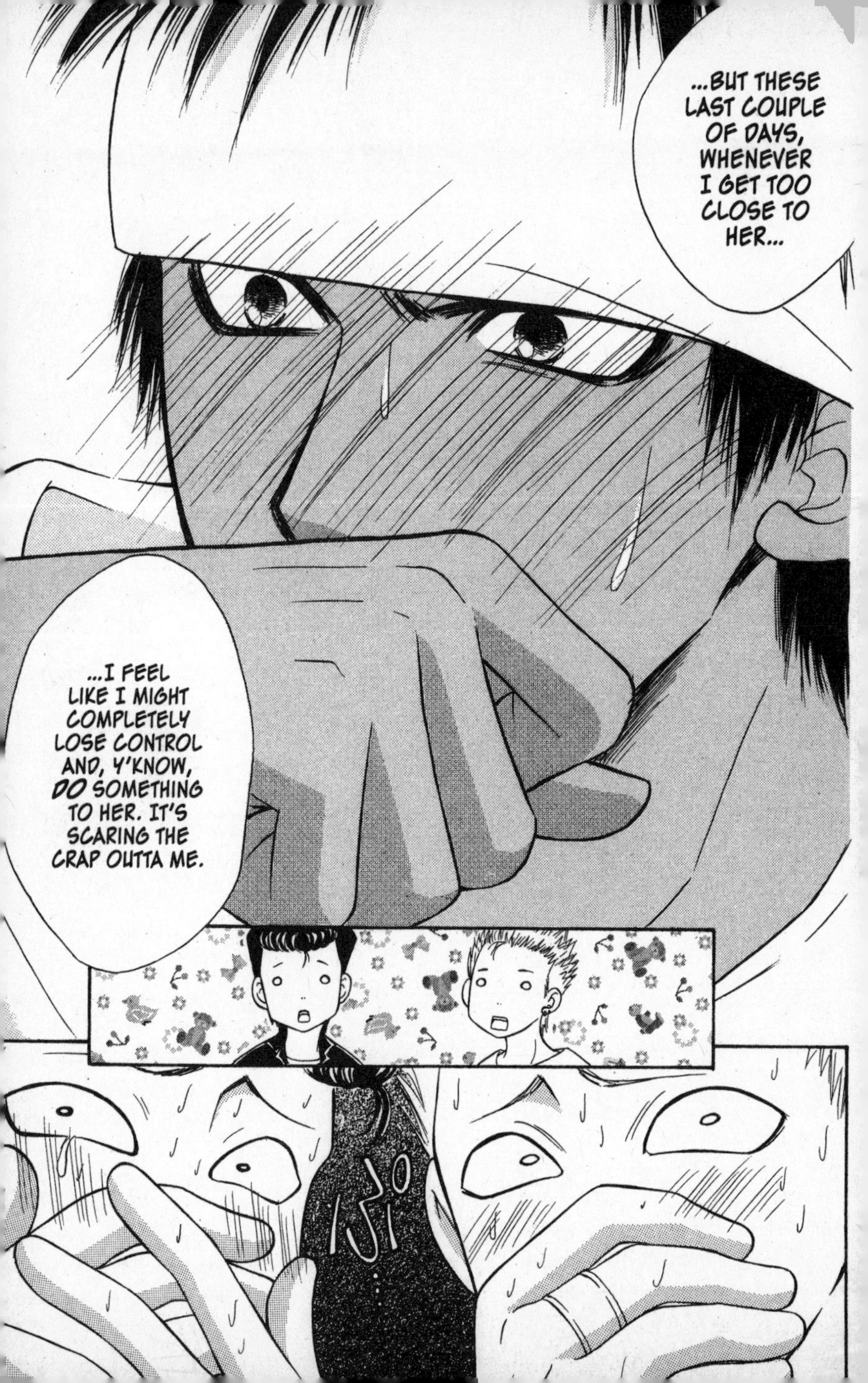
...BUT THESE LAST COUPLE OF DAYS, WHENEVER I GET TOO CLOSE TO HER...
...I FEEL LIKE I MIGHT COMPLETELY LOSE CONTROL AND, Y'KNOW, DO SOMETHING TO HER. IT'S SCARING THE CRAP OUTTA ME.

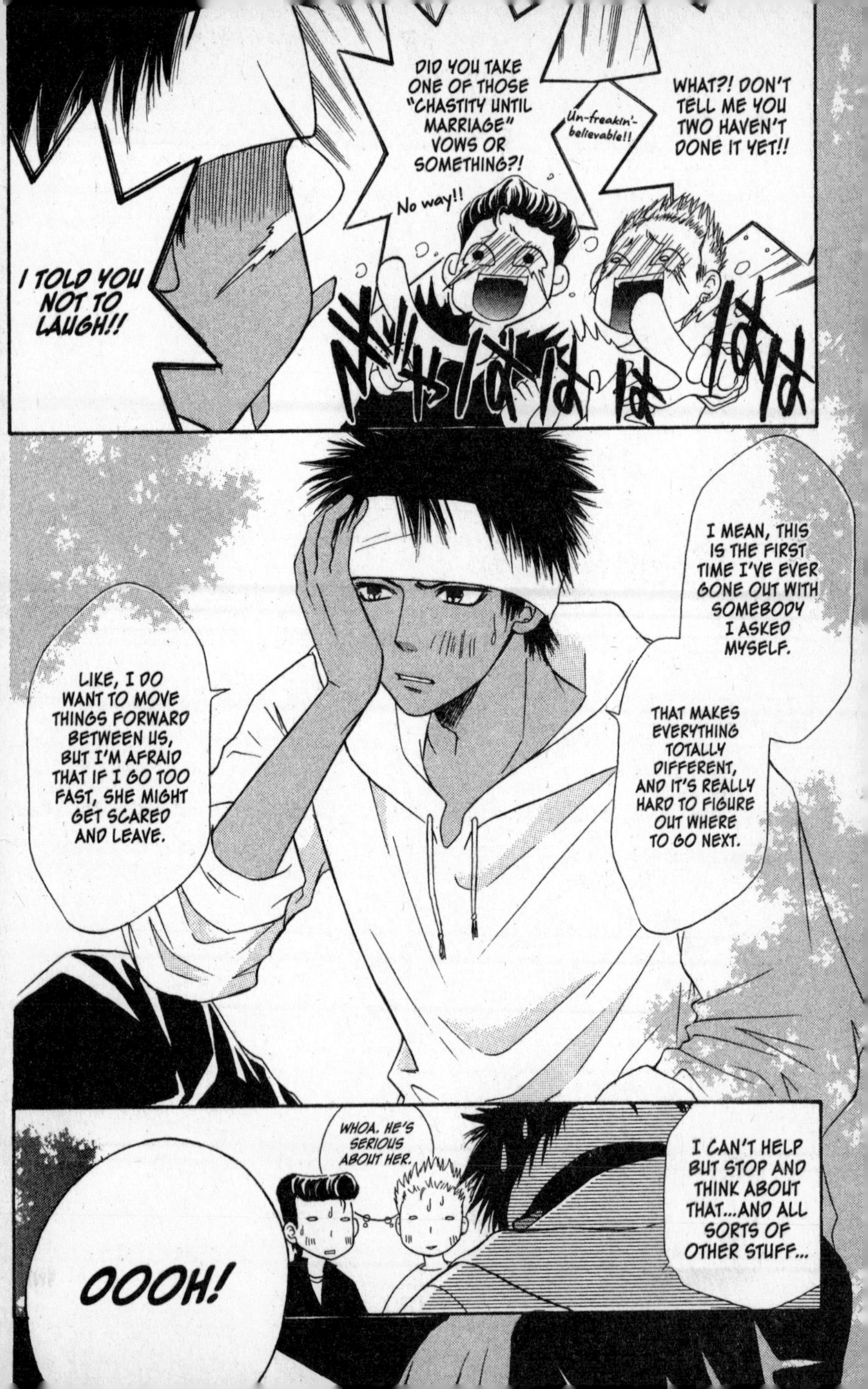
WHAT?! DON'T TELL ME YOU TWO HAVEN'T DONE IT YET!!
Un-freakin'-believable!!
DID YOU TAKE ONE OF THOSE "CHASTITY UNTIL MARRIAGE" VOWS OR SOMETHING?!
No way!!
ぎゃははは は はは
I TOLD YOU NOT TO LAUGH!!
I MEAN, THIS IS THE FIRST TIME I'VE EVER GONE OUT WITH SOMEBODY I ASKED MYSELF.
THAT MAKES EVERYTHING TOTALLY DIFFERENT, AND IT'S REALLY HARD TO FIGURE OUT WHERE TO GO NEXT.
LIKE, I DO WANT TO MOVE THINGS FORWARD BETWEEN US, BUT I'M AFRAID THAT IF I GO TOO FAST, SHE MIGHT GET SCARED AND LEAVE.
I CAN'T HELP BUT STOP AND THINK ABOUT THAT...AND ALL SORTS OF OTHER STUFF...
WHOA. HE'S SERIOUS ABOUT HER.
OOOH!

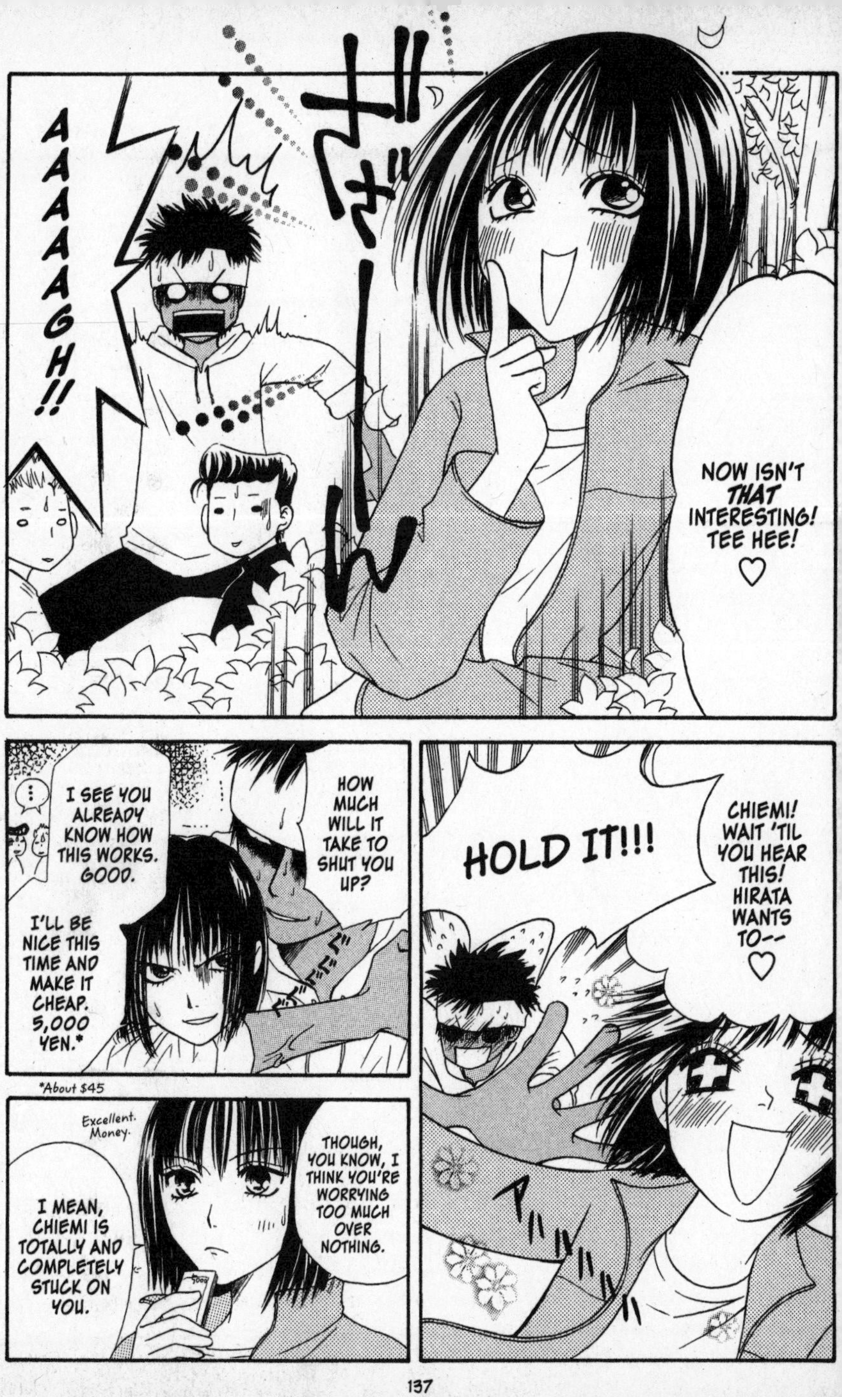
AAAAAAAGH!!
NOW ISN'T *THAT* INTERESTING! TEE HEE! ♡
HOLD IT!!!
CHIEMI! WAIT 'TIL YOU HEAR THIS! HIRATA WANTS TO-- ♡
HOW MUCH WILL IT TAKE TO SHUT YOU UP?
I SEE YOU ALREADY KNOW HOW THIS WORKS. GOOD.
...
I'LL BE NICE THIS TIME AND MAKE IT CHEAP. 5,000 YEN.*
THOUGH, YOU KNOW, I THINK YOU'RE WORRYING TOO MUCH OVER NOTHING.
Excellent. Money.
I MEAN, CHIEMI IS TOTALLY AND COMPLETELY STUCK ON YOU.

*About $45

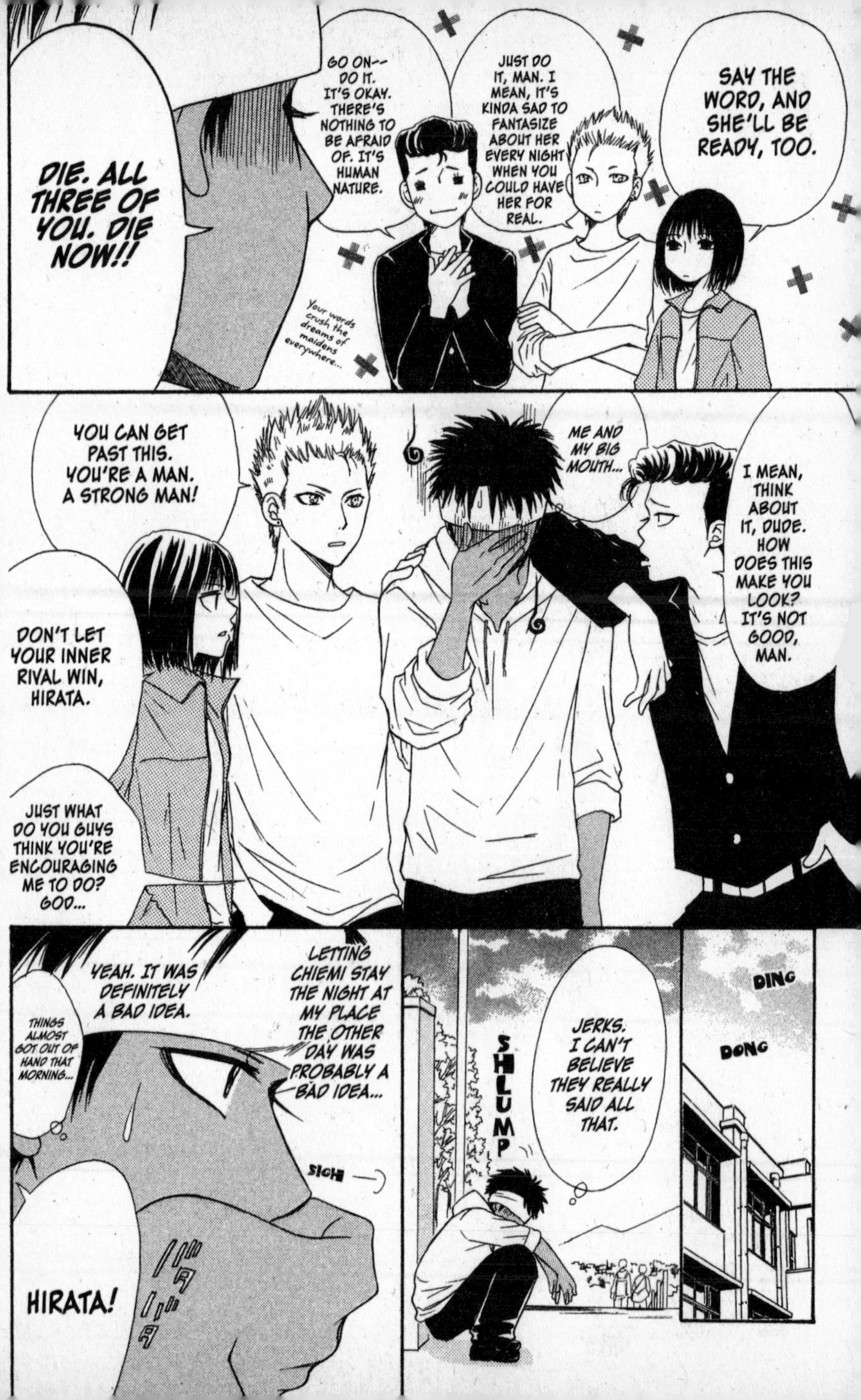
SAY THE WORD, AND SHE'LL BE READY, TOO.
JUST DO IT, MAN. I MEAN, IT'S KINDA SAD TO FANTASIZE ABOUT HER EVERY NIGHT WHEN YOU COULD HAVE HER FOR REAL.
GO ON-- DO IT. IT'S OKAY. THERE'S NOTHING TO BE AFRAID OF. IT'S HUMAN NATURE.
DIE. ALL THREE OF YOU. DIE NOW!!
Your words crush the dreams of maidens everywhere...
I MEAN, THINK ABOUT IT, DUDE. HOW DOES THIS MAKE YOU LOOK? IT'S NOT GOOD, MAN.
ME AND MY BIG MOUTH...
YOU CAN GET PAST THIS. YOU'RE A MAN. A STRONG MAN!
DON'T LET YOUR INNER RIVAL WIN, HIRATA.
JUST WHAT DO YOU GUYS THINK YOU'RE ENCOURAGING ME TO DO? GOD...
DING
DONG
JERKS. I CAN'T BELIEVE THEY REALLY SAID ALL THAT.
SHLUMP
SIGH
LETTING CHIEMI STAY THE NIGHT AT MY PLACE THE OTHER DAY WAS PROBABLY A BAD IDEA...
YEAH. IT WAS DEFINITELY A BAD IDEA.
THINGS ALMOST GOT OUT OF HAND THAT MORNING...
HIRATA!

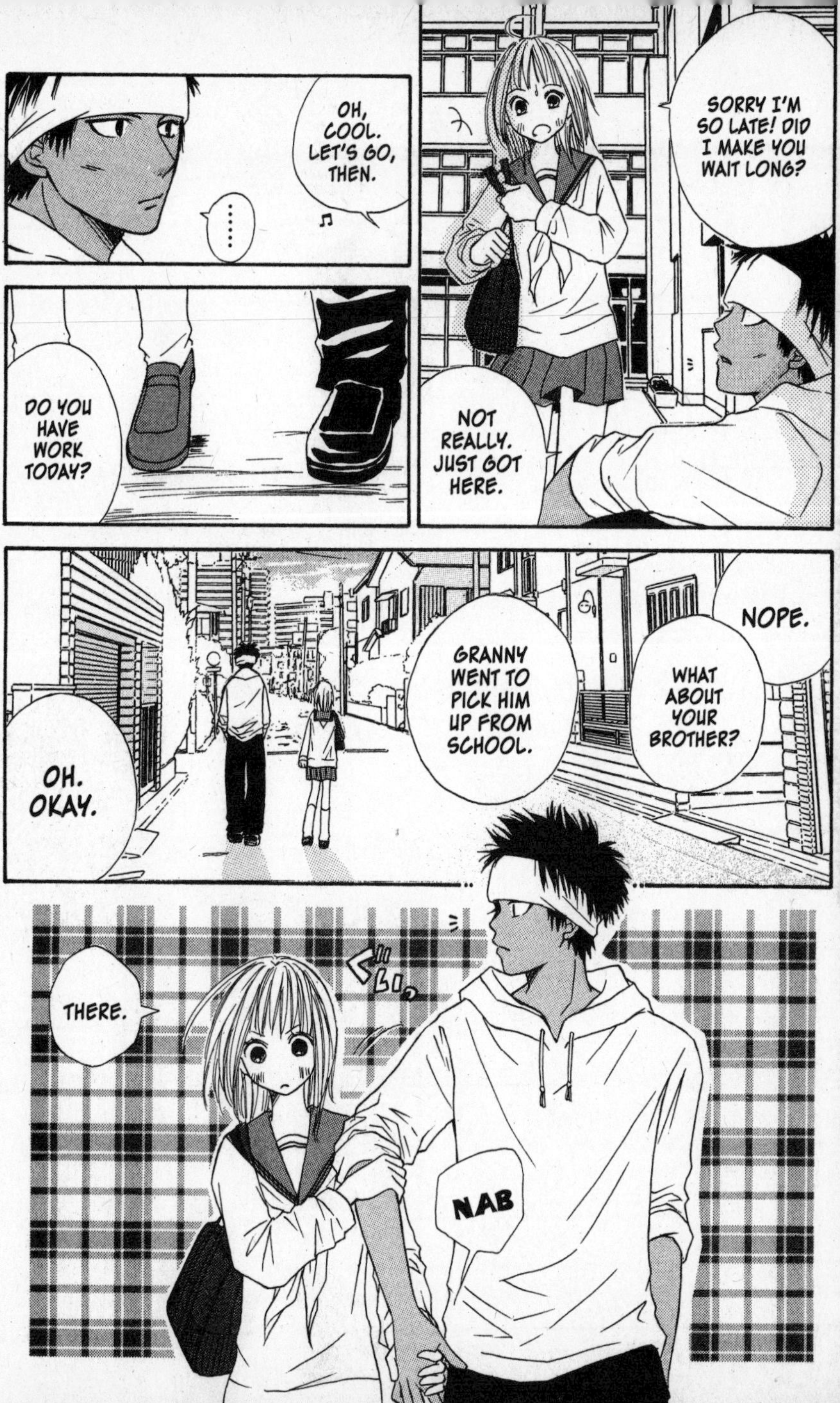
SORRY I'M SO LATE! DID I MAKE YOU WAIT LONG?
NOT REALLY. JUST GOT HERE.
OH, COOL. LET'S GO, THEN.
......
DO YOU HAVE WORK TODAY?
NOPE.
WHAT ABOUT YOUR BROTHER?
GRANNY WENT TO PICK HIM UP FROM SCHOOL.
OH. OKAY.
NAB
THERE.

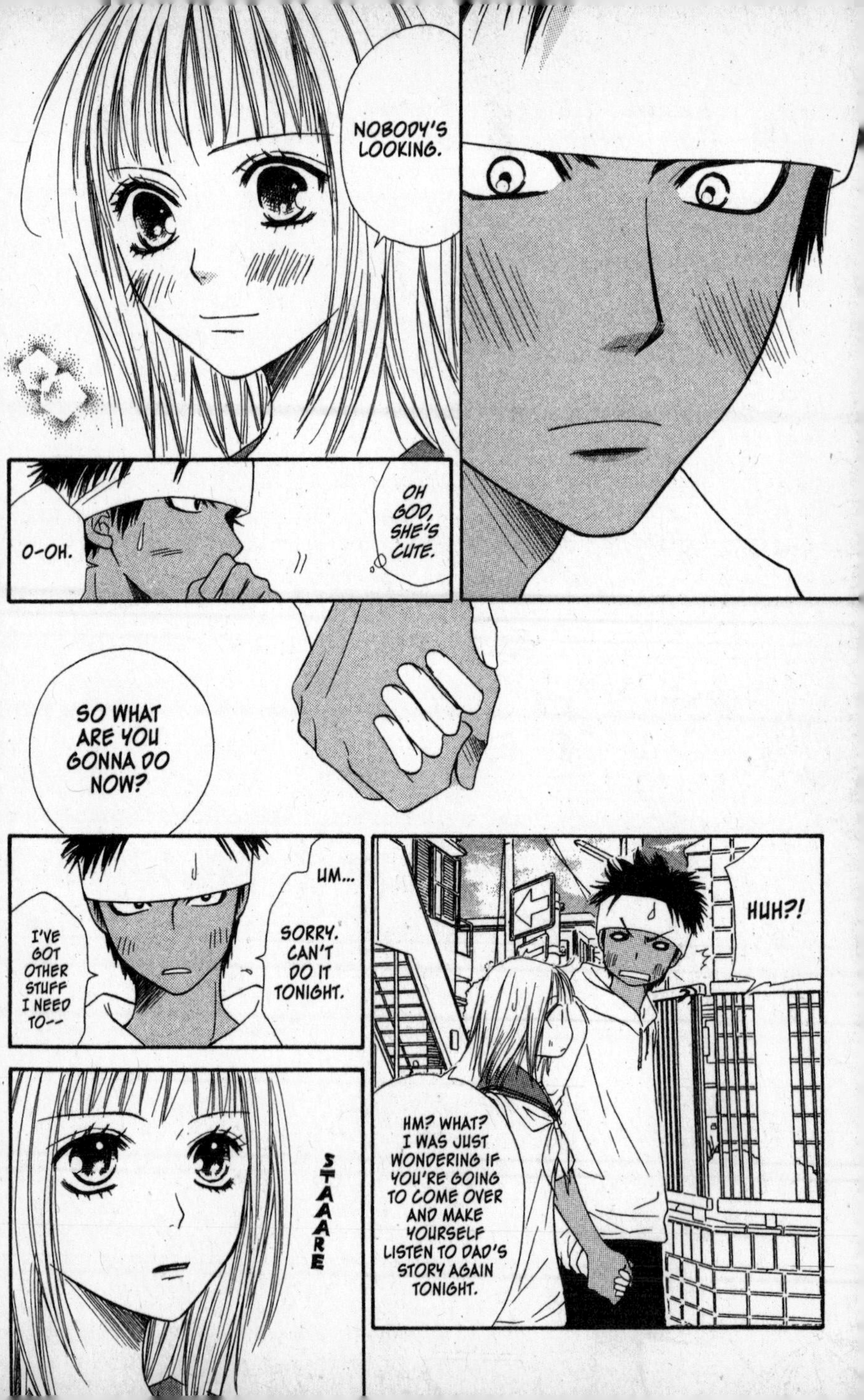
NOBODY'S LOOKING.
OH GOD, SHE'S CUTE.
O-OH.
SO WHAT ARE YOU GONNA DO NOW?
HUH?!
HM? WHAT? I WAS JUST WONDERING IF YOU'RE GOING TO COME OVER AND MAKE YOURSELF LISTEN TO DAD'S STORY AGAIN TONIGHT.
UM...
SORRY. CAN'T DO IT TONIGHT.
I'VE GOT OTHER STUFF I NEED TO--
STAAAARE

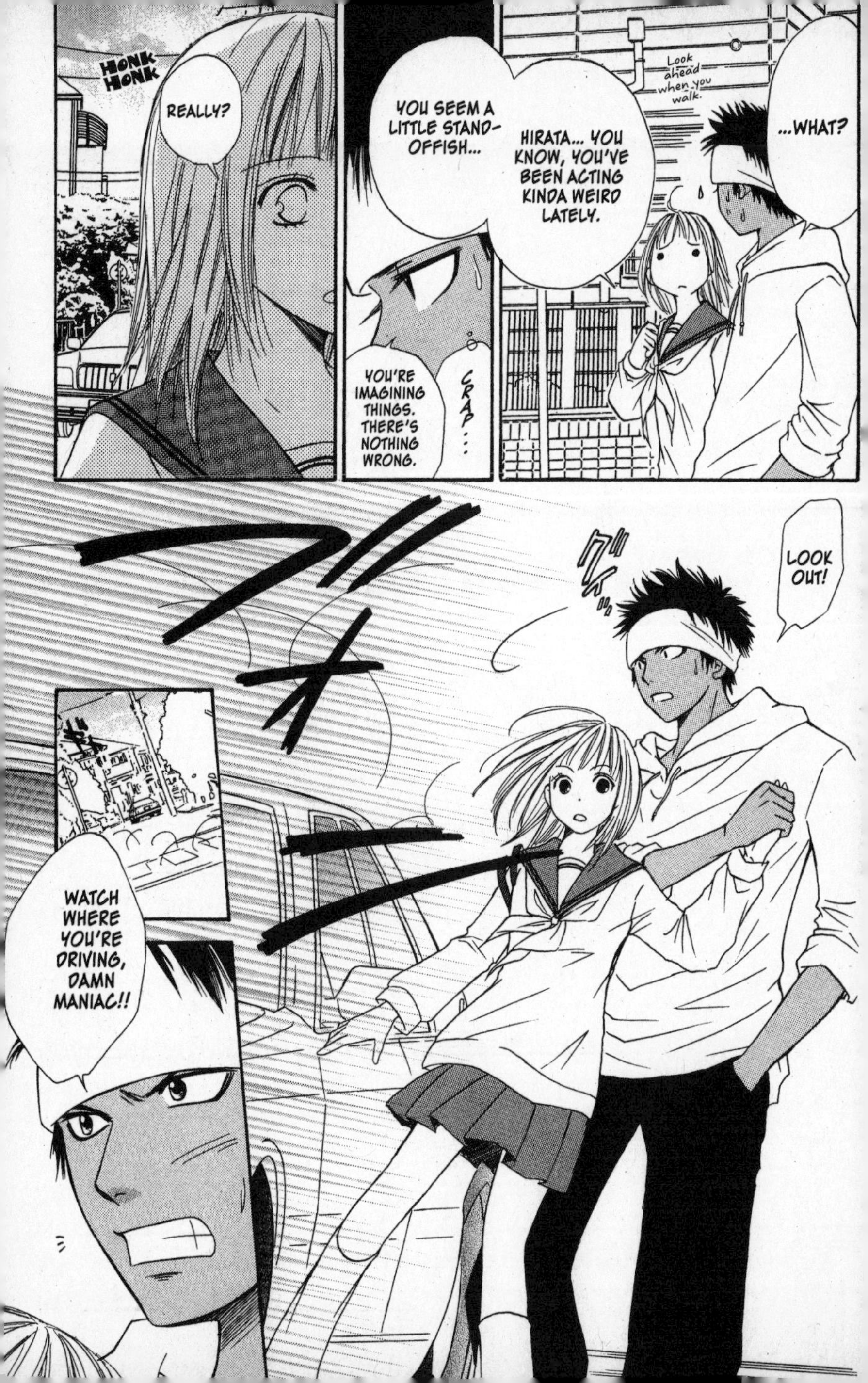
HIRATA... YOU KNOW, YOU'VE BEEN ACTING KINDA WEIRD LATELY.
...WHAT?
Look ahead when you walk.
YOU SEEM A LITTLE STAND-OFFISH...
YOU'RE IMAGINING THINGS. THERE'S NOTHING WRONG.
CRAP...
HONK HONK
REALLY?
LOOK OUT!
WATCH WHERE YOU'RE DRIVING, DAMN MANIAC!!

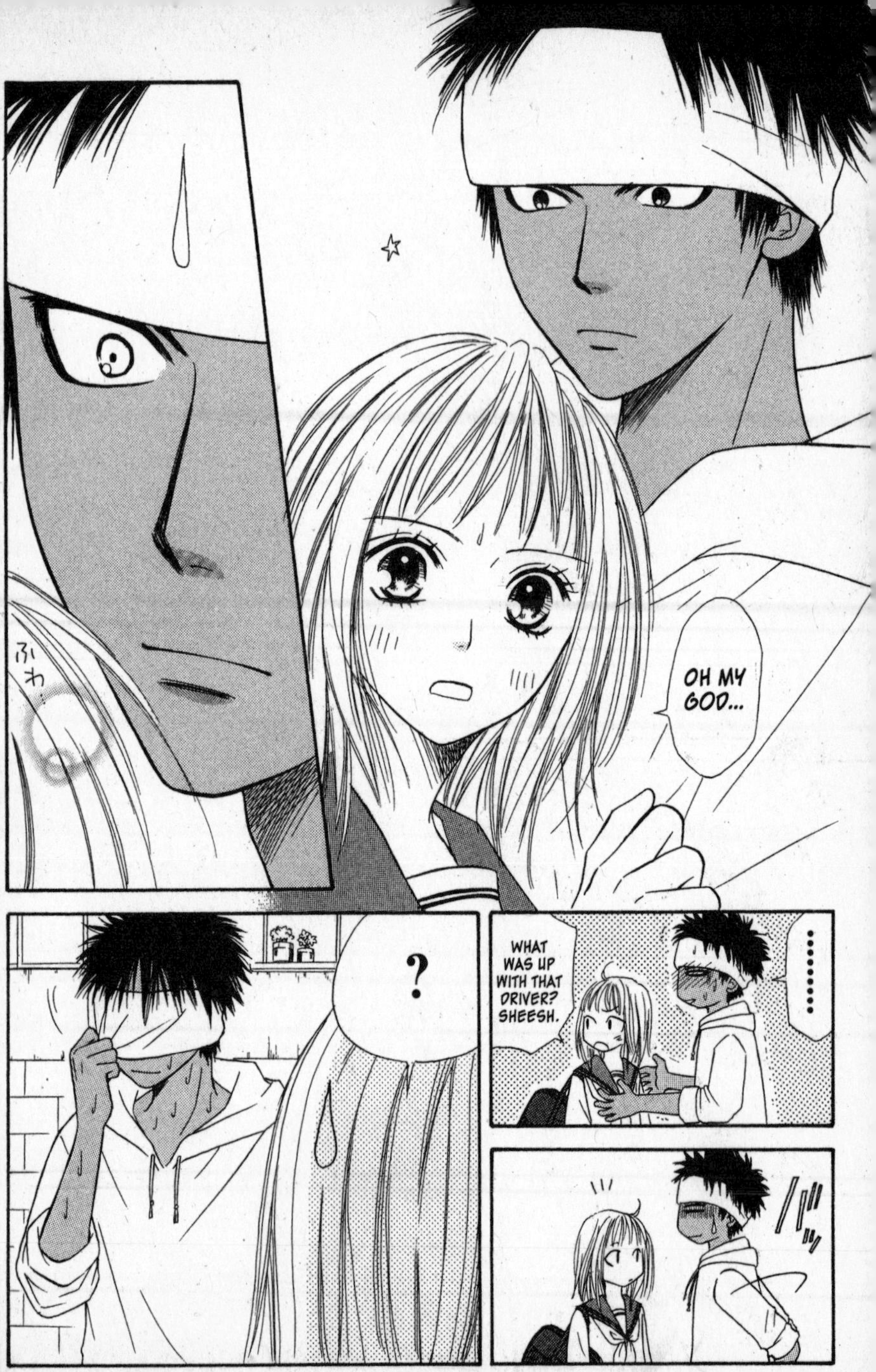
OH MY GOD...
ふわ
....
WHAT WAS UP WITH THAT DRIVER? SHEESH.
?

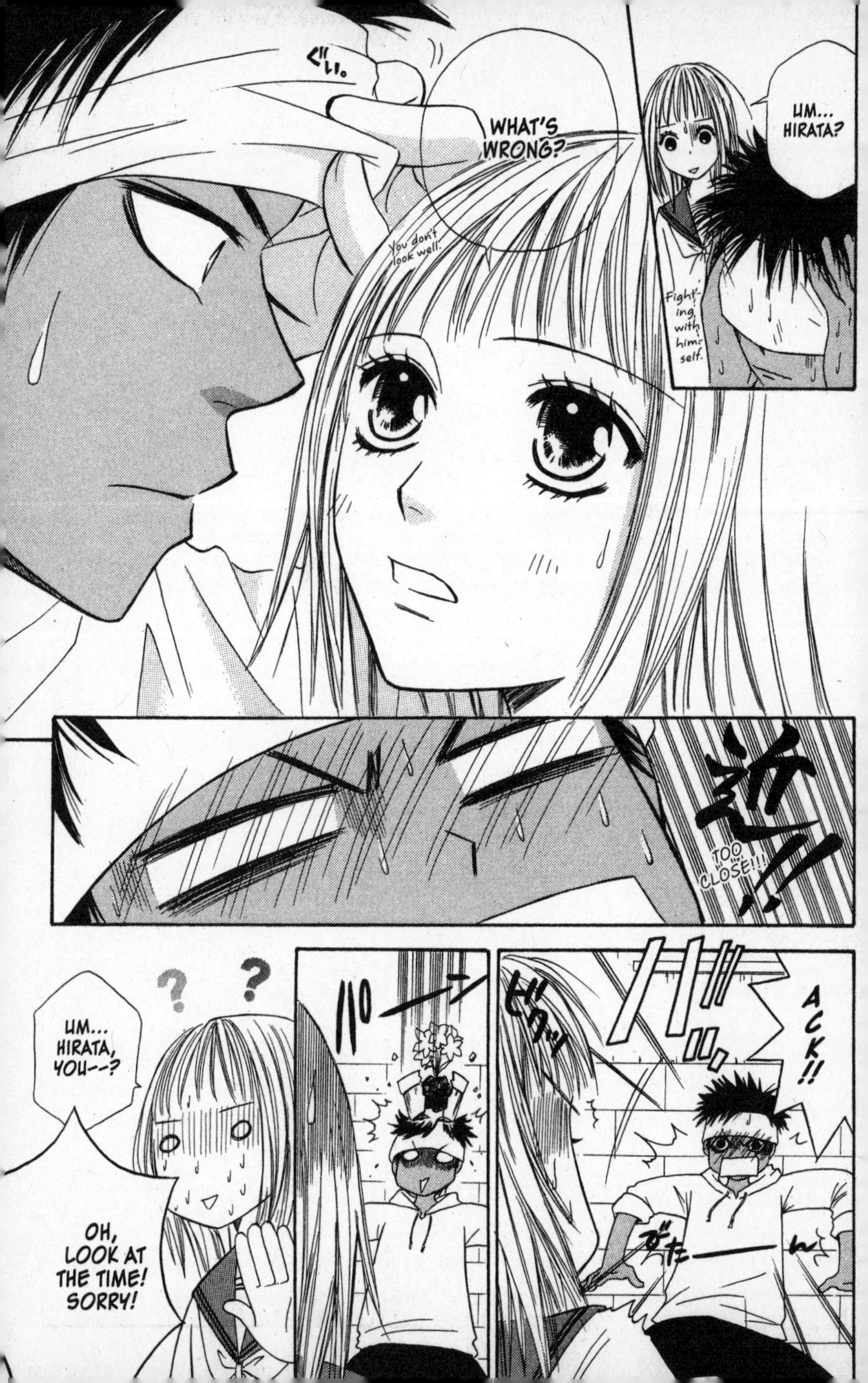
UM... HIRATA?
Fighting with himself.
ぐいっ
WHAT'S WRONG?
You don't look well.
近!!
TOO CLOSE!!!
ACK!!
UM... HIRATA, YOU--?
OH, LOOK AT THE TIME! SORRY!

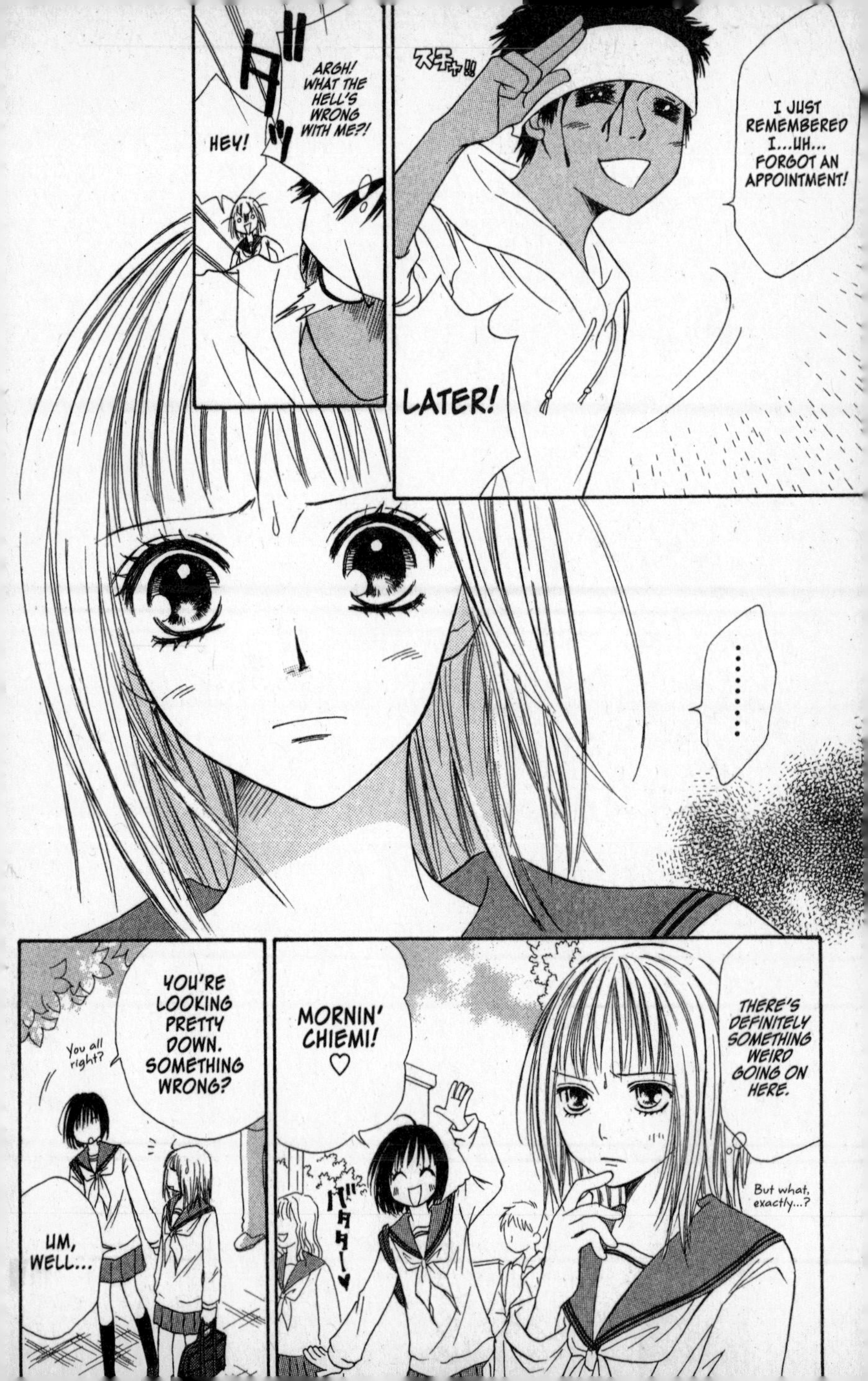
スチャ!!
I JUST REMEMBERED I...UH... FORGOT AN APPOINTMENT!
LATER!
ダッ
ARGH! WHAT THE HELL'S WRONG WITH ME?!
HEY!
......
THERE'S DEFINITELY SOMETHING WEIRD GOING ON HERE.
But what, exactly...?
MORNIN' CHIEMI! ♡
バタター♥
YOU'RE LOOKING PRETTY DOWN. SOMETHING WRONG?
You all right?
UM, WELL...

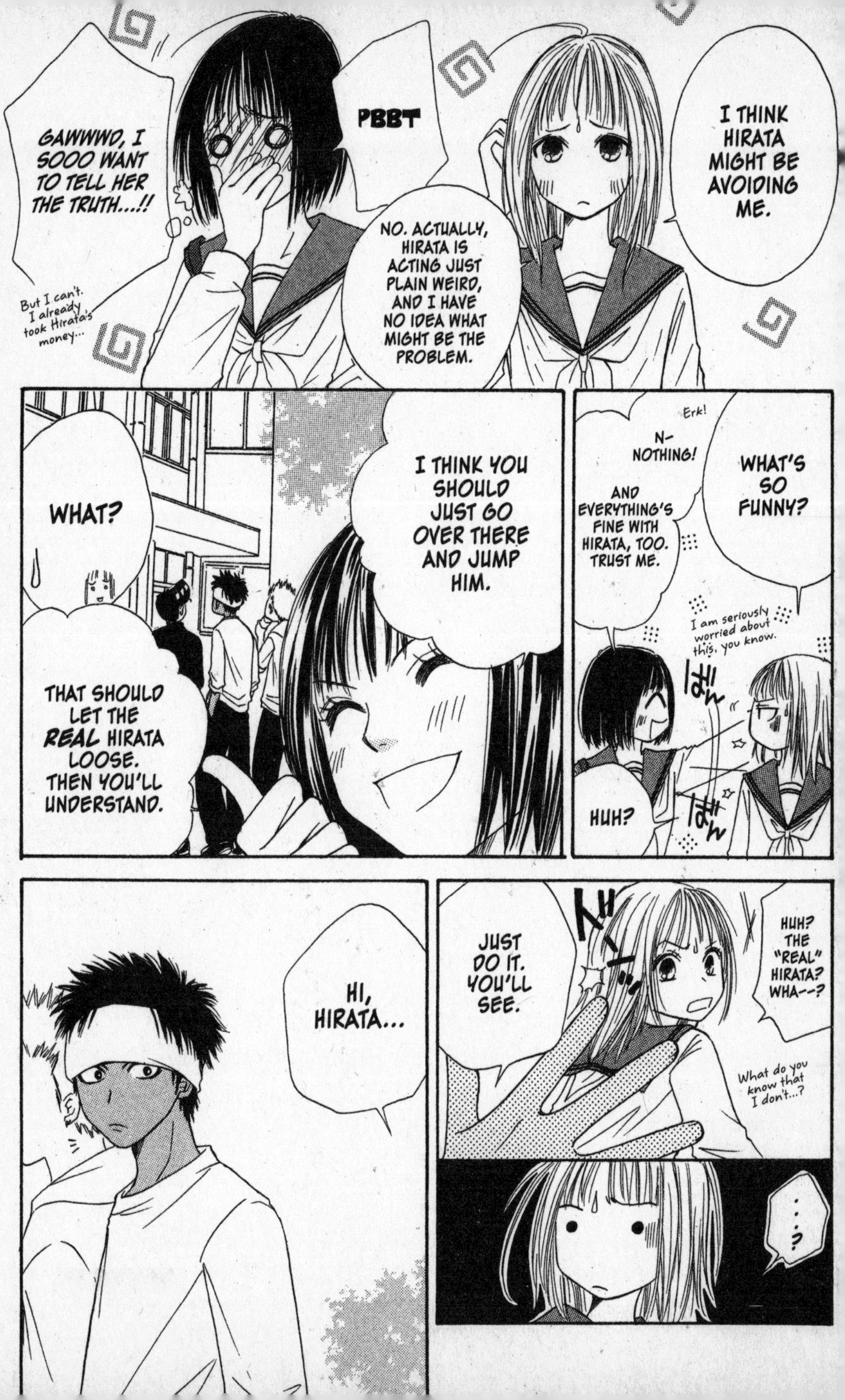
I THINK HIRATA MIGHT BE AVOIDING ME.
NO. ACTUALLY, HIRATA IS ACTING JUST PLAIN WEIRD, AND I HAVE NO IDEA WHAT MIGHT BE THE PROBLEM.
PBBT
GAWWWD, I SOOO WANT TO TELL HER THE TRUTH...!!
But I can't. I already took Hirata's money...
WHAT'S SO FUNNY?
Erk!
N-NOTHING!
AND EVERYTHING'S FINE WITH HIRATA, TOO. TRUST ME.
I am seriously worried about this, you know.
ばん
ばん
HUH?
I THINK YOU SHOULD JUST GO OVER THERE AND JUMP HIM.
WHAT?
THAT SHOULD LET THE REAL HIRATA LOOSE. THEN YOU'LL UNDERSTAND.
HUH? THE "REAL" HIRATA? WHA--?
JUST DO IT. YOU'LL SEE.
What do you know that I don't...?
...?
HI, HIRATA...

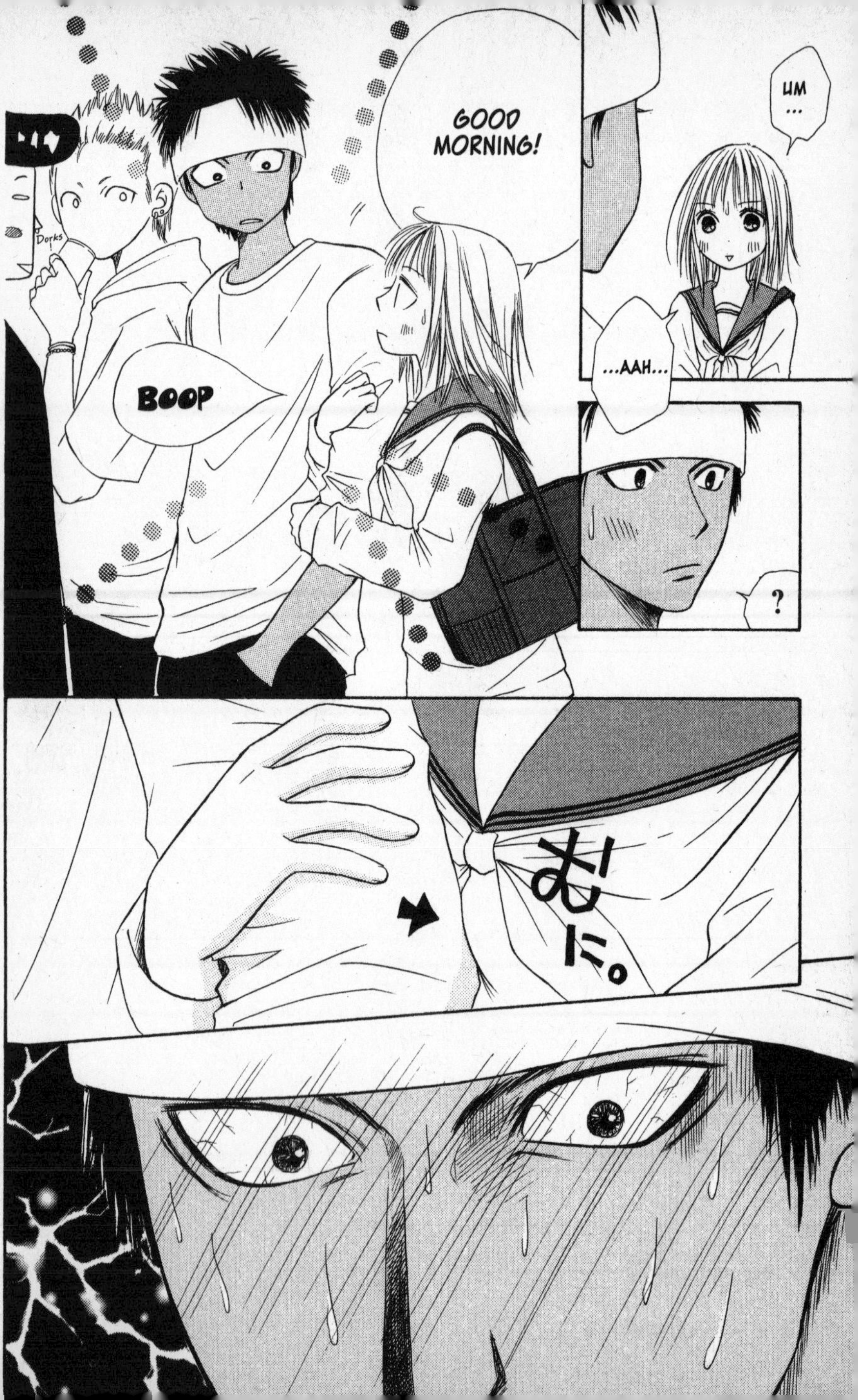
UM ...
...AAH...
?
GOOD MORNING!
BOOP
Dorks !
むに。

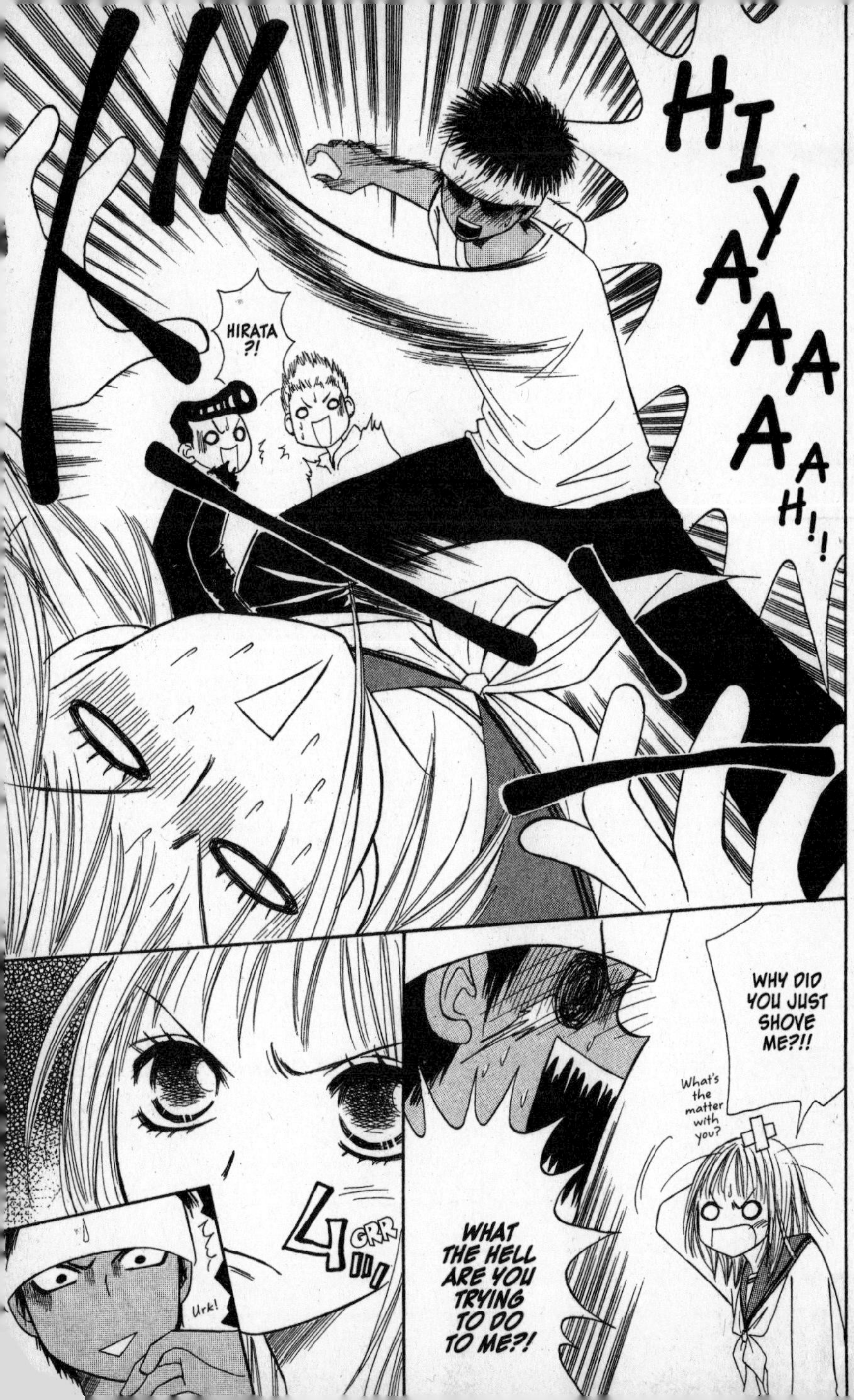
HIYAAAAAAH!!
HIRATA?!
WHY DID YOU JUST SHOVE ME?!!
What's the matter with you?
WHAT THE HELL ARE YOU TRYING TO DO TO ME?!
GRR
Urk!

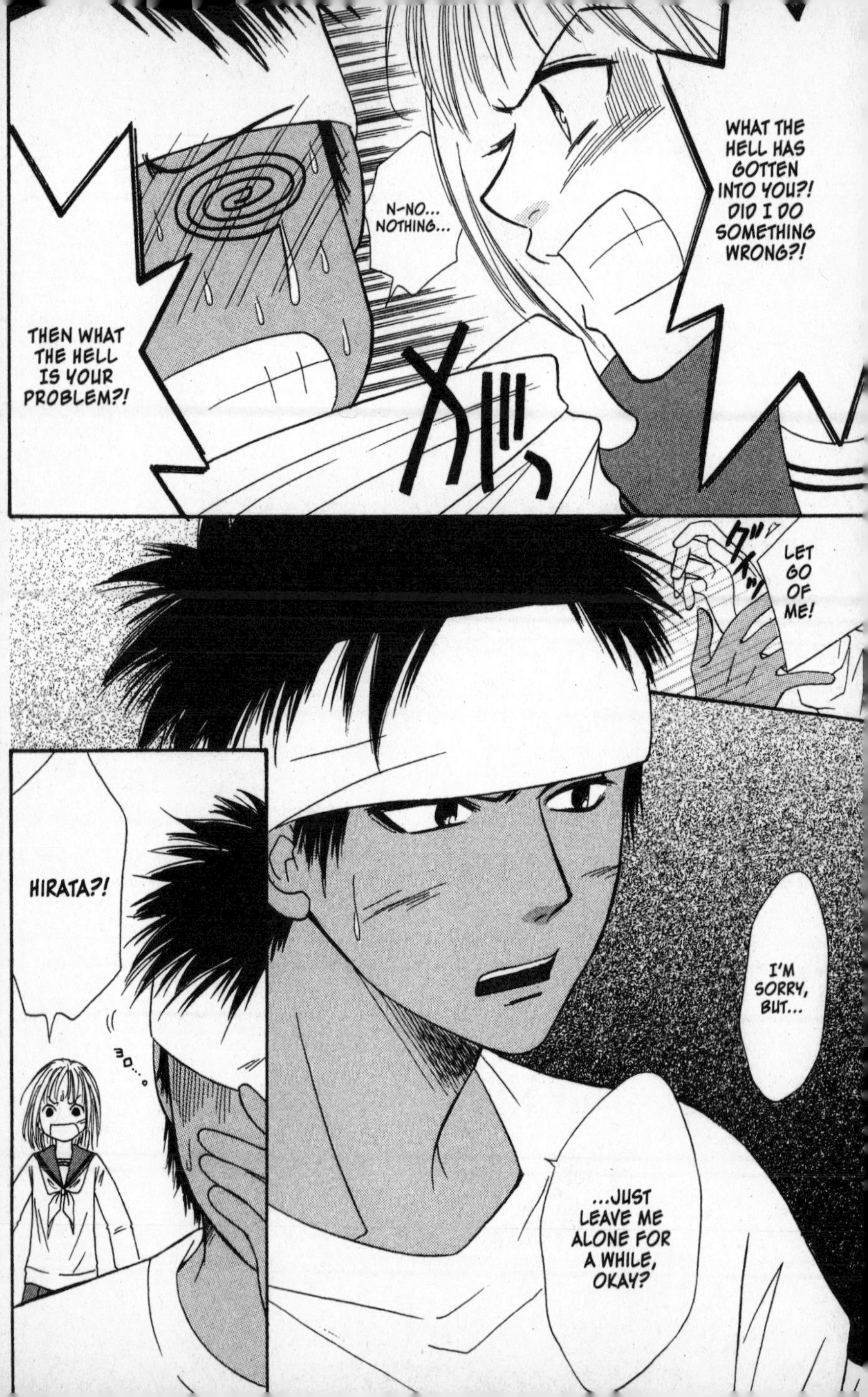
WHAT THE HELL HAS GOTTEN INTO YOU?! DID I DO SOMETHING WRONG?!
N-NO... NOTHING...
THEN WHAT THE HELL IS YOUR PROBLEM?!
LET GO OF ME!
I'M SORRY, BUT...
...JUST LEAVE ME ALONE FOR A WHILE, OKAY?
HIRATA?!

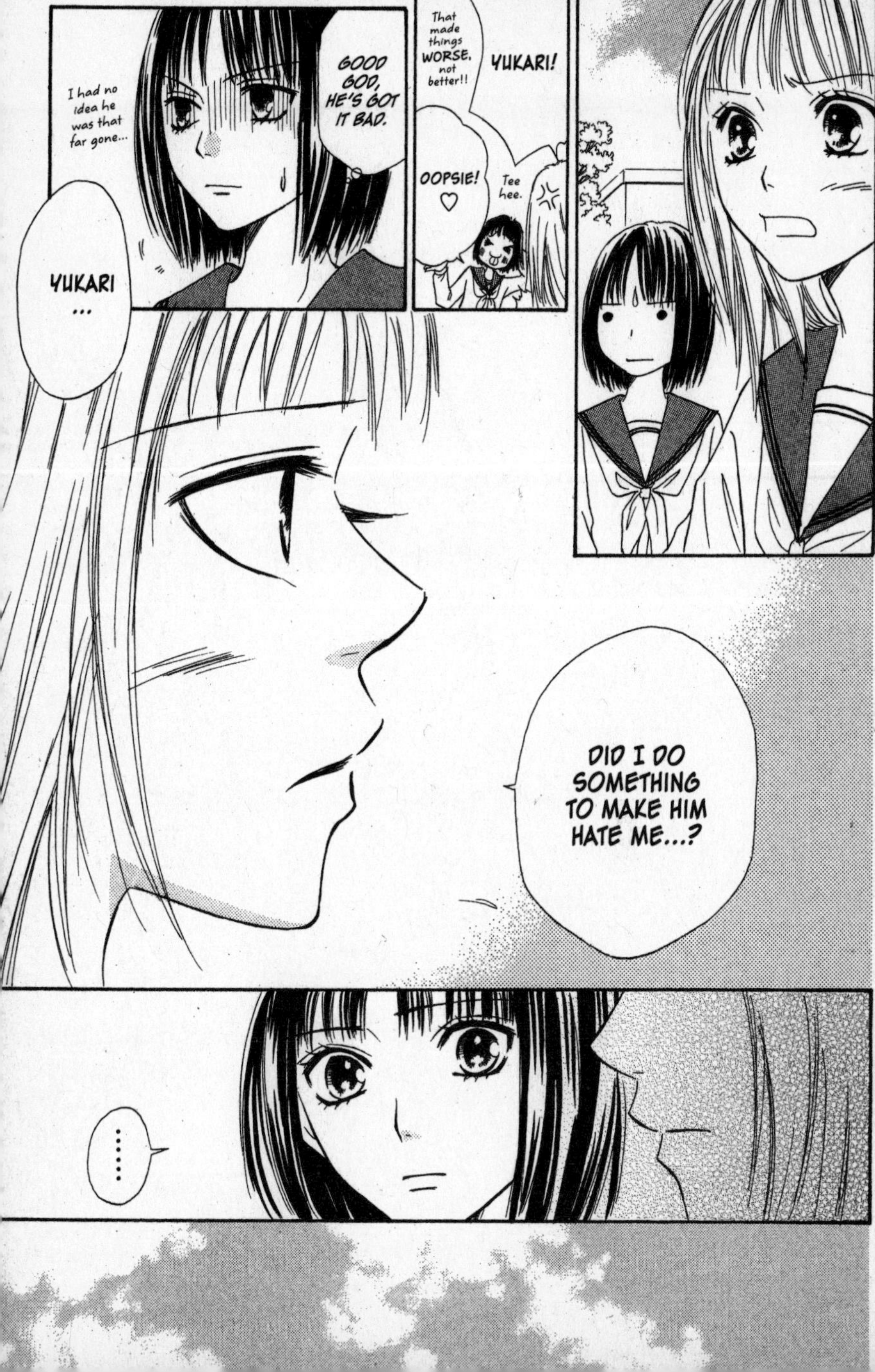
YUKARI!
That made things WORSE, not better!!
Tee hee.
OOPSIE! ♡
GOOD GOD, HE'S GOT IT BAD.
I had no idea he was that far gone...
YUKARI ...
DID I DO SOMETHING TO MAKE HIM HATE ME...?
......

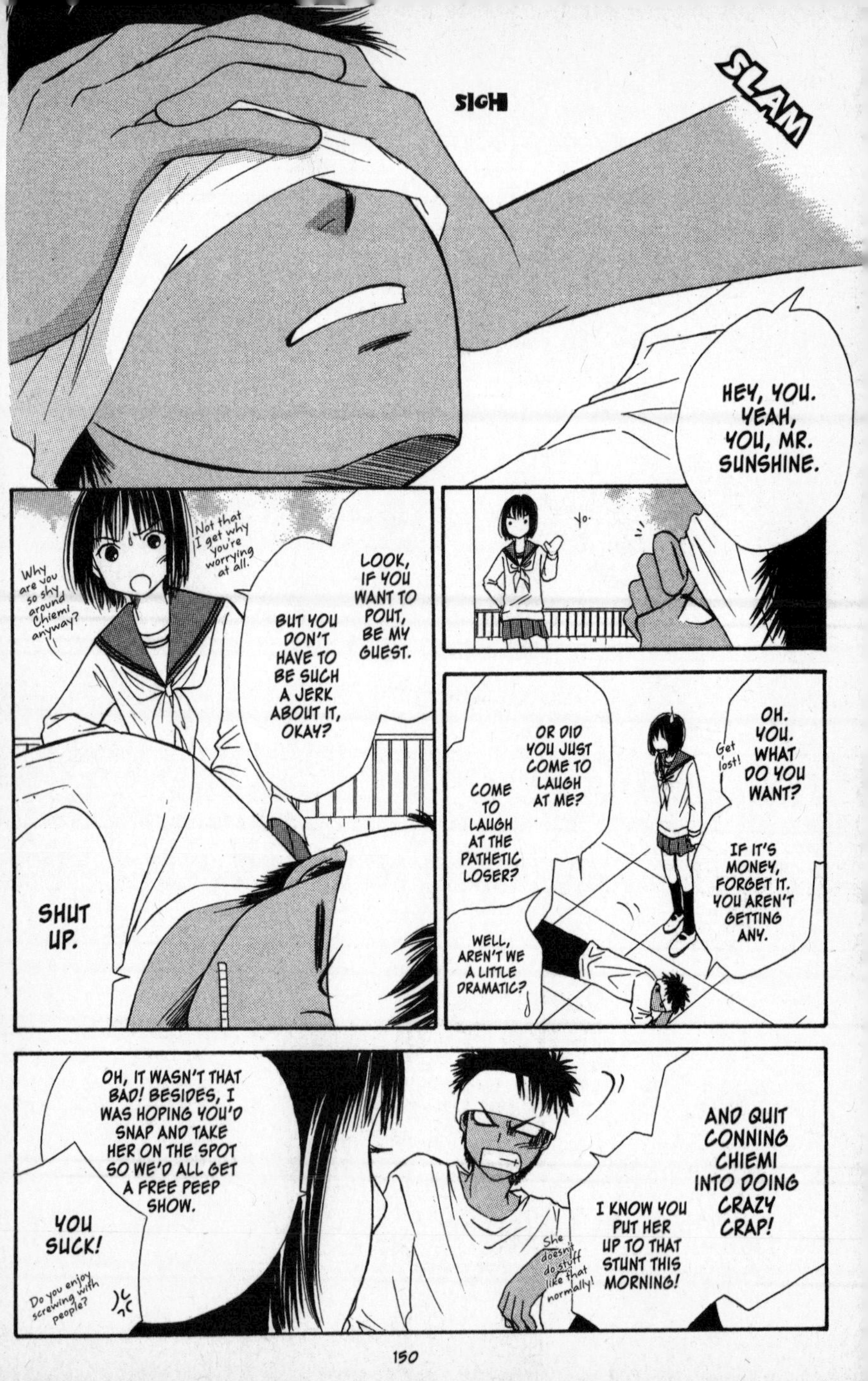
SLAM
SIGH
HEY, YOU. YEAH, YOU, MR. SUNSHINE.
Yo.
OH. YOU. WHAT DO YOU WANT?
Get lost!
IF IT'S MONEY, FORGET IT. YOU AREN'T GETTING ANY.
OR DID YOU JUST COME TO LAUGH AT ME?
COME TO LAUGH AT THE PATHETIC LOSER?
WELL, AREN'T WE A LITTLE DRAMATIC?
LOOK, IF YOU WANT TO POUT, BE MY GUEST.
BUT YOU DON'T HAVE TO BE SUCH A JERK ABOUT IT, OKAY?
Not that I get why you're worrying at all.
Why are you so shy around Chiemi anyway?
SHUT UP.
AND QUIT CONNING CHIEMI INTO DOING CRAZY CRAP!
I KNOW YOU PUT HER UP TO THAT STUNT THIS MORNING!
She doesn't do stuff like that normally!
OH, IT WASN'T THAT BAD! BESIDES, I WAS HOPING YOU'D SNAP AND TAKE HER ON THE SPOT SO WE'D ALL GET A FREE PEEP SHOW.
YOU SUCK!
Do you enjoy screwing with people?

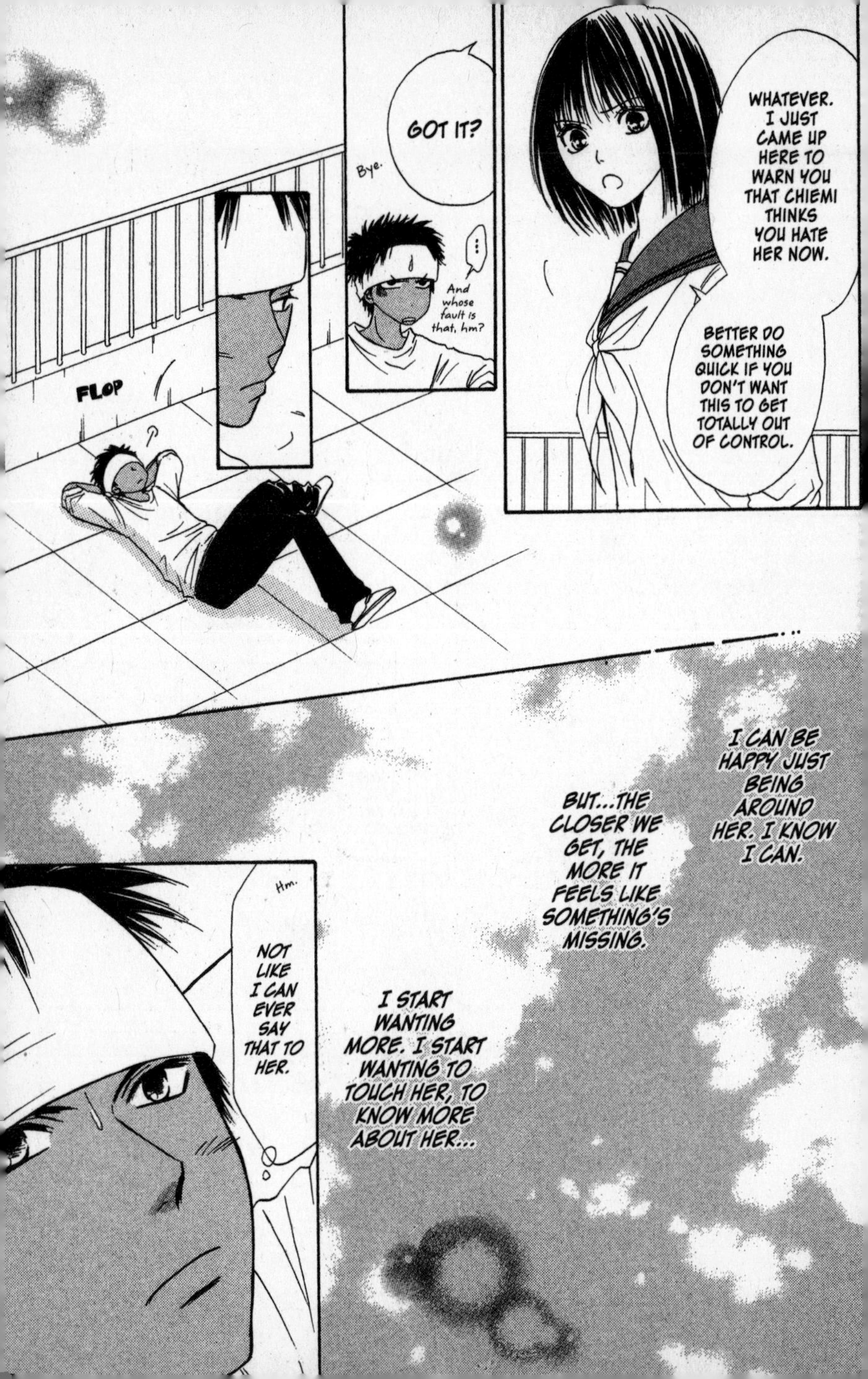
WHATEVER. I JUST CAME UP HERE TO WARN YOU THAT CHIEMI THINKS YOU HATE HER NOW.
BETTER DO SOMETHING QUICK IF YOU DON'T WANT THIS TO GET TOTALLY OUT OF CONTROL.
GOT IT?
Bye.
...
And whose fault is that, hm?
FLOP
?
I CAN BE HAPPY JUST BEING AROUND HER. I KNOW I CAN.
BUT...THE CLOSER WE GET, THE MORE IT FEELS LIKE SOMETHING'S MISSING.
I START WANTING MORE. I START WANTING TO TOUCH HER, TO KNOW MORE ABOUT HER...
Hm.
NOT LIKE I CAN EVER SAY THAT TO HER.

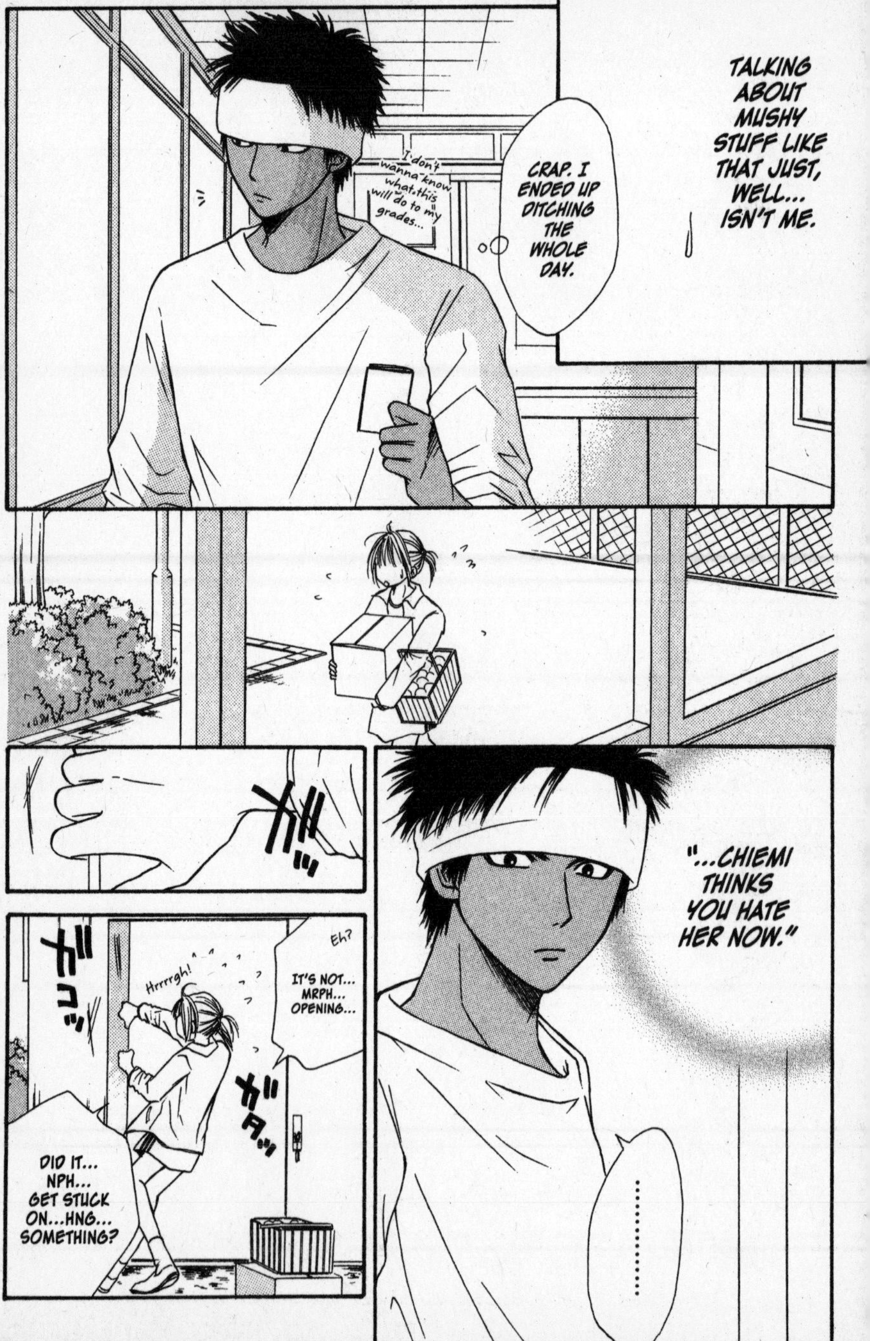
TALKING ABOUT MUSHY STUFF LIKE THAT JUST, WELL... ISN'T ME.
CRAP. I ENDED UP DITCHING THE WHOLE DAY.
I don't wanna know what this will do to my grades...
"...CHIEMI THINKS YOU HATE HER NOW."
......
Eh?
IT'S NOT... MRPH... OPENING...
Hrrrrgh!
DID IT... NPH... GET STUCK ON...HNG... SOMETHING?

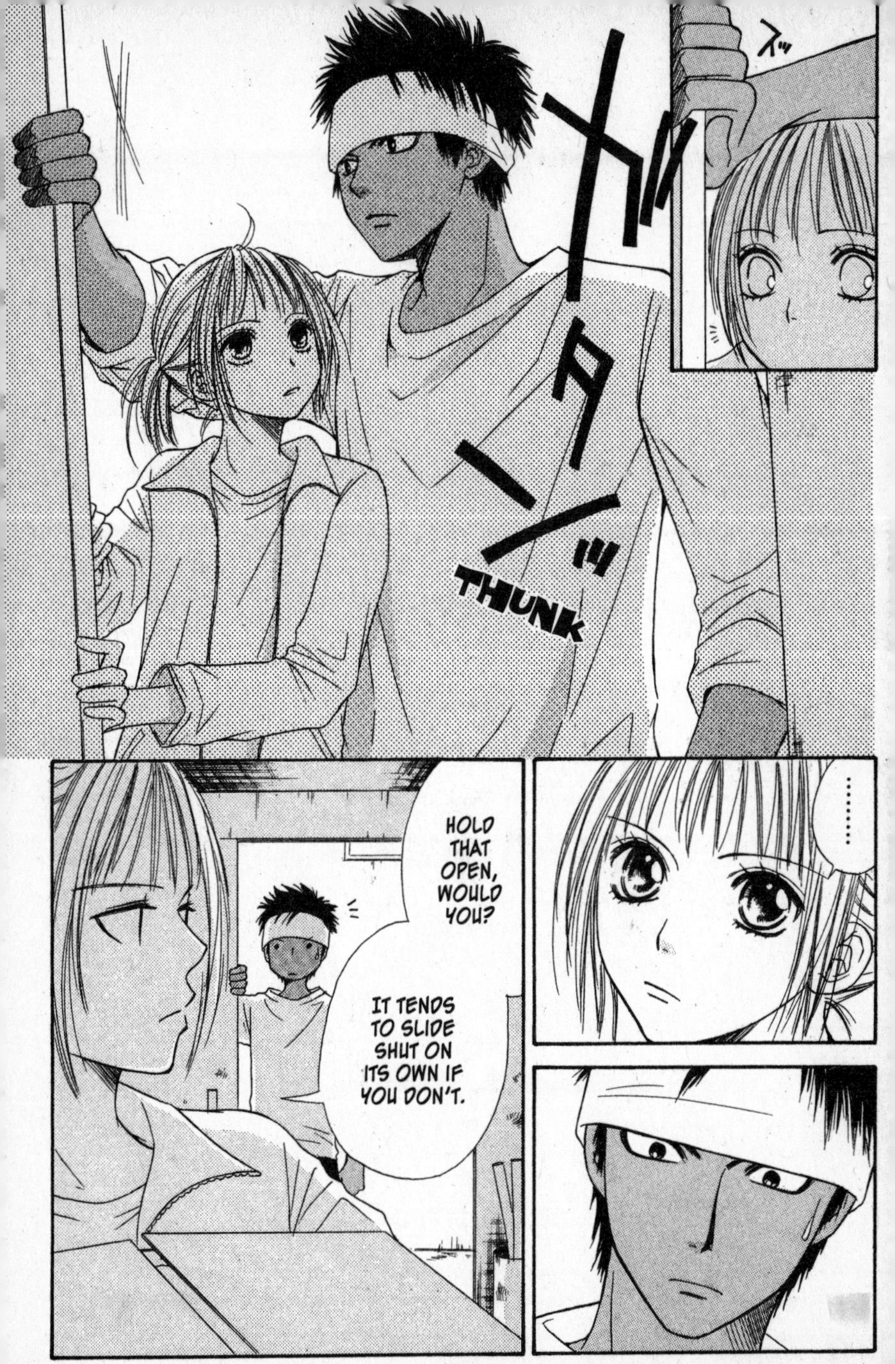
THUNK
......
HOLD THAT OPEN, WOULD YOU?
IT TENDS TO SLIDE SHUT ON ITS OWN IF YOU DON'T.

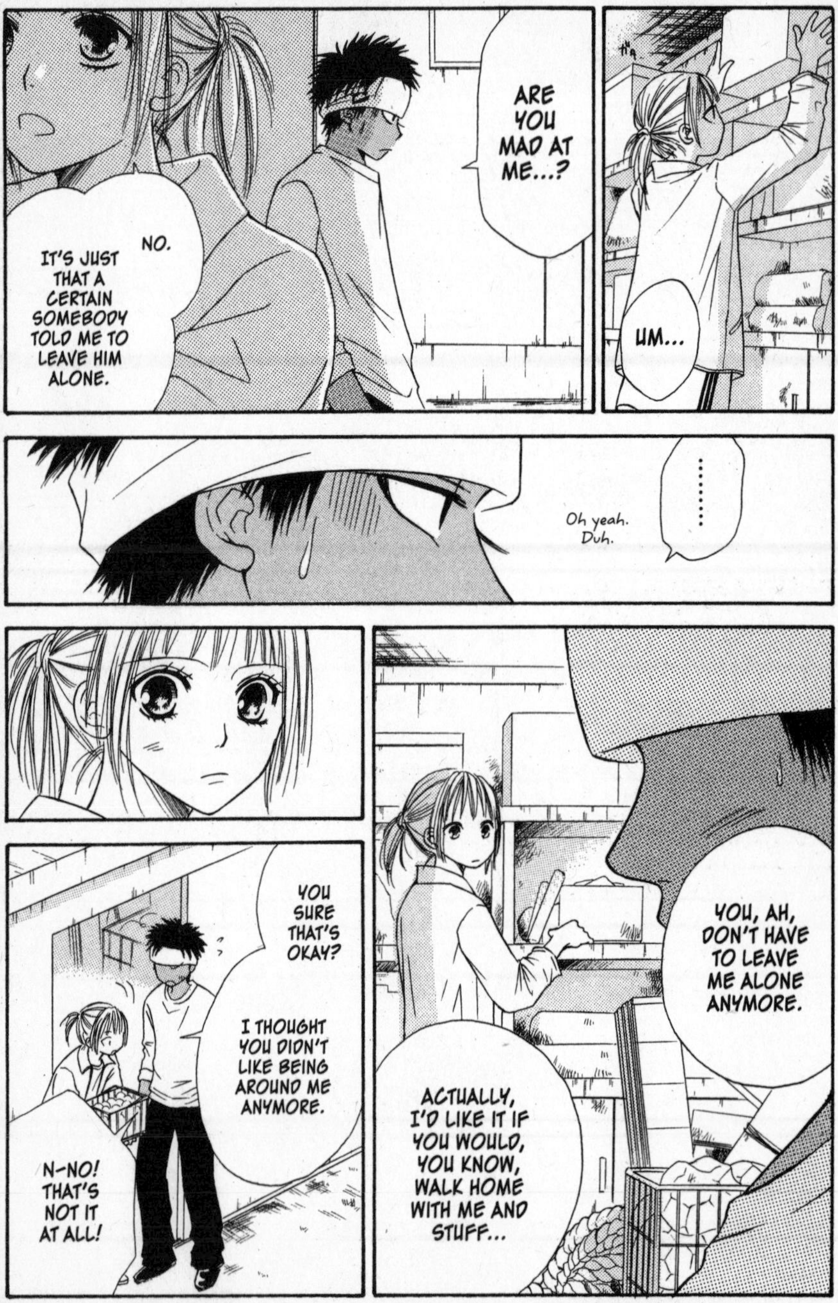
UM...
ARE YOU MAD AT ME...?
NO.
IT'S JUST THAT A CERTAIN SOMEBODY TOLD ME TO LEAVE HIM ALONE.
......
Oh yeah. Duh.
YOU, AH, DON'T HAVE TO LEAVE ME ALONE ANYMORE.
ACTUALLY, I'D LIKE IT IF YOU WOULD, YOU KNOW, WALK HOME WITH ME AND STUFF...
YOU SURE THAT'S OKAY?
I THOUGHT YOU DIDN'T LIKE BEING AROUND ME ANYMORE.
N-NO! THAT'S NOT IT AT ALL!

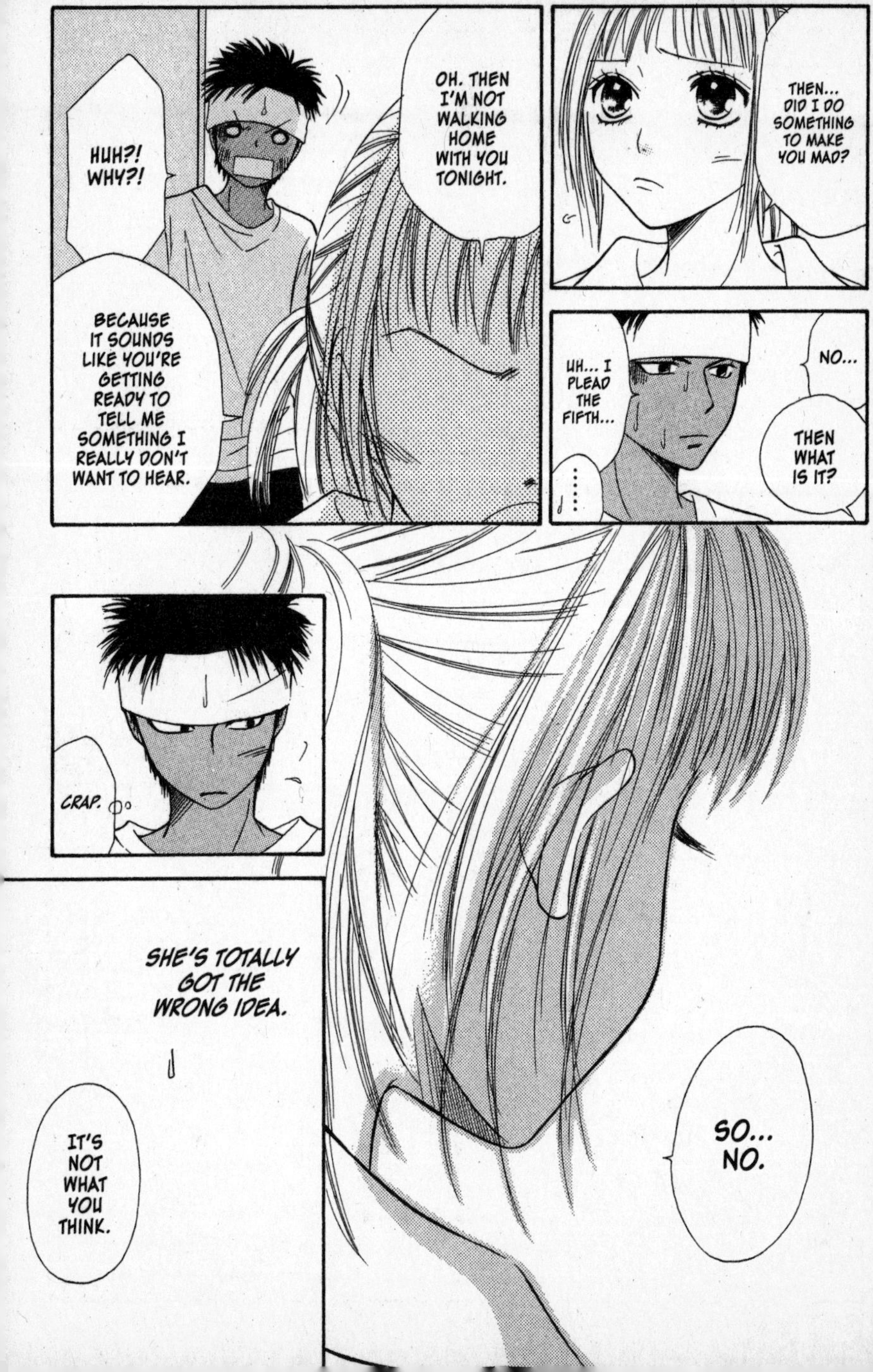
THEN... DID I DO SOMETHING TO MAKE YOU MAD?
NO...
THEN WHAT IS IT?
UH... I PLEAD THE FIFTH...
......
OH. THEN I'M NOT WALKING HOME WITH YOU TONIGHT.
HUH?! WHY?!
BECAUSE IT SOUNDS LIKE YOU'RE GETTING READY TO TELL ME SOMETHING I REALLY DON'T WANT TO HEAR.
SO... NO.
CRAP.
SHE'S TOTALLY GOT THE WRONG IDEA.
IT'S NOT WHAT YOU THINK.

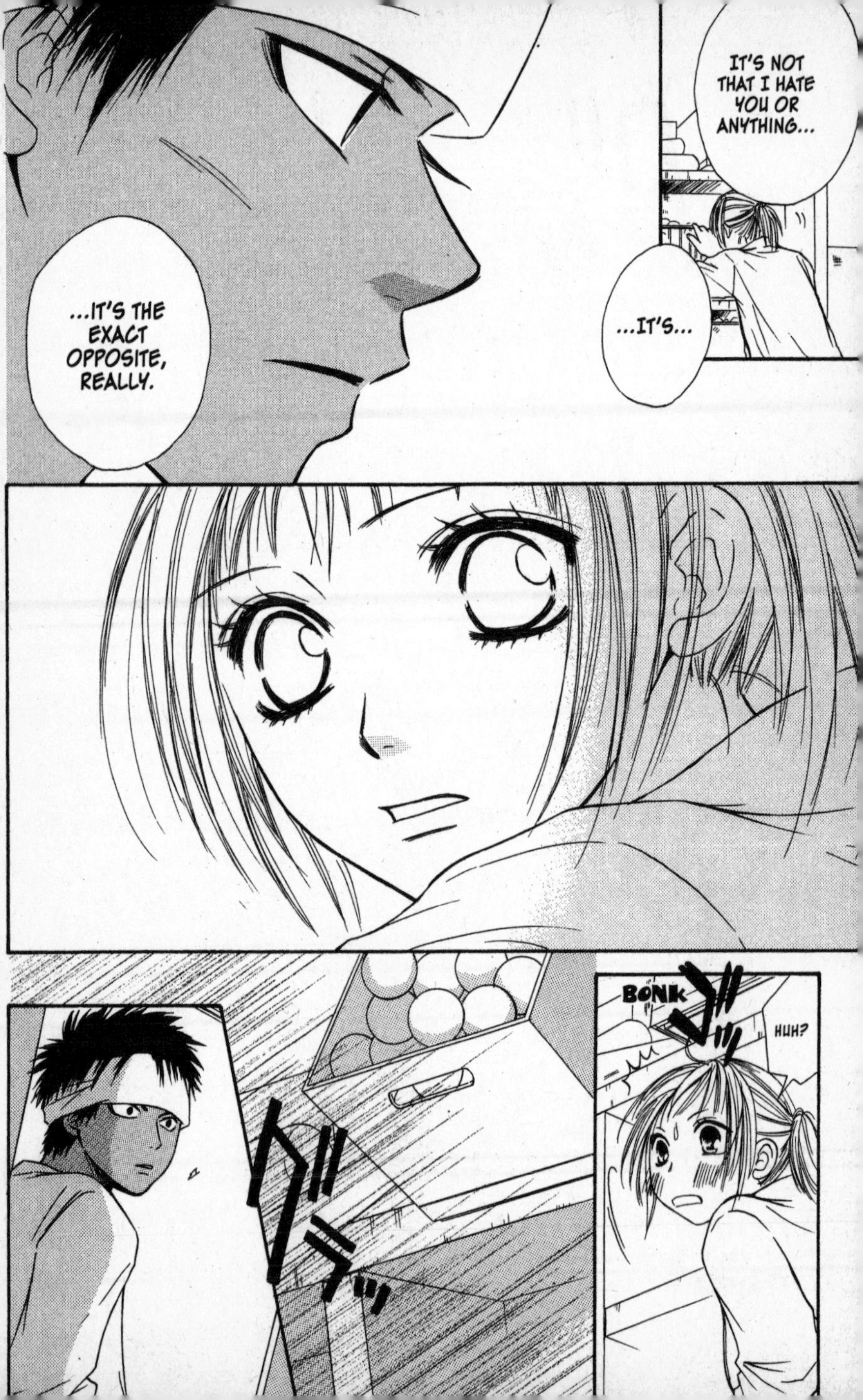
IT'S NOT THAT I HATE YOU OR ANYTHING...
...IT'S...
...IT'S THE EXACT OPPOSITE, REALLY.
BONK
HUH?

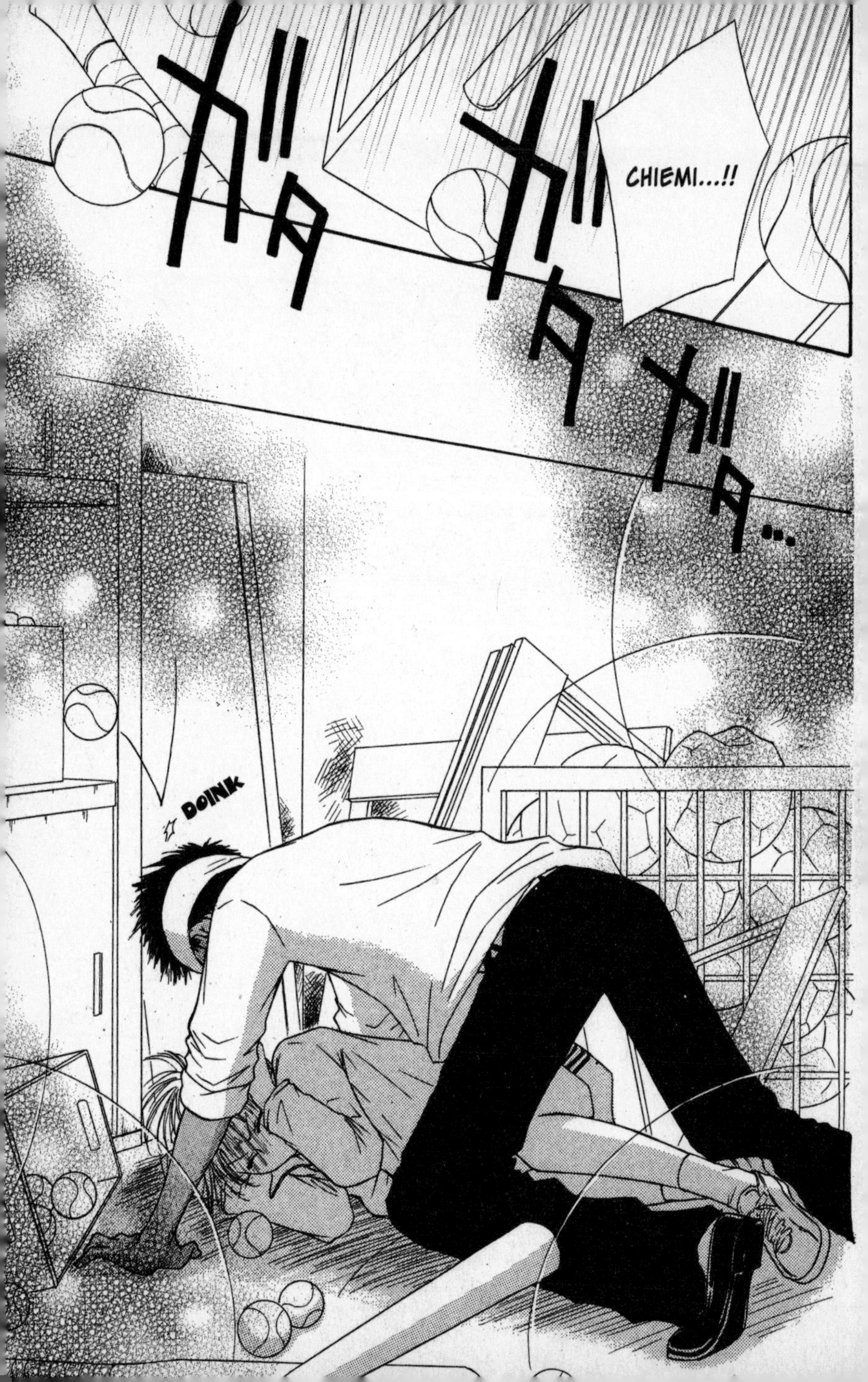
CHIEMI...!!
ガタ
ガタ
ガタ...
DOINK

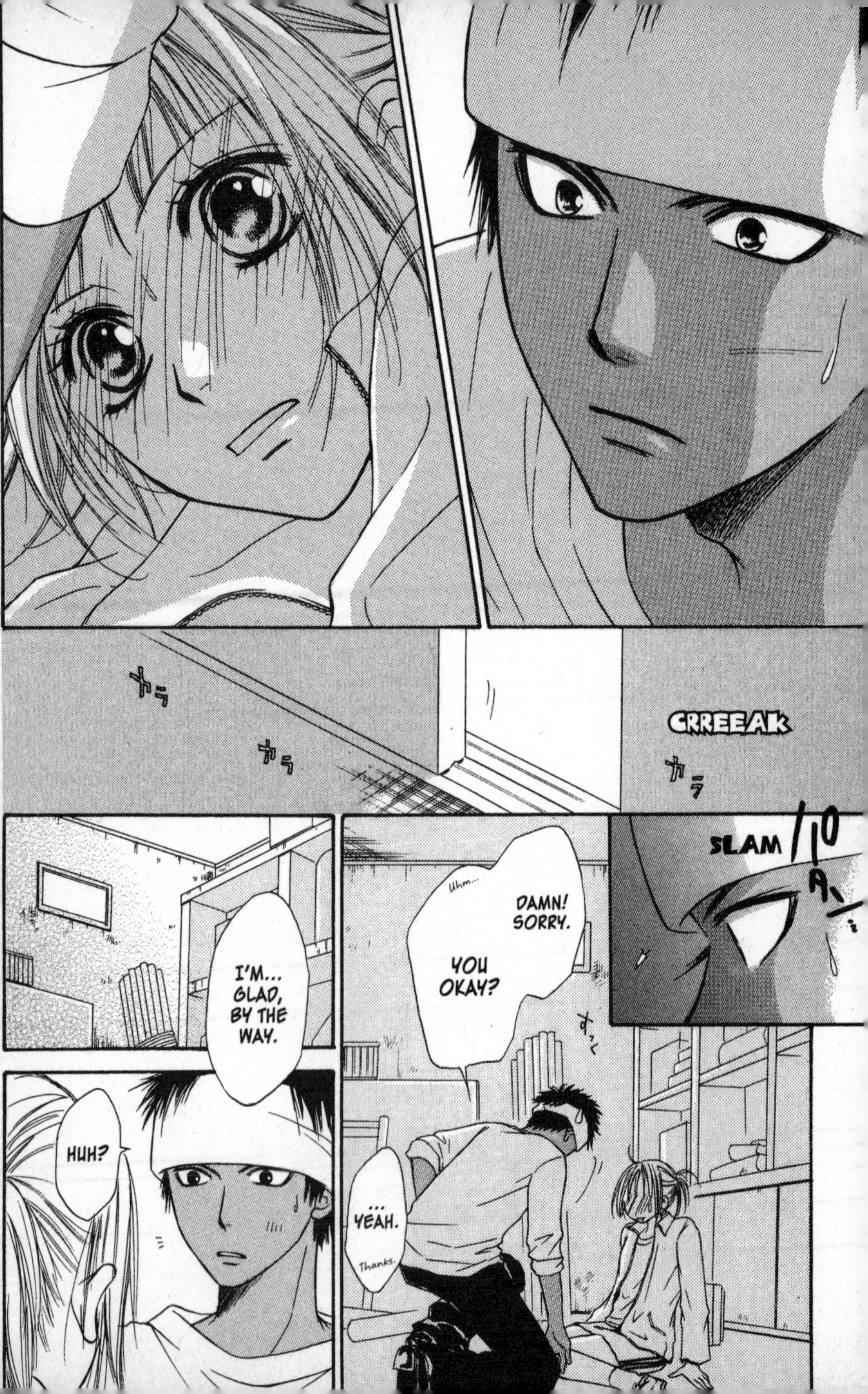

CRREEAK
SLAM
Uhm...
DAMN! SORRY.
YOU OKAY?
...YEAH.
Thanks.
I'M... GLAD, BY THE WAY.
HUH?

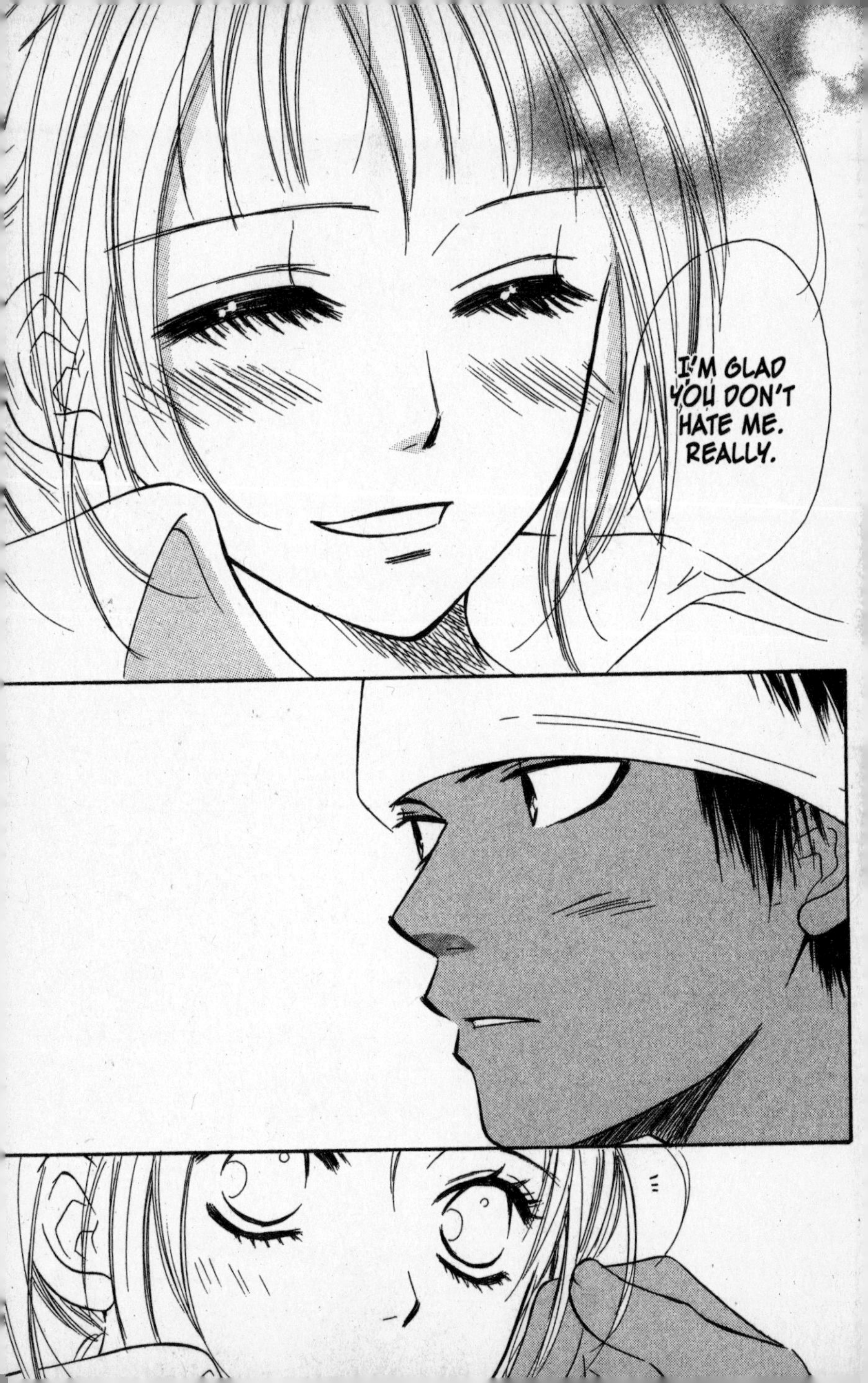
I'M GLAD YOU DON'T HATE ME. REALLY.

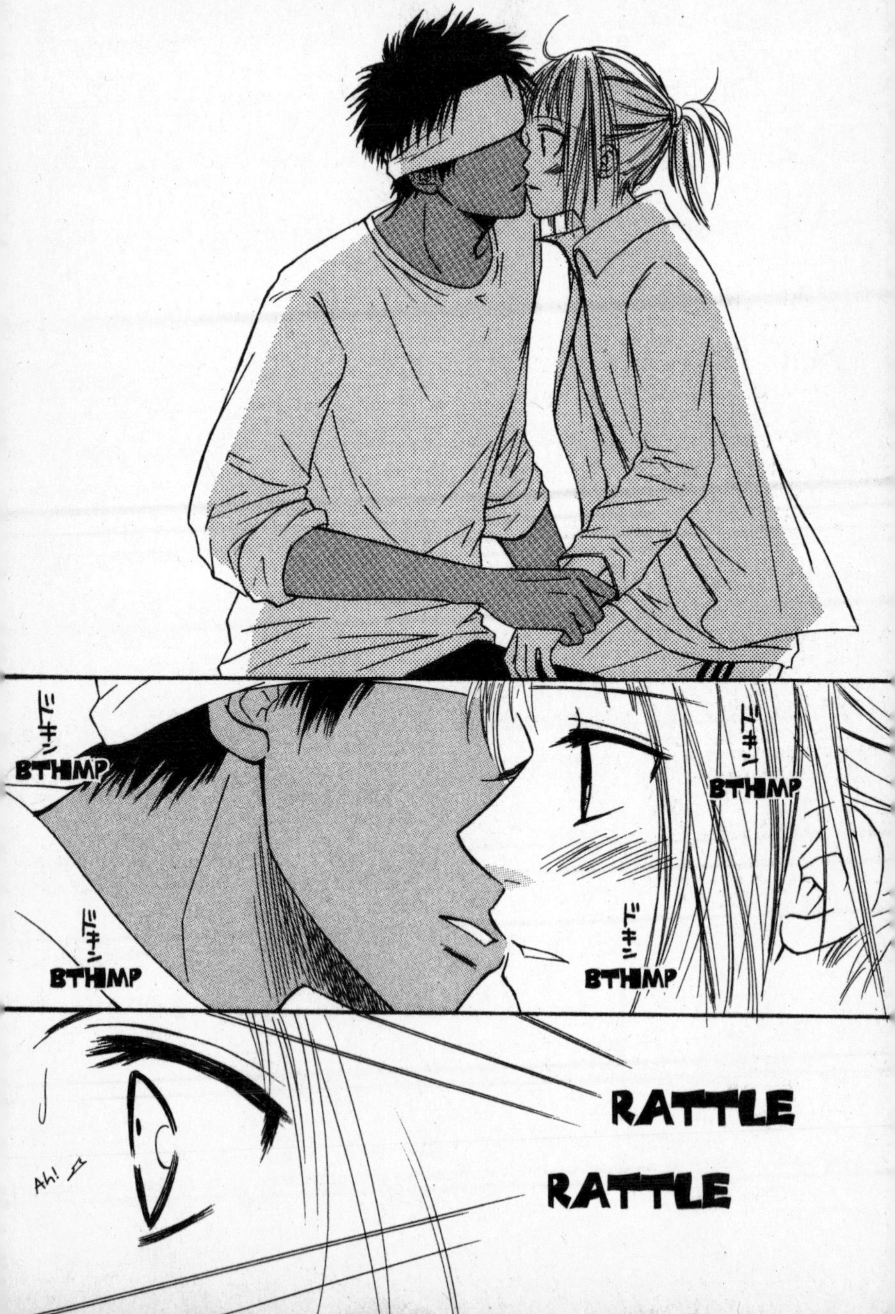
ドキン
BTHMP
ドキン
BTHMP
ドキン
BTHMP
ドキン
BTHMP
RATTLE
RATTLE
Ah!

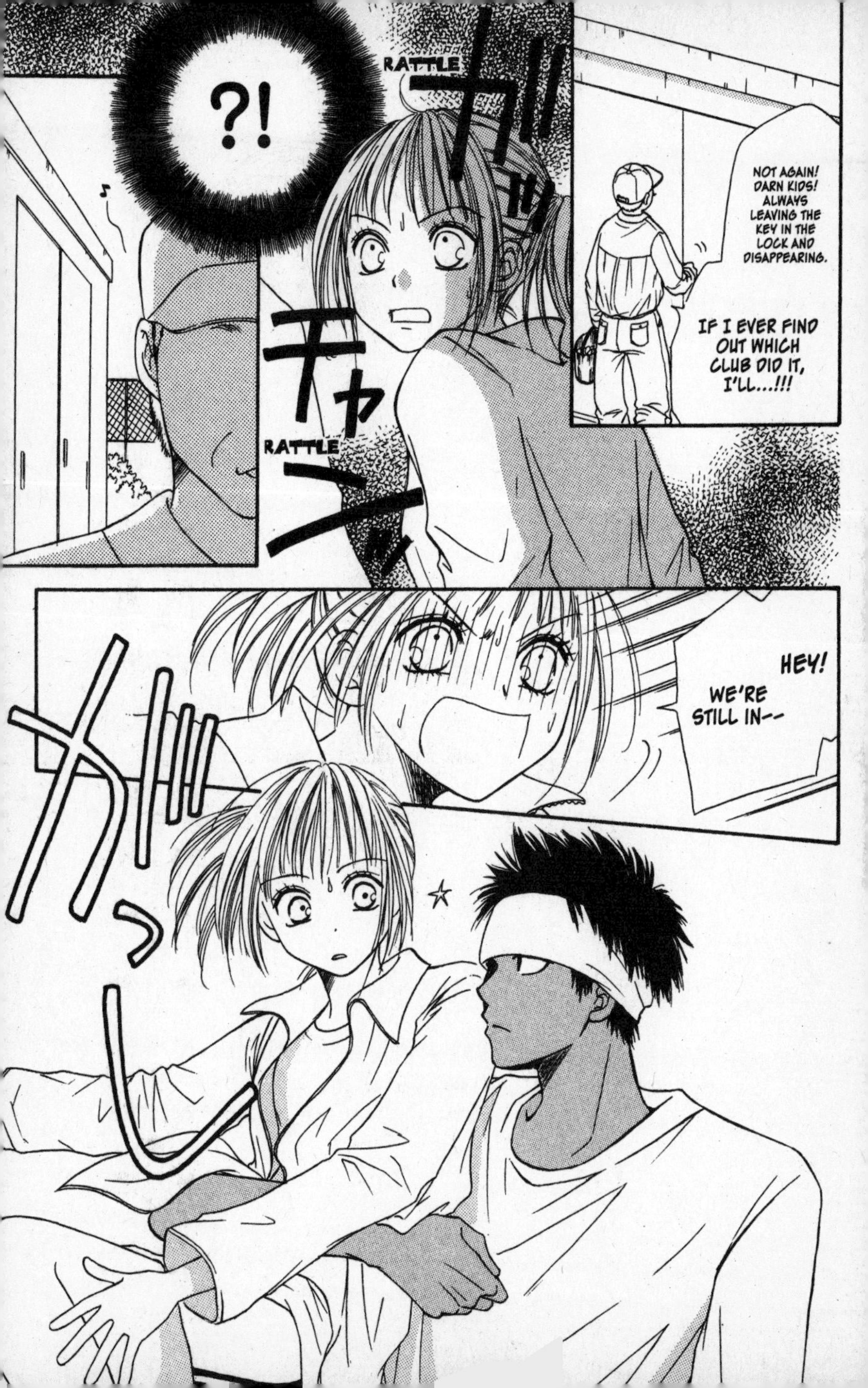
NOT AGAIN! DARN KIDS! ALWAYS LEAVING THE KEY IN THE LOCK AND DISAPPEARING.
IF I EVER FIND OUT WHICH CLUB DID IT, I'LL...!!!
RATTLE
?!
RATTLE
HEY!
WE'RE STILL IN--

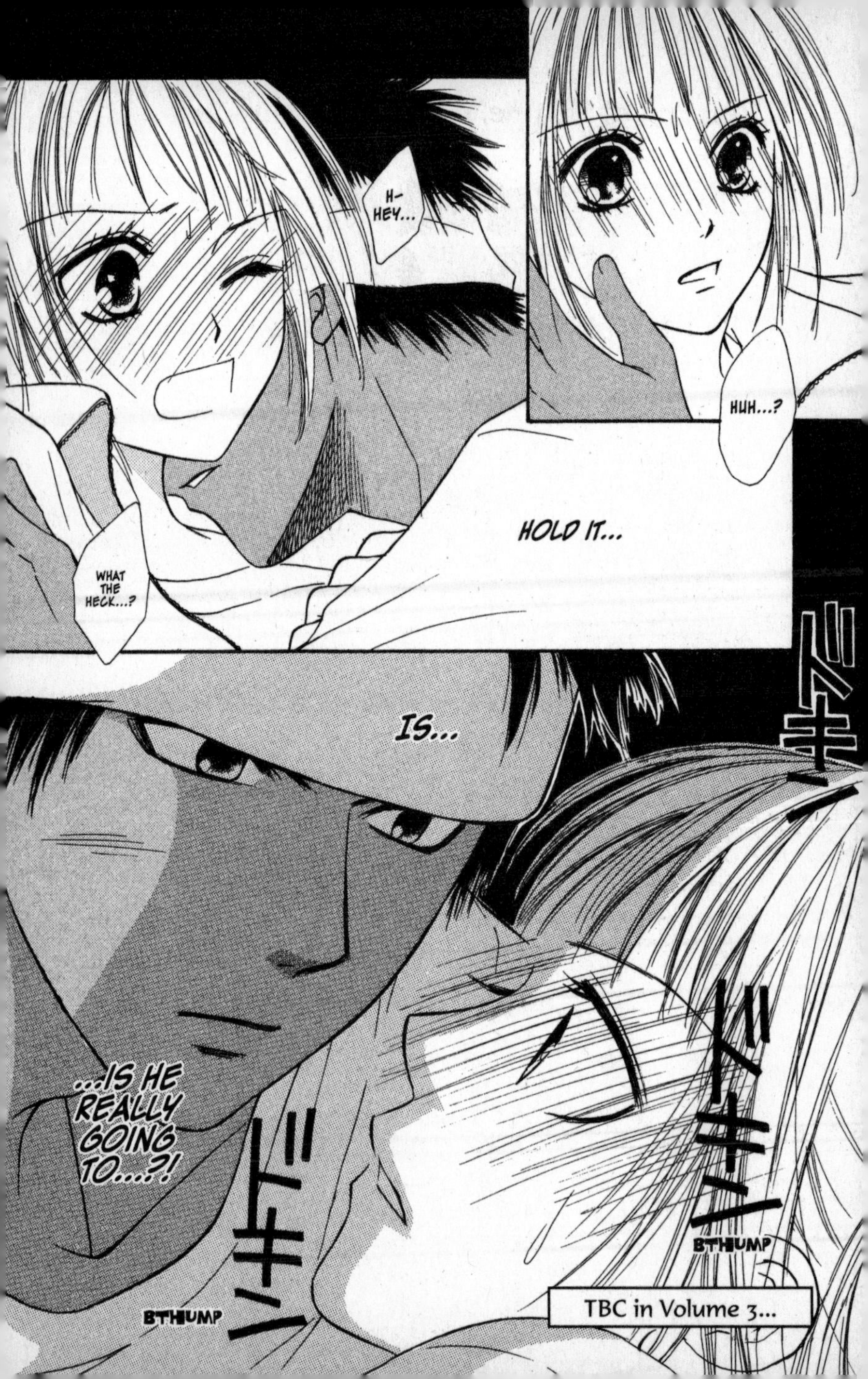
HUH...?
H-HEY...
WHAT THE HECK...?
HOLD IT...
IS...
...IS HE REALLY GOING TO...?!
ドキン
BTHUMP
ドキン
BTHUMP
TBC in Volume 3...

An End-of-Volume, Long-Winded Production...

LEGEND OF A GREAT FATHER, A GREAT MAN

~SPECIAL~

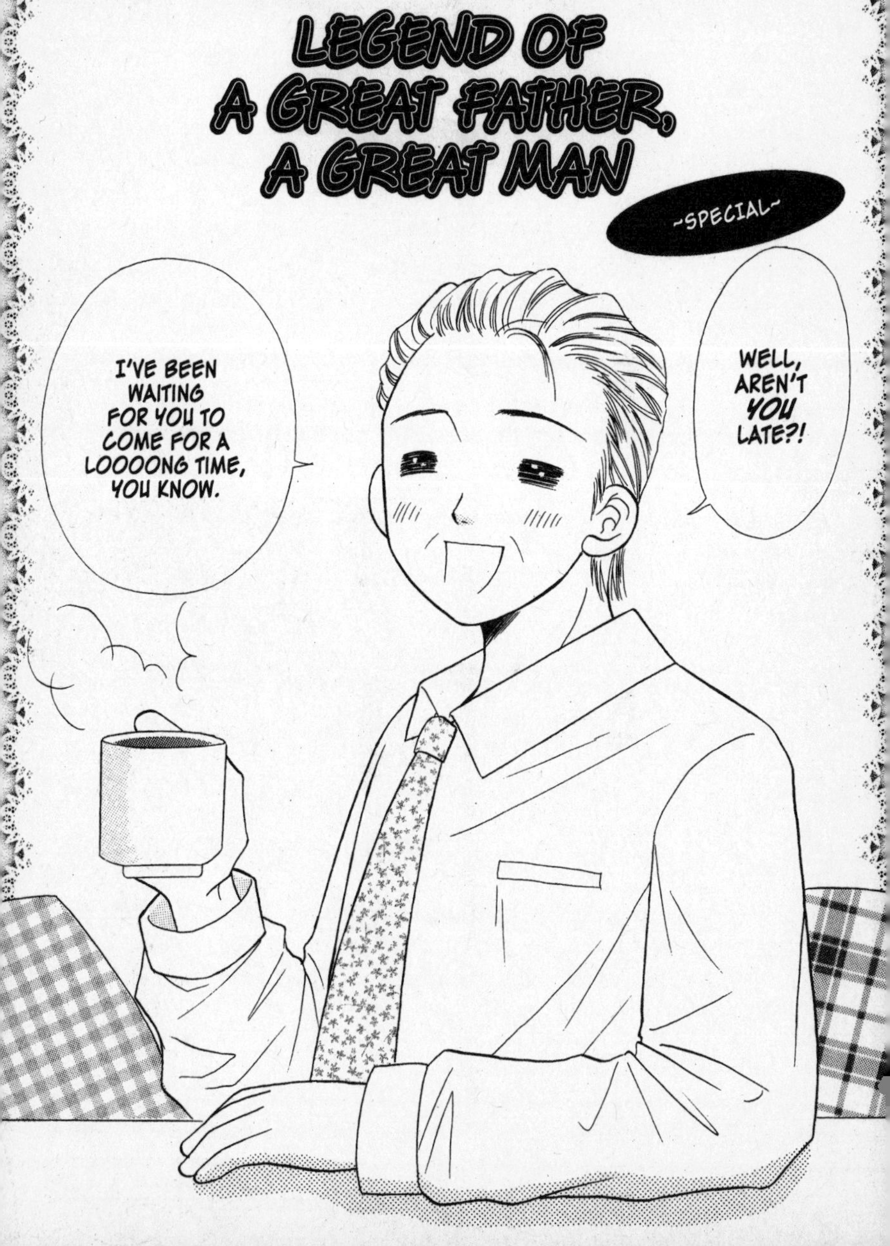
WELL, AREN'T *YOU* LATE?!
I'VE BEEN WAITING FOR YOU TO COME FOR A LOOOONG TIME, YOU KNOW.

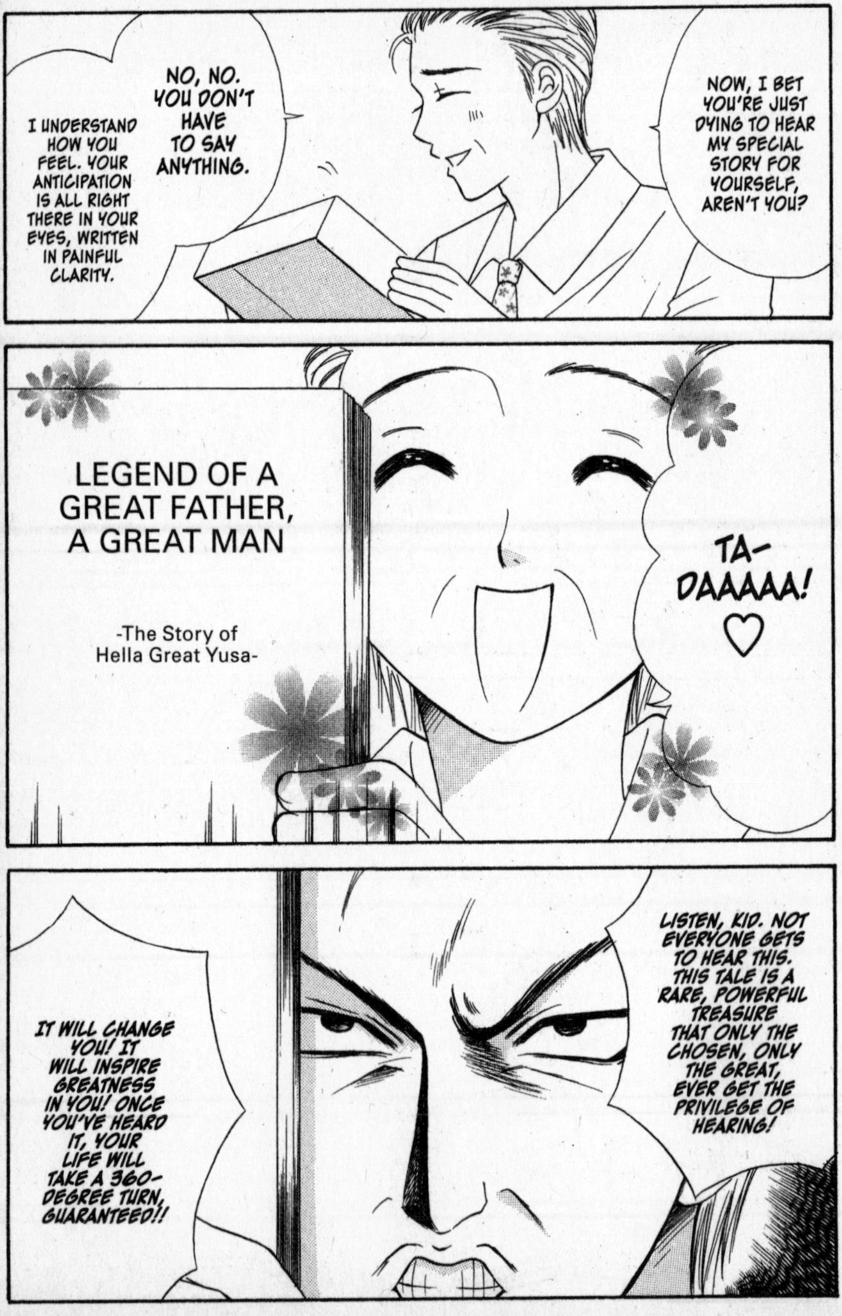
NOW, I BET YOU'RE JUST DYING TO HEAR MY SPECIAL STORY FOR YOURSELF, AREN'T YOU?
NO, NO. YOU DON'T HAVE TO SAY ANYTHING.
I UNDERSTAND HOW YOU FEEL. YOUR ANTICIPATION IS ALL RIGHT THERE IN YOUR EYES, WRITTEN IN PAINFUL CLARITY.
TA-DAAAAA! ♡
LEGEND OF A GREAT FATHER, A GREAT MAN
-The Story of Hella Great Yusa-
LISTEN, KID. NOT EVERYONE GETS TO HEAR THIS. THIS TALE IS A RARE, POWERFUL TREASURE THAT ONLY THE CHOSEN, ONLY THE GREAT, EVER GET THE PRIVILEGE OF HEARING!
IT WILL CHANGE YOU! IT WILL INSPIRE GREATNESS IN YOU! ONCE YOU'VE HEARD IT, YOUR LIFE WILL TAKE A 360-DEGREE TURN, GUARANTEED!!

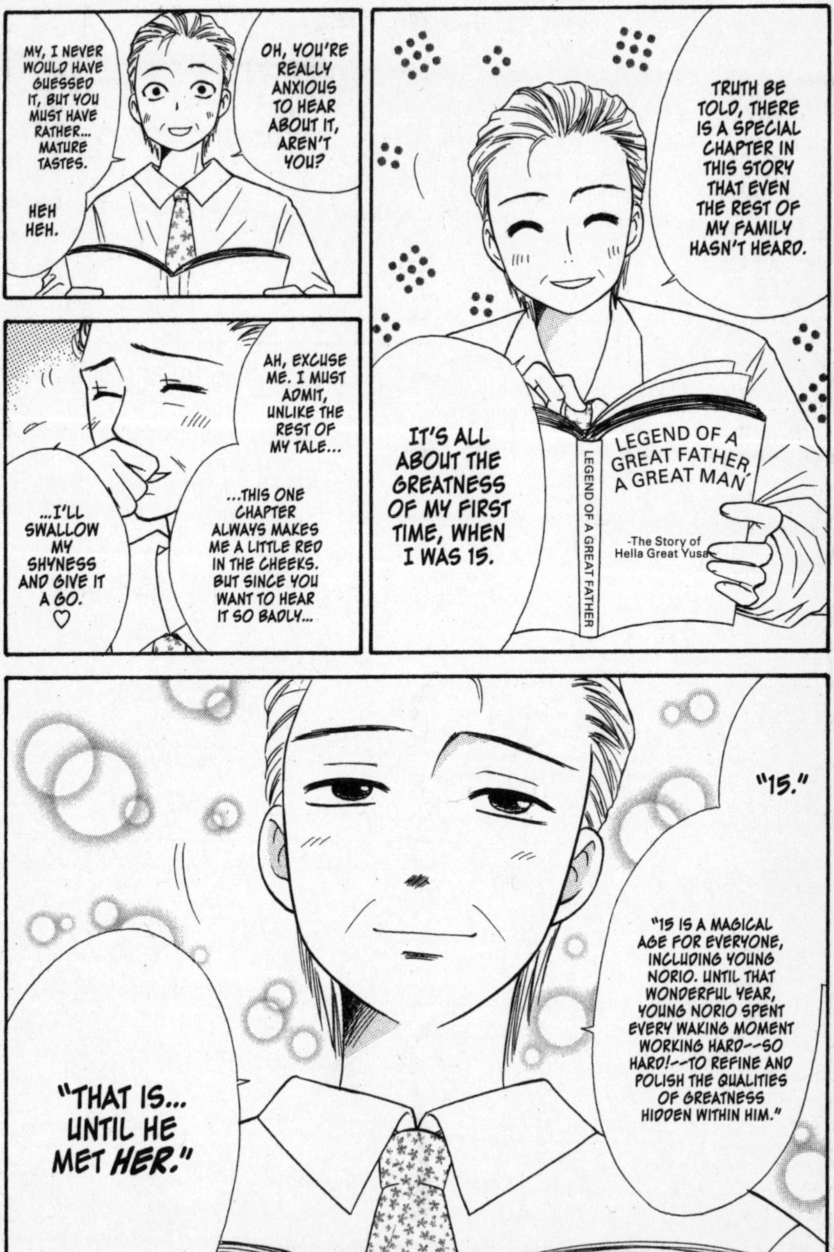
TRUTH BE TOLD, THERE IS A SPECIAL CHAPTER IN THIS STORY THAT EVEN THE REST OF MY FAMILY HASN'T HEARD.
IT'S ALL ABOUT THE GREATNESS OF MY FIRST TIME, WHEN I WAS 15.
LEGEND OF A GREAT FATHER, A GREAT MAN
-The Story of Hella Great Yusa-
LEGEND OF A GREAT FATHER
OH, YOU'RE REALLY ANXIOUS TO HEAR ABOUT IT, AREN'T YOU?
MY, I NEVER WOULD HAVE GUESSED IT, BUT YOU MUST HAVE RATHER... MATURE TASTES.
HEH HEH.
AH, EXCUSE ME. I MUST ADMIT, UNLIKE THE REST OF MY TALE...
...THIS ONE CHAPTER ALWAYS MAKES ME A LITTLE RED IN THE CHEEKS. BUT SINCE YOU WANT TO HEAR IT SO BADLY...
...I'LL SWALLOW MY SHYNESS AND GIVE IT A GO. ♡
"15."
"15 IS A MAGICAL AGE FOR EVERYONE, INCLUDING YOUNG NORIO. UNTIL THAT WONDERFUL YEAR, YOUNG NORIO SPENT EVERY WAKING MOMENT WORKING HARD--SO HARD!--TO REFINE AND POLISH THE QUALITIES OF GREATNESS HIDDEN WITHIN HIM."
"THAT IS... UNTIL HE MET HER."

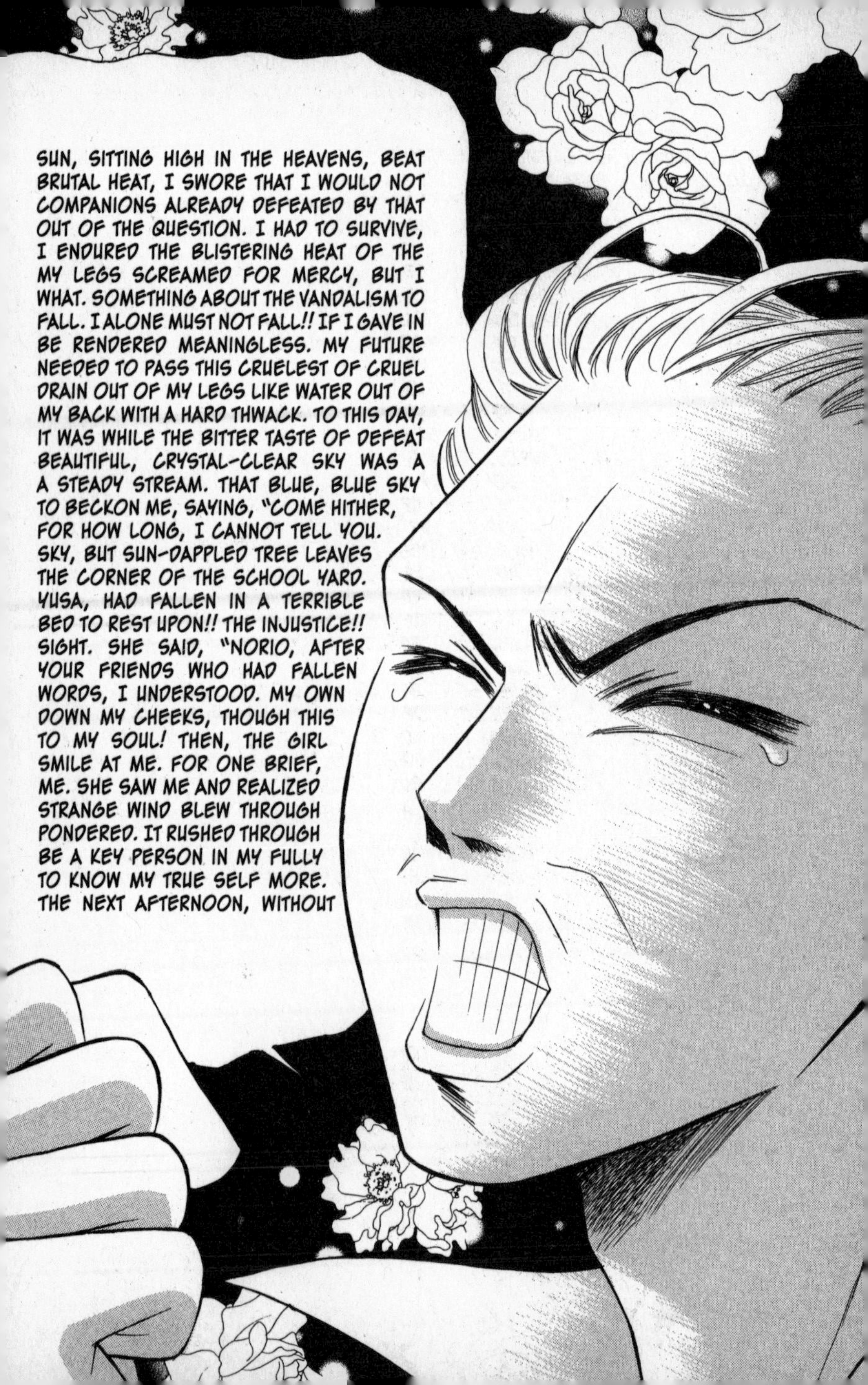
SUN, SITTING HIGH IN THE HEAVENS, BEAT
BRUTAL HEAT, I SWORE THAT I WOULD NOT
COMPANIONS ALREADY DEFEATED BY THAT
OUT OF THE QUESTION. I HAD TO SURVIVE,
I ENDURED THE BLISTERING HEAT OF THE
MY LEGS SCREAMED FOR MERCY, BUT I
WHAT. SOMETHING ABOUT THE VANDALISM TO
FALL. I ALONE MUST NOT FALL!! IF I GAVE IN
BE RENDERED MEANINGLESS. MY FUTURE
NEEDED TO PASS THIS CRUELEST OF CRUEL
DRAIN OUT OF MY LEGS LIKE WATER OUT OF
MY BACK WITH A HARD THWACK. TO THIS DAY,
IT WAS WHILE THE BITTER TASTE OF DEFEAT
BEAUTIFUL, CRYSTAL-CLEAR SKY WAS A
A STEADY STREAM. THAT BLUE, BLUE SKY
TO BECKON ME, SAYING, "COME HITHER,
FOR HOW LONG, I CANNOT TELL YOU.
SKY, BUT SUN-DAPPLED TREE LEAVES
THE CORNER OF THE SCHOOL YARD.
YUSA, HAD FALLEN IN A TERRIBLE
BED TO REST UPON!! THE INJUSTICE!!
SIGHT. SHE SAID, "NORIO, AFTER
YOUR FRIENDS WHO HAD FALLEN
WORDS, I UNDERSTOOD. MY OWN
DOWN MY CHEEKS, THOUGH THIS
TO MY SOUL! THEN, THE GIRL
SMILE AT ME. FOR ONE BRIEF,
ME. SHE SAW ME AND REALIZED
STRANGE WIND BLEW THROUGH
PONDERED. IT RUSHED THROUGH
BE A KEY PERSON IN MY FULLY
TO KNOW MY TRUE SELF MORE.
THE NEXT AFTERNOON, WITHOUT

IT WAS A STIFLINGLY HOT SUMMER DAY WHEN THE PRINCIPAL CALLED US OUTSIDE. THE
DOWN MERCILESSLY, PUMMELING ME WITH ITS HOT RAYS! BUT DESPITE THE HARSH,
LOSE. I HAD TO STAND TALL AND STRONG! ALL THE HOPES, ALL THE DREAMS OF MY
CRUEL SUN RESTED SQUARELY UPON MY YOUNG BUT WORTHY SHOULDERS. LOSING WAS
FOR THEIR SAKES! TIME PASSED, BUT STILL I STOOD, STRONG AND HARD AS A ROCK.
MERCILESS SUN FOR WHAT FELT LIKE AN ETERNITY. SWEAT POURED DOWN MY BACK AND
ENDURED!! THE PRINCIPAL DRONED ON, TALKING ABOUT SOMETHING I DON'T REMEMBER
THE RABBIT CAGES, MAYBE. BUT THAT IS NOT IMPORTANT. I JUST KNEW THAT I MUST NOT
TO THE HARSH GAZE OF THE SUN, EVERYTHING I WAS, EVERYTHING I STOOD FOR, WOULD
WAS ON THE LINE, FOR I KNEW THAT IF I WAS EVER TO ACHIEVE TRUE GREATNESS, I
TRIALS. BUT! AT THAT VERY MOMENT, MY VISION WAVERED, TILTED. I FELT THE STRENGTH
A BURST BALLOON. MY WEARY BODY BETRAYED ME, AND THE GROUND SLAMMED INTO
I REMEMBER STARING UP AT THAT SKY THAT DAY AND WONDERING AT HOW VERY BLUE
BURNED AT THE BACK OF MY THROAT. IT WAS THE ONLY TIME IN MY LIFE WHEN SUCH A
THING OF SORROW. TEARS THE COLOR OF THAT SKY TRICKLED DOWN MY CHEEKS IN
SADDENED ME TO NO END, BUT LOOKING UP INTO ITS SAPPHIRE DEPTHS, IT SEEMED
WOUNDED WARRIOR. LET ME SOOTHE YOUR PAIN." THEN, I LOST CONSCIOUSNESS.
ALL I KNOW IS THAT WHEN I OPENED MY EYES, IT WASN'T THE DEEP BLUE VOID OF THE
THAT FILLED MY VISION. SOMEONE HAD CARRIED ME INTO THE SHADE OF A TREE IN
THE FIRST THOUGHT THAT FILLED MY MIND WAS ANGER! RAGE! I, I, THE HELLA GREAT
BATTLE WITH A MERCILESS FOE, AND NO ONE HAD SEEN FIT EVEN TO GIVE ME A SOFT
THE INSULT!! BUT THEN A BEAUTIFUL GIRL BEARING A DAMP TOWEL LEANED INTO MY
YOU FAINTED, YOU MUMBLED SOMETHING ABOUT NOT NEEDING A BED, ABOUT LETTING
BEFORE YOU HAVE ALL THE BEDS. SO I BROUGHT YOU OVER HERE." HEARING HER
GREATNESS STRUCK ME TO THE VERY CORE OF MY BEING. TEARS ONCE AGAIN COURSED
TIME IN JOY. I REALIZED THAT I MAY ALREADY BE A GREAT MAN, ALL THE WAY DOWN
SPOKE AGAIN: "NORIO, YOU'RE AWFULLY...DIFFERENT." AND SHE SMILED A BEAUTIFUL
FLEETING MOMENT, I DOUBTED MY EARS. BUT THEN I KNEW. THIS GIRL UNDERSTOOD
THE MAGNITUDE OF GREATNESS WITHIN ME! AT THAT MOMENT OF COMPREHENSION, A
MY SOUL. A VERY WARM, GENTLE WIND THAT FELT OF SPRING. WHAT WAS THAT WIND, I
MY SOUL EVERY TIME I LOOKED INTO THAT GIRL'S EYES. I CONCLUDED THAT SHE MIGHT
REALIZING THE LATENT GREATNESS THAT SLEPT WITHIN ME. TO KNOW HER MORE WAS
THAT STRANGE, SPRING WIND IN MY HEART ENCOURAGED ME TO DO STRANGE THINGS.
KNOWING WHY, I WENT TO THE GIRLS' LOCKER ROOM...

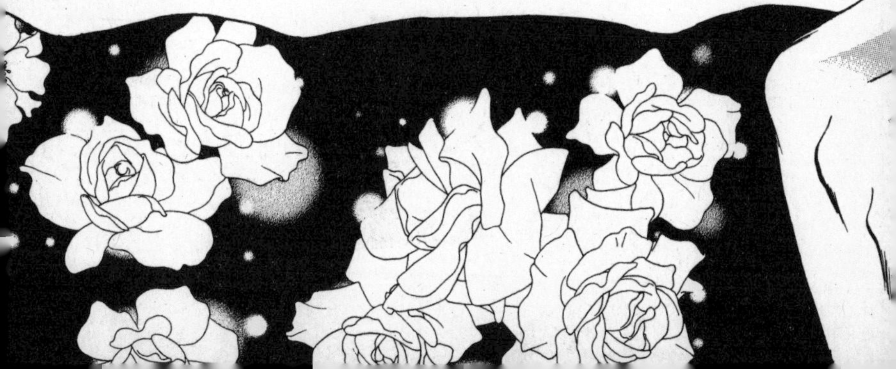

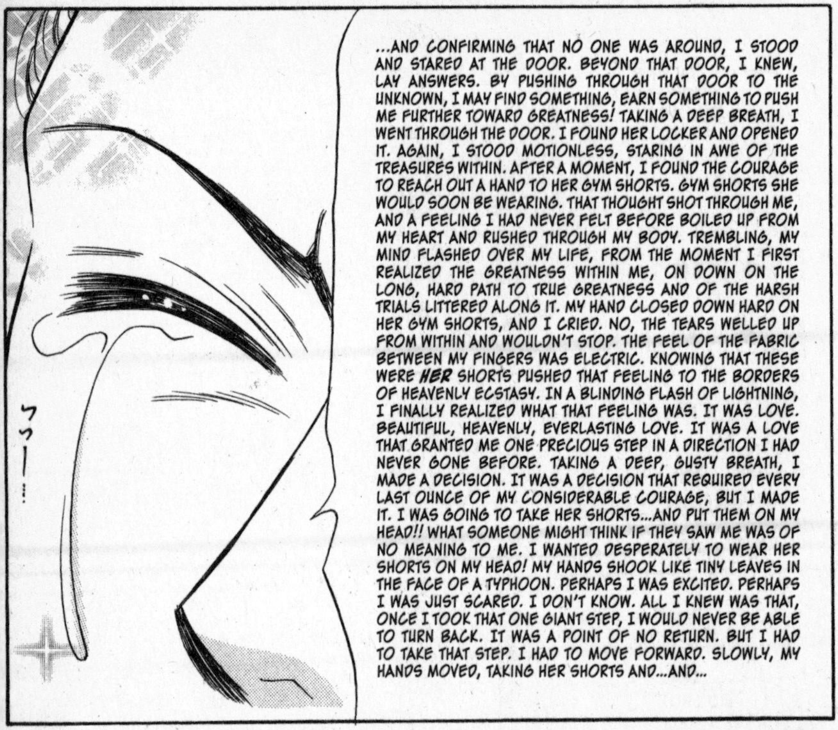
...AND CONFIRMING THAT NO ONE WAS AROUND, I STOOD AND STARED AT THE DOOR. BEYOND THAT DOOR, I KNEW, LAY ANSWERS. BY PUSHING THROUGH THAT DOOR TO THE UNKNOWN, I MAY FIND SOMETHING, EARN SOMETHING TO PUSH ME FURTHER TOWARD GREATNESS! TAKING A DEEP BREATH, I WENT THROUGH THE DOOR. I FOUND HER LOCKER AND OPENED IT. AGAIN, I STOOD MOTIONLESS, STARING IN AWE OF THE TREASURES WITHIN. AFTER A MOMENT, I FOUND THE COURAGE TO REACH OUT A HAND TO HER GYM SHORTS. GYM SHORTS SHE WOULD SOON BE WEARING. THAT THOUGHT SHOT THROUGH ME, AND A FEELING I HAD NEVER FELT BEFORE BOILED UP FROM MY HEART AND RUSHED THROUGH MY BODY. TREMBLING, MY MIND FLASHED OVER MY LIFE, FROM THE MOMENT I FIRST REALIZED THE GREATNESS WITHIN ME, ON DOWN ON THE LONG, HARD PATH TO TRUE GREATNESS AND OF THE HARSH TRIALS LITTERED ALONG IT. MY HAND CLOSED DOWN HARD ON HER GYM SHORTS, AND I CRIED. NO, THE TEARS WELLED UP FROM WITHIN AND WOULDN'T STOP. THE FEEL OF THE FABRIC BETWEEN MY FINGERS WAS ELECTRIC. KNOWING THAT THESE WERE ***HER*** SHORTS PUSHED THAT FEELING TO THE BORDERS OF HEAVENLY ECSTASY. IN A BLINDING FLASH OF LIGHTNING, I FINALLY REALIZED WHAT THAT FEELING WAS. IT WAS LOVE. BEAUTIFUL, HEAVENLY, EVERLASTING LOVE. IT WAS A LOVE THAT GRANTED ME ONE PRECIOUS STEP IN A DIRECTION I HAD NEVER GONE BEFORE. TAKING A DEEP, GUSTY BREATH, I MADE A DECISION. IT WAS A DECISION THAT REQUIRED EVERY LAST OUNCE OF MY CONSIDERABLE COURAGE, BUT I MADE IT. I WAS GOING TO TAKE HER SHORTS...AND PUT THEM ON MY HEAD!! WHAT SOMEONE MIGHT THINK IF THEY SAW ME WAS OF NO MEANING TO ME. I WANTED DESPERATELY TO WEAR HER SHORTS ON MY HEAD! MY HANDS SHOOK LIKE TINY LEAVES IN THE FACE OF A TYPHOON. PERHAPS I WAS EXCITED. PERHAPS I WAS JUST SCARED. I DON'T KNOW. ALL I KNEW WAS THAT, ONCE I TOOK THAT ONE GIANT STEP, I WOULD NEVER BE ABLE TO TURN BACK. IT WAS A POINT OF NO RETURN. BUT I HAD TO TAKE THAT STEP. I HAD TO MOVE FORWARD. SLOWLY, MY HANDS MOVED, TAKING HER SHORTS AND...AND...
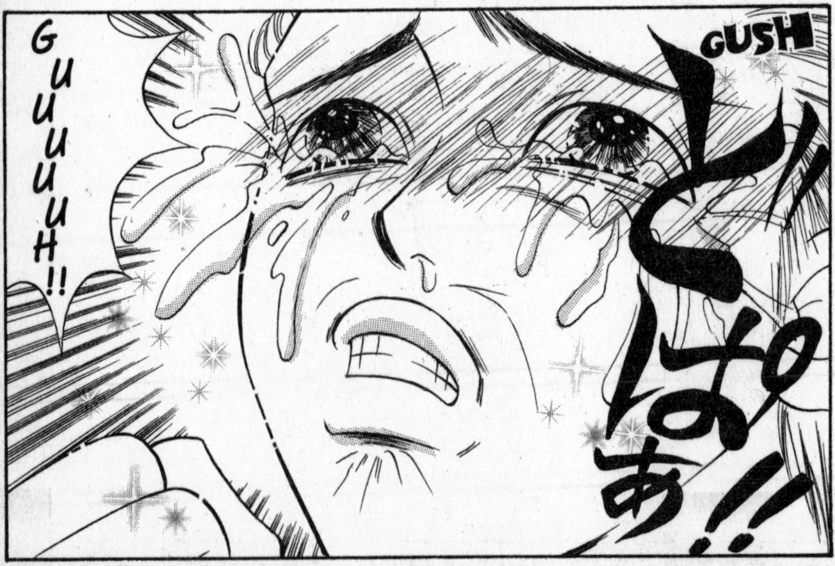
GUSH
GUUUUUH!!

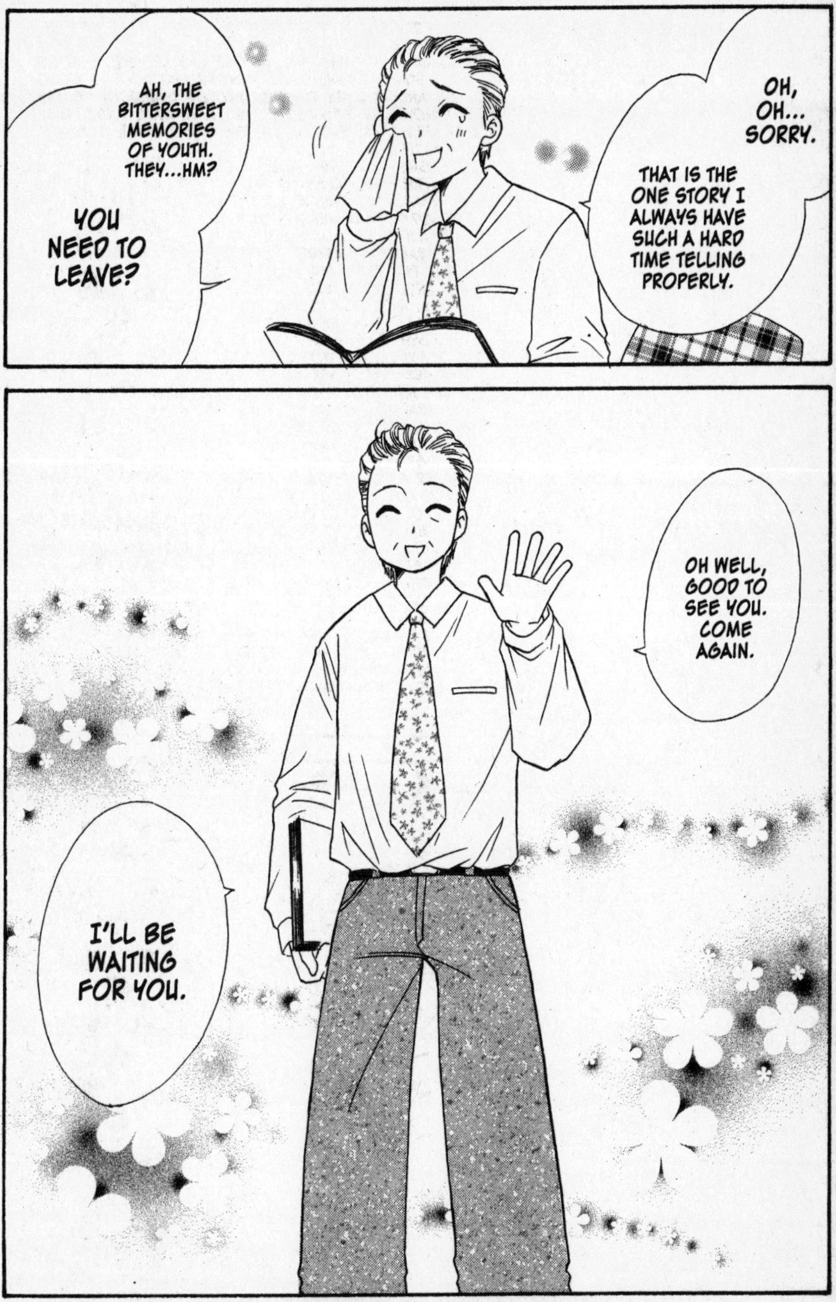
AH, THE BITTERSWEET MEMORIES OF YOUTH. THEY...HM?
YOU NEED TO LEAVE?
OH, OH... SORRY.
THAT IS THE ONE STORY I ALWAYS HAVE SUCH A HARD TIME TELLING PROPERLY.
OH WELL, GOOD TO SEE YOU. COME AGAIN.
I'LL BE WAITING FOR YOU.

LEGEND OF A GREAT FATHER, A GREAT MAN SPECIAL / END

IN THE NEXT...

LOVE ATTACK

JUNAI TOKKO TAICHO!

TALK ABOUT STUCK BETWEEN A ROCK AND A HARD PLACE!
NOT ONLY IS CHIEMI LOCKED INSIDE THE TENNIS CLUB
STORAGE SHED, BUT HIRATA'S LOCKED IN WITH HER AND
COMPLETELY UNDER THE CONTROL OF HIS RAGING
HORMONES! A DUMB-BELL UPSIDE THE HEAD SOLVES
THE HORMONE PROBLEM (I KNOW! SHUCKS!), BUT THE
PROBLEM OF BEING STUCK IN A CLAUSTROPHOBIA-
INDUCING SPACE LINGERS ON UNTIL RESCUE ARRIVES
IN THE MOST INOPPORTUNE TIME POSSIBLE!

WORLD'S SCARIEST COUPLE VS. STORAGE SHED

COMING IN AUGUST OF 2008!

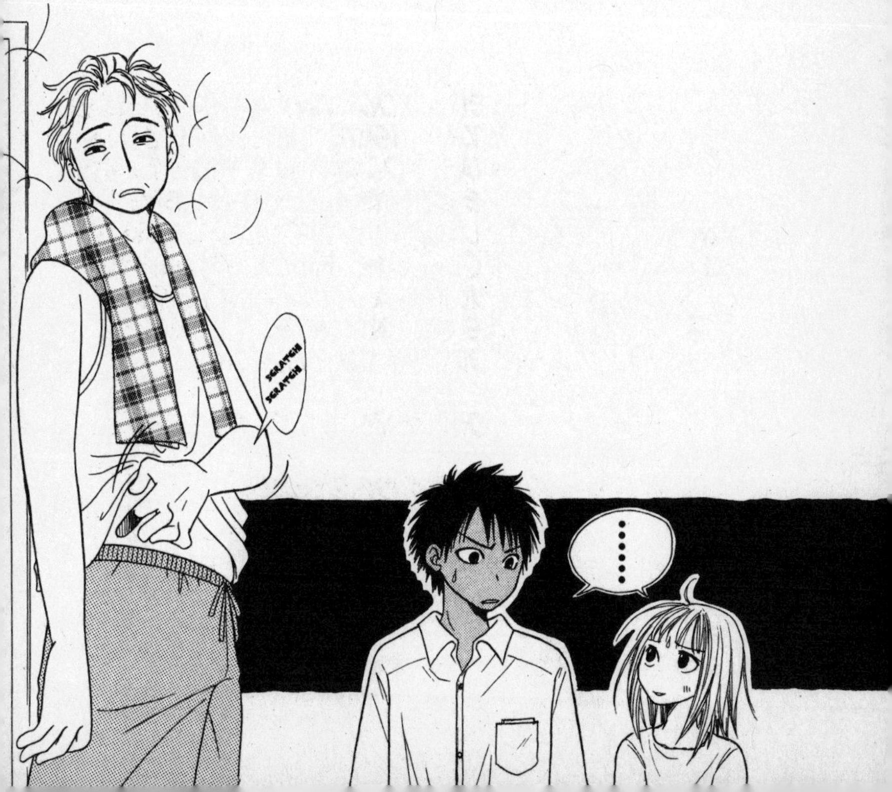
SCRATCH SCRATCH
......

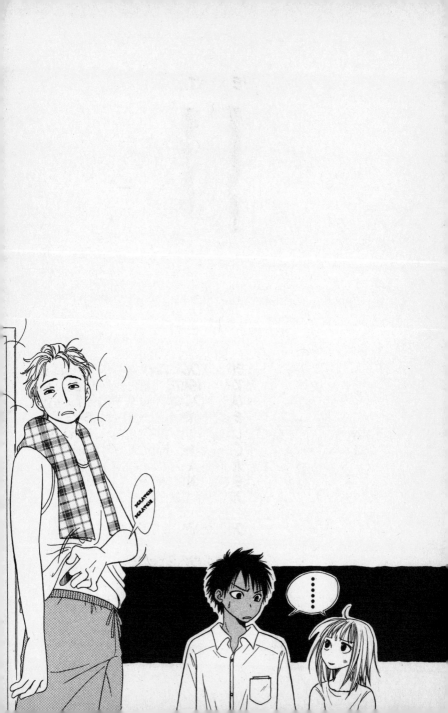

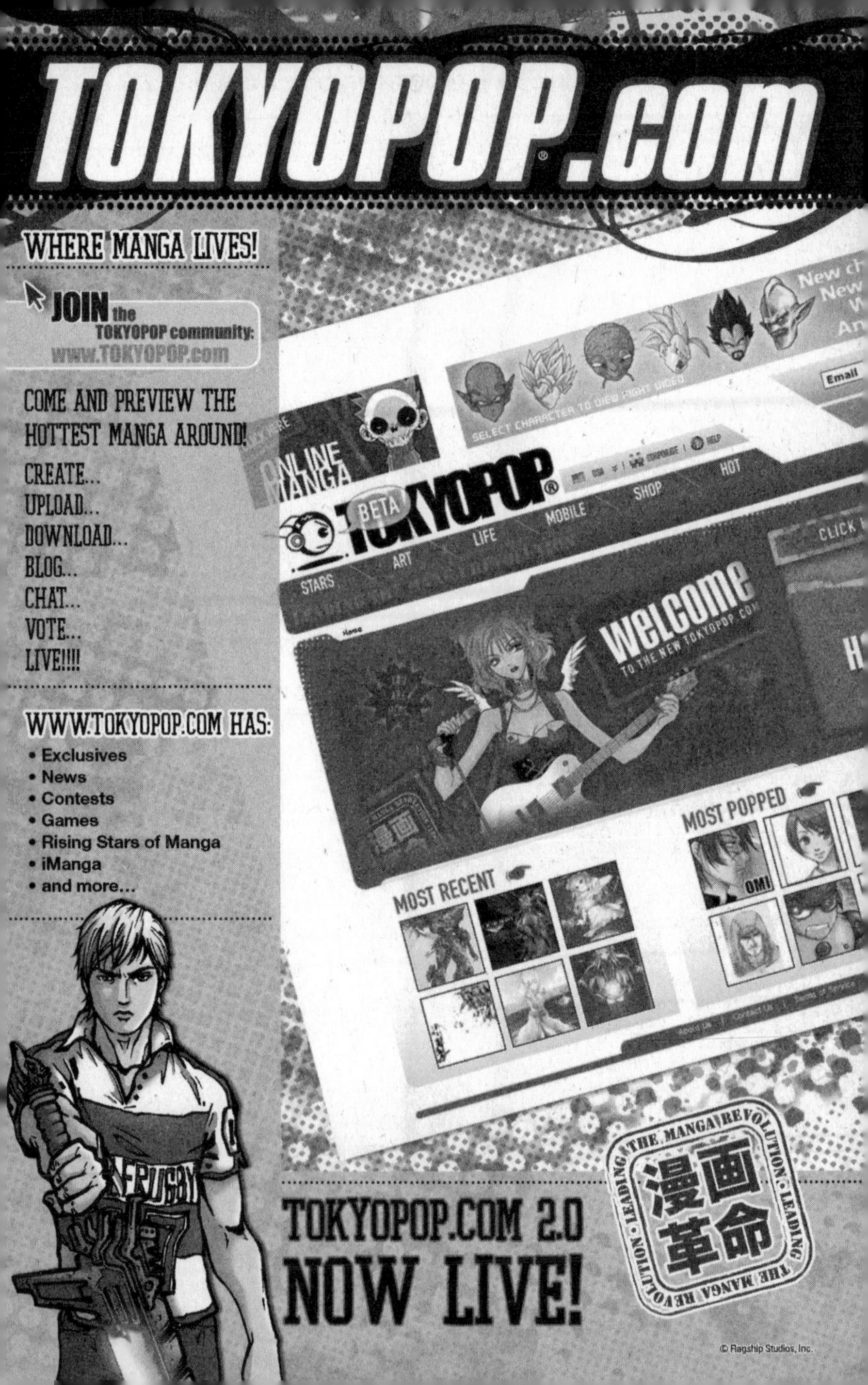
TOKYOPOP.com
WHERE MANGA LIVES!
JOIN the TOKYOPOP community:
www.TOKYOPOP.com
COME AND PREVIEW THE HOTTEST MANGA AROUND!
CREATE...
UPLOAD...
DOWNLOAD...
BLOG...
CHAT...
VOTE...
LIVE!!!!
WWW.TOKYOPOP.COM HAS:
• Exclusives
• News
• Contests
• Games
• Rising Stars of Manga
• iManga
• and more...
TOKYOPOP.COM 2.0
NOW LIVE!
THE MANGA REVOLUTION • LEADING THE MANGA REVOLUTION • LEADING
漫画革命
© Flagship Studios, Inc.

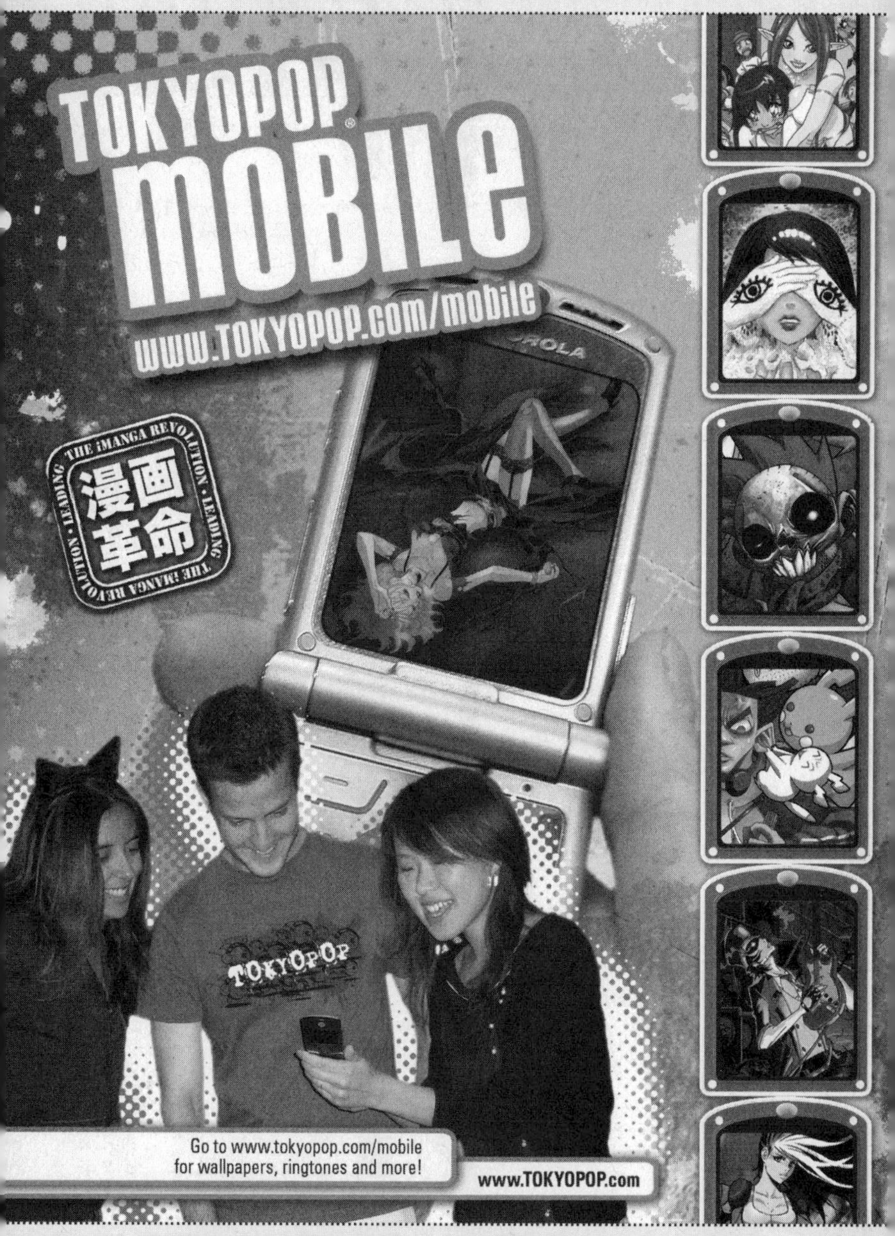
TOKYOPOP® MOBILE
www.TOKYOPOP.com/mobile
THE iMANGA REVOLUTION · LEADING
漫画革命
LEADING · THE iMANGA REVOLUTION
TOKYOPOP
Go to www.tokyopop.com/mobile
for wallpapers, ringtones and more!
www.TOKYOPOP.com

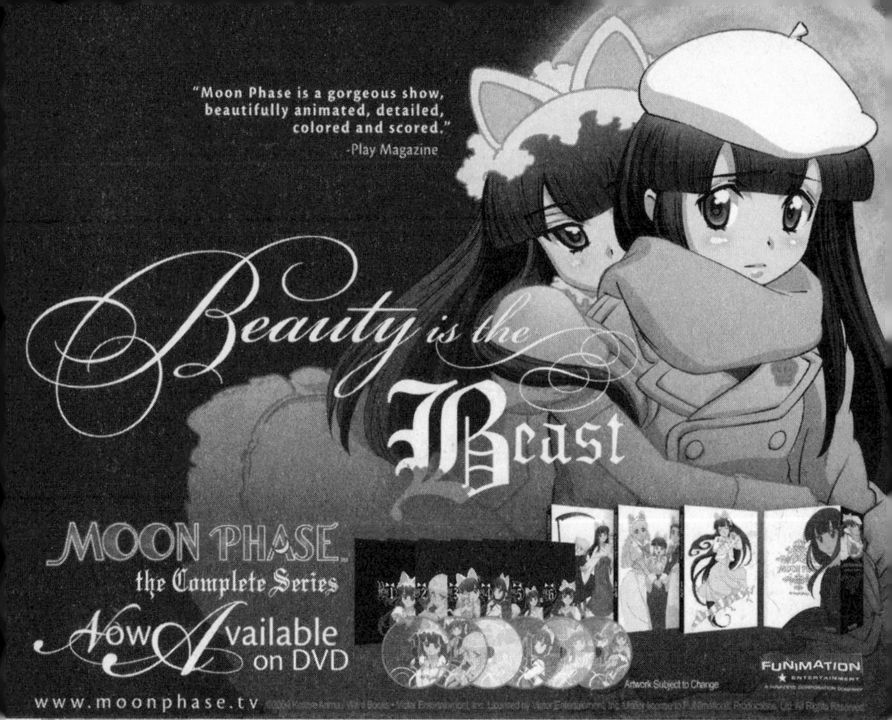
"Moon Phase is a gorgeous show, beautifully animated, detailed, colored and scored."
-Play Magazine
Beauty is the Beast
MOON PHASE
the Complete Series
Now Available on DVD
Artwork Subject to Change
FUNIMATION ENTERTAINMENT
www.moonphase.tv
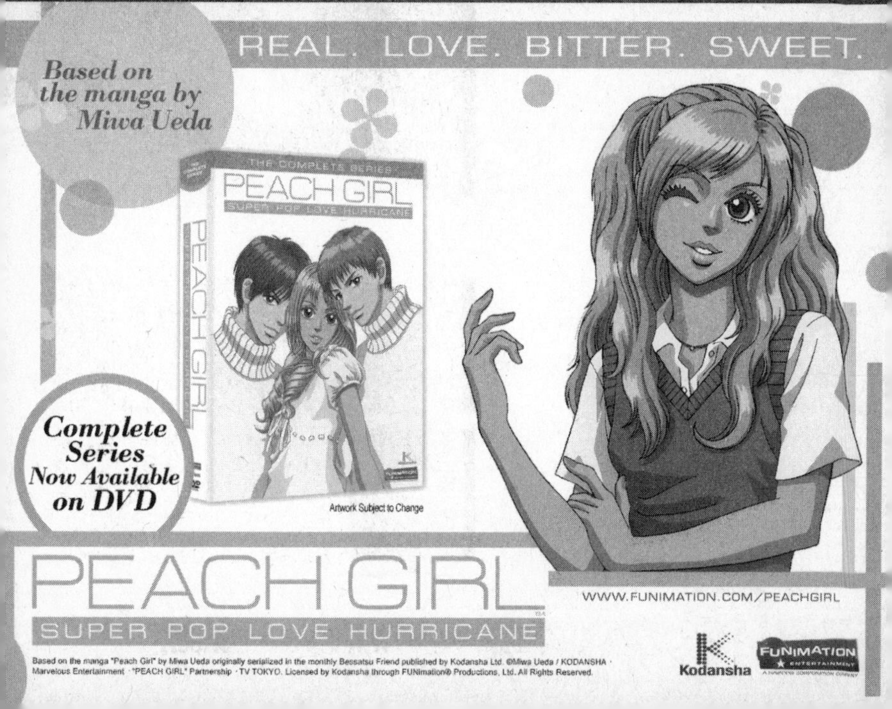
REAL. LOVE. BITTER. SWEET.
Based on the manga by Miwa Ueda
THE COMPLETE SERIES
PEACH GIRL
SUPER POP LOVE HURRICANE
Complete Series Now Available on DVD
Artwork Subject to Change
PEACH GIRL
SUPER POP LOVE HURRICANE
WWW.FUNIMATION.COM/PEACHGIRL
Based on the manga "Peach Girl" by Miwa Ueda originally serialized in the monthly Bessatsu Friend published by Kodansha Ltd. ©Miwa Ueda / KODANSHA · Marvelous Entertainment · "PEACH GIRL" Partnership · TV TOKYO. Licensed by Kodansha through FUNimation® Productions, Ltd. All Rights Reserved.
Kodansha
FUNIMATION ENTERTAINMENT

STOP!

This is the back of the book.
You wouldn't want to spoil a great ending!

This book is printed "manga-style," in the authentic Japanese right-to-left format. Since none of the artwork has been flipped or altered, readers get to experience the story just as the creator intended. You've been asking for it, so TOKYOPOP® delivered: authentic, hot-off-the-press, and far more fun!

DIRECTIONS

If this is your first time reading manga-style, here's a quick guide to help you understand how it works.

It's easy... just start in the top right panel and follow the numbers. Have fun, and look for more 100% authentic manga from TOKYOPOP®!